Children and Their Changing Media Environment

A European Comparative Study

LR/LE?

LEA's COMMUNICATION SERIES
Jennings Bryant/Dolf Zillmann, General Editors

For a complete list of titles in LEA's Communication Series, please contact Lawrence Erlbaum Associates, Publishers.

Children and Their Changing Media Environment

A European Comparative Study

Edited by

SONIA LIVINGSTONE
MOIRA BOVILL
The London School of Economics and Political Science

LEA
2001

LAWRENCE ERLBAUM ASSOCIATES, PUBLISHERS
Mahwah, New Jersey   London

Lawrence Erlbaum Associates, Inc., Publishers
10 Industrial Avenue
Mahwah, New Jersey 07430

Cover design by Kathryn Houghtaling Lacey

Library of Congress Cataloging-in-Publication Data

Children and their changing media environment : a European comparative study / edited
By Sonia Livingstone, Moira Bovill.
      p. cm.
   Includes bibliographical references and index.
   ISBN 0-8058-3498-2 (cloth : alk. paper) – ISBN 0-8058-3499-0 (pbk. : alk. paper)
   1.   Mass media and children—Europe—Cross-cultural studies. 2. Technology and children—Europe—Cross-cultural studies. 3. Computers and children—Europe—Cross-cultural studies. 4. Information society—Europe—Cross-cultural studies. I. Livingstone, Sonia. II. Bovill, Moira.

   HQ784.M3 C453 2001
   302.23'083'094—dc21

                                                                                         2001023048

Books published by Lawrence Erlbaum Associates are printed on acid-free paper, and their bindings are chosen for strength and durability.

Printed in the United States of America
10   9   8   7   6   5   4   3   2

Contents

v

Preface

The domestic television screen is being transformed into the site of a multimedia culture integrating telecommunications, broadcasting, computing, and video. Already, satellite and cable television, interactive video and electronic games, the personal computer and the Internet are central to the daily lives of children and young people. Yet little is known about the meanings, uses, and impacts of these new technologies. This volume brings together researchers from 12 countries—Belgium, Denmark, Finland, France, Germany, the United Kingdom, Israel, Italy, the Netherlands, Spain, Sweden, and Switzerland.[1] We present new findings about the diffusion and significance of new media and information technologies among children and young people.

Forty years ago, Himmelweit, Oppenheim, and Vince's *Television and the child* (1958), together with Schramm's *Television in the lives of our children* (1961), set the scene for researchers, parents, teachers, and policymakers as they came to grips with the introduction of television in the United Kingdom and America, respectively. This volume was inspired by parallels between the arrival in the family home of television in the 1950s and the present-day arrival of new media. Today, similar questions are being asked and similar hopes and fears expressed. On the other hand, much has changed and is still changing. This seemed, therefore, a good moment to take stock and ask: What is the place of media in children and young people's lives today?

Some issues are familiar, being revisited as each new medium is introduced. Others are new. What are the impacts of new information and communication technologies on older mass media? What new opportunities for integrating learning, socializing, and playing are being facilitated? Will some be excluded from these opportunities while others live in an increasingly information-rich environment? Will the growing importance of the media add to the variety and pleasure in young people's lives, or will this contribute to their withdrawal from traditional leisure activities and even from social and political participation? Will the media strengthen local identities with locally produced programming or will they support the emergence of transnational identities—European, Western, global, etc.?

---

[1]Although Israel is strictly not part of Europe, its inclusion strengthens our representation of Mediterranean countries.

Empirical research is needed to understand the balance between the opportunities and dangers of new media. The contributors to this book argue that such questions—intellectual, empirical, and policy-related— can be productively addressed through comparative, cross-national research. This allows us to ask about the similarities and differences in children and young people's media environments within and between European countries. It also allows us to relate the similarities and differences in media use to cross-national differences in family structure, education systems, or civic culture, and so forth. Comparative work is not lightly undertaken, and this volume aims to illuminate the comparative research process itself, as well as to produce a complex picture of the place of media and information technologies in the lives and experiences of European children and young people at the turn of the century. To achieve this, we interviewed and surveyed some 11,000 6- to 16-year-olds around Europe as well as many of their parents and teachers, as part of the project. We thank them all here for their cooperation and participation.

ACKNOWLEDGMENTS

Many people contributed to the project presented in this volume during the past 5 years; the project has encompassed researchers and their universities, funding bodies, and academic colleagues across 12 countries. We are particularly indebted to the vision of Jay Blumler who, together with Colin Shaw, Andrea Millwood Hargrave, and colleagues at the Broadcasting Standards Council (now, Broadcasting Standards Commission), originally inspired this European project and who obtained the initial funding to make this possible. Thus we thank the European Parliament, the European Commission, and the European Science Foundation for their vital support throughout the conduct of the European comparative work. Thanks are also due to George Gaskell at the London School of Economics and Political Science (LSE) who worked with us on the original design for the project, to our research assistant Kate Holden, to David Scott for his help with the British database, and to Robert Kubey and Linda Bathgate at Lawrence Erlbaum Associates for seeing this book through to publication. The comparative work depended on a series of meetings around Europe, and we acknowledge here the efforts of the research teams and their departments and universities who worked hard to make these events both successful and pleasurable. As editors of this volume, we must express our gratitude to all the colleagues whose work is included in this volume. They have shown great enthusiasm and patience in working with us: We have learned much from them about their countries and research traditions and hope in the process to have made our small contribution to furthering European collaborative research. In particular, we would like to thank Pierangelo Peri and Mario Callegaro from the University of Trento, Italy, for their efforts in constructing a common database for use by all teams. We also note with great regret that the untimely death of Renato Porro meant that an Italian-authored chapter for this volume was not possible. Last but not least, we thank the many friends and colleagues with whom we have compared notes, asked advice, and discussed the challenges posed by this project. Particularly, we would like to thank our partners, Peter Lunt and David Bovill, for their sustained and always intelligent support throughout the production of this volume.

REFERENCES

Himmelweit, H. T., Oppenheim, A. N., & Vince, P. (1958). *Television and the child: An empirical study of the effect of television on the young.* London and New York: Oxford University Press.
Schramm, W., Lyle, J., & Parker, E. B. (1961). *Television in the lives of our children.* Stanford, CA: Stanford University Press.

Sonia Livingstone
Moira Bovill

Foreword

Jay Blumler
University of Leeds (emeritus)
University of Maryland (emeritus)

I write as a proud godfather[1] of what emerges from this meaty volume as a meaty project—remarkable in substantive scope, cross-national scale, organizational effectiveness, and integration of fully analyzed data with fully considered theory. The result is a thoroughly contextualized study of youngsters' thoroughly mediated childhoods across the diverse social, cultural, and communication systems of Europe.

This work deserves a place on the shelves of all media scholars for at least three reasons. First, it provides a definitive account, wide-ranging and richly explored, of the role of the new media (alongside and amidst their audiovisual and print predecessors) in the lives, identities, and social relations of young Europeans in the late 1990s. Although initially conceived as a follow-up in multimedia conditions to the early postwar study of *Television and the Child* (Himmelweit, Oppenheim, & Vince, 1958), the investigators soon realized that they had to attempt something more ambitious. After all, television researchers of the 1950s and 1960s could concentrate on the coming of a single, finite new medium. In retrospect, even its far-reaching impact now seems like a big rock thrown into a more or less placid pool. In contrast, however, the sweep of the changes occurring since the 1980s has been *environmental*, involving a host of social trends and media developments, interacting with and on each other. Such a situation is more like a storm of numerous stones raining continually down on a seething sea of shifting and cross-cutting tides!

All credit, then, to Sonia Livingstone, Moira Bovill, and their colleagues for having plunged into and made so much convincing sense of this maelstrom! They knew that its taming required a holistic study design, which they fashioned with great care. In gist, approximately 11,000 children and adolescents (spanning 6- to 16-years-of-age) were asked through comparable questionnaires (for qualitative data in 32 topic areas) and

---

[1]Other godparents included Colin Shaw, director, and Andrea Millwood Hargrave, research director, of the then Broadcasting Standards Council (now Commission).

interview guides (for qualitative material) about their access to, time spent with, uses of, and meanings ascribed to a range of new and old media within three different settings—those of home and family (including their own bedrooms), peer relationships, and school. The findings from all this, their commonalities and differences as well as their numerous linkages of interconnection, are masterfully presented and interpreted in the chapters that follow.

Second, this study is a model of high quality communications research in general. Among its many achievements, readers should appreciate: its integrative interweaving of quantitative and qualitative evidence; its productive passages of conceptual innovation (as in the comparisons in chapter 11 of private and public pathways to computer usage at home and school); its creative use of findings to extend or modify the conventional wisdom available in a body of literature (as in the discussion in chapter 12 of the differing media content preferences of boys and girls); its careful specification of the study's policy implications; and all that must have been involved in enabling the authors to shed their national skins and trawl the full data set for comparative insights theme by theme. Also exemplary is the fusion of child-centered with media-centered perspectives in this work. The notion that the media both shapes and are shaped by surrounding social conditions should be adhered to more often in other subareas of communications research.

Third, this is a veritable handbook of how to go about, and what can be gotten out of, well-designed comparative media research. Within its pages, all the team's *comparative* expectations, procedures, problems, routes of analysis, data, and findings are on transparent display. Perhaps two main strategic lessons emerge from this material. One is that it confirms that the comparative element should not be treated as a post-hoc add-on after the substantive terms of a topic of research have been worked out. Instead, much prior reflection must be devoted to the contributions one expects of cross-national comparisons in the case concerned. The other key point is the pay-off value of cultivating what may be termed *system-sensitivity*. This is not just a matter of discretely and descriptively comparing isolated bits and pieces of empirical phenomena situated in two or more locales. Rather, it involves the kind of persistent effort that all these scholars have made to understand how systemic institutional and cultural contexts may have shaped such phenomena.

The study also illustrates three main contributions to knowledge that comparative communications research is uniquely suited to make. One is to extend the range of settings within which the validity of generalizations can be tested. Thus, it transpires that the classic stratification variables of social class, gender, and age do differentiate children's relations to the media in all 12 countries surveyed in the research—though in varying respects (meticulously plotted by the investigators) and with some intriguing "wrinkles." There is major policy relevance, for example, in the discovery that, although the children in high socioeconomic status (SES) households are more likely to have computers at home, working-class youngsters with such access spend as much time using them for "serious" purposes as do their better-off peers. Also, after finding many more similarities than differences in the significance of new media for your Europeans overall, the cross-national spread of the project has allowed its authors to conclude that a more or less common media-impregnated culture of childhood and youth is emerging throughout the advanced industrialized societies of Europe.

In addition, only comparative research can identify the effects of differences in how societies are organized at a macro level. Although we are accustomed to thinking of Europe as a patchwork of diverse institutional arrangements and cultures, our understanding of the consequences of cross-national variation in such "system conditions" is remarkably thin. However, the outcomes of this study make impressive strides toward filling this gap, both negatively (e.g., in finding no relationship between levels of national economic development and rates of new media diffusion) and positively. Among a number of systemic discriminators in this research, the most powerful appears to be the distinction between societies with peer-oriented cultures (in mainly Nordic and Protestant countries) and those with family-oriented ones (mainly South European and Catholic).

Finally, there is a contribution that is specially suited to our dynamic times. This is to take some trend believed to be cross-nationally in train, to chart its advance in different societies, and to ask how far its development is being accelerated, modified, or withstood by key features of their social structures or cultures. The value of such an approach is demonstrated by the concluding chapter's fascinating discussion of the impact on young Europeans' relations to new media of the processes of individualization, privatization, and globalization that have been unleashed in late modernity.

REFERENCES

Himmelweit, H. T., Oppenheim, A. N., & Vince, P. (1958). *Television and the child: An empirical study of the effect of television on the young.* London and New York: Oxford University Press.

RESEARCHING YOUNG PEOPLE AND THE CHANGING MEDIA ENVIRONMENT

1

Childhood in Europe: Contexts for Comparison

Sonia Livingstone
Leen d'Haenens
Uwe Hasebrink

LOCATING THE MEDIA IN CHILDREN AND YOUNG PEOPLE'S LIVES

By 4 p.m. on a dreary English afternoon, 8-year-old Sophie has been picked up from school by her mother, driven home, and is now watching Children's BBC while having her tea in the living room. Her 4-year old sister, who will start school next year, is annoying her by chatting throughout the program; her older brother is off in his bedroom, watching television there while doing his homework. Her counterpart in Spain, Maria, finished school several hours ago and is spending the afternoon and early evening at an after-school club before returning to her family for the evening. In Finland, Pertti—also 8—walked home from school with friends a little while ago, and, delighted to find the house empty, is enjoying a quiet chance at the family computer before everyone else gets back. Danish Gitte went off to the library after school to complete her homework on the Internet there, as well as to change her books: Although she only recently started school, she is already adept at combining new and old media.

In sketching these scenarios, have we just drawn on familiar, even unfortunate, national stereotypes? Or do the commonly noted differences in daily life across Europe, including school hours, maternal working patterns, trends in urbanization, cost of living, and even the weather, make a real difference to the quality of children's daily lives and, of central interest here, to the role of media in their lives? Stereotypes tend to overstate differences, and it may be more important to recognize that young people across Europe share a common pattern in their daily lives, balancing time at school, with family, with friends, and, accompanying much of this, with media. Yet commonalities also are easily presumed, and few of us are good at identifying what, if anything, is nationally specific about our everyday lives. Ask Maria or her parents what is typically Spanish about her life, and she'll be hard put to tell you, but compare her daily routine with that of Pertti or Sophie and differences may become apparent.

Researchers also find it difficult to articulate which aspects of everyday life are specific to their country. Academic research literatures build up through national or regional publications, with "international" publications often restricted to the English language. Without deliberate strategies for comparison, it is difficult to recognize how taken-for-granted aspects of everyday life may be distinctive whereas features considered nationally significant may in fact be shared with other countries (Chisholm, 1995). Comparative research aims to enhance understanding by improving an understanding of one's own country, gaining knowledge of other countries and, perhaps most valuable, examining how common, or transnational, processes operate under specific conditions in different national contexts (Øyen, 1990; Teune, 1990).

For this volume, we compared 12 countries in order to observe both similarities and differences, attempting to interpret these within an appropriate national and/or European context. The comparative research project on which this volume is based was guided by five key aims:

1. To chart current access and use for new media at home (and, in less detail, at school).
2. To provide a comprehensive account of domestic leisure and media activities.
3. To understand the meaning of the changing media environment for children (and, in less detail, parents).
4. To map access to and uses of media in relation to social inequalities and social exclusion.
5. To provide a baseline of media use against which to measure future changes.

To address these research questions, the meanings boys and girls of diverse ages and social backgrounds attach to media and media use have been related to a unique data set in which media ownership and practices were measured and the use of space and time documented. This integration of qualitative and quantitative methods, together with the challenges of conducting such a project cross-nationally, are discussed in chapter 2. Here we begin with some theoretical considerations.

DEVELOPING A RESEARCH FRAMEWORK

In many respects, the 8 year old children with whom we began once lived in distinct universes, speaking different languages, being taught within different educational systems, watching different television programs, listening to different music. Some of these differences are still present—language, for example—whereas others have been transformed in recent years, most obviously television and music. As some changes take place, these have unintended consequences, so that, for example, although national language remains central to national culture, English is gaining ground as a second language throughout Europe. It may appear that cross-national differences are diminishing and, moreover, that the media contribute to this process, but the media are by no means the sole or even most important influence here. In Europe, the historical and cultural trajectories that shape national cultures heavily overlap and intersect. Many macrosocial structures within Europe—economy, politics, civic society, religion, family—share a common history and are shaped by common factors. Although acknowledging this broader perspective, our focus in this volume is on how the media fit into this bigger picture: How do the media play their distinctive role in shaping, as well as being shaped by, children's and young people's identity and culture, and their relations with family, peers, school, and community?

Today, not only do political and policy developments attempt to define these children and young people as *European citizens*, but commercial and cultural trends attempt to reorient them all—to a greater or lesser extent—toward American or globalized culture (Schlesinger, 1997). The media play a key role here; popular music is ever more global, television shows them how people live in other parts of the world, and the Internet allows e-pals and chat groups among young people around the world. As Western society becomes increasingly information-based, we suggest that two trends make an academic volume on children's and young people's media environments valuable at the present time. First, the media are playing an ever greater role in children's leisure, whether measured in terms of family income, use of time and space, or importance within the conduct of social relations. Second, the media are extending their influence throughout children's lives so that children's leisure can no longer be clearly separated from their education, their employment prospects, their participation in public activities, or their participation within the private realm of the family. To put the point concretely, buying children personal computers may not only affect how much television they watch, but may also have consequences for their job prospects, family conversation, use of parks and shopping malls, confidence at school, and so on, as, too, may being unable to afford to buy a personal computer, or the decision to buy a games machine instead.

Child-centered Versus Media-centered Approaches

Although researching "new media" means studying a moving target, our focus is on the domestic screen, including the video recorder, multiple television channels, the personal computer, electronic games, e-mail, and the Internet. Our priority is to understand the meanings, uses, and impacts of the screen in the lives of children and young people, first by placing it in its everyday context (including nonscreen media and other leisure activities) and second, by viewing the screen where possible from a child-centered perspective (rather than that of the household, family, or school). These two priorities are linked, for although contexts both shape and are shaped by the actors within them, rather than passively containing them, one distinctive feature of children's lives is that they have relatively little control over the parameters of their "lifeworld." Thus, children may diverge from adults in their perceptions of everyday practices precisely because their actions represent tactics to resist or reinvent the adult-created contexts in which they live (Graue & Walsh, 1998).

Two starting points are readily available in framing an understanding of children's and young people's media environment (Drotner, 1993). We can begin with children and young people, and ask how the media fit into their lives, or we can begin with the media, and ask what impacts they are having on children and young people.

The *child-centered* approach directs us toward the many parameters of young people's lifeworld. It is valuable for putting the media in context, for playing down some of the hype surrounding new media by "putting them in their place," and so for refusing to reify children in terms of media use (as addicts, nerds, fans, etc; cf. Buckingham, 1993). Within children's lifeworld, our present focus is on the *home*, this being the primary location for media use for younger children and an important location across our 6 to 16 age range. However, we also seek to contextualize domestic media use by asking about school, peer culture, and community contexts. On occasion, this is invaluable: If one compared British and Finnish children for their access to the Internet at home, one would conclude that differences in Internet access are rather less dramatic than if one also considered the much greater access that Finnish children obtain in public locations such as schools, libraries, cafés, and so forth. Trying to be less media-centered and more contextualized also has its dangers, and a focus on childhood and youth per se may lead to the neglect of the media altogether (a tendency apparent in the so-called "new sociology of childhood;" cf. James, Jenks, & Prout, 1998).

The *media-centered* approach takes its agenda from technological developments. It tends to be more sensitive to the medium- or content-specific characteristics of different media, tracing the chain of influence from diffusion through both commercial and public domains to access in the home, then to actual use and, eventually, to impacts on children and young people (e.g., Rogers, 1986). However, it tends to neglect those diverse factors that lead to different meanings or practices for media in different contexts of use. Moreover, a media-centered approach often focuses on just one medium (although several exceptions exist; e.g., Edelstein, 1982), tending to construct noncommensurate images of children and young people. We hear of the oppositional youth culture of the music fan, the imaginative world of the reader, the aggressive world of the video game player, the mindless world of the television viewer, and so forth, ignoring the way that, as we see later in this volume, children and young people construct diverse lifestyles from a mix of different media, rarely if ever making use of just one medium. For this reason, we stress the notion of the *media environment* throughout this volume.

Given that there are advantages both to seeing the media as figure and childhood as ground, and vice versa, one should attempt to keep both perspectives in mind. Ultimately, contexts of childhood and youth shape the meanings, uses, and impacts of media just as these, in turn, contribute to shaping the experience of childhood and youth. Neither of these starting points, however, is easily defined, and both *children* and *media* are terms that are culturally variable, complicating cross-national comparisons. Certainly, the lack of a single term to cover our chosen age range (6 to 16) is indicative of socially constructed distinctions between child and youth, minor and adult, dependency and autonomy. Similarly, the shift from what were traditionally termed *mass media* but are now labeled *information and communication technologies* marks a diversification in media available in the home, including ever more interactive and convergent forms of domestic media technology.

Although debates about both children and media are rife with suppositions about social change, neither of these perspectives is wholly satisfactory in its account of change. The child-oriented or contextual approach tends to argue against change, seeing the media as fitting into pre-existing meaning systems and practices. The media-oriented approach tends to overstate the case for technology-driven change, construing this in terms of linear, causal effects brought about by the insertion of media into everyday life. In this project, we argue that despite the plausibility of claims regarding the social transformation of childhood and youth, as well as the claimed radical break between mass media and interactive media, the case for change should not be overstated. Each decade sees dramatic technological change; however, in many respects children's lives are as they were 20 or even 40 years ago. Children grow up, watch television, ride their bikes, argue with their parents, study hard, or become disaffected with school, just as they always did. The portrait of children's lives in *Television and the Child* (Himmelweit, Oppenheim, & Vince, 1958) is recognizable 40 years on: Then, just as we find today, children prefer to play outside with their friends than use the media, mainly watching television to relieve boredom; and when they do watch television, then as now children prefer to watch prime-time programs, rather than those made specifically for children, whereas their parents and teachers wish they would read more books instead.

Mediated Childhoods in Late Modernity

More subtle changes may be observed in relation to both children and media, however. These concern postwar transformations in time, space, and social relations (Thompson, 1995; Ziehe, 1994). For example, in many countries children no longer walk to school or play in the streets as freely as they once did. Yet although their lives may be less locally grounded, they are simultaneously becoming global citizens, increasingly in touch with other places and people in the world. This is particularly apparent once they reach adolescence, with transnational entertainment media now playing a key role in young people's identity formation and peer culture. In the family, too, larger changes are occurring. Comparing young people's lives with the childhood and youth of their parents, the divorce rate has escalated, more women engage in paid work, and the structure of families has diversified. More children are better off but more, too, are poorer. More young people are going into further or higher education whereas entry into the workplace is more difficult, with the prospect of a job for life diminishing (Lagree, 1995). Even larger changes are also at work, as globalizing economic, political, and technological developments challenge the autonomy of the nation state. What are the consequences of such changes for children, young people, and their use of media? Does lack of freedom to play outside influence time spent watching television? Do global media encourage consumerist values? How does children's new-found expertise with computers affect parental authority?

Such questions open up a third starting point for researching children and young people's changing media environment. This goes beyond the child-centered and media-centered approaches by encompassing debates about childhood and youth, as well as those concerning media and information technologies, within the broader set of concerns commonly theorized as "late modernity" (Fornäs & Bolin, 1994; Giddens, 1991; Reimer, 1995; Thompson, 1995). Theorists of late modernity stress the convergence of historically linked processes, operating at both the institutional and individual level, which although not necessarily constituting a break with the past, suggest a new array of opportunities and dangers across diverse spheres of social life. From the point of view of children and young people, these changes have resulted in a reconsideration during the twentieth century of their status as citizens within Western society. Most notably, the United Nations Convention on the Rights of the Child ratified a wide range of children's rights, although this stress on children's rights is paralleled in other spheres by a growing perception of children as a market.

UNIVERSITY OF WOLVERHAMPTON
Harrison Learning Centre

ITEMS ISSUED:

Customer ID: WPP62911732

Title: Children and their changing media
environment : a European comparative study
ID: 762308183X
Due: 13/12/2016 23:59

Total items: 1
Total fines: £2.40
06/12/2016 11:23
Issued: 9
Overdue: 0

Thank you for using Self Service.
Please keep your receipt.

Overdue books are fined at 40p per day for
1 week loans, 10p per day for long loans.

Giddens (1991) noted that, "Modern institutions differ from all preceding forms of social order in respect of their dynamism, the degree to which they undercut traditional habits and customs, and their global impact" (p. 1). To conceptualize these complex changes, we found three trends to be particularly pertinent in guiding our research. Each gives rise to a set of debates and dilemmas regarding its potential opportunities and dangers. Here we focus on privatization, individualization, and globalization, specifically as they help us understand children's and young people's position in relation to new media technologies. We hope that insofar as our findings relate to these broader social trends, the present study of children and young people can also inform that bigger debate.

Privatization refers to the retreat from publically accessible spaces where people are conceptualized as citizens (e.g., Meyrowitz, 1985) and to the parallel shift toward domestic spaces, where people are conceptualized as consumers or audiences (or, as Habermas (1962/1989) put it, to the refeudalization of the public sphere by commercial interests). For example, one observable trend for children is the growth of protectionist practices that serve to restrict their access to public spaces while enhancing the attractions of privatized forms of leisure, whether at home or in commercial leisure centers.

One may suppose, therefore, that the family would be of growing importance to children, yet although the family home remains all-important as a vital resource for leisure as well as sustenance, the process of individualization ensures that within this home, family members are increasingly "living together separately" (Flichy, 1995), leading Giddens (1993), among others, to write of "a democratization of the private sphere" (p. 184). *Individualization* refers to the shift away from traditionally important sociostructural determinants of identity and behavior toward more diversified notions of lifestyle (Reimer, 1995; Ziehe, 1994). Individuals are seen as placing increasing stress on constructing a project of the self independent of such traditional structures of identity as socioeconomic status, gender, region, or age, where these are, in any case, breaking down or becoming blurred.

Buchner (1990) noted that by the end of the twentieth century, "every child is increasingly expected to behave in an 'individualized way' . . . children must somehow orient themselves to an *anticipated* life course. The more childhood in the family is eclipsed by influences and orientation patterns from outside the family . . . the more independent the opportunity (and drive) to making up one's own mind, making one's own choice . . . described here as the *biographization* of the life course" (pp. 77–78). Thus privatization and individualization represent different ways of conceptualizing changes in social relations, the former focusing on the private versus the public or civic sphere whereas the latter focuses on individual versus communal but socially stratified culture. The position of the home is both complex and changing: Although traditionally private and socially stratified by class, gender, and age, privatization makes the home of increasing importance as a site of leisure and work, whereas individualism means that children are ever less inheriting their cultural possibilities and preferences from their parents. The position of the media is also shifting: Traditionally part of the public and communal sphere in Europe especially, they are becoming commercialized, thereby potentially undermining public and communal culture by offering more opportunities for individual lifestyle choices.

Thus commercialized forms of peer culture and media culture are increasingly penetrating the family home. For many observers, this is particularly of concern in relation to children and young people insofar as children are ever more construed as a valuable market in their own right as well as a key driver of consumption in the home. The media represent not only the means whereby consumer messages reach children but are themselves increasingly indistinguishable from them, as programs promote toy tie-ins, as electronic games are comarketed with fast-food offers, and so on (cf. Kinder, 1991; Kline, 1993). What is most notable about the growth in consumerism is that it increasingly involves global brands and products. Hence, our third trend is that of *globalization*. Although this refers to several processes—economic and political as well as cultural—we are here interested in the strengthening of global culture, or global identities, at the expense of national culture and identity (Tomlinson, 1999). The globalization of culture leads to many questions regarding national identity, linguistic boundaries, or moral traditions, and these are often expressed as anxieties in relation to young people. Not only are their preferences for British music, Australian soaps, Japanese cartoons, or American films seen as the "weak link" through which external "threats" make their entry, but also, being young, children are seen as harbingers of the future for national cultures.

Adopting a Comparative Perspective

In comparing countries, one faces opposing temptations. One invites the conclusion that children, and media, are much the same everywhere, and that observed variations are trivial. The other invites the conclusion that "societies and cultures are fundamentally non-comparable and certainly cannot be evaluated against each other" (Chisholm, 1995, p. 22). The advantages and disadvantages of cross-national comparisons depend on how countries are compared, with different models striking a different balance between the search for commonalities (or *universalism*) and the identification of difference (or *relativism*). In the history of comparative research, many strategies have been found more or less useful in different circumstances (Øyen, 1990). Kohn (1989) offered a useful classification of these approaches.

First is the search for commonalities. Here the focus is on testing the generality of findings across different national contexts. An example of this is research on the common gender differences to be found in different countries (e.g., Gibbons, Lynn, & Stiles, 1997; see also chapter 12, this volume). The role of the family provides another example: As a recent 14-nation European study found, "the national reports . . . all bear witness to the importance of families and kinship relations with respect to reproduction and no evidence is given for declining functions" (Dahlström, 1989, p. 41; although see chapter 7 for some within-Europe differences). The second and converse strategy is of rather less interest here, for its idiographic focus leads researchers to treat each country as the primary object of study, using the particularities of one country to contrast with or reveal the different characteristics of others.

For reasons of parsimony, the comparisons made within this volume begin with this first model, assuming in particular that gender, age, and socio-economic status (SES) are likely to operate in similar ways across national contexts. When universals are expected, their confirmation is useful, but it is their contradiction that is often most interesting. For example, as social inequalities in household income are greater in some countries than others, we find not constant but greater within-country differences in domestic media ownership by SES for those countries (see chapter 3).

Clearly, any contradiction of universalist assumptions demands explanation. One way of approaching this is to adopt what Kohn (1989) labeled the *transnational* comparative model, treating nations as components of a larger system and so seeking more abstract or generalized accounts of observed differences. In line with the earlier theoretical discussion about the cultural shifts in society, and hence in contexts of childhood and youth, some of the chapters that follow consider the ways in which European countries are subject to the conditions of late modernity. Given the considerable similarities among the countries being compared here in their degree of modernization, this perspective is of only limited value in accounting for cross-national differences, though it offers an insightful interpretative framework. Nonetheless, the key processes of privatization, individualization, and globalization just discussed do illuminate certain findings in which different media are refracted or appropriated by different groups of children and young people in different contexts. For example, chapter 8 seeks to account for the United Kingdom's relative lead in the possession and use of personalized screen media in terms of privatization and individualization within the home and the society.

However, the model of comparative analysis to which we have devoted most attention treats countries as the *unit* of analysis, where each takes a position along key dimensions of social and cultural analysis (see Blumler, McLeod, & Rosengren, 1992). Also positioned between the extremes of universalism and relativism, yet taking a less abstract approach than the transnational model, this model investigates how social phenomena can be systematically related to the characteristics of the different countries. The selection of countries is critical to this model: We aimed to compare countries that differ moderately but not hugely and that, rather than being selected arbitrarily, are already bound together by the common regional and policy concerns of Europe (a similar justification is offered by Qvortrup, 1989).

In this chapter we identify two subtypes of this model—child-centered and media-centered—each focused on different sources of cross-national variation, in order to frame our analysis. Thus, we examine whether dimensions of cultural difference (such as variations in family structure, or national wealth, or linguistic uniformity/diversity) or dimensions of the media environment in each country are systematically related to observed differences in patterns of media use across our 12 European countries (see Appendix A). This allows us to ask such child-centered questions as: Do children who live in wealthier countries have greater access to the Internet? Are children living in larger language communities less open to American/global media? It also allows us to ask more media-centered questions. For example, do children brought up in countries with strong public service broadcasting traditions show greater interest in national programming? Or, now that the personal computer has entered the home, is the amount of reading done by children less affected in countries that place less stress on screen entertainment?

In what follows, we examine first the contexts for children's lives across Europe and second, we map media environments across Europe, focusing on the electronic screen. In both cases, our aim is to identify key dimensions that discriminate among countries, or groups of countries, in order to facilitate the thematic cross-national comparisons that form the substantive chapters of this volume. We caution, however, that there is no easy way to place boundaries around "context." Our comparison involves countries that are broadly comparable in degree of modernization and global positioning; however, we can only provide a brief and necessarily selective overview of some of the key dimensions along which the 12 countries vary, and we include nation-by-nation tables only where cross-national differences are marked.

As there are many demographic and cultural dimensions on which European countries can be compared, we considered an attempt at broad country groupings premature for the child-centered model; rather, the cross-national comparisons in the chapters to follow will probably be best interpreted in relation to specific social indicators. However, the variables relating to the media-centered model are more strongly interrelated, allowing us to draw out a tentative grouping of countries according to their media environments and, in consequence, suggest some substantive hypotheses to be examined in chapters to follow. We approach this process with caution, noting the difficulties in constructing country groupings (Teune, 1990). Most notably, variance within countries is often greater than that between them. However, without these groupings, it would prove difficult to explore cross-national hypotheses about the diffusion and consequences of new media that abound in academic and policy domains.

DEMOGRAPHIC AND CULTURAL CONTEXTS FOR CHILDHOOD IN EUROPE

In conducting comparative research, facts and figures referring to the amount of time children spend with particular media need to be carefully interpreted in the context of the available media and the policies that regulate them. They also need to be interpreted in the context of a wide range of cultural factors that frame the everyday lives of young people and their families in different countries. For although European countries differ in media provision, these differences are in turn partly explained by national wealth or socioeconomic indicators and partly they reflect differing structures of childhood and youth at all levels from individual domestic practices to national policy matters. Crucially, then, our stress on contextualization enables us to perceive the child as a complex human being acting in many different circles: at home, at school, with peers, at the sports club, in his or her own country, in Europe, in the world. Let us examine some of these demographic and cultural factors.

Population Stability

Population-wise (Table 1.1), Europe is made up of five largish countries (France, Germany, the United Kingdom, Italy, and Spain), with Germany well ahead with some 82 million inhabitants. The rest are small countries, with only the Netherlands qualifying as a middle-sized country. Urbanization is highest in Belgium and Israel, and lowest in Switzerland, Finland, and Italy. This is modestly correlated with population density, the Netherlands being the most crowded, followed closely by Belgium (with a population density equal to that of Japan) and then by three of the big five: the United Kingdom, Germany, and Italy; the least crowded countries are Sweden and Finland.

National Wealth

When looking at the real Gross Domestic Product (GDP) per capita in purchasing power (Table 1.1), Spanish and Israeli families rank among the poorest, with Sweden, Finland, Italy, and the United Kingdom next, showing lower than average income levels; Switzerland and Denmark are among the most highly ranked European countries.

TABLE 1.1
Population Characteristics and National Wealth

	Total Population (000s)	Urban Population as % of Total	Population Density (Inhabitants/ sq. km)	Real GDP per capita in PPP$	Real GDP per capita Poorest 20% Share in PPP$, 1980-1994	Real GDP per capita Richest 20% Share in PPP$, 1980-1994	Richest 20% to Poorest 20%, 1980-1994
Belgium	1014	97	333	22,750	7,718	35,172	4.6
Denmark	5270	85	122	23,690	5,454	38,986	7.1
Finland	5154	63	15	20,150	5,141	30,682	6.0
France	58683	75	108	22,030	5,359	40,098	7.5
Germany	82133	87	230	21,260	6,594	37,963	5.8
Great Britain	58649	89	244	20,730	3,963	38,164	9.6
Italy	57369	67	191	20,290	6,174	37,228	6.0
Israel	5984	91	259	18,150	4,539	29,957	6.6
Netherlands	15678	89	379	21,110	7,109	31,992	4.5
Spain	39628	77	78	15,930	5,669	24,998	4.4
Sweden	8875	83	20	19,790	7,160	33,026	4.6
Switzerland	7299	61	172	25,240	5,907	50,666	8.6

Source Population: http://www.unicef.org (last update, 01/12/99, United Nations Population Division).
Source Urbanization: http//www.undp.org/hdro/iurban.htm (1995).
Source Population Density: Eurostat Yearbook '97; central Bureau of Statistics, Government of Israel, 1996.
Note. GDP = Gross domestic product; PPP$ = purchasing power parities in US$, based on comparisons among prices of consumer goods.
Source the Human Development Report 1999, data from 1997.

For questions of information technology diffusion and social exclusion, it may be more important to know how hierarchical European societies are. If we consider the disparity between the income levels of the richest 20% and the poorest 20%, we see that disparities are least in Spain, the Netherlands, and Belgium, whereas they are greatest in the United Kingdom and Switzerland. It is worth noting that the United Kingdom has the lowest income levels among its poorest 20% group and its richest 20% ranks among Europe's richest. On the other hand, Switzerland's top 20% share group enjoys Europe's highest income levels by far, and its poorest 20% are better off than the United Kingdom's. During the 1980s and 1990s, the earnings inequality increased most in the United Kingdom and least in the Nordic countries (United Nations Development Program, 1999).

Purchasing power or lack thereof is clearly linked to (un)employment, and high and persistent unemployment is undoubtedly one of Europe's major problems. Of the countries under study, Switzerland has the lowest unemployment rate, and Spain has the highest (*Europe in Figures*, 1995). Finland, France, and Italy are three more countries with an unemployment rate above 10%. Across Europe, more women than men are jobless, and youth unemployment is twice as high as the average.

Family Characteristics

Regardless of how youth is defined, the percentage of young people in the population is slowly but surely falling across Europe. However, the percentage of the population under 20 years of age is comparable among the countries in our study (about one in four). Israel has a clearly younger population (35%); both Italy's (21%) and Germany's (22%) populations are relatively older. The prospects are that Europe is becoming a "grey" continent: life expectancy rates are rising while birth rates are falling (Table 1.2). Italy and Spain, traditionally associated with big families, now have among Europe's lowest birth rates; the highest birth rate is to be found in Sweden. Today, the average European family includes no more than one or two children; Italy's single-child family figure is Europe's highest.

This slump in births is affected by economic, social, and religious factors. Traditionally fecund countries such as Italy and Spain show similar patterns: a clear decline in the Catholic church's influence and gains in wealth since World War II have led to the postponement of marriage and child rearing. The mean age of women giving birth across the European countries in our study is 28 to 29 years. Although there is little cross-national variation in the marriage rate (which stands at approximately 5 marriages per 1000 people; *Eurostat Yearbook '97*), secularization has increased the frequency of divorce. Although the average is approximately 2 divorces per 1000 people (in 1995; *Europe in Figures*), it is still lowest in the Mediterranean countries

TABLE 1.2

Family Characteristics: Birth Rate (per 1000); Families by Number of Children as % of all Families; Single-Parent Households; Working Mothers

	Birth Rate (per 1000)	Families With One Child	Families With Two Children	Families With Three+ Children	Single Parent Families as % of all Families	Proportion of Employed Mothers (%)
Belgium	11.8	32	24	11	31.6	60
Denmark	12.0	23	19	5	38.3	73
Finland	12.5	30	24	10	30.3	54
France	12.4	28	23	13	24.5	54
Germany	9.2	32	23	7	30.0	41
Great Britain	12.9	27	24	11	35.8	45
Italy	9.6	34	29	11	21.8	41
Israel	21.4	14	20	26	18.8	71
Netherlands	12.3	25	27	12	24.7	48
Spain	9.8	28	31	19	16.4	35
Sweden	13.6	21	19	8	37.7	67
Switzerland	12.3	25	24	10	23.2	n/a

Source Birth Rate: *Europe in Figures* (1995-2000); *Central Bureau of Statistics, Government of Israel, 1997.*
Source Percentage of Only Children, Families with Two, Three, or More Children: *Eurostat Yearbook '97* (figures based upon 1991).
Source Single Parents: Eurostat Yearbook '97; Central Bureau of Statistics, Government of Israel, 1997.
Source Finland: http//www.stat.fi/tk/tp/tasku/vaes/oen.html
Source for Proportion of Mothers Who Are Employed (with a 3-year-old child): Eurostat, UOE, and Labour Force Survey in *Key Data on Education in the European Union* (1997), data from 1994-1995. *Central Bureau of Statistics, Government of Israel, 1997 (for Jewish population only).*
Source for single parent families: calculated from data in Eurostat '97.

(fewer than one divorce per 1000) and highest in the United Kingdom and the Nordic countries (between 2 and 3 divorces per 1000). Consequently, the number of children being raised by a single parent is also growing; highest in the United Kingdom, lowest in Spain.

The situation of women in the workforce varies widely across the countries: Swedish women are by far the most numerous in the workforce (about 9 in 10 are employed), whereas in Italy and Spain only 3 to 4 out of 10 women are in the job market. The other countries stand somewhere in the middle, with 5 women out of 10 (BE-vlg, DE, FR, IS, NL)[1] or even 6 to 7 in 10 in the workforce (CH, DK, GB). Although in all countries under scrutiny the female component of the labor force has risen during recent decades, the cross-national differences appear relatively stable (compare with Boh, 1989). The proportion of mothers who are employed, be it part-time or full-time, follows a similar pattern (highest in Denmark and Sweden, lowest in Spain and Italy). The relatively low rates of working mothers (with a 3-year-old child) in Germany, the United Kingdom, and the Netherlands may be explained in part by the relative lack of day-care facilities in those countries. Provision of day-care and after-school facilities for children varies considerably across Europe: such facilities are far more available in Nordic countries than in Mediterranean countries. Although, broadly speaking, men are increasingly encouraged to participate in family care, women remain the main domestic caregivers (and continue to be persistently seen as such, which makes change extremely difficult).[2]

Cultural Diversity and Religion

In a fast-globalizing world, European societies become more and more heterogeneous owing to migration flows from North Africa and east and central Europe. On the other hand, regionalist forces fueled by feelings of identity

---

[1]Throughout this volume, we have adopted the international convention of identifying countries by two letters, as follows: Flanders (BE-vlg), Denmark (DK), Finland (FI), France (FR), Germany (DE), Israel (IL), Italy (IT), the Netherlands (NL), Spain (ES), Sweden (SE), Switzerland (CH), United Kingdom (GB).

[2]In Europe, Finland has traveled the furthest: after a 12-month maternity leave, either parent is offered the possibility to stay at home until the child is 3 years old, including financial compensation and job guarantees after those 3 years. If the parents prefer to continue to work outside, it is the community's responsibility to arrange for child care while the parents are out working. Some Nordic countries have legislation allowing parents to reduce their daily working hours to take care of family commitments: Finland allows parents of children under age 4, Sweden parents with children under age 10, to shorten each workday by 2 hours, to be dedicated to child care. Indeed, flexible work schedules on the one hand and expanding public day-care centers on the other allow mothers (and fathers) to more easily combine paid work with family commitments. Germany offers "flexitime" practices; in Sweden part-time work while children are still very young can always be turned into full-time employment whenever wanted. Employers, traditionally unsupportive of such arrangements, now allow employees to work out of their homes or to bring "home to work," by providing child care at the workplace (United Nations Development Program, 1995).

and alienation are stronger in some countries than others. Finland has one of Europe's most homogeneous populations (*Europe in Figures*, and Council of Europe's *Recent demographic developments in Europe*, 1997), as does Israel with 80% of the population Jewish. Switzerland and Belgium have the largest number of foreign nationals, one reason being the high proportion of white-collar workers (often European Union Member State nationals) hired by European and international institutions located in Brussels and Geneva. The European country currently attracting the most immigrants is Germany, followed by Italy, with incoming migration significantly higher than outgoing migration.

When it comes to religion (cf. *Europe in Figures*), countries can be grouped differently: some countries are very homogeneous (Italy and Spain are mainly Catholic; Denmark and Sweden are mainly Lutheran). Others, like Germany and Switzerland, show a more diverse picture. Declining religiosity, especially strong in the United Kingdom and the Netherlands, has consequences both for society (e.g., higher divorce rates) and for specifically media-related activities (e.g., Protestants have traditionally shown more reticence towards the media, especially television, than has the relatively more permissive Catholic church).

Education

A country's willingness to invest in the future can be gauged by its support for its education system (Table 1.3). Of European countries involved in our study, Denmark spends the largest share of GNP on education and Germany spends the smallest. Judging from its education budget as part of the total state expenditure, the Italian government spends the least on education, followed by Germany, whereas the Swiss government spends the most. Empowerment of women also starts with education. Therefore it is encouraging to see that in both upper secondary and post-18 higher education, females have caught up with and in some cases overtaken males, most especially in Sweden and France and least in Germany and, to a lesser extent, the Netherlands. However, undoubtedly the biggest media-related budget issue at present throughout Europe in education circles is to get more computers into primary and secondary schools (one PC per 10 to 15 pupils is generally the target). The current status of *SchoolNet* in Europe, which depends on partnerships between governments and the private sector, has more to do with an accumulation of regional initiatives than a full-fledged network (see chapter 10).

The age at which compulsory schooling ends ranges from 14 to 16 years. In Belgium, Germany, and the Netherlands it is 18 years if part-time schooling is also taken into account. Compulsory schooling may begin before the age of 6 (Table 1.3). The duration of compulsory education throughout Europe ranges from 8 or 9 years (DK, FI, IT, SW) to 12 or 13 years (BE-vlg, DE,

TABLE 1.3

Education: Public Expenditure; Organization of School Time (at age 10); Gender Inequalities

Country	% GNP Spent on Education	% Total Government Expenditure Spent on Education	Combined Enrollment at First, Second, and Third Levels of Education	Duration (years) of Compulsory Schooling	Daily Load (min/day at School)	Annual Load (hours/year) at School	Female Participation in Education (number girls per 100 boys in upper secondary education), 1993-1994	Female Participation in Education (number girls per 100 boys in higher education), 1993-1994
Belgium	5.7	10.2	100	9 f/t + 3 p/t	280	948	97	97
Denmark	8.3	12.6	89	9	216	720	101	105
Finland	7.6	11.9	99	9	207-225	656-713	125	113
France	5.9	10.8	92	10	282	846	96	120
Germany	4.7	9.4	88	9 f/t + 3 p/t	227	712	85	73
Great Britain	5.5	11.4	100	11	295	903	115	100
Italy	4.9	8.8	82	8	270	900	99	106
Israel	6.6	12.3	80	10	300	1193-1476	n/a	n/a
Netherlands	5.3	9.5	98	11 f/t + 2 p/t	300	1000	84	86
Spain	5.0	12.6	92	10	270	810	111	104
Sweden	8.0	11.0	100	9	240	760	114	120
Switzerland	5.5	15.6	79	9	165-317	529-1120	n/a	n/a

Note. f/t = full time, p/t = part time.
Source: Spending on Education; UNDP 1998 (based upon 1995). Source: Combined First-, Second-, and Third-Level Gross Enrollment Ratios (i.e., primary, secondary, and post-18 education): UNDP 1999.
Source: Duration of Compulsory Schooling: Youth in the European Union. From Education to Working Life. Eurostat 1997 and Education Across the European Union—Statistics and Indicators. Eurostat 1996 (based upon 1996).
Source: Eurydice. Organisation of School Time. Brussels. Eurydice European Unit, 1997.
Source for female participation in education: Education Across the European Union—Statistics and Indicators, Eurostat (1996) and Youth in the European Union, From Education to working life (Eurostat).

NL); France, Spain, and Israel occupy an intermediate position with 10 years of compulsory education. Clearly, cross-cultural differences in the structuring of the school day may also affect the amounts of time spent with media. Across all countries, children spend 5 days a week at school, except for Italy, where they spend 6. The average daily load of hours spent at school shows more variety: Danish and German children spend the least time in the classroom every day, whereas Dutch, British, French, and Belgian children spend the most time there. This pattern persists on an annual basis: Dutch children spend up to 1,000 hours a year in the classroom, but the figure for German children is a mere 712 hours.

MAPPING MEDIA ENVIRONMENTS ACROSS EUROPE

Further to the prior demographic, social, cultural, and economic factors that structure everyday life for young people in Europe, the contextualization of children's media use also requires an understanding of the media environments in the countries being studied. Unfortunately, there is no consensus among researchers on how to define *media environment*, and the few approaches that do systematically classify European countries (e.g., McCain, 1986) can only provide some hints to guide our comparative study. Thus in order to construct a meaningful and pragmatic classification of European countries, we begin with economic, political, and technological aspects of the media environment that are likely to determine the conditions within which children and young people in Europe develop their own patterns of media use. For the most part, such statistics as are available concern the adult population; clearly it is information about children and young people that is lacking, this being the gap that the present volume seeks to fill. Thus, given our focus on the domestic screen, we first examine the television environment in our 12 European countries. Second, we analyze similarities and differences with regard to new screen-based technologies. Third, we examine everyday media use to identify orientations toward the different media.

The Television Environment

Before dealing with differences between European countries, we should emphasize one important commonality of European broadcasting systems that contrasts with, particularly, the United States of America. As a rule, European broadcasting landscapes are organized as "dual systems" with public service broadcasters not just being a supplement to commercial but a central (and until recently, the only) pillar of the broadcasting system. One aspect of this position of public broadcasting is the availability of advertising-free and thus less commercialized children's programming in many

European countries (Blumler & Biltereyst, 1997). However, in recent years public broadcasters have been facing increasing competition by global (American) commercial children's channels like Cartoon Network, The Disney Channel, Nickelodeon, and Fox Kids Network (Table 1.4). These channels, where they are available, are generally successful, setting a trend toward thematic channels for children. This trend is furthered by the advent of digital television—all the digital bouquets available so far in Europe include at least one children's channel. In order to compete with these new channels, some public broadcasters have started thematic children's channels themselves (e.g., Kinderkanal in Germany and RaiSat 2 in Italy). At the same time, we are seeing a reduction in air time for children's programs on the main public service channels. Nevertheless, in 1997–1998 (during our empirical field work), children's television in Europe was characterized by public broadcasters providing nationally distributed noncommercial children's programs on their main channels, together with a few commercial global competitors, available in households with cable or satellite equipment.

Beyond these commonalities mentioned so far, media environments in Europe are shaped by characteristics of the respective media markets. We can group countries according to three criteria: the size of the language markets, technical infrastructure, and the distribution of new technologies (see Fig. 1.1).

For media products, language plays a significant role: The bigger the number of native speakers of a given language, the bigger the potential market for media products in this language. As a consequence, it might be expected that media environments for bigger language communities would provide more options than those for smaller communities. In addition, and for the same reasons, imported television programs in countries with bigger languages are usually dubbed, whereas in countries with smaller languages they are usually subtitled. In Fig. 1.1 we first differentiate between "big" and "small" language communities. In each of the six countries belonging to bigger language communities (CH, DE, ES, FR, GB, IT), the vast majority of television channels available are broadcast in their national language. As other studies show (e.g., Eurobarometer, 1994), knowledge of foreign languages is lower than in the other group of countries with smaller languages (BE-vlg, DK, FI, IL, NL, SE).

In the 1980s and early 1990s, the development of television in European countries was influenced by the technical infrastructure, the main factor in that period being cable distribution. This, then, provides us with a second criterion for grouping the countries. Due to marked differences in cable policies, the quantity of television channels available differs considerably across Europe. For example, in Belgium and the Netherlands, relatively small countries with the highest population density in Europe, cable technology has represented an appropriate means of broadcast distribution;

TABLE 1.4
Children's Television Channels in Europe

Channel	Shareholder	Country (Launch date)	Subscribers*
Canal J	MCM Euromisique et al.	FR (1985)	2.5
Carlton Kids	Carlton Comms.	GB (1998)	0.1
Cartoon Network	Turner Network	NL/BE. (1977), FR/BE-cf. (1998), IT/CH (1998), GB (1993), DK/SE (1997), ES (1997)	8.3
Channel 6	Nova Communications	IL (1989)	1.1
The Disney Channel	Walt Disney Co	IT (1998), ES (1998), GB (1995)	5.4
Fox Kids	Fox Family Worldwide	NL (1998), BE-cf. (1999), Nordic (1998), ES (1998), FR (1997), GB (1996)	14.4
Junior	Kirch Group	DE (1996)	0.1
Junior TV	Orsini Family	IT (1985)	16.7
Kinderkanal	ARD/ZDF	DE (1997)	23.0
Kindernet	n.d.	NL (1988)	6.3
K-toon	Kirch Group	DE (1996)	0.1
Manga	Groupe AB	FR (1998)	0.5
Nickelodeon	Viacom (& partners)	Nordic (1997), ES (1999), GB (1993)	6.6
Panda	TPS Multicanal	ES (1996)	0.3
RaiSat2	RAI	IT (1997)	0.8
Super RTL	CLT-Ufa, Walt Disney Co	DE (1995)	21.5
TCC	Flextech	Nordic (n.d.)	0.6
Télétoon	TPS	FR (1997)	1.3
Trouble	Flextech	GB (1996)	n.d.

Note. *In millions of households; total number in the countries mentioned in the table. Source: *Screen Digest,* May 1999, pp. 105-107.

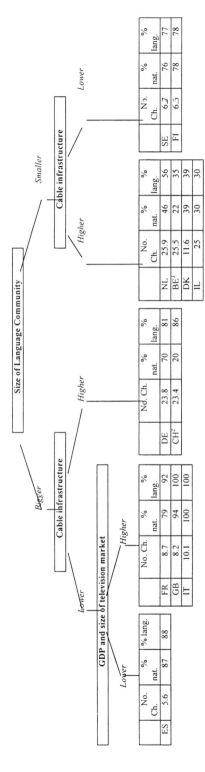

FIG. 1.1.   Grouping countries according to their television environment.[1]

[1]These figures result from calculations that draw on information provided in IP (ed.): Television 97, European Key Facts (Neuilly-sur-Seine) (Figures for Israel were estimated on the basis of national data). Channels listed for each country are weighted according to their technical distribution across the population and summed for the following categories: a) Total number of channels available ("No. Ch."); among these b) percentage of national channels ("% nat."), and c) percentage of national, foreign and pan-European channels distributed in the native language ("% lang."). The numbers of channels are to be read as "number of channels available for the average television household;" they do not represent the total number of channels. In order to take technical distribution into account, channels were weighted by the percentage of television households they reach. For example, a channel covering 100% of the country was counted as 1.0, another channel reaching 50% of the television households was counted as 0.5.

[2]Figures for the German speaking Switzerland. Figures for the French and Italian speaking parts of Switzerland are similar, except that the foreign channels are not German but French or Italian respectively.

[3]Figures for the Flemish Community of Belgium.

almost 100% of the television households in these countries are connected to cable. Switzerland and Germany also have high cable density. In these four countries, most viewers live in a multichannel environment with more than 23 channels available on average. The key difference between Belgium and the Netherlands on the one hand and Germany and Switzerland on the other is that in the latter "big language" countries, the majority of channels available are in their native language.[3] From the viewpoint of children, it is worth noting that more channels generally means more dedicated children's channels are available, whether national or transnational. It also means more variation, and hence possibly more inequality, across households within countries with many channels.

The Nordic countries have experienced a rapid growth of channel availability by cable and especially by satellite over the last few years, among them Denmark. Despite its significantly lower number of channels available, Denmark has been grouped together with Belgium, the Netherlands, and Israel because of these countries' similarities with regard to the significance of foreign channels and foreign language offers. In this group, fewer than half of the channels available are national channels. This contrasts with the situation in Sweden and Finland, where there are fewer channels available and a stronger focus on national channels.

Compared to the multichannel environments in Germany and Switzerland, the other bigger language countries provide much fewer channels. Cable and satellite reception is relatively rare here, especially in Italy and Spain. The United Kingdom and France are experiencing a rapid growth of satellite as well as cable distribution, but nevertheless the figures are far below those of the other countries in our study. Within this group of four "bigger" countries, a further differentiation may be made by separating Spain from the others because of its smaller national television market and thus smaller number of domestic channels.

Distribution of New Technologies

Beyond the differences outlined for television environments, there are marked differences in media provision both between and within European states in relation to newer forms of media. In the information age, the central issue is the extent to which the network society has become a reality in Europe. Politicians and policy-makers view information and communication technologies (ICT's) as a top priority: ICT's bring economic development, and

---

[3]Germany and Switzerland differ in other ways, however. Unlike Germany, Switzerland is a relatively small country whose different language communities share the same language as a bigger country. Thus we find the "next-door-giant" problem: The many foreign channels available in their own language cause heavy competition for national broadcasters; hence only a small number of the channels available for Swiss households are national channels.

scenarios in which disadvantaged groups are permanently excluded from the benefits of information technology must therefore be avoided (see e.g., Bangemann, 1994). In order to assess the preparedness of different countries for the demands of a network society, the World Economic Forum (1996) published a ranking of countries that is based on the number of phone lines, mobile phones, television density, cable and satellite connections, PC penetration, and the overall maturity of business use of new technologies. Within this ranking, 5 of the European countries involved in this study are among the first 10 (FI 2nd, DK 3rd, SE 5th, CH 7th, and NL 10th). A middle group is made up by Germany (13th), the United Kingdom (14th), and Belgium (15th). According to the World Economic Forum's criteria, France (20th), Israel (22nd), Italy (23rd), and Spain (25th) seem to be less prepared for the network society.

More specifically, let us now examine Internet penetration in Europe. Although always lagging far behind the United States in this respect, Europe has now definitely taken to the Net. In May 1998, 23 million people were on-line in Europe according to various surveys (e.g., the NUA Internet Survey, 1998). Because of the high growth rate of Internet adoption in Europe, any research soon becomes out of date and estimates of the numbers on-line are inevitably inexact as surveys abound and very different measures are used. The Information Society Project Office (ISPO), in cooperation with Eurobarometer, conducted a Europe-wide public opinion survey that included questions on familiarity with and appreciation of media in order to go beyond the fragmentary picture given by national surveys to facilitate pan-European comparisons. Table 1.5 shows that Internet use differs widely between European countries: Nordic countries and the Netherlands are early adopters, followed by the United Kingdom (see also chapter 3). The situation for the use of mobile phones is similar to this, with the exception that for this new tool, the Netherlands does not belong to the top group.

One further factor that might explain differences in the significance of new information technologies is the English language (see also chapter 13). Among the pioneers are exactly those European countries that are closest to the English language, either because it is their native language or because they belong to the smaller language communities who have had to use English for international communication: This might make it easier to approach the new information technologies and services, many of them being in English.

Patterns of Media Orientations

As a further step we can examine the cultural aspect of media environments. Within Europe, different patterns of media orientations have developed regarding, for example, the average reach and amount of use of both old and new media. As Table 1.5 shows, several European countries focus heavily on television (ES, GB, IT). Households in these countries often have more than

TABLE 1.5
Use of New and Old Media

	BE	CH	DE	DK	ES	FI	FR	GB	IL	IT	NL	SE
Availability and use of new media												
1 Individuals (15+) using PC at home (%, 1997)	25	n.a.	26	**50**	24	34	*19*	38	n.d.	25	**53**	**48**
2 Individuals (15+) using the Internet/WWW at home (%, 1997)	3.4	n.a.	4.4	8.9	1.8	9.5	*2.0*	5.9	n.d.	*3.1*	**10.7**	**18.5**
3 Individuals using the Internet/WWW in office (% of those employed)	7.9	n.a.	8.8	**19.8**	3.0	**20.5**	*4.4*	12.2	n.d.	8.0	**19.7**	**27.3**
4 Individuals (15+) using Mobile Phone at home/for private reasons (%, 1997)	*14*	n.a.	*11*	**34**	*14*	**44**	*9*	25	n.d.	22	15	**55**
Orientations toward different old media												
5 TV households with 2 TV sets or more (% of TV households, 1997)	*18*	*20*	*23*	42	58	46	37	**79**	n.d.	50	38	39
6 Average daily TV viewing (in min, 1997, adults)	168	*128*	196	162	**218**	150	193	**228**	151*	**217**	157	149
7 Average daily radio listening (in min, 1996, adults)	187	*190*	174	139	*101*	**213**	192	154	140	172	179	174
8 Circulation of newspapers 1996 (copies per 1000 inhabitants)	*163*	*357*	*318*	311	*105*	*456*	*182*	330	n.d.	*105*	307	*438*
9 Daily reach of newspapers 1998 (%)	*52*	**85**	79	78	38	**87**	50	74	83	42	72	**84**
10 Use of news in different media (% saying "everyday"):												
Newspapers	33	n.a.	60	61	34	**70**	27	50	69	32	64	**76**
Television	66	n.a.	65	70	68	**80**	56	**73**	n.d.	**82**	77	69
Radio	50	n.a.	54	**73**	42	53	38	48	n.d.	23	56	58

Notes. 1-4: Information Society Project Office (ISPO): Measuring Information Society 1997. (http://www.ispo.cec.be/infosoc/promo/pubs/poll97; access October 1999).

5-6: IP (1998): Television 98. European Key Facts. Neuilly-sur-Seine, August 1998; for Israel: OTOT, May 1999 (data for 1998).

   7: GEAR 1997: for Israel: OTOT, May 1999 (data for 1998).

   8: Gustafsson/Weibull (1997), p. 255.

   9: BDZV (1998): Zeitungen 98. Bonn: Advertisers Association of Israel (1977).

 10: Eurobarometer No. 46, autumn 1996; Advertisers Association of Israel (1997).

one television set (see row 5), and the individual amount of viewing adds up to more than 3 hours per day (row 6). On the other hand, despite their multi-channel environment, people in German-speaking Switzerland watch 1½ hours less. Radio listening times show a rather complementary picture: people in Finland, France, Switzerland, and Flanders reach the highest usage figures. Differences with regard to newspaper reading are even more significant. There are substantial differences between newspaper-oriented countries (especially CH, FI, SE) with a daily reach of around 85% and other countries where newspapers reach only half of the population or even less (ES, FR, IT). These patterns of orientations are supported by indicators from other sources: as the Eurobarometer survey showed, adults across Europe differ in where they seek their news (row 10).

Conclusion

As a conclusion of this overview of media-related comparative indicators, we propose a pragmatic classification for relating the results of our comparative study to the media environments in Europe. Because this study on children and young people is particularly interested in new technologies, this criterion is taken as the primary one to group the countries involved.

First, there is a group with Spain, Italy, and France, characterized by a focus on national television and relatively low figures in new technologies. This classification is mainly based on cable and satellite television and the availability of PCs and the Internet as the globalized new technologies.[4]

The second group is less homogeneous than the first, being made up of Germany, Switzerland, Belgium, and Israel, all countries with a multichannel environment and moderate use of new technologies, but with different preferences with regard to television and newspapers.

Third, the United Kingdom is treated as a group on its own: Contrary to the pattern observed elsewhere, it combines a heavy orientation toward television with rather high figures for new technologies.

Finally, the fourth group, with the Nordic countries and the Netherlands, includes those countries that are seen as the pioneers of new technologies. The new technologies are integrated to a media environment that is characterized by a focus on newspapers (and radio) and less importance of television. Together with the United Kingdom, they are also countries with a strong public service television tradition, though a link to new technologies here is unclear.

---

[4]Thus, this does not take into account rather specific technologies (e.g., Minitel in France) that could be interpreted as very high availability of computers. Given the leading role today taken by France and Spain in digital television, this classification might be a surprise, but in 1997–1998, when our empirical work was completed, digital television was not yet a part of children's media environment in any country.

A BRIEF NOTE ON THE REPORTING
OF FINDINGS IN THIS VOLUME

The 12 countries included in this volume were selected so as to ensure representation from across (western) Europe, the point being to include countries that vary along the key dimensions of European Union policy debate
(size, wealth, linguistic and ethnic diversity, geography); beyond this theoretical consideration, country selection was also, inevitably, partly serendip-
itous. However, the comparative analysis is organized around genuine collaboration to address key themes, with each chapter analyzing data
produced by all countries in relation to a specific intellectual and empirical
theme, instead of the rather easier reporting of a series of national projects
according to a common agenda, a process that leaves the drawing of comparative conclusions to the reader. In opting for direct cross-national comparisons by chapter theme, we must acknowledge the effort, generosity, and
commitment of all national team members to pooling data and ideas during
the production of this volume. All team members and their national funders
are acknowledged in Appendix B.

REFERENCES

Bangemann, M. (1994). *Europe and the global information society: Recommendations to the Euro-
pean Council prepared by members of the high-level group on the information society*. Brussels:
European Council.
Blumler, J. G., McLeod, J. M., & Rosengren, K. E. (1992). An introduction to comparative com-
munication research. In J. G. Blumler, J. M. McLeod, and K. E. Rosengren (Eds.), *Compara-
tively speaking: communication and culture across space and time*. Newbury Park, CA: Sage.
Blumler, J. G., & Biltereyst, D. (1997, Winter). Trends in children's television. *Diffusion*, 27–30.
Boh, K. (1989). European family life patterns—A reappraisal. In K. Boh, M. Bak, C. Clason, M.
Pankratova, J. Qvortrup, G. B. Sgritta, & K. Waerness, (Eds.), *Changing patterns of European
family life*. London: Routledge.
Buchner, P. (1990). Growing up in the Eighties: Changes in the social biography of childhood in
the FRG. In L. Chisholm, P. Buchner, H.-H. Kruger, & P. Brown (Eds.), *Childhood, youth and
social change: A comparative perspective* (pp. 71–84). London: Falmer Press.
Buckingham, D. (1993). *Reading audiences: Young people and the media*. Manchester: Manchester
University Press.
Bundesverband Deutscher Zeitungsverleger (BDZV). (1998). *Zeitungen 98* [Newspapers 1998].
Bonn: ZV Zeitungs-Verlag Service GmbH.
Chisholm, L. (1995). European youth research: Tour de force or turmbau zu babel? In L.
Chisholm, P. Buchner, H.-H. Kruger, & M. Bois-Reymond (Eds.), *Growing up in Europe: Con-
temporary horizons in childhood and youth studies* (pp. 21–32). Berlin: Walter de Gruyter.
Dahlström, E. (1989). Theories and ideologies of family functions, gender relations and human
reproduction. In K. Boh, M. Bak, C. Clason, M. Pankratova, J. Qvortrup, G. B. Sgritta, & K.
Waerness (Eds.), *Changing patterns of European family life* (pp. 31–52). London: Routledge.
Drotner, K. (1993). Media ethnography: An other story? *Nordicom, 2*, 1–13.
Edelstein, A. S. (Ed.). (1982). *Comparative communication research*. Beverly Hills, CA: Sage.

European Commission (1997a). *Key data on education in the European Union.* Luxembourg: Office for Official Publications of the European Communities.

European Commission (1997b). *Youth in the European Union—from education to working life.* Luxembourg: Office for Official Publications of the European Communities.

Eurostat (1997). *Eurostat yearbook—A statistical eye on Europe 1986–1996.* Luxembourg: Office for Official Publications of the European Communities.

Flichy, P. (1995). *Dynamics of modern communication: the shaping and impact of new communication technologies.* London: Sage.

Fornäs, J., & Bolin, G. (Eds.). (1994). *Youth culture in late modernity.* Beverly Hills, CA: Sage.

Gibbons, J. L., Lynn, M., & Stiles, D. A. (1997). Cross-national gender differences in adolescents' preferences for free-time activities. *Cross-Cultural Research: The Journal of Comparative Social Science, 31*(1), 55–69.

Giddens, A. (1991). *Modernity and self-identity: Self and society in the late modern age.* Cambridge: Polity Press.

Giddens, A. (1993). *The transformation of intimacy: Sexuality, love and eroticism in modern societies.* Cambridge: Polity Press.

Graue, M. E., & Walsh, D. J. (1998). *Studying children in context: Theories, methods and ethics.* Thousand Oaks, CA: Sage.

Group of European Audience Researchers (GEAR) (1997). *Euro-Factsheets.* Vienna: ORF.

Gustafsson, K. E., & Weibull, L. (1997). European newspaper readership: Structure and development. *Communications, 22*(3), 249–273.

Habermas, J. (1989). *The structural transformation of the public sphere.* Cambridge, MA: MIT Press.

Himmelweit, H. T., Oppenheim, A. N., & Vince, P. (1958). *Television and the child: An empirical study of the effect of television on the young.* London and New York: Oxford University Press.

Information Society Project Office (ISPO): *Measuring Information Society 1997.* (http://www.ispo.cec.be/infosoc/promo/pubs/poll97; access October 1999).

IP (1998). *Television 98. European Key Facts.* Neuilly-sur-Seine, August 1998

James, A., Jenks, C., & Prout, A. (1998). *Theorizing childhood.* Cambridge: Cambridge University Press.

Kinder, M. (1991). *Playing with power in movies, television and video games: From Muppet Babies to Teenage Mutant Ninja Turtles.* Berkeley, CA: University of California Press.

Kline, S. (1993). *Out of the garden: Toys, TV, and children's culture in the age of marketing.* London and New York: Verso.

Kohn, M. L. (1989). Introduction. In M. L. Kohn (Ed.), *Cross-national research in sociology* (pp. 17–31). Newbury Park, CA: Sage.

Lagree, J.-C. (1995). Young people and employment in the European Community: Convergence or divergence? In L. Chisholm, B. Buchner, H.-H. Kruger, & M. Bois-Reymond (Eds.), *Growing up in Europe: Contemporary horizons in childhood and youth studies.* Berlin: Walter de Gruyter.

McCain, T. (1986). Patterns of Media Use in Europe: Identifying Country Clusters. In: *European Journal of Communication 1*, No. 2, pp. 231–250

Meyrowitz, J. (1985). *No sense of place: The impact of electronic media on social behavior.* New York: Oxford University Press.

NUA Internet Survey (1998). (http://www.nua.ie/surveys/how_many_online/europe.html)

Øyen, E. (1990). The imperfection of comparisons. In E. Øyen (Ed.), *Comparative methodology: Theory and practice in international social research.* London: Sage.

Qvortrup, J. (1989). Comparative research and its problems. In K. Boh, M. Bak, C. Clason, M. Pankratova, J. Qvortrup, G. B. Sgritta, & K. Waerness (Eds.), *Changing patterns of European family life.* London: Routledge.

Reimer, B. (1995). Youth and modern lifestyles. In J. Fornas & G. Bolin (Eds.), *Youth culture in late modernity.* London: Sage.

Rogers, E. M. (1986). *Communication technology: The new media in society.* New York: The Free Press.

Schlesinger, P. (1997). From cultural defence to political culture: media, politics and collective identity in the European Union. *Media, Culture and Society, 19*, 369–391.

Teune, H. (1990). Comparing countries: Lessons learned. In E. Øyen (Ed.), *Comparative methodology: Theory and practice in international social research.* London: Sage.

Thompson, J. B. (1995). *The media and modernity: a social theory of the media.* Cambridge: Polity.

Tomlinson, J. (1999). *Globalisation and culture.* Chicago: University of Chicago Press.

United Nations Development Program (1995). *Human development report.* New York: United Nations.

United Nations Development Program (1999). *Human development report.* New York: United Nations.

World Economic Forum (1996): *Global competitiveness report 1996.* Geneva.

Ziehe, T. (1994). From living standard to life style. *Young: Nordic Journal of Youth Research, 2*(2), 2–16.

Doing Comparative Research
With Children and Young People

Sonia Livingstone
Dafna Lemish

APPROACHING THE TASK

Despite widespread speculation about the changing media environment, when we began our research many things were unknown about children's and young people's use of media, especially the new media. In this project, we wanted to discover the facts and figures, and the meanings and experiences, associated with media access and use. We also wanted to understand the social contexts of access and use in terms of family, friends, and school, and we wanted to get a handle on the consequences of use for different young people and in different contexts. In this chapter, we elaborate the methods used in the comparative project with the primary aim of making our working procedures transparent. We learned a lot from designing and conducting this large-scale comparative project and hope that others may benefit from our experience, particularly as cross-national projects are becoming increasingly common in Europe and elsewhere.

To outline first the project design, we interviewed children and young people from 12 countries in Europe, from those just starting school at 6 years old to those coming to the end of their school career at 16 years old. Some live in rural surroundings, others in suburbs, others in city centers, and they come from households that vary considerably in income and social class. In all, we surveyed some 11,000 6 to 16-year-olds in four age bands (6–7, 9–10,

12–13, and 15–16 years).[1] Where funding allowed, we surveyed them face-to-face; many others completed questionnaires in their classrooms. Using qualitative, in-depth interviewing, we interviewed several hundred more. Their willing, often enthusiastic, participation in our project and their readiness to answer our questions at length added to the quality of the material collected. They were keen to contribute to a book about children and new media, and felt this addressed issues of importance to them.

Because our research questions centered on children's and young people's access to, use of, and attitudes toward 16 distinct media, the result is a very large data set that has the potential to address some complex issues. Our primary task was to document which young people have access to which media and how they use them in different European countries. This provides important baseline data against which future changes may be measured. In addition, having documented access and use during 1997 and 1998, we took the opportunity to segment the sample and recombine the variables in more complex ways to understand the more enduring patterns and trends. For we also wanted, more tentatively, to trace the consequences of technological and societal developments for children and young people, to identify new opportunities and dangers, to critique misleading claims, and to inform debate.

RESEARCHING CHILDREN AND YOUNG PEOPLE

Research on the uses of the domestic screen is generally conducted on households, by surveying adults. Yet parents and children may have different stories to tell about their everyday lives. Asking parents is not enough, nor is it satisfactory to treat children and young people as a homogeneous group, but what, if anything, is specific about researching children and young people? Despite the pervasive call to give children a "voice" in social research (Buckingham, 1993; Greig & Taylor, 1999; Ireland & Holloway, 1996; Mahon, Glendinning, Clarke, & Craig, 1996; Morrow & Richards, 1996), children are still perceived by many researchers as powerless subjects, incompetent according to cognitive and emotional developmental criteria, and so incapable of accurately describing and analyzing their own experiences. Adults, be they researchers, parents, or teachers, thus serve as informants for children's everyday lives. Yet their accounts may be misleading as a guide to understanding children's practices, pleasures, and meanings. For example, in the British study we asked both parents and children how much

---

[1]In fact in five countries (DE, DK, FR, GB and NL), the whole age range from 6 to 17 was sampled and in Sweden, the whole range from 7 to 17. This resulted in an overall total of around 14,600 children and young people taking part in the survey research.

time children spent with different media (Livingstone & Bovill, 1999). We found that parents claim somewhat lower television viewing for their children but higher reading times, compared with the times reported by their children. Here a social desirability effect operating on the part of parents would seem at least as plausible as the normative claim that children are simply unreliable respondents.

How we perceive children affects how we study them. In this project, we invited children and young people to recount their own world view in regard to the area of their lives in which they are the most powerful and knowledgeable—their leisure culture. Rather than "testing" their perceptions, evaluating their media usage, or imposing our preconceptions on "appropriate" behaviors, we were interested in hearing their own stories, from their own perspective, freed from adult value judgments. In this sense, our research is not merely "on" children but "with" them and "for" them (Hood, Kelley, & Mayall, 1996). Nonetheless, doing research with children is not an easy task, and we were constantly challenged by some major questions involving age, language, location, context, and ethics. We discuss next how each of these issues was handled in our research design.

Age

In many respects, the age boundaries dividing *children* from *young people* and both from *adults* are culturally constructed, with the education system, family law, the labor market, and cultural traditions all playing their part (James, Jenks, & Prout, 1998). Hence, rather than apply a cognitive–developmental approach to the variable of age (thus implicitly measuring children's performance against adult standards), we chose to treat our four separate age bands as objects of study in their own right. Thus we assume that each child is capable of providing valid and insightful information, provided that he or she is approached appropriately and that the data are interpreted carefully.

The question of age also raises that of the power differential between child and researcher. The latter runs the risk of collecting data that fit adult prior expectations whereas what the child is actually trying to convey, or is able to convey, about his or her world is missed (Graue & Walsh, 1998). To overcome such difficulties, we used various methods, adapted to the wide range of ages in our study. For example, some teams (e.g., the United Kingdom and Italy) used illustrative cards with pictures of media on them in interviews with the youngest children, and invited them to draw pictures. In all countries, face-to-face interviews conducted with children of different ages employed different wordings of the same questions and different interviewing practices. Following pilot work, two versions of the self-completion questionnaires were developed, designed to adjust to different competencies and experiences. In those countries where the questionnaires were administrated in the classrooms, 6- to 8-year-olds were interviewed individually and older children received the version for self-completion. Generally, the youngest children were treated rather differently from the rest: Certain questions, such as those estimating time spent with media, were not asked for this age group and other questions were asked in a simpler form or with more restricted response options.

Language

Key to the conduct of age-appropriate research is attention to the use of language, for there are dangers in researching children if language, a form of "performance," is used to evaluate competence (Buckingham, 1991; Hodge & Tripp, 1986). Children's production of linguistic utterances may fail to represent, sometimes overrepresenting and sometimes underrepresenting, their understandings and feelings (Lemish, 1997). In our study, we accept children's discourse in the personal interviews, and their responses to the questionnaires, as representative of what they chose to share with us about their leisure (Rudd, 1992). Thus their perceptions, expressed in their own words, were the center of our concern. This is not to say that we have analyzed their talk at face value, but we have not undervalued their accounts either.

In the qualitative work, the terms children use to discuss media in particular were of central interest. The metaphors they used to describe, the values they imputed to, and the expectations they associated with different media allowed us insight into their perspectives on new and old media. Indeed, it emerged clearly from these interviews that even the terms *old* and *new* reflect adult rather than child perspectives. In the quantitative survey it was important to ensure, for key terminology such as that of computers (though some difficulties arose also for other media, given changes in technology), that we both understood, and were understood by, the children we interviewed. The fact that "computer" for many children means "games machine" tells us much about the place of computers in children's lives and is not simply to be seen as an example of a restricted or careless use of language.

Location

In researching children, it is important to pay attention to where, as well as how, the research takes place. Thus, children's responses to, and cooperation with, the research process should be understood in relation to the particular social context (Buckingham, 1993; Rudd, 1992). For example, we know that children, like adults, interact differently in individual settings versus group situations, at home as opposed to in a formal school setting, or with an adult who is perceived as a guest in the home or an adult who is perceived as another authoritative "school" person. For various reasons, both conceptual and practical, our research took place in a variety of settings. Pilot work demonstrated that children and young people reveal different aspects of themselves and their relationship with the media, depending on where they are interviewed. At home alone, more personal idiosyncratic reactions are more easily admitted to a sympathetic interviewer. At home with their family, the impact of parents and siblings on behavior is most easily observed. Group interviews in schools give the opportunity to witness peer pressure in action, whereas interviews in the classroom may reveal more academic efforts to "explain" or "understand." The advantages and disadvantages of each context were considered and integrated into the analysis.

Context

Where to interview children raises the broader question of contextualizing findings. Having eschewed a cognitive–developmental approach, our stress was on recognizing that children are positioned within a particular social context that both shapes and is shaped by their activities within it. If possible, we needed to research not just children but also their parents and teachers; we needed to relate screen media to print and music and to relate the home to the community and the school. Survey questions to children therefore embraced the two worlds of home and school and covered a wide spectrum of leisure activities both inside and outside the home. In the majority of the 12 countries, qualitative interviews with parents were integrated into research findings and, in some, interviews with teachers were also achieved. Without putting media use into context, it is difficult to interpret one's observations or to identify the appropriate dimensions with which to compare demographic groups, media, or nations. Without context, how does one decide if 50% of 6- to 7-year-olds having their own television set is a high or a low figure, and how does one understand why the 50% figure obtained in the United Kingdom is higher than the 25% obtained in Sweden? In analyzing children's media use, we also used the secondary data discussed in the previous chapter to elaborate two kinds of cuts through the larger context: one media-centered (how media vary by country), the other society-centered (how societies vary by country).

Ethics

Our respect for children's views demands sensitivity to ethical issues (Morrow & Richards, 1996). Each team followed the ethical guidelines required in their country, including the attainment of informed consent from children and parents in the case of home- and school-based interviews (Holmes, 1998). Respondents' anonymity was guaranteed and upheld in the use of all research tools. Furthermore, children were allowed to drop in or out at any stage of the interview and/or when completing the questionnaire, and to refrain from answering questions with which they felt uncomfortable. We try hard in this book to provide a fair account of our findings and to represent the children's voice authentically.

ON ADOPTING A MULTIMETHOD DESIGN

Given the breadth of our research agenda and our stress on contextualizing media use, the combination of both qualitative and quantitative methods was essential to ensure the quality and interpretability of the data obtained. For practical reasons, the balance between, and timing of, qualitative and quantitative phases varied across the different national teams. The advantages of integrating qualitative and quantitative data are well rehearsed in the methodological literature, offering the opportunity for triangulation of different methods onto a common object of inquiry (Flick, 1998). At various points in our cross-national project, each of the following approaches was adopted.

Qualitative Phase Precedes Quantitative Phase

Here, the qualitative research supports the design and construction of quantitative research instruments, playing a prior, subordinate role in order to improve and strengthen the validity of the quantitative study. Indeed, the use of qualitative in-depth interviews with children was crucial in providing us with insights and understandings that, to a large degree, shaped many of our decisions regarding the quantitative questionnaire, in terms of both its construction and interpretation. In the initial focus group discussions, for example, we experimented with different ways of referring to the media (e.g., "home computer" or "PC;" "multimedia computer" or "CD-ROM") and different ways of estimating time spent with media. In using what we learned to inform the design, construction, and phrasing of the survey, in effect we treated this part of the qualitative research as a pilot study for the quantitative. Moreover, given the difficulties of designing a research instrument that worked equally well with very different kinds of children across a diversity of national settings, the process of sharing insights from the qualitative work carried out in each country was vital in ensuring that the survey made sense on its administration.

Complementarity

This approach assumes that different research questions are best addressed by drawing on the strengths of different methods. Thus some questions are seen as best pursued through qualitative methods, and quantitative methods are most appropriately used for other parts of the project. According to this view, each approach stands in its own right, rather than being subordinated to the other. For example, we considered the questions about children's perceptions of media—such as, how do children distinguish between old and new media, or national and imported programs—were best pursued by very open, qualitative methods. Here we as researchers provided no prior indication of appropriate or expected answers. By contrast, the questions about the relative importance of sociostructural factors (such as gender, social class, age) in framing the use of different media were better researched quantitatively. Here the survey provided direct comparability across individuals, allowing us to map these complex contingencies (as in the finding that those with media-rich bedrooms, who tend to be older and financially better off, also spend more time in their bedrooms, particularly if they are girls).

Mutuality

Rather than using different methods for different questions, the focus here is precisely on using both kinds of data to illuminate the same research question. Thus, quantitative research is used to interpret the qualitative and vice versa. For the former, the crucial concern is with representativeness. It is all too easy, when conducting qualitative research, to find several children in a row sharing the same experience and assume, therefore, that this is a common or normative experience. Similarly, it is easy to regard a detailed case study as full of unique characteristics, when a look at the related survey findings might reveal how widespread such characteristics actually are. Implicit claims for representativeness may be usefully "tested" against the survey findings to provide a sense of common or infrequent responses, to explore patterns of response, and to guard against implicit and unchecked assumptions about frequency distributions embedded in qualitative analysis (Lewis, 1997).

Conversely, qualitative research is often needed to interpret quantitative findings, for although it is often assumed that figures speak for themselves, this is far from the case. Because the researcher is at a distance from the research participants, and because a good survey instrument often asks the same related questions several times over, albeit in different ways, surveys commonly throw up puzzles and contradictions: Why do items expected to intercorrelate not do so, why does the apparently same question asked in two ways generate different findings, etc. Qualitative research can often be scrutinized for some insights here, as well as providing a check on the validity of findings, a guide for what to look for in the quantitative data set, and a means of contextualizing bald facts.

As the research process incorporated both qualitative and quantitative methods, we next describe each in turn.

QUALITATIVE METHODS AND DESIGN ISSUES

In keeping with the epistemology of qualitative research, we attempted to build on our understandings of children's media environment through use of an inductive discovery process based on grounded theory (Glaser & Strauss, 1967). This approach is particularly useful in research situations where researchers are unwilling to impose an a priori theoretical framework onto the data. Such research seeks to build theoretical insights from the bottom up by adopting a contextualized, holistic, process-oriented perspective that aims to respect each individual's interpretation of his or her own experiences. The taken-for-granted aspects of everyday life are granted legitimacy as topics for study and reflection, including those centered around the private sphere, the subjective, and the emotional.

To give an example from our in-home interviews in the United Kingdom and Israel, we were frustrated by the difficulty of determining how parents regulate media use. Parents were much more likely than their children to claim that there were rules about media use in the family. Children were more likely to talk in terms of media habits, focusing on the practices that render rules unenforceable and/or irrelevant to family activities. It was tempting to decide on an interpretation of rules halfway between the parents' and children's accounts, but the point, of course, is that what is occurring is not simply the partial enforcement of some half-hearted rules, but a continual activity—engaged in by both parents and children—of negotiating access to and the meanings of shared space, time, and resources, and, consequently, negotiating identities, relationships, and domestic power (Corsaro, 1997). In short, the point of listening to children is not just a liberal fancy, but stresses the importance of discovering children's definitions, conceptions, priorities, and assumptions rather than assuming that they endorse an adult understanding but express it imperfectly. Children act, interact, support each other, negotiate with others, get involved, or avoid situations all according to their understandings of the social world.

Children's Interview Schedule

Within the nine countries (CH, DK, ES, FI, FR, GB, IL, IT, and SE) that completed the qualitative research phase, a common set of questions were established and an interview guide drawn up by the British team. This included questions initially of particular interest to one or several teams that ultimately proved valuable for all. For example, questions such as "What's it like living around here?" and "What's it like being your age?" were suggested to put children at their ease at the beginning of the interview. In fact, when subsequently similar questions were asked in the survey, these generated some valuable context that supported cross-cultural comparisons (e.g., chapter 8). Although detailed interview guides were prepared, with simplified versions being drawn up for the youngest children, these were not intended to be followed verbatim in any interview, as the priority was for discussion to develop naturally, following the children's lead and exploring the topics of most interest to them. However, the interviewers were expected to ensure that all topics addressed in the guides were covered in the groups as a whole. An outline of topics addressed is shown in Table 2.1.

Interviewing: Who and Where?

In an attempt to account for national diversity, an effort was made in each country to include basic national divisions. We did so by interviewing children representing the various cultural profiles (according mainly to gender, social class, ethnicity, urban/rural, and geographical location). For a variety of reasons, different national teams made different decisions about the types of interviews to be conducted. For example, in Israel a quota for religious families was set, whereas in the United Kingdom (where religion plays a less central role in national life; see chapter 1) this was not an important criterion. Similarly, in Israel interviews with the whole family present proved highly productive, whereas in other countries this was felt likely to inhibit discussion and parents and children were interviewed separately. Although several teams used multiple qualitative methods here, the final data set includes individual, family, or peer-group interviews, conducted at home, at school, or elsewhere. Interviewing children and young people individually in their homes gave us access to their domestic media environment, so that the place of the media in the lives of children and their families could be observed directly. In this setting, discussion of media use and family rules about media arose naturally and could be pursued in context and in depth. Interviewing in schools, on the other hand, allowed us to observe the peer context in the

TABLE 2.1
Outline of Interview Schedule

Topics for open-ended discussion

- The area where children live—freedom and facilities in public spaced
- Being their age
- Media use in context of other activities—considered as enjoyable/boring things to do
- Meanings of a range of media—spontaneous associations, conceptual maps, definitions of old and new media
- Social contexts of media use, especially domestic practices and friendship networks
- Changes in access—recent acquisitions, future desires for media
- Television content, including a focus on one selected genre—soaps/music/sport, etc.
- Computer use and games content, including the Internet
- Emerging media issues—global media products, consumer and peer pressure
- Expectations of the media future

---

group situation, thereby revealing other aspects of media meanings for children. Notwithstanding some peer pressure, we found that most children were able to express their individuality in the groups at school.

The type of qualitative research undertaken by each national team and the numbers involved are shown in Table 2.2.

Data Analysis and Presentation

As is the nature of such a project, massive amounts of interview data were produced, all of which were transcribed verbatim. Following immersion in these transcripts, each team developed analytical categories, enabling data to be coded and analyzed more manageably. In this data reduction process, we used simple categories involving people, behaviors, places, times, and technologies, as well as more complex categories covering aspects such as key concepts, attitudes, relationships, and gratifications attached to media.

The most innovative, yet difficult, aspect of the qualitative research was the attempt at a comparative, cross-national analysis. As this material was available in various languages, most of which could not be read by the other collaborating teams, we were dependent on each national team making their interpretation and analysis available in English. As has been already outlined, a typical process of qualitative data categorization involves two levels: first, the participants' own account, as transcribed from interviews; and second, the researcher's own account, which is based on the first account but

TABLE 2.2
Qualitative Interviews

Country	Type of Interview	Numbers of Interviewees
BE-vlg	None	-
CH	Groups in school (German-speaking region only)	80
DE	None	-
DK	Groups in school and day clubs	100
	Individual interviews in home	50
ES	Groups in school	50
	Individual interviews	25
FI	Groups in school	350
FR	Groups in school	150
	Individual interviews at home	50
GB	Groups in school	150
	Individual interviews at home	50
IL	Groups in school and at home	82
	Family interviews at home	44
IT	Groups at school	250
NL	None	-
SE	Individual interviews in school	20
	Groups in school	80

provides a "thick description" (Geertz, 1973) that incorporates his or her own interpretation. In our project, we added a third level, namely a comparative analysis resulting from an ongoing process of negotiation between team members themselves and between the "country team" and other teams. This third level of comparison allowed the researchers to look at the more general trends in each country, rather than focus on the contextualized, often noncomparable details of each situation. In practice, this was a difficult, often bumpy road to take, resulting at times in direct conflicts of interpretation. However, in the long run, both agreements and disagreements contributed greatly to our ability to probe even deeper into the children's world and to consider the multiplicity of possible meanings it carries.

Applying evaluative criteria for qualitative research (such as the common questions of validity, reliability, and generalizability) is always a thorny issue. As is commonly practiced, each researcher was expected to report in detail on his or her role in the research situation and to apply a "disciplined subjectivity." Triangulation of data from various sources and validation of conclusions by the study's participants themselves were often applied (Lindlof, 1995). Here, we have attempted to follow the guidelines offered by Anderson (1987): to engage not only in a description of media-related activities, but also to document the meanings they have for our children, to provide firsthand information from the children themselves; to present evidence of a committed study on our part (with investment of time, effort, thought, self-reflection); to present as complete a picture as possible so as to address most possible questions that may arise for the interested reader; and to convey respect for the participants' perspectives, both the children and the researchers.

Representing our qualitative findings as comprehensively as they deserve in this book has been no easy task. The thematic approach adopted for each chapter does not allow for a detailed account of qualitative data and its interpretation. In searching for the most economical illustration to present, one can easily be tempted to chose the most vivid, striking examples, ones that tend to be noticed but do not necessarily represent the typical occurrence of the phenomenon discussed. Practical constraints may also result in the presentation of decontextualized, fragmented data, rather than an integral part of the presentation. We have attempted to use the qualitative illustrations as representative exemplars (Lindlof, 1995): those that attempt to capture as many features as possible of the phenomenon and to provide the reader with better access to its understanding. However, perhaps inevitably, the complexity of both the issues at hand and the comparative design resulted in diversity in standards of application of these principles and guidelines. We urge the readers to use their own judgments in evaluating our work and to cross-examine our interpretations. It should nevertheless be stressed that shared insights from the qualitative phase of our research have informed and illuminated every stage of the project. It thus has made a significant, if not immediately apparent, contribution to every chapter in this book.

QUANTITATIVE METHODS AND DESIGN ISSUES

As Lewis (1997) noted, many claims made about media use are implicitly if not explicitly quantitative in nature. We are commonly concerned with discovering frequency of media use, with comparing the degree of use of one group compared with another, and with putting some figures into the academic and policy debate, while not prejudging whether these figures will confirm or confound prior assumptions. Quantification also permits a search for patterns: Over and above simple figures, one can seek for trends and tendencies, revealing a more nuanced and complex picture of media use.

Children's Survey Questionnaire

Notwithstanding these difficulties, the promise of surveying a large number of children and young people across Europe and asking them many questions of academic and policy interest was worth our efforts, even if the figures we produced were ball-park figures and if the comparisons made must be treated with care. Not only were our initial research aims broad, but also our 12 national teams combined considerable multidisciplinary expertise as well as previous research within the field; hence the final survey instrument represented a wide range of issues and questions.

Areas covered by the survey are shown in Table 2.3. The majority of the national teams included most of these questions; the main questions on media ownership and use were asked by all twelve.

The survey questionnaire was produced in two versions—a face-to-face interview and a self-completion questionnaire. The selected questions were translated into their own languages and then piloted by the national teams. The final instrument was lengthy for two reasons. First, we measured key variables (e.g., media exposure) using a series of questions to increase reliability (see Appendix C for details). Second, we invited a considerable amount of background information to contextualize our findings. However, children's willingness to answer many questions placed a practical limit on the questionnaire length (on average, this took 45 minutes to complete).

Where appropriate, we distinguished between the different uses of a medium. Hence, we measured time spent using "the PC—not for games," distinguishing this from "playing electronic games" (whether on the PC or another medium). We also distinguished between types of reading activity, and focused particularly on time spent reading "books—not for school." As it proved difficult for children to distinguish which medium they listened to music on, we simply asked about time spent "listening to music." For television, days of the

TABLE 2.3
Areas Covered by Survey Questionnaire

Access	• Satisfaction with local amenities, freedom within local environment • Ownership (in bedroom and/or elsewhere in the home) and use of each of 16 media • Access to computers and the Internet in school
Time	• Leisure activities engaged in (19 listed, including 7 non-media related) • Typical number of days per week spent on each of 16 media in leisure time • Length of time spent (hours/minutes) which these media on a typical day • Times of day television switched on/watched in the home • Time spent on use of computers at school • Bedtime, and proportion of leisure time at home spent in bedroom
Use/modes of engagement	• Which media child uses personally, which child would miss most, which want to get next birthday • Which media child chooses when bored/wants to relax/wants excitement/wants not to feel left out/which does child concentrate on • Which media child talks about to friends and which are parents keen for child to do • Which media child finds best for following main interest (names in Values/Interests) • For media-related good (books, magazines, comics, music tapes, etc., computer games, videos, clothes, toys, things you collect), which does child buy with own money and which does child swap with friends • For television, how often/when does child flick channels • What are computers at home/in school used for and what is the Internet used for
Content	• Name of favorite television program(s) • Understanding of who program is for (older/younger people), whether child talks to friends about it, whether parents keen for child to watch it • Type of favorite electronic game
Social context of use	• Who child spends most of free time with • Who usually watches favorite television programs/plays electronic games with • Who asks for advice about computers • How often do things with parents (eat main mail/watch TV/play or make things/talk about things that matter/talk about things on news) • Whether child visits friends to use (which) media not available at home
Parental mediation (for father/mother separately)	• For each of watching television/videos, using/playing on computer, listening to music, making telephone calls, reading books and going out, for which is child told when can/can't do and which media do parents talk to child about
Attitudes Values/interests	• Which of 14 topics interests the child most • Perceptions of what makes someone child's age popular • What will be most/least important to child when grown up
Background and personality	• Who child lives with • If lived abroad where they would prefer • Whether child worries/gets bored/likes being the way they are/finds it hard to make friends.

week made a difference: thus, with some cross-national variation, we asked about time spent watching television on weekdays, on Saturdays, and on Sundays (see Appendix C).

Sampling

All 12 participating countries completed the survey as shown in Table 2.4. All national teams aimed for representative sampling within their country, but limited funding made for some practical compromises, particularly for those surveys administered as self-completion questionnaires through schools, though most encompass the geographic and regional diversity of their country. Quotas were set for age, gender, and social class. However, for a variety of practical reasons, the achieved samples were imperfectly balanced (see Table 2.5). These imbalances make it inappropriate for us to collapse the data across countries or age bands in this volume. This is because first, the samples are neither representative of the relative size of the countries concerned, nor are countries equally represented (e.g., the Swiss, Danish, and Swedish samples are half as large again as those of some other countries) and second, not only are age bands discontinuous, but they are not all equally represented in each

TABLE 2.4
Survey Sample Type and Size, by Country

	Type of Survey	Sample Size
BE-vlg	In school	608
CH	In school	1131
DE	In home face-to-face	829
DK	In school	1391
ES	In school	937
FI	In school	753
FR	In school	931
GB	In home face-to-face	871
IL	In school	904
IT	In school	825
NL	In home telephone	893
SE	In school	1295
Total		11368

Note. Comparisons conducted throughout this volume are based on data collected from discontinuous age bands (as to maximize the age range covered while economizing on research costs). In fact, many samples were larger than reported in this volume, as some countries surveyed children in the entire age range 6 to 17.

The definition of the population is not always obvious. The key points to note here are that the Swiss sample included all three language communities, the Belgian sample included just Flanders (the Dutch-speaking part of Belgium), Israel had only sampled from the Jewish population (approximately 80% of total) when this volume was prepared, Finland excluded the Swedish-speaking population (approximately 5% of total), and the United Kingdom includes Northern Ireland.

TABLE 2.5
Demographic Characteristics of Samples, by Country (Percentages)

	BE-vlg	CH	DE	DK	ES	FI	FR	GB	IL	IT	NL	SE
Gender												
Boy	50	46	55	47	49	49	50	51	47	45	50	51
Girl	50	54	45	53	51	51	50	49	53	55	50	49
N	608	1126	829	1392	936	753	931	871	900	825	893	1294
Age												
6-7	19	7	20	15	22	25	27	23	24	-	25	11
9-10	22	31	25	27	24	26	18	24	23	-	25	27
12-13	25	29	28	30	28	24	28	27	26	49	25	29
15-16	34	32	27	28	27	25	27	26	26	51	25	33
N	608	1131	829	1391	937	753	931	871	904	825	893	1295
SES												
High	41	17	28	56	NA	39	22	17	20	26	20	33
Medium	38	60	41	33		34	47	27	55	51	38	46
Low	21	23	32	11		27	30	56	25	23	42	21
N	608	1086	373	1321		737	899	868	896	757	893	825

country (e.g., the Italian sample includes none under 12). Consequently, caution should be exercised in interpreting gender and SES groupings. Where an "all" figure is provided, unless otherwise stated, this is an average of the averages, calculated by giving an equal weight to each country rather than a simple average over all respondents across Europe. Thus, "all" figures should not be taken as simply representative of "European children." In addition, caution should be exercised in interpreting any grouping such as gender or SES as these are based on an aggregate of the four age bands.

There are particular difficulties surrounding the classification of socioeconomic status (SES) and no cross-national standard definition. In most cases, SES was derived from information about the income, employment, and educational levels of parents, though in a few countries classification was based on information about the school. Each country then classified their sample into high, medium, and low SES in a manner that made most sense in terms of their country, resulting in some discrepancies in the proportions assigned to each category. We cannot therefore assume direct comparability between the three categories across different countries, although we can compare trends within countries with confidence.

Data Interpretation

Care is required when interpreting the survey findings. In our analyses in this volume, and depending on the issue at hand, we may report findings for a particular age group, or we may report findings only for those who have access to a medium, or only for those who actually use it. These distinctions make a difference, and for different research questions we try to present the data that are most relevant. Furthermore, one must beware of overinterpreting small variations in the data: Given our large sample size, many of our findings are statistically significant, but this may not make them socially significant, and thus only findings that we judged both sizeable and reliable (as well as being statistically significant at $p < 0.05$) are given attention in this volume.[2]

Analytically, a contextual focus invites several kinds of analysis beyond the straightforward description of media use by categories of children and/or categories of media. First, one can consider combinations or clusters or typologies of media use. Thus we may explore how children and young people combine media to construct their own media-leisure environments (e.g., chapter 5). Further, the conditional analysis of data allows one to explore how media use is conditional on certain contextual factors (thus, for example, in chapter 8 we show how children who have a television in their bedroom watch in a different way from those who do not).

CONDUCTING RESEARCH IN COMPARATIVE PERSPECTIVE

Early on, our project generated a heuristic metaphor for collaborative work. Our "flower" model discriminated the directly comparable data collected (the flower center) from additional national variations (the petals). Thus for both qualitative and quantitative phases, we could construct shared instruments (survey questions, interview schedules) while permitting countries to add their own petals that would not be involved in subsequent comparisons. A "tree" model might capture the process event better: Here, the "roots" represent the multiple intellectual disciplines and methodological preferences that sustained the project, these feeding into a common "trunk" (namely, shared aims, design, sampling, schedules, survey questions). The main "branches" were generally agreed also, these being the themes that form the empirical chapters of this book; the "twigs" allow for national variations on a theme. These variations are telling in themselves—the Israeli team added

---

[2]For all statistical comparisons, we have adopted the convention, unless otherwise stated, of noting significant differences as follows: bold = $p < 0.001$; underline = $p < 0.01$; italics = $p < 0.05$.

questions about national identity and globalization versus localization; the British team added questions about media regulation—but are not addressed within this volume.

Such talk of flowers and trees may seem fanciful, but in fact, a key lesson learned about the conduct of comparative research is the importance of evolving a common conceptual language, necessary to co-orient participants to that temporary academic community, "the international project team." Funding for regular meetings was vital for this process, for ad hoc meetings and e-mail can supplement but do not suffice to create and sustain a comparative framework. Each national team obtained funding for its national project, and the network as a whole received pan-European grants for meetings from the European Parliament, the European Commission's Youth for Europe Programme and the European Science Foundation. Such funding matters more for some types of collaboration than others: The present project is neither a collection of national studies (as in Coleman & Rollet, 1997; Lull, 1988), nor was it constructed by one team and imposed, top-down, on all others; rather we wished to draw on the multidisciplinarity and the multinational nature of the project by determining appropriate theories and methods through discussion. In essence, if one believes in national variation in key concepts and measures as well as in the object of study, and if one believes in the importance of local contextualization of findings, one cannot just design a questionnaire in one country and then hand it out in the others, despite the apparent simplicity of this strategy. However, a hard lesson from the present comparison has been of the importance of not underestimating the very considerable collaborative work that must then be put into both codesigning and, especially, cointerpreting the comparative findings (Blumler, McCleod, & Rosengren, 1992).

In practical terms, the workshops were therefore indispensable. In all, we held eight main meetings, at approximately 6-month intervals over the 4 years of the project's duration, as well as several additional meetings with two or three teams. These served as fora for negotiating differences in opinion, a quality assurance check on the standard and comparability of work, and a context for the interpretation of comparative findings. In addition, in these meetings we constructed interview schedules, the survey questionnaire, coding schemes, data interpretation, discussion of chapter drafts, etc. It proved beneficial academically also to hold the workshops in different countries (as required by the European Commission and the European Science Foundation), allowing us to gain a "feel" for different cultural environments. Between meetings, it proved vital to have one nominated link person who acted as the central node in the supporting e-mail network. Comparative conference presentations and interim publications supported the development of conclusions satisfactory for all (e.g., Livingstone, 1998). Moreover, in writing this volume, the chapters have been circulated in draft form from country to country and in each, researchers have taken the time to check data concerning their own country, correct misunderstandings, explain surprising or interesting findings, and provide qualitative exemplars. Despite its many satisfactions, research remains a laborious, intensive, time-consuming process: We must here, once again, acknowledge the very considerable generosity and good will required of, and freely given by, all team members to ensure the completion of this comparative project.

Nonetheless, despite our best efforts, a number of problems remained. Anticipating the consequences of inevitable design compromises is one; contextualizing the emergent differences across national studies is another. Qualitative and quantitative phases posed different problems. Superficially at least, cross-national research appears easier to conduct using quantitative rather than qualitative methods. By its very nature, quantitative research is oriented toward a standardized output, whereas qualitative research is, conversely, necessarily receptive to the variable and contingent factors encountered during the conduct of the research, placing it in tension with the principle of comparability or equivalence of methods (Samuel, 1985; Steiner, 1995). We found it easier to specify and check on the conduct of the survey in each of our 12 countries than we did the qualitative research. Researchers everywhere, it seems, share an understanding of the decisions involved in selecting quota or random samples, face-to-face interviews, or self-completion questionnaires, and the construction of a Statistical Package for the Social Sciences (SPSS) data file. However, researchers everywhere do not necessarily conduct or interpret a focus group interview in a standard fashion.

Quantitative and qualitative data also differ in how readily they may be shared and compared cross-nationally. Initially the data from surveys in each of the 12 countries were summarized and circulated as a series of standardized cross-tabulations. Subsequently our survey data were combined into a single, albeit very large, file containing data from 10 nations, some 11,000 children in all; Indeed, the production of this common file was crucial to the quantitative comparisons.[3] However, our qualitative data remain as collections of the tapes and transcripts, in nine different languages, each in the country where it was collected, along with the handwritten notes, children's pictures, and other contextual information that accompany them. The multiplicity of languages meant that reading each others' transcripts was not practicable, and so any sharing of these data was filtered through the translations, interpretations, and summaries of the researchers involved. Thus, as noted earlier, the comparative qualitative work was conducted at a secondary level of analysis, through each team's own immersion in their data and the inherent reduction process involved in the creation of prioritized, sensible categories.

---

[3]Unfortunately, national funds were not available to enable the data from Denmark and France to be prepared for inclusion in the comparative database.

Yet although it is hard to overstate the demands and difficulties of comparing cross-national qualitative research, and it is perhaps here that we have been least successful, it would be misleading to underplay the difficulties of comparing apparently comparable statistics. For example, we faced problems of slight differences in phrasing, whether inadvertent or unavoidable, problems of question routing (so that base sizes, or subgroup definitions, might vary) as well as problems in constructing composite variables. As discussed earlier, social class categories mean different things in different countries, and even age is complicated by cross-national variation in its mapping onto the school year. In short, behind the rows and columns of standardized tables lie a series of decisions, not always exactly parallel in every country, that determine their meaning.

OVERVIEW

In sum, the 12 participating countries in this project completed a survey on a nationally representative sample of children and young people, using mutually agreed core questions. In addition, in nine countries in-depth individual and group interviews were held, allowing for qualitative and quantitative methods to be combined. These interviews were similarly based on a mutually agreed interviewing schedule. In this chapter, we outlined our rationale for determining the comparative research design as well as some of the methodological consequences of stressing the importance of contextualizing findings within a cultural and historical framework.

As discussed in the previous chapter, contexts can be seen as nested, with local contexts (the home, street, school) embedded within larger, overlapping contexts (community, region, nation). However, contextualizing findings is not so easy, and the question of where context stops, in practical terms at least, is far from obvious in advance; thus an enormous body of data is easily generated and rather less easily analyzed. Similarly, although the theoretical justification for conducting cross-national comparative research is strong, as discussed in the previous chapter, we have here reflected on some of the practical difficulties in implementing comparative research, some of which were apparent at the outset (language and funding, for example), whereas others (differing interview practices, differing ethical requirements, for example) became apparent only later.

Despite these difficulties, the advantages of collecting cross-national data according to a common framework and using common instruments are obvious. For both logistical and financial reasons, cross-national projects do not often combine depth and breadth on such a scale as the present project. Thus we hope that this attempt to compare contextualized investigations of media use in each of 12 nations is of value to our readers.

REFERENCES

Anderson, J. A. (1987). *Communication research: Issues and methods.* New York: McGraw-Hill.

Blumler, J. G., McLeod, J. M., & Rosengren, K. E. (Eds.). (1992). *Comparatively speaking: Communication and culture across space and time.* Newbury Park, CA: Sage.

Buckingham, D. (1991). What are words worth? Interpreting children's talk about television. *Cultural Studies, 5*(2), 228–245.

Buckingham, D. (1993). *Children talking television: The making of television literacy.* London: Falmer Press.

Coleman, J. A., & Rollet, B. (Eds.). (1997). *Television in Europe.* Exeter: Intellect.

Corsaro, W. A. (1997). *The sociology of childhood.* Thousand Oaks, CA: Pine Forge Press.

Flick, U. (1998). *An introduction to qualitative research.* London: Sage.

Geertz, C. (1973). *The interpretation of cultures.* New York: Selected Books.

Glaser, B. G., & Strauss, A. (1967). *The discovery of grounded theory.* Chicago: Aldine.

Graue, M. E., & Walsh, D. J. (1998). *Studying children in context: Theories, methods and ethics.* Thousand Oaks, CA: Sage.

Greig, A., & Taylor, J. (1999). *Doing research with children.* London: Sage.

Hodge, B., & Tripp, D. (1986). *Children and television: A semiotic approach.* Cambridge: Polity Press.

Holmes, R. M. (1998). *Fieldwork and children.* Thousand Oaks, CA: Sage.

Hood, S., Kelley, P., & Mayall, B. (1996). Children as research subjects: A risky enterprise. *Children and Society, 10*, 117–128.

Ireland, L., & Holloway, I. (1996). Qualitative health research with children. *Children and Society, 10*, 155–164.

James, A., Jenks, C., & Prout, A. (1998). *Theorizing childhood.* Cambridge, England: Cambridge University Press.

Lemish, D. (1997). Kindergartners' understanding of television: A cross cultural comparison. *Communication Studies, 48*(2), 109–126.

Lewis, J. (1997). What counts in cultural studies. *Media, Culture and Society, 19*, 83–97.

Lindlof, T. R. (1995). *Qualitative communication research methods.* Thousand Oaks, CA: Sage Publications.

Livingstone, S. (1998). Young People and the New Media in Europe. *European Journal of Communication, 13*(4), 435–592.

Livingstone, S., & Bovill, M. (1990). Young people, new media. An LSE Report, available from http://psych.lse.ac.uk/young_people.

Lull, J. (Ed.). (1988). *World families watch television.* Newbury Park, CA: Sage.

Mahon, A., Glendinning, C., Clarke, K., & Craig, G. (1996). Researching children: methods and ethics. *Children & Society, 10*, 145–154.

Morrow, V., & Richards, M. (1996). The ethics of social research with children: An overview. *Children & Society, 10*, 90–105.

Rudd, D. (1992). Children and television: A critical note on theory and method. *Media, Culture and Society, 14*, 313–320.

Samuel, N. (1985). Is there a distinct cross-national comparative sociology, method and methodology? In L. Hantrais, S. Mangen, & M. O'Brien (Eds.), *Doing cross-national research* (pp. 3–10). Aston: Aston Modern Languages Club.

Steiner, I. (1995). Growing up in twelve cities: The families in which pupils live. In L. Chisholm, P. Buchner, H.-H. Kruger, & M. Bois-Reymond (Eds.), *Growing up in Europe: Contemporary horizons in childhood and youth studies* (pp. 73–82). Berlin: Walter de Gruyter.

II

A TIME AND PLACE
FOR NEW MEDIA

3

Old and New Media:
Access and Ownership in the Home

Leen d'Haenens

In this chapter we look into the media environment in the homes and bedrooms of children and teenagers in 11 European countries and Israel. Information about media *in the household* enables us to map out the adoption of new media (in the light of old media) among those groups known to be relatively early media adopters, that is, families with children. In addition, we have information about *the personal ownership* by children of media. We are therefore able to contribute a detailed comparative account of how far the diffusion process has advanced for families as a whole in our 12 countries, and for children within these families. Has the information age really arrived, we ask, in the day-to-day media worlds of European children and adolescents?

Particular attention is focused, however, on the emergence of new media: This is explored in the light of access to, and ownership of, older media. "New" media are defined in terms of the technology used (more interactivity; convergence of telecommunications, broadcasting, and computing) and the services offered (more choices; convergence of information, entertainment, and education), in terms of social diffusion processes (early adopters own and/or use new media, whereas older media are available to a mass market), and in terms of historical change (despite becoming rapidly familiar, new media are still new in relation to the pace of social and cultural change; see Livingstone, Gaskell, & Bovill, 1997; Silverstone, 1997). We are particularly interested in mapping access and ownership of information and communication technologies (ICTs) because these are said to restructure the traditional dimensions of time and space within which people live and interact and to "offer the prospect of greater opportunities for finding employment, seeking advice, challenging orthodoxy, meeting like minds and constructing one's own sense of self" (Loader, 1998, p. 10). Furthermore, the pace of technological change—though possibly not social change—is speeding up. The Human Development Report (1999) cited the time new technologies have taken from inception to achieve 50 million users (defined as widespread acceptance). Radio reached this number of users in 38 years, the personal computer in 16 years, television in 13 years, whereas it has taken only 4 years for the World Wide Web to attract 50 million people worldwide. In other words, the Internet is undoubtedly the fastest-growing communication tool so far.

One of the primary concerns in the information age is the issue of disparity between the so-called "information-poor" and "information-advantaged" nations or groups within society. It is therefore of considerable interest that chapter 1 of this book already documented an uneven spread of media provision at the national level between European states, particularly with respect to the newest forms of media.

Rogers (1995) provided us with a model of the diffusion process that helps to make sense of these differences. His model focused on the relative speed with which an innovation is adopted, measured in terms of the length of time required for a certain percentage of potential users to adopt. Most adoption rates are S-shaped. However, variations occur in the slope of the S. When the diffusion takes place relatively rapidly, then the S-curve is quite steep. Conversely, a more gradual S-curve is indicative of a slower diffusion process. The S-shaped diffusion curve "takes off" at between 10% to 25% adoption, when interpersonal networks become activated so that a critical mass of users starts to develop. This critical mass is achieved when a sufficient number of individuals have become users, ensuring that the innovation's further rate of adoption becomes self-sustaining. Before this happens, the rate of adoption is slow. Afterward, it starts to accelerate.

The model identified five adopter categories, which map onto the diffusion of innovation curve, depending on how late or early individuals become users. First to take up the new medium are the *innovators*, those few venturesome individuals who are able to cope with uncertainty and willing to accept early setbacks. They represent the first 2.5% of adopters in Rogers's system. Next come the *early adopters*: this group consists of respected opinion leaders, and represents the addition of a further 13.5% of users in Rogers's model. At a later stage still, the *early majority* become users. Such individuals are not opinion leaders, but represent an important stage in the adoption process, as they make up a third of the total system. Next come the *late majority*, skeptical individuals who require convincing and who constitute a further third of the total system. Finally we are left with the *laggards*, the recalcitrant sixth of the total system who are traditionalists, suspicious of innovations.

The national statistics quoted in chapter 1 (Table 1.5) suggest that, in the case of the Internet, our 12 countries are still (in 1997) to be located at an early phase on Rogers's S-shaped diffusion curve. Only innovators in Spain and France are so far using it, and even in Sweden, the country with most users, the early majority are hardly as yet involved. As regards the diffusion of domestic computers, the range is between 24% (in Spain) and 53% (in the Netherlands), placing all countries at the "early majority" stage when we can expect fairly rapid expansion.

The northern European countries are clearly the leaders in the field, at a more advanced stage in the diffusion process both for the Internet and computers in general. If we look at stand-alone machines rather than networked ones, as many as half of the individuals aged 15 and older use a PC at home in the Netherlands, Denmark, and Sweden (see chapter 1, Table 1.5). Similarly, in Sweden almost one in five individuals aged 15 and older have access to the Internet from home; in the Netherlands and Finland, the proportion is one in ten. Figures are substantially lower for all other countries under scrutiny. Such figures are, of course, difficult to interpret, as the data have not always been gathered in exactly the same way and at the same time for each country; hence the need for our present research. Moreover, patterns of access and use differ between countries, complicating things still further (see chapter 4). In the case of Finland, for example, statistics for access at home or in the office may be misleading as an indicator of Internet access because there is extensive and well-used provision of Internet facilities in public places, such as libraries, which should be taken into account.

The fact that old and new media emerged in very different policy climates may explain why such unequal access to computers and advanced telecommunications infrastructure has occurred across the various European countries. The diffusion of old media was supported by universal and public service policies, whereas the new media have been emerging in times of privatization, with heavily indebted governments leaving the development of the necessary infrastructure almost entirely to the market (see e.g., Van Dijk, 1999). However, the new, interactive media are considerably more expensive than older media because, among other things, they become obsolete at a much faster rate and constantly require ever more powerful equipment and software (see Loader, 1998; Van Dijk, 1999). As a result, Holderness (1995), among many others, identified a direct link between nations' ability to become connected and to gather and disseminate information on the one hand, and their material position on the other hand (expressed in Gross National Product per capita, for instance). "For the vast majority of the world's population, the possibility of constructing virtual identities is entirely dependent upon their material situation. Clearly most people are not free to choose but instead are subject to a variety of social and economic conditions which act to structure and articulate their opportunities for action" (Loader, 1998, p. 10).

Our multinational project allows us to consider whether social and economic indicators at the national level can explain, at least in part, some of the differences in new media penetration within households with children across Europe. Spanish and Israeli families, for example, have the lowest income and purchasing power on average (see chapter 1, Table 1.1). Sweden, Finland, Italy, and the United Kingdom come next, showing rather low average income levels. Switzerland, on the other hand, ranks highest, followed by Denmark and Belgium. Are these differences reflected in the percentage of families and children with new media in each country?

In addition, we are able to explore in detail the effect of income stratification at the microlevel of the family. In 11 of the 12 countries, we have information about the socioeconomic status (SES) of the household. Although these measures have been collected in somewhat different ways, all are based on information about family income and level of education (see chapter 2). Are these, we ask, reliable predictors of media provision in the household? Our hypothesis is that the impact of SES is likely to be influenced by the degree of social stratification between countries (see chapter 1). The more hierarchical a society is, the more pivotal the SES of a child's parents is likely to be in terms of new media penetration. Countries may be defined as more or less hierarchical in terms of the income gap between the poorest 20% and the richest 20%: the bigger the disparity, the more hierarchical the society. Countries such as the United Kingdom, Switzerland, and, to a lesser extent, France, belong to the highest category. Least hierarchical are the Netherlands, Belgium, and Spain.

However, research suggests, as we might expect, that material wealth is not the only discriminating factor. As Loader (1998) commented, "The 'information-poor' are no more an homogeneous social phenomenon than their wealthier counterparts. Fragmented and divided by gender, race, disability, class, location or religion, their experience of ICT will vary enormously as will their opportunities to utilize it" (p. 9). In this chapter, we therefore explore two additional demographic factors that may be supposed to have an impact on young people's media ownership—age and gender. Our assumption is that boys will be more oriented toward new, interactive media than girls and therefore will own more new media than girls. In other words, boys probably have a lower threshold for adoption of new media than girls. As regards the age of the child, this too is expected to have an effect on children's media ownership. In other words, the older the child, the more likely he or she will be to own media personally. Access in the home is likely to be less affected.

RESULTS: KEY COMPARATIVE FINDINGS

This section examines the media environment of the child at home and distinguishes between access somewhere in the household and personal ownership by the child of media equipment in the bedroom. Access is, of course, a necessary, but not sufficient, condition of use, and for more detailed figures concerning proportions of users and indications of time spent with the different media, we refer the reader to chapter 4.

As we see, an exclusive focus on media access in the home tells only part of the story. The bedroom represents an experiment with identity, an opportunity both to exercise personal control and to manage relations with family and friends (see chapter 8). Having media in this location indicates a far closer integration of a medium into a child's life and may be taken to imply personal ownership by the child. We primarily adopt a medium-focused approach and map general trends of current access and ownership in both the child's home and bedroom across the 12 countries under study. For each medium, we take into account gender-, age- and SES-related trends in ownership. Thus Tables 3.1 to 3.9 show access at home and in the bedroom for familiar and new, interactive media forms, by gender and age of the child for each, and SES of the family, for 11 of the 12 countries under study. Finally, we include children's responses to three complementary questions related to ownership that can be seen as reflecting the relative importance of different media in children's lives: Which medium[1] would you miss most (see Table 3.10). Which medium would you like most as your next birthday present (see Table 3.11). Which medium do you buy with your pocket money (see Table 3.12).

Current Media Access and Ownership

Television and Video. Our survey shows that access in the home to a television set and to a video recorder (VCR) is very similar from one country to another. Television is the most pervasive medium in European households: about 90% of children have access to a television set in their homes. A slightly smaller proportion of homes (between 7 and 9 in every 10) have a VCR. Access to a VCR in the home is lowest in Switzerland, where fewest have television sets and, less expectedly, in Spain.

However, in contrast to the nearly universal access to television in the home, having a television set in one's bedroom varies considerably from one country to the other. A television set is most frequently part of the child's bedroom equipment in the United Kingdom and Denmark (three in every five children have one). Sets in children's bedrooms are found least often in Switzerland (only one in five have one). Understandably children are more likely to own a VCR in countries where a television set is standard equipment in the bedroom (e.g., UK, DK, SE) and least likely to own one in Switzerland.

As we would expect, neither the age nor the gender of the child, nor the socioeconomic status of the family is associated with having a family television

---

[1]One medium only—except for the Danish children, who were allowed to give multiple responses.

TABLE 3.1
Percentage Having Television Set (1) Anywhere at Home (H); (2) in Own Bedroom (B); by
Country, Gender, Age, and SES

		Gender		Age				SES		
		M	*F*	*6-7*	*9-10*	*12-13*	*15-16*	*H*	*M*	*L*
BE(vlg)	H	93	96	92	91	**97**	**97**	94	94	97
	B	**33**	**19**	**6**	**14**	**30**	**41**	29	22	28
CH	H	90	90	**93**	83	**92**	**95**	**90**	**92**	**90**
	B	24	14	**16**	9	**16**	**29**	**16**	**18**	**25**
DE	H	96	95	*93*	*95*	*95*	*97*	99	95	93
	B	**44**	**36**	**18**	**29**	**44**	**62**	38	45	38
DK	H	98	98	100	98	98	98	99	99	97
	B	64	56	32	58	72	84	58	62	59
ES	H	96	97	*98*	*94*	*96*	*98*	-	-	-
	B	*34*	27	20	27	36	32	-	-	-
FI	H	96	94	97	92	95	96	96	95	94
	B	**45**	**31**	**21**	**30**	**42**	**60**	31	43	43
FR	H	98	99	99	99	98	100	98	99	99
	B	32	24	16	25	30	40	16	31	31
GB	H	100	100	100	100	100	100	100	100	100
	B	**70**	**57**	**50**	**57**	**69**	**75**	**45**	**61**	**71**
IL	H	95	93	*95*	*90*	*92*	*97*	95	93	95
	B	*40*	*33*	*28*	*33*	*42*	*40*	33	38	37
IT	H	*97*	*99*	-	-	97	98	98	98	98
	B	57	48	-	-	52	54	**44**	**52**	**66**
NL	H	98	99	99	97	100	97	98	99	98
	B	31	28	**12**	**20**	**39**	**48**	**22**	**25**	**38**
SE	H	**96**	**98**	**100**	**96**	**95**	**98**	99	97	97
	B	**56**	**41**	**24**	**39**	**51**	**64**	43	47	53

Note. Bold $p < 0.001$, underlined $p < 0.01$, italics $p < -.005$.

TABLE 3.2
Percentage Having Video Recorder (1) Anywhere at Home (H); (2) in Own Bedroom (B); by Country, Gender, Age, and SES

		Gender		Age				SES		
		M	*F*	*6-7*	*9-10*	*12-13*	*15-16*	*H*	*M*	*L*
BE(vlg)										
	H	88	88	88	84	87	91	88	87	90
	B	**16**	**8**	<u>5</u>	<u>9</u>	<u>11</u>	<u>19</u>	14	13	7
CH										
	H	73	71	**78**	**57**	**75**	**83**	**80**	**74**	**68**
	B	10	8	*6*	5	*9*	*10*	7	*9*	*9*
DE										
	H	87	87	86	84	89	88	*19*	*90*	*80*
	B	16	11	**5**	**6**	**10**	**21**	<u>12</u>	*9*	<u>9</u>
DK										
	H	92	92	91	92	91	95	92	93	89
	B	32	27	12	28	32	50	30	29	31
ES										
	H	71	76	**78**	**54**	**76**	**85**	-	-	-
	B	11	8	7	11	9	10	-	-	-
FI										
	H	91	90	92	92	86	93	91	92	89
	B	17	12	**6**	**14**	**17**	**22**	12	15	18
FR										
	H	93	91	91	92	92	91	91	93	90
	B	11	6	4	8	14	9	8	9	10
GB										
	H	96	96	94	96	97	96	99	97	94
	B	25	*18*	**11**	**18**	**24**	**32**	**10**	**19**	**26**
IL										
	H	83	82	*83*	*75*	*82*	*87*	86	81	82
	B	*17*	12	12	18	16	*10*	10	13	16
IT										
	H	90	90	-	-	91	90	93	90	88
	B	22	*15*	-	-	19	17	17	17	17
NL										
	H	92	92	95	92	91	90	89	93	93
	B	5	4	2	2	*5*	8	5	2	6
SE										
	H	92	92	**97**	**90**	**92**	**92**	95	92	92
	B	**25**	**16**	**8**	**11**	**19**	**36**	*16*	*20*	*25*

Note. Bold $p < 0.001$, underlined $p < 0.01$, italics $p < 0.005$.

TABLE 3.3
Percentage Having Cable/Satellite (1) Anywhere at Home (H); (2) in Own Bedroom (B); by
Country, Gender, Age, and SES

		Gender		Age				SES		
		M	*F*	*6-7*	*9-10*	*12-13*	*15-16*	*H*	*M*	*L*
BE(vlg)	H	-	-	-	-	-	-	-	-	-
	B	-	-	-	-	-	-	-	-	-
CH	H	*51*	*48*	*29*	*42*	**50**	**63**	*57*	*50*	*46*
	B	*12*	*6*	4	4	7	16	*7*	8	12
DE	H	83	83	*74*	*83*	**85**	**87**	86	86	78
	B	30	25	**6**	**19**	**33**	**45**	*24*	*31*	*29*
DK	H	58	48	52	50	55	56	52	55	50
	B	27	16	10	19	28	31	22	21	20
ES	H	21	21	*14*	24	25	*21*	-	-	-
	B	4	3	3	2	3	5	-	-	-
FI	H	38	31	*40*	29	*32*	38	36	36	31
	B	*11*	*6*	**2**	**6**	**8**	**17**	9	9	8
FR	H	25	22	26	26	24	19	23	23	23
	B	3	3	3	2	3	3	2	3	3
GB	H	42	38	45	38	37	42	35	42	41
	B	5	5	5	2	5	8	5	4	6
IL	H	73	70	*70*	*61*	*75*	*77*	**68**	**78**	**62**
	B	30	25	**16**	**21**	**37**	**33**	28	28	25
IT	H	23	18	-	-	22	19	**27**	**20**	**13**
	B	7	*3*	-	-	6	4	4	5	4
NL	H	-	-	-	-	-	-	-	-	-
	B	-	-	-	-	-	-	-	-	-
SE	H	66	62	**63**	**50**	**65**	**76**	72	58	61
	B	*24*	*18*	**8**	**10**	**23**	**33**	21	18	19

Note. Bold $p < 0.001$, underlined $p < 0.01$, italics $p < 0.005$.

TABLE 3.4
Percentage Having Books (1) Anywhere at Home (H); (2) in Own Bedroom (B); by Country, Gender, Age, and SES

		Gender		Age				SES		
		M	*F*	*6-7*	*9-10*	*12-13*	*15-16*	*H*	*M*	*L*
BE(vlg)	H	*93*	*98*	95	96	99	93	93	97	96
	B	**77**	**89**	**86**	**81**	**89**	**73**	83	87	77
CH	H	90	94	**98**	**88**	**95**	**93**	**98**	**94**	**86**
	B	84	89	90	84	89	87	**95**	**89**	**76**
DE	H	95	94	*93*	*94*	*95*	*96*	99	97	92
	B	85	87	*82*	*83*	*88*	*89*	**92**	**87**	**77**
DK	H	94	97	99	92	96	94	96	96	91
	B	82	86	83	86	83	85	84	79	69
ES	H	93	95	**96**	**86**	**96**	**97**	-	-	-
	B	*83*	88	<u>84</u>	<u>79</u>	<u>89</u>	<u>90</u>	-	-	-
FI	H	95	97	98	94	93	97	97	97	93
	B	**83**	**91**	*83*	*86*	88	90	*91*	*85*	*84*
FR	H	98	99	99	100	98	98	100	99	98
	B	91	96	93	95	94	92	96	95	90
GB	H	85	88	92	86	87	83	**97**	**91**	**82**
	B	60	65	68	63	64	57	**77**	**67**	**56**
IL	H	89	<u>91</u>	<u>94</u>	<u>84</u>	<u>90</u>	<u>89</u>	91	90	89
	B	73	<u>77</u>	<u>78</u>	<u>77</u>	<u>74</u>	<u>73</u>	*82*	*75*	*70*
IT	H	**89**	**94**	-	-	92	92	**97**	**93**	**86**
	B	69	75	-	-	74	71	*80*	*72*	*68*
NL	H	100	99	99	99	99	99	100	99	99
	B	94	96	<u>96</u>	<u>98</u>	<u>96</u>	<u>90</u>	<u>96</u>	<u>97</u>	<u>92</u>
SE	H	**92**	**98**	**100**	96	94	95	98	97	94
	B	**84**	**96**	*94*	*91*	89	87	96	92	86

Note. Bold $p < 0.001$, underlined $p < 0.01$, italics $p < 0.05$.

TABLE 3.5
Percentage Having Telephone (1) Anywhere at Home (H); (2) in Own Bedroom (B); by Country, Gender, Age, and SES

		Gender		Age				SES		
		M	F	6-7	9-10	12-13	15-16	H	M	L
BE(vlg)	H	85	90	84	85	92	89	86	89	90
	B	11	9	**3**	**5**	**10**	**18**	11	8	11
CH	H	90	89	**90**	**86**	**90**	**93**	**94**	**91**	**87**
	B	6	7	**1**	**4**	**5**	**11**	**11**	**6**	**5**
DE	H	89	87	*86*	*86*	*90*	*90*	93	88	86
	B	5	4	*2*	*3*	*6*	*6*	*9*	*4*	*1*
DK	H	95	96	100	91	93	96	96	96	92
	B	15	18	1	11	22	35	17	16	17
ES	H	86	86	**87**	**76**	**87**	**92**	-	-	-
	B	11	11	<u>5</u>	<u>9</u>	<u>13</u>	<u>14</u>	-	-	-
FI	H	*94*	*98*	97	96	94	97	98	96	93
	B	15	18	**4**	**10**	**24**	**30**	14	16	20
FR	H	97	97	97	96	98	97	100	97	96
	B	9	6	6	4	11	9	9	7	7
GB	H	92	94	95	93	94	90	**99**	**98**	**87**
	B	5	5	*4*	*2*	*6*	*8*	3	6	6
IL	H	93	92	**95**	**82**	**93**	**98**	95	92	92
	B	39	40	**22**	**34**	**44**	**56**	44	41	34
IT	H	97	98	-	-	98	97	99	98	97
	B	39	37	-	-	35	41	39	40	34
NL	H	99	99	99	99	99	100	98	99	99
	B	4	4	3	2	4	6	7	*3*	*3*
SE	H	<u>95</u>	<u>97</u>	99	95	95	96	98	98	95
	B	47	50	<u>17</u>	<u>31</u>	<u>59</u>	<u>66</u>	52	48	41

Note. Bold $p < 0.001$, underlined $p < 0.01$, italics $p < 0.05$.

TABLE 3.6
Percentage Having Television-Linked Games Machine (1) Anywhere at Home (H); (2) in Own
Bedroom (B) by Gender, Country, Age, and SES

		Gender		Age				SES		
		M	F	6-7	9-10	12-13	15-16	H	M	L
BE(vlg)	H	56	43	37	42	56	59	49	51	48
	B	30	14	11	18	22	30	23	20	23
CH	H	51	32	29	39	47	38	41	41	40
	B	27	10	10	14	20	19	17	18	20
DE	H	37	24	16	35	39	32	32	31	30
	B	25	13	10	21	24	20	19	19	22
DK	H	49	31	39	49	38	33	40	36	54
	B	33	14	17	32	24	19	23	20	34
ES	H	62	45	41	46	62	61	-	-	-
	B	44	22	20	29	42	37	-	-	-
FI	H	50	36	36	50	47	38	34	48	51
	B	28	12	12	25	22	20	12	25	25
FR	H	66	48	48	58	65	59	45	61	61
	B	34	16	14	26	35	25	16	26	28
GB	H	78	57	64	66	74	66	53	66	73
	B	47	20	24	32	42	36	18	31	41
IL	H	44	34	35	39	42	39	39	39	38
	B	24	13	13	22	20	18	15	18	20
IT	H	55	38	-	-	56	39	47	45	56
	B	39	20	-	-	34	24	28	28	33
NL	H	56	39	36	53	58	42	42	41	55
	B	25	9	9	15	23	21	12	13	23
SE	H	70	55	53	64	68	61	59	63	72
	B	45	22	14	33	41	35	27	32	42

Note. Bold $p < 0.001$, underlined $p < 0.01$, italics $p < 0.05$.

TABLE 3.7
Percentage Having PC of Any Type (1) Anywhere at Home (H); (2) in Own Bedroom (B); by Country, Gender, Age, and SES

		Gender		Age				SES		
		M	F	6-7	9-10	12-13	15-16	H	M	L
BE(vlg)	H	*92*	*93*	92	92	92	93	92	91	94
	B	*21*	*15*	7	**11**	**20**	**28**	22	16	15
CH	H	61	59	**2**	**56**	**64**	**72**	**91**	**64**	**29**
	B	**24**	**14**	**0**	**15**	**18**	**27**	**28**	**19**	**9**
DE	H	_56_	_43_	**34**	**45**	**55**	**63**	**70**	**45**	**39**
	B	**24**	**12**	**4**	**12**	**24**	**32**	_23_	_16_	_19_
DK	H	-	-	-	-	-	-	-	-	-
	B	-	-	-	-	-	-	-	-	-
ES	H	54	53	**48**	**43**	**55**	**68**	-	-	-
	B	21	17	**7**	**16**	**18**	**29**	-	-	-
FI	H	_74_	_65_	*61*	*60*	*73*	*74*	**83**	65	55
	B	**37**	**11**	**10**	**26**	**29**	**30**	27	24	19
FR	H	-	-	-	-	-	-	-	-	-
	B	-	-	-	-	-	-	-	-	-
GB	H	50	55	49	53	51	55	**76**	**60**	**41**
	B	**17**	**9**	10	13	12	16	13	11	14
IL	H	**83**	**66**	72	75	71	77	**81**	**78**	**61**
	B	**50**	**21**	29	37	38	34	25	37	34
IT	H	**59**	**43**	-	-	53	48	**69**	**50**	**32**
	B	**40**	**21**	-	-	31	28	32	31	26
NL	H	83	85	**76**	**85**	**84**	**90**	92	88	76
	B	**15**	7	_5_	_8_	_14_	_15_	12	9	12
SE	H	70	62	59	57	69	71	**82**	**67**	**61**
	B	**30**	**14**	**8**	**16**	**25**	**31**	24	21	22

Note. Bold $p < 0.001$, underlined $p < 0.01$, italics $p < 0.05$.

TABLE 3.8
Percentage Having PC With CD-ROM (1) Anywhere at Home (H); (2) in Own Bedroom (B); by
Country, Gender, Age, and SES

		Gender		Age				SES		
		M	F	6-7	9-10	12-13	15-16	H	M	L
BE(vlg)	H	*44*	*34*	**31**	**24**	**51**	**47**	40	39	36
	B	**13**	**5**	**2**	**3**	**12**	**16**	*12*	7	8
	H	44	41	**0**	**39**	**46**	**52**	**74**	**45**	**16**
	B	15	7	0	8	10	14	**17**	**11**	**5**
	H	*44*	*34*	**24**	**34**	**45**	**50**	**58**	**35**	**27**
	B	**19**	**7**	**1**	**6**	**18**	**26**	_17_	_13_	_9_
DK	H	59	46	33	56	61	62	56	46	47
	B	23	8	3	17	19	26	16	16	14
ES	H	40	38	**29**	**32**	**42**	**51**	-	-	-
	B	15	11	3	10	13	22	-	-	-
FI	H	**53**	**39**	**33**	**47**	**54**	**48**	**61**	**44**	**28**
	B	**23**	**5**	**5**	**14**	**18**	**19**	_19_	_14_	_8_
FR	H	26	18	20	11	31	21	43	21	10
	B	5	3	3	1	8	3	5	5	2
GB	H	30	31	31	31	32	30	**55**	**40**	**19**
	B	6	2	3	2	6	4	7	4	3
IL	H	**63**	**45**	50	52	57	55	**65**	**57**	**39**
	B	39	14	20	25	30	26	23	28	22
IT	H	**44**	**27**	-	-	*39*	*34*	**50**	**34**	**20**
	B	**31**	**14**	-	-	23	20	26	23	15
NL	H	48	43	39	47	47	48	_53_	_48_	_39_
	B	4	2	*1*	2	*3*	7	5	2	4
SE	H	53	41	_27_	_43_	_51_	_55_	64	44	42
	B	**22**	**7**	**2**	**9**	**16**	_23_	15	13	17

Note. Bold $p < 0.001$, underlined $p < 0.01$, italics $p < 0.05$.

TABLE 3.9
Percentage Having PC With Modem (1) Anywhere at Home (H); (2) in Own Bedroom (B); by Country, Gender, Age, and SES

		Gender		Age				SES		
		M	*F*	*6-7*	*9-10*	*12-13*	*15-16*	*H*	*M*	*L*
BE(vlg)	H	*21*	*13*	15	13	20	19	19	15	15
	B	**6**	**1**	*1*	*1*	*4*	6	4	3	3
CH	H	20	13	**2**	**19**	**17**	**16**	**34**	**15**	**7**
	B	<u>5</u>	<u>1</u>	0	2	2	4	**6**	**3**	**1**
DE	H	10	8	8	8	10	9	<u>17</u>	<u>5</u>	<u>7</u>
	B	2	1	0	0	1	3	<u>2</u>	<u>1</u>	<u>0</u>
DK	H	29	21	10	27	27	26	29	17	21
	B	7	2	1	5	5	7	5	3	5
ES	H	10	7	*4*	*8*	*11*	*11*	-	-	-
	B	2	2	0	1	4	3	-	-	-
FI	H	**32**	**19**	19	24	31	29	**37**	**20**	**17**
	B	**11**	**2**	<u>2</u>	<u>5</u>	<u>8</u>	<u>11</u>	9	5	*4*
FR	H	10	5	7	4	12	5	13	7	3
	B	3	1	1	1	4	1	2	2	1
GB	H	9	5	6	7	9	7	**17**	**10**	**3**
	B	2	1	1	1	1	1	1	2	1
IL	H	**39**	**24**	*25*	*28*	*33*	*36*	**43**	**32**	**18**
	B	26	6	12	13	17	17	15	16	15
IT	H	*12*	7	-	-	10	10	**15**	**8**	**6**
	B	2	4	-	-	5	6	7	5	3
NL	H	19	17	18	18	15	20	**28**	**22**	**9**
	B	*2*	*0*	<u>1</u>	<u>1</u>	<u>0</u>	<u>3</u>	2	0	1
SE	H	32	29	<u>18</u>	<u>25</u>	<u>33</u>	<u>38</u>	**45**	**29**	**16**
	B	**11**	4	**1**	3	8	13	7	8	6

Note. Bold $p < 0.001$, underlined $p < 0.01$, italics $p < 0.05$.

TABLE 3.10
What Would You Miss Most? Top Three Choices (Percentage of Those With Medium in Home); by Country, Gender, Age, and SES

	Gender		Age				SES		
	M	F	6-7	9-10	12-13	15-16	H	M	L
BE (vlg)	33% Hi-fi 19% Radio 10% TV	46% Hi-fi 25% Radio 6% TV	42% Radio 10% Books 9% G mach	37% Radio 25% Hi-fi 8% G mach	42% Hi-fi 20% Radio 7% G mach	54% Hi-fi 12% TV 10% Radio	46% Hi-fi 18% Radio 9% TV	32% Hi-fi 25% Radio 9% G mach	37% Hi-fi 24% Radio 9% TV
CH	32% Hi-fi 15% G mach 14% Books	46% Hi-fi 20% Books 12% Radio	38% Books 29% Hi-fi 25% G mach	27% Hi-fi 23% Books 16% Radio	38% Hi-fi 15% Books 10% TV	49% Hi-fi 12% Books 10% Radio 10% PC 10% G mach	34% Hi-fi 22% Books 11% Radio	42% Hi-fi 17% Books 10% Radio 10% G mach	35% Hi-fi 15% Books 13% Radio
DE	32% Hi-fi 27% TV 23% G mach	48% Hi-fi 26% TV 15% Radio	53% Hi-fi 41% G mach 15% Radio	42% Hi-fi 22% G mach 21% TV	38% Hi-fi 27% TV 19% G mach	40% TV 29% Hi-fi 22% PC	40% Hi-fi 27% TV 16% Radio	35% Hi-fi 30% TV 22% G mach	32% Hi-fi 32% TV 31% G mach
ES	42% TV 23% PC 16% G mach	39% TV 15% Phone 14% Hi-fi	53% TV 23% G mach 15% Books	37% TV 24% PC 18% G mach	34% TV 20% PC 12% Phone	39% TV 17% Hi-fi 16% Phone	N/A	N/A	N/A
FI	42% TV 38% PC 12% G mach	40% TV 27% Phone 20% Hi-fi	N/A	36% PC 29% TV 17% Phone	50% TV 18% PC 15% Hi-fi	44% TV 23% Phone 17% PC	34% TV 23% PC 16% Hi-fi	44% TV 24% PC 17% Phone	46% TV 23% PC 15% Phone
GB	56% TV 15% PC 14% G mach	50% TV 20% PC 12% Phone	46% TV 33% G mach 25% PC	59% TV 15% PC 12% G mach	58% TV 11% Hi-fi 10% G mach	45% TV 27% Hi-fi 14% Phone	56% TV 13% Phone 11% PC	56% TV 23% Phone 15% PC	51% TV 19% Hi-fi 13% G mach
IL	38% TV 28% PC 10% Hi-fi	38% TV 25% Phone 14% PC	38% PC 34% TV 13% Books	33% TV 24% PC 13% Phone	47% TV 21% Phone 14% PC	36% TV 29% Phone 20% Hi-fi	35% TV 25% Phone 16% PC	38% TV 26% PC 16% Phone	39% TV 19% Phone 14% Hi-fi
IT	30% TV 23% PC 17% Hi-fi	26% TV 22% Phone 19% Hi-fi	N/A	N/A	32% TV 17% PC 16% Phone	23% TV 23% Hi-fi 18% Phone	23% TV 18% Hi-fi 19% Phone	27% TV 20% Hi-fi 17% Phone	33% TV 16% Phone 15% Hi-fi
NL	38% TV 16% PC 9% Radio	36% TV 12% Radio 12% Hi-fi	41% TV 16% PC 15% G mach	39% TV 12% Books 9% Radio	42% TV 11% Radio 10% Hi-fi	26% TV 17% Hi-fi 16% Phone	36% TV 15% Books 11% PC	36% TV 12% PC 10% Radio	38% TV 13% Radio 10% Hi-fi
SE	41% TV 18% PC 11% Phone	38% TV 32% Phone 8% Hi-fi 8% Books	32% TV 25% PC 25% G mach	35% TV 15% Phone 14% PC	42% TV 27% Phone 9% PC	44% TV 27% Phone 10% PC	34% TV 26% Phone 12% PC	41% TV 20% Phone 10% PC	39% TV 20% PC 17% Phone

TABLE 3.11

What Would You Like to Get on Next Birthday? Top Three Choices (Percentage of Those Without Item in Own Room); by Country, Gender, Age, and SES

	Gender		Age				SES		
	M	F	6-7	9-10	12-13	15-16	H	M	L
BE (vlg)	21% TV 17% Internet 16% CDR	24% TV 19% Pager 18% G'boy	29% TV 18% CDR 15% G'boy	19% TV 25% G' boy 15% Internet	19% G'boy 18% TV 15% Internet 15% Pager	25% TV 20% *Books* 18% Internet	21% TV 16% Internet 13% G'boy 13% Books	19% TV 18% Books 17% G' boy	33% TV 21% Internet 16% G'boy
CH	21% CDR 15% Camc 14% TV	20% Phone 18% TV 14% CDR	N/A	17% TV 14% CDR 13% G mach	18% Camc 18% CDR 14% TV	20% TV 20% CDR 18% Phone	19% TV 16% CDR 15% Internet	17% CDR 15% TV 14% Phone 14% Camc	19% CDR 14% TV 14% Camc 14% Phone
DE	33% TV 17% CDR 14% G mach	42% TV 13% Per ster 11% CDR	32% G'boy 31% TV 13% G'boy	36% TV 19% CDR 16% Hi-fi	34% TV 27% CDR 13% Hi-fi	40% TV 22% CDR 15% Per ster	36% TV 20% CDR 20% *Hi-fi*	28% TV 21% CDR 18% G'boy	40% TV 21% G'boy 16% G mach
ES	27% CDR 10% G mach 12% CB/sat	25% CDR 10% Camc 10% Internet 10% Hi-fi	27% G mach 15% Camc 14% G'boy 14% CDR	24% CDR 17% G mach 12% G'boy	36% CDR 14% Per ster 11% Cb/sat 11% Internet	27% CDR 16% Cb/sat 16% Internet	N/A	N/A	N/A

FI	23 CDR 19% Gmach 12% Internet	19% TV 19% Mob ph 16% Per ster	24% Gmach 19% PC 16% Per ster	21% CDR 15% Gmach 11% Per ster 11% TV	29% CDR 17% TV 18% Mob ph	32% Mob ph 18% CDR 16% TV	17% CDR 14% TV 14% Mob ph	18% CDR 14% Internet 13% TV	15% Mob ph 19% CDR 13% Gmach
GB	23% Gmach 13% CDR 13% PC	22% TV 15% CDR 14% Mob ph	19% TV 16% G'boy 15% Gmach	16% TV 16% Gmach 15% CDR	20% TV 16% CDR 17% Hi-fi	17% Mob ph 5% CDR 15% Per ster	17% TV 13% Gmach 13% Camc	16% Gmach 16% CDR 15% TV	18% TV 15% CDR 14% PC
IL	25% TV 18% CDR 18% Camc	31% TV 17% CDR 16% Camc	24% TV 17% CDR 12% Gmach	34% TV 18% CDR 13% Per ster	28% TV 25% CDR 19% Hi-fi	33% Hi-fi 24% TV 26% Camc	32% TV 23% Camc 15% CDR	28% TV 17% CDR 14% Hi-fi	21% Camc 17% Hi-fi 15% TV
IT	27% CDR 24% Internet 15% Mob ph	19% Internet 7% Camc 17% CDR	N/A	N/A	28% CDR 21% Internet 14% Camc	22% Internet 18% Camc 15% Mod ph	23% Internet 23% Hi-fi 17% Camc	25% Internet 23% CDR 14% Camc	24% CDR 18% Camc 15% Internet
NL	22% PC 16% TV 10% Gmach 10% T'text	30% TV 17% Hi-fi 11% T'text	17% TV 17% Gmach 15% G'boy	30% TV 15% Hi-fi 11% PC	25% TV 25% Hi-fi 20% PC	3% Hi-fi 16% TV 16% t'text	23% TV 13% PC 11% Hi-fi	23% TV 16% Hi-fi 14% PC	23% TV 18% Hi-fi 15% PC
SE	26% PC 19% TV 12% Cb/sat	26% TV 18% Hi-fi 17% Mob ph	25% PC 22% Gmach 18% TV	27% TV 14% PC 14% Mob ph	22% PC 20% TV 15% Mob ph	26% PC 23% TV 18% Internet	28% TV 18% PC 13% Mob ph	24% TV 19% PC 12% Mob ph 12% Internet	22% Hi-fi 21% PC 16% Internet

Note. Figures in italics indicate small base size and must be regarded with caution.

TABLE 3.12

What Would You Buy With Your Own Money? Top Three Choices (Percentage of Those Without Item in Own Room); by Country, Gender, Age, and SES

	Gender		Age				SES		
	M	F	6-7	9-10	12-13	15-16	H	M	L
BE (vlg)	65% Music 43% C game 41% Comics	67% Music 45% Mags 36% Books	24% Comics 21% Books 16% Video	45% Music 41% Comics 33% Books	82% Music 54% Comics 49% C game	92% Music 49% Mags 37% C game	75% Music 40% Mags 39% Comics	56% Music 39% Comics 33% Books	65% Music 36% Books 33% Comics
CH	48% Music 39% C game 23% Videos	53% Music 27% Mags 20% Books	6% Books 4% C game 2% Mags 2% comics	N/A	71% Music 37% C game 32% Books	80% Music 39% Mags 39% C game	60% Music 33% C game 30% Mags	50% Music 24% C game 22% Mags	49% Music 22% C game 16% Mags
DE	34% Music 25% C game 23% Mags	38% Music 35% Mags 21% Books	17% Comics 5% Music 5% Mags	24% Mags 21% C game 19% Music	44% Music 39% Mags 23% C game	64% Music 40% Mags 22% C game	39% Music 36% Mags 18% Books	34% Music 28% Mags 18% Comics	32% Music 24% Mags 15% C game
ES	43% C game 40% Music 31% Mags	46% Music 44% Mags 34% Books	20% Books 11% Comics 11% Videos 11% Music	43% Books 34% C game 30% Mags	48% Music 48% Mags 41% C game	66% Music 56% Mags 29% Books	N/A	N/A	N/A

FI	32% Music 25% C game 19% Videos	39% Music 23% Mags 13% Books	N/A	N/A	65% Music 37% C game 32% Videos	74% Music 34% Mags 31% Videos	33% Music 16% C game 15% Mags 15% Videos	36% Music 19% C game 17% Videos	39% Music 17% Mags 13% Videos
GB	59% Music 45% C game 32% Mags	63% Music 51% Mags 27% Books	29% C game 28% Videos 27% Books	31% Mags 27% Books 24% C game	58% Mags 56% Music 29% C game	84% Music 61% Mags 37% C game	71% Music 48% Mags 33% Books 33% C game	60% Music 41% Mags 33% Books	58% Music 40% Mags 28% C game
IL	51% Music 37% C game 23% Videos	52% Music 22% Books 19% Videos	35% C game 23% Music 21% Videos	40% Music 34% Books 24% C game	60% Music 2% C game 22% Videos	72% Music 20% Books 19% Videos	57% Music 28% Books 22% C game	49% Music 28% C game 23% Videos	54% Music 27% C game 23% Books
IT	72% Music 48% C game 54% Comics	65% Music 54% Mags 40% Books	N/A	N/A	61% Music 52% Comics 50% Mags	72% Music 52% Mags 40% Books	75% Music 52% Mags 49% Comics	66% Music 50% Mags 45% Comics	65% Music 51% Mags 39% Comics
NL	54% Music 50% C game 28% Mags 28% Comics	61% Music 45% Mags 42% Books	16% Books 11% C game 8% Music	48% Music 45% Books 35% C game	78% Music 52% Mags 46% C game	92% Music 63% Mags 43% C game	55% Music 39% Books 38% Mags 38% C game	58% Music 40% Mags 34% Books 34% C game	58% Music 36% C game 33% Mags
SE	54% Music 34% C game 27% Videos	56% Music 35% Mags 34% Books	14% Comics 12% Music 8% C game	38% Music 29% Books 26% Comics	66% Music 33% Mags 25% Comics	76% Music 34% Mags 27% Videos	58% Music 28% Mags 27% Books	56% Music 27% Mags 24% Books	53% Music 27% Comics 23% Books

set, which as we noted is almost universal in European homes. However, younger children and, more interestingly, girls are less likely to have a set in their own room. In general, there is also a tendency for children from richer, high SES homes to be *less* likely to have their own set. This is the case in 8 of the 11 countries for which we have information (CH, DE, FI, FR, GB, IT, NL, and SE). In Flanders, Denmark, and Israel, on the other hand, there are no observable SES-related trends.

Family ownership of a VCR is not influenced by the gender of the child, nor are there any consistent patterns associated with the age of the child. Nor is there any association between SES and ownership of a VCR in the majority of countries. Only in Switzerland and Germany, where ownership of a VCR is slightly less common, are poorer, low SES families less likely to have one. On the other hand, replicating the pattern for personal ownership by the child of a television set, older children and boys are more likely to have one in their bedroom. Similarly, in the United Kingdom and Sweden (where household ownership is higher) children in the most affluent families are *less* likely to have a VCR in their own rooms.

Cable/satellite.   There are striking differences among our 12 countries in the number of homes with cable or satellite subscription. Variations in the broadcasting markets, country size, and language spoken in the countries under study account for these differences (see also chapter 1). In Flanders and the Netherlands, television signals are almost always carried through cable as cable penetration is among the highest in the world (over 90%); satellite reception is therefore negligible. As a result, questions about cable/satellite were not asked in these countries. Overall, in Table 3.3 two groups of countries can be distinguished: in Denmark, Germany, Israel, and Sweden, more than half of families have access to cable or satellite television. Interestingly, this degree of access for children in Sweden is higher than we would expect from the national data presented in chapter 1. In Germany penetration is particularly high, with four in every five families connected. In all other countries, households have moderate to low access.

Cable or satellite television access is much rarer in the child's bedroom: It is least common in France, Italy, Spain, and the United Kingdom (where apparently cable and satellite television are almost entirely confined to the living-room). In Germany and Israel, on the other hand, over a third of young people over the age of 12 have access to cable or satellite television in their own rooms.

We expected the balance of the genders in the family to have some influence on subscription to cable or satellite television, in view of the wider coverage of sport on such channels. However, only in Switzerland and Denmark are families with boys more likely to have subscribed. There is a trend in the majority of countries, however, for boys to be slightly more likely than girls to have cable or satellite access in their own rooms. We find wider penetration among families with older children only in Switzerland and Germany, although the usual finding that older children are more likely to own media personally is true for cable or satellite access also in the majority of countries. The cost of subscription doubtless underpins the finding that the poorest, low SES families are less likely to have cable or satellite in the majority of countries. The United Kingdom is an interesting exception to this rule.

Television-linked Games Machines. Television-linked games machines are most common in the United Kingdom and Sweden, where about two thirds of households with children have one somewhere in the home. They are least common in Germany, where less than one third of homes are so equipped. Examination of personal ownership of games machines reveals dramatically that in all countries, these are predominantly a male interest. Twice as many boys as girls own a television-linked games machine. Moreover, as we shall see, among those with access to a games machine in the home, boys are far more likely than girls to buy computer games with their own pocket money (see Table 3.12). In the majority of countries, personal ownership of games machines peaks at about age 12 to 13. However, this is not the case in Flanders, where more 15- to 16-year-olds own games machines than any other age group. In most countries, children from lower SES households are more likely to have a games machine either in the home or in the bedroom than higher SES children. Exceptions are Flanders, Switzerland, Germany, and Israel, where there are no SES-related differences in the home, although in Switzerland and Germany there is a slight tendency for children from lower SES families to be more likely to have a games machine in the bedroom.

Personal Computer. Access to a personal computer of some kind in the home varies considerably from one country to the next. Flanders and the Netherlands appear to have the widest distribution with, respectively, nine and eight in every ten families having a PC of some sort in the home. Israel comes next with three quarters of families owning a PC. In Switzerland, Finland, and Sweden, about six in every ten families do so, leaving Germany, the United Kingdom, Spain, and Italy trailing with only half of families owning a PC of some kind. Variations in diffusion patterns often, although not always, go hand-in-hand with different rates of hardware upgrading: Thus, families in the United Kingdom, together with those in France,[2] are least likely to have an up-graded PC with a CD-ROM drive (only 30% and 22% respectively do so).

---

[2]Because data for France and Denmark are not included in the comparative data base, we have not been able to calculate the numbers having access to a PC with or without a CD-ROM drive (a PC of any kind). However, figures show that in France, only half of children have PC's without a CD-ROM drive, compared with three quarters of children in Denmark.

Similarly, families in Israel and Denmark are particularly likely to own an upgraded PC (just over half do so in both countries) and those in Sweden and the Netherlands are not far behind (46% and 45% respectively). On the other hand, in Flanders, where ownership of a PC of some kind is particularly high, families are no more likely to own a PC with a CD-ROM drive than families in Germany, where overall PC ownership is low (39% do so in both cases).

The age and gender of the child and the SES of the family all have an effect on children's access in the home. In general, the older the child, the more likely the family is to have a PC. This is particularly likely to be the case where PCs with a CD-ROM drive are concerned. Only in France, the United Kingdom, and the Netherlands are families with younger children equally likely to own a PC with a CD-ROM drive. As we would predict, the gender of the child is less likely to affect access to a PC somewhere in the home. Only in Italy and Israel, and, to a lesser extent, in Germany and Finland, do boys have more access to a PC of some kind somewhere in the home than girls. However, gender differences are clearer when the purchase of a multimedia PC with a CD-ROM drive or a modem is involved: In most countries, parents seem more inclined to purchase a multimedia PC if they have a son as opposed to a daughter. Most influential of all is the SES of the family. The family's SES is a strong predictor of access to a PC in the house in eight out of ten countries, and the gap between SES groups widens with regard to access to PC peripherals such as a CD-ROM drive or a modem. Differences are particularly large in Germany, Switzerland, Italy, and the United Kingdom, but somewhat less pronounced in Finland, Israel, the Netherlands, and Sweden. Only in Flanders does the SES of the family apparently make no difference to the likelihood of owning a PC.

Personal ownership of PCs by children and young people differs considerably from country to country: The relative ratios of children having a computer in the bedroom compared to families having a computer in the house also varies. For example, in the Netherlands and Flanders, where the vast majority of families with children have a PC somewhere in the home, few children have one in their own bedroom. In most other countries, although access at home is lower, proportionately more children have their own PC. Overall, PCs are least likely to be found in the child's bedroom in the United Kingdom and the Netherlands. Just over one in every ten children has his or her own PC in these two countries, compared, for example, with Israel, where around a third of young people have their own PC. Ownership of a PC by children and young people is also high in Finland, where a quarter do so, and in Italy, where the figure is three in every ten (although in the latter case the sample is restricted to older children who are more likely to have their own equipment).

Having a PC in the bedroom in all cases increases steadily with age. There is also a clear gender effect: many more boys than girls have a PC (be it a PC of any type or a multimedia PC) in their own bedroom. Interestingly, however, SES-related differences are far less pronounced than is the case with access in the home generally. Only in Switzerland are children from low SES homes much less likely to have a PC of some kind in their own room. In Finland, Germany, and to a lesser extent Flanders, PCs with CD-ROM drives are also less frequent in the bedrooms of children from lower SES families.

The Internet. Internet access is evolving fast, and studying its diffusion is consequently rather like attempting to fire at a moving target. Nevertheless, the snapshot provided by our research provides interesting evidence of national differences at an early stage in the diffusion process. The Nordic countries tend to be the leaders in Europe with regard to Internet access among families with children, as we would expect from the high Internet penetration in these countries (see chapter 1, Table 1.5). Israeli families are also very keen on having Internet access at home. A quarter or more families in Israel,[3] Sweden, Denmark, and Finland have PCs equipped with a modem, placing them at the very top of the "take off" stage in Rogers's model. By way of contrast, in Germany, Spain, France, and the United Kingdom, fewer than one in every ten families have such access. The figure is about two in ten for Flanders, Switzerland, Italy, and the Netherlands. As regards demographic differences, there is a tendency for families with older children, and families with girls, to have greater Internet access. However, the SES of the family is the most influential factor. The most affluent families are two or three times more likely to have Internet access than those with the lowest income. The discrepancy is highest in Switzerland, France, and the United Kingdom, where families in the highest grade are five times more likely to have Internet access than those in the lowest grade. Only in Flanders and Denmark are SES-related differences negligible.

Internet access in the child's bedroom is still rare: Well under 10% of European children, or Israeli girls, have personal access in their bedroom to a PC connected to a modem. On the other hand, as many as a quarter of Israeli boys have it. Although the difference between Israeli boys and girls is particularly dramatic, a consistent gender difference can be noted. Only in Spain are girls as likely as boys to have their own modem. The influence of age and social status is not so clearly discernible. Only in Switzerland are children from less affluent families significantly less likely to have personal access to the Internet. However, in most countries 15- to 16-year-olds are more likely to have a modem.

Books. Books (defined in the survey as "a shelf of books, not for school") are, like television, omnipresent in homes in all 12 countries. They are particularly popular in the Netherlands, where almost every home has its shelf

---

[3] As already mentioned in chapter 2, the Israeli sample only included Jewish children; Internet access among Arab children is probably much lower.

of books. Only in the United Kingdom are books found in fewer than nine out of ten homes with children, and only in the United Kingdom and Switzerland, countries with the greatest degree of social stratification, are children in lower SES families less likely to have books somewhere in the home. Families with older children are not more likely to have books somewhere in the home, and books are found in roughly equal proportions in households with boys and girls, although there is a slight tendency for families with girls to be more likely to have them.

Unsurprisingly, personal ownership of books by children reflects national patterns for books within the family home generally. A shelf of books can be found in the bedrooms of most children everywhere and books are, next to radio, the most pervasive bedroom medium. In the Netherlands, almost every child owns books, whereas in the United Kingdom, only two thirds of children do so. However, SES-related differences are more strongly marked than in the case of books in the home generally. Everywhere, children from high SES families are more likely to have books in their bedrooms. Differences are smallest in the Netherlands, Sweden, Finland, Flanders, and France, and largest in the United Kingdom and Switzerland. There are also interesting age and gender effects. For example, everywhere girls are somewhat more likely than boys to have books in the bedroom. The influence of age is less uniform, and seems to be influenced by cultural factors. In Flanders, the Netherlands, and the United Kingdom, there is a distinct falling off in the numbers of children owning books after the age of 13. However, in Germany, Spain, and Finland, personal ownership of books increases with age.

Telephone. Telephone access in the home is nearly universal in all countries, although in the United Kingdom, Switzerland, and Germany, children from lower SES families are less likely to have it. On the other hand, telephones are rarely found in children's bedrooms, with the exception of Sweden, where almost half have their own telephone line, and Israel and Italy, where almost two in every five do so. In the case of the first two countries, this is related to the high level of Internet access in children's bedrooms. Although boys are consistently more likely than girls to have new media in their own rooms, there is no such gender difference for the telephone. There is, however, a clear and universal age trend: Teenagers are much more likely to have their own telephone line.

Relative Importance of Different Media in Children's Lives

It may be presumed that the presence of media in the home reflects at least some degree of interest. However, children may have little to do with their parents' decisions about what to buy. In order to get more insight into the comparative value attached by children to the ownership of different media, we turned to a number of other questions they answered about their media-related preferences and behavior.

For example, which one, out of a list of about 16 media, would children and young people miss most?[4] It must be acknowledged that there was a considerable spread of answers, indicating that young people's media tastes are quite diverse, but the importance of television in children's lives is very clear. In the majority of countries, both boys and girls are most likely by far to name television: Girls are next most likely to name older media such as the hi-fi or the telephone, whereas boys name a computer of some kind. There are also some consistent age- and a few SES-related trends. For example, the popularity of the hi-fi and the telephone increases with age, whereas that of the games machine and books decreases. Similarly, books tend to appear more often in the rankings of children from high SES families and games machines in those of children from lower SES families. Interestingly, the SES of the family makes little difference to children's attachment to television: Only in Finland are high SES children noticeably less likely to say they would miss television most, although there is a trend in that direction in Germany and Italy.

However, the most striking finding to emerge involves national differences in the popularity of both television and computers (see Table 3.10). Confirming the United Kingdom's strong screen orientation (see chapter 1), half or more British children in every demographic group say that they would miss television most. Similarly underlining the Nordic edge in ICTs, PCs are particularly popular with boys in Finland, with little difference in the numbers naming television and a PC as the thing they would miss most. In stark contrast, television does not figure at all among the top three choices of either boys or girls in Switzerland. It is only the second most common choice in Germany and the third most common in Flanders. Moreover, PCs do not rank in the top three choices for boys in any of these three countries. In each it is music media (the hi-fi or the radio) that are most likely to be missed. Young people in Switzerland appear to have a particularly traditional culture, with books ranked second to the hi-fi in almost all demographic groups and ranked first amongst 6- to 7-year-olds. The only other countries where books are ever ranked among the top three media are Spain, Israel, and the Netherlands, and in all three cases, books are mentioned only by younger children.

---

[4]Television set, cable/satellite television, Teletext, VCR, radio, hi-fi, personal stereo, Gameboy, television-linked games machine, PC (not able to take CD-ROMs), PC (able to take CD-ROMs), Internet link/modem, telephone, mobile phone, shelf of books, camcorder. In addition, in France, Minitel was included on the list, as was a pager in Flanders, the Netherlands, and Switzerland, and interactive television in Spain.

Taking a different perspective and focusing on those media that children do not yet own personally, we asked which they would most like to get as a birthday present. How, we wondered, would their choices be influenced by their age, gender, and the SES of their families? What would be the effect of the country's position on Rogers's diffusion curve? Would those few children who did not yet have an item currently owned by most other children be more likely to want it than children living in an environment where that item was comparatively rare?

At this point it is important to note that only those children who did not already have an item in their own room were entered into the analysis. This means that the figures in Table 3.11 are not distorted by the fact that, for example, only one in five Swiss children, compared with one in three British children, own their own television set. We expected that some of the less expensive items (books for example) would seldom be selected. However, we have the opportunity to compare their relative popularity in different countries and with different demographic groups.

The lower recorded percentages for any one item indicate that here we have even greater diversity in choices made. However, once again there are clear national differences. In Italy, a television set does not figure among the top three choices of either boys or girls. In Spain, only a small proportion of boys show an interest in having cable or satellite. In stark contrast, more than a third of German children at present without a set of their own express a desire to have one. This can be compared with the finding that in Germany, children are *least* likely to miss television if they already have it. These results are intriguing and probably reflect very different patterns of family life and viewing habits. In Germany, although as yet comparatively few children actually own their own sets (see Table 3.1), particularly large numbers of children already spend half or more of their waking time at home in their own rooms (see chapter 8, Table 8.1). German children are also more likely than children in other countries to watch their favorite program alone (see chapter 8, Table 8.5). This suggests that German children prefer a more individualized style of television viewing, and that there is an appetite among young people for their own set and the resultant control over what they can watch. In Italy and Spain, on the other hand, very few children usually watch alone. Thus different styles of family interaction and different viewing patterns may make personal ownership valued in Germany, but render it meaningless in a country such as Italy or Spain.

The comparative lack of interest in ownership of a television set is compensated for in Spain and Italy by particularly high levels of interest in multimedia computers and, in Italy, in the Internet. Interest in acquiring a PC with a CD-ROM drive is high overall, but there are indications that children in different countries have been alerted to their desirability in different degrees. For example, in the United Kingdom with its screen entertainment culture, interest in PCs is eclipsed by interest in television-linked games machines (see Livingstone & Bovill, 1999). In the Netherlands, where family ownership of basic PCs is high but ownership of multimedia PCs rare, even boys seem unaware of their possibilities. Despite being offered the choice of a PC able to take CD-ROMs, Dutch boys choose the basic PC. There is also evidence of what we might consider fads or more idiosyncratic national interests, such as the interest of older Flemish girls in pagers and Dutch children in teletext.

There are predictable gender- and age-related differences, but few consistent SES-related trends. Thus, only in Flanders are children from low SES families much more likely to want their own television set. Moreover, this trend is reversed in Israel, where children from high SES families are the most likely to want one. However, girls are consistently more likely to be interested in acquiring their own television set, hi-fi, personal stereo, or mobile phone, whereas boys show more interest in computers and games machines. Interest in Gameboys and games machines fades, but interest in the Internet increases with age. Intriguingly, in eight out of the ten countries, young people seem most interested in acquiring computers between the ages of 12 and 13.

When we turn to what children and young people tell us about the media they buy with their own money, several interesting points emerge.[5] Girls in every country, and boys everywhere except in Spain, are most likely to spend their own money on music tapes or CDs. Second on the list for boys (first for Spanish boys) come computer games, with videos or comics as the third most common choice. For girls the second most common purchase is a magazine, and books take third place. It is striking that books never appear among the top three items bought by boys, just as computer games never appear high on girls' lists. There are also noticeable age-related effects. For example, buying music tapes or CDs and magazines becomes much more common among teenagers, whereas book and comic buying tends to drop off among this age group. Books are also more often the choice of children from higher SES families. On the other hand, there are few indications of differences between countries. Older teenagers in Italy, Spain, and Israel are more likely than those in other countries to buy books with their own money; the reverse is true for Finnish children, who tend to borrow a lot of books from libraries. Otherwise, cross-national similarities outweigh differences.

---

[5]Children were asked whether they bought books, magazines, comics, music CDs/tapes/ records, computer/video games, or videos for themselves out of their own pocket money. Answers do not, therefore, reflect the regularity of purchases or the number of occasions on which items are bought.

CONCLUSIONS AND DISCUSSION

All in all, television remains the most pervasive medium in European homes. Almost all families with children have a television set as well as a shelf of books somewhere in the home, and, as we saw, it is also the medium European children are most likely to say they would miss. Other chapters in this book show that it is also the medium children spend most time with by far (see chapter 4) and the medium young people and their parents in all countries are most likely to talk about (see chapter 7).

However, although in all countries the majority of children have their own books, personal ownership by children of their own television set is much rarer. In only two countries, the United Kingdom and Denmark, do as many as two of every three children have their own set. Uniquely, British children are as likely to have a television set in their own room as they are to have a shelf of books. It will be interesting to see whether this British pattern represents the future for children in other European countries. Rogers's model suggests that personal ownership of a television set by children in other European countries has reached the point where we can expect rapid expansion. However, children are not themselves in control of expensive purchases such as television sets, and purchase of such items for a child may tell us as much or indeed more about parents' needs and priorities. It is, after all, not only the child whose interests are served by having a television set in the bedroom—parents' privacy and access to programs they prefer are also ensured.

Our data also show that the PC has achieved a high degree of prominence in the lives of most children, particularly in northern European countries and among Jewish youths in Israel. Even in the four countries with comparatively low access figures—Italy, the United Kingdom, Spain, and Germany—about half of the children have a computer somewhere at home. In the latter two countries, this represents almost twice the proportion recorded for adults as whole (see chapter 1, Table 1.5), confirming that families with children are leading the field in adoption of domestic computers. Families with boys seem particularly likely to invest in the most up-to-date computers. In Israel, Sweden, Finland, and Denmark, the majority of boys have a computer with a CD-ROM drive somewhere at home. On the other hand, only in Israel, Sweden, Denmark, and Finland is Internet access among families with children widespread enough to be beginning to involve the "early majority" of families. Once again the United Kingdom, Spain, and Germany together with France lag furthest behind, with fewer than one in ten families having Internet access at home.

Personal ownership of computers by children themselves is still comparatively rare, although no country is at Rogers's earliest stage: In most, personal ownership of a computer by boys has already begun to involve the "early majority." However, as yet only a tiny minority of children have Internet access. The one exception is the case of Israeli boys, two in every five of whom already have access to the Internet in their own room.

Our findings confirm striking discrepancies between the rankings of some countries produced by the World Economic Forum in 1996 (see chapter 1, p. 25) and the media realities in children's homes and bedrooms. For example, the high ranking of Switzerland (marginally below the Nordic countries) for overall preparedness for the networked society (see chapter 1) is not reflected in our study. Swiss figures for family Internet access are well below those of Sweden, Finland, and Israel. Similarly, many more Flemish children than Swiss children have access to a computer somewhere at home, although Belgium is regarded by the World Economic Forum as only a middle-ranking country.

Likewise, the distinction between Germany and the United Kingdom on the one hand (middle-ranking countries according to the World Economic Forum) and Spain and Italy (low-ranking) on the other is not confirmed when we consider the media environment of children in the home. Figures in Germany and the United Kingdom for home ownership of computers are comparable to those in Italy or Spain: In all four countries, in about half of families with children, there is a computer somewhere in the home. Whether or not we conclude that the situation at the domestic level is much worse than we would expect in Germany or the United Kingdom, or much better than we would expect in Italy and Spain, is a matter of judgment.

The very low World Economic Forum ranking for Israel looks particularly misleading, as our data show that Israeli children enjoy very high domestic access to PCs—including expanded, multimedia PCs—not only in the home but also in their own bedrooms. However, it should be remembered that our Israeli sample was limited to Jewish families, and the poorer Arab population is not represented.

Only in the case of France do the figures for home access and the World Economics Forum statistics agree unequivocally, suggesting that France is particularly ill-equipped. For example, at the time of our survey in 1997, less than a quarter of French families had an up-to-date computer with CD-ROM access in the home, compared with about half of Danish, Finnish, Swedish, Dutch, and Israeli families. Paradoxically, France's position in 1997 can be at least partly attributed to the pioneering, but ultimately tangential, Minitel experience, not to a natural resistance to innovation. As a result, France has recently been rapidly making up for lost time. Diffusion patterns are, of course, heavily dependent on government policy and pricing strategies of both hardware and software, among other factors. The high rate of home PC ownership in the Netherlands, for example, can be seen as the result of the many home PC projects set up by companies in the recent past. Similarly, in Flanders the government is making major efforts to create a beneficial climate for companies in the ICT sector.

Although, as already outlined, there are major national variations in the domestic access that children and young people have to media, within each country we noted very similar demographic patterns. Most important, however, are the differences between the demographic factors that influence personal ownership of media by the child and those that influence family ownership of media.

For most media, ownership at the level of the family varies little according to the age or gender of the child, but is generally associated with SES. Generally, high SES is associated with high levels of ownership (as in the case of computers and the Internet) but occasionally this pattern is reversed (as in the case of television-linked games machines). By contrast, personal ownership of media by the child depends primarily on the child's age and/or gender and there are few SES-related differences.

Looking first at the kinds of media found in boys' and girls' bedrooms, our empirical investigation confirms our earlier hypothesis that boys are earlier adopters than girls of new, interactive media. Although girls are less likely than boys to own most media personally, including television sets and video recorders, the difference is particularly marked in the case of computers and games machines. Only in the case of books are girls a little more likely to possess their own. Our survey suggests that these discrepancies reflect girls' interests and not simply parental prejudice. Asked which medium they would miss most, television tops the list for girls in most countries, and older media such as the telephone, books, and audio media come next. Only in Israel does the PC figure among girls' top three choices. On the other hand, a PC or a games machine is listed among the top three choices for boys in all but one of our countries. Again, whereas boys are more likely to buy computer games with their own money, girls, who tend to read more and listen more to music than boys do (see chapter 4), are much more likely to buy books and magazines, and somewhat more likely to buy CDs, tapes, or records.

Focusing on how the age of the child influences which media are likely to be found in the bedroom, the general finding is that older children are more likely to own most media. In particular, personal ownership by children of PCs and screen entertainment media (television sets, access to cable or satellite channels, and video recorders) increases dramatically with age. On the other hand, ownership of television-linked games machines peaks in the majority of countries between the ages of 12 and 13, and ownership of books reverses the pattern, with younger children more likely to have a shelf of books in their own rooms. In only three countries—Germany, Spain, and Finland—does ownership of books increase slightly with age. Asked which medium they would miss most and which they would most like to have as a birthday gift, children confirmed that these differences in ownership reflect their preferences. For example, books are more likely to be named by primary school children as the medium they would miss most (see Table 3.10). Game-boys and games machines are most popular as a birthday gift among younger children, who are also more likely to name these as the medium they would miss most. Teenagers, on the other hand, are much more likely to name television, the hi-fi, or the telephone as the things they would miss most (see Table 3.10).

Turning now to media in the home, we find that, as predicted, the age and gender of the child are not important in the case of media that parents are equally likely to use, such as television, video recorders, telephones, or books. For obvious reasons, a major exception is the television-linked games machine, a favorite boys' toy: These are consistently more likely to be found among families with boys. Furthermore, there is an overall tendency for families with boys to be more inclined to have a computer of any type in the home, and these gender-related differences are more marked for the more up-to-date machines. Parents seem more inclined to purchase a multimedia PC if they have a son as opposed to a daughter. Chapter 10, which centers on PC use in schools, and chapter 11, which focuses on the use of new media, show us the extent to which PC access in school is compensating for this inequality. Similarly, the age of the child is consistently related to family ownership of media only in the case of computers. In most countries, families with older children are much more likely to have a PC of some type.

On the other hand, SES has considerable influence on family ownership of a number of media: Video recorders, cable or satellite television, telephones, books, and computers are all less frequently found in low SES families. There is only one exception—in more than half our countries, high SES families are less likely to have games machines.

Our hypothesis that the influence of SES was likely to be linked to the degree of social stratification within a country is, however, only partly confirmed. As we expected, in Flanders, ranked with Spain and the Netherlands as one of the least hierarchical countries, there are no SES-related differences in ownership of any of the media we asked about. Conversely, countries such as Switzerland and the United Kingdom, where the income gap between the poorest 20% and the richest 20% is particularly marked (see chapter 1), do show very large disparities: In Switzerland, for example, three times as many high SES compared with low SES families have a PC. The poorest families in these two countries are also less likely to own a telephone or a video recorder. Interestingly, in the United Kingdom, Switzerland, and Italy, books are also less likely to be found in low SES homes, suggesting that in these countries there may be a strong link between our measure of SES and the family's cultural capital.

In summary, there are certain consistent patterns that cut across national differences; particularly, the more restricted access to ICTs of low SES families, the tendency for girls to be less likely than boys to own most media, girls' greater interest in books, and boys' greater interest in, and superior access to, new interactive media. However, there is also a considerable body of evidence that media have been integrated into family life in very different ways in different countries. Differential uptake by different demographic groups to particular media suggests that media ownership is not a simple matter, but is influenced by complex social and cultural as well as economic factors. Thus, for Swiss and British families, as we saw, a love of books seems to be related to SES. On the other hand, in France, a highly hierarchical society comparable to Switzerland or the United Kingdom, all families, regardless of SES, are equally likely to have books somewhere in the home. British children stand out as screen entertainment fans, with the highest percentage of children having a television set in their own rooms and the lowest percentage owning books. The leading position of countries such as Denmark, Finland, Sweden, and Israel in access to the Internet, or the widespread ownership by families of PCs in the Netherlands and Flanders, are also clearly the product of a multiplicity of factors, including the needs of more isolated, small language communities as well as commercial and government policy.

In conclusion, we need to remind ourselves that having access to a medium at home does not necessarily imply use. It may very well be that children choose not to use a given medium at all during their leisure time, even though it is readily available (see chapter 5). Conversely, physical unavailability within the home is not necessarily an insurmountable barrier to leisure time use: Many young people find ways around it, such as going to a library or a friend's house to surf the Net or borrow a book. Moreover, actual time spent with different media varies greatly. The following chapter addresses the question of how much time is actually spent with different media in different countries, allowing us to determine how far the information on media access and ownership within the home presages media use.

REFERENCES

Holderness, M. (1995). *The Internet: Superhighway or dirt-track for the south?* London: Panos Institute; available at *http://www.oneworld.org/panos/panos*_internet_press.htm.

Livingstone, S., Gaskell, G., & Bovill, M. (1997). Europäische Fernseh-Kinder in veränderten Medienwelten [European television children in changing media worlds]. *Television, 10*(2), 4–12.

Livingstone, S., & Bovill, M. (1999). *Young people, new media. An LSE Report.* Available from http://psych.lse.ac.uk/young_people.

Loader, B. D. (Ed.). (1998). *Cyberspace divide. Equality, agency and policy in the information society.* London: Routledge.

Rogers, E. M. (1995). *Diffusion of innovations* (4th ed.). New York: The Free Press.

Silverstone, R. S. (1997). "New Media in European households." In U. T. Lange & K. Goldhammer (Eds.), *Exploring the limits: Europe's changing communication environment* (pp. 113–134). Berlin: Springer-Verlag.

Human Development Report (1999). New York: United Nations Development Program.

Van Dijk, J. (1999). *Network society, social aspects of new media.* London: Sage.

4

Children's Use of Different Media: For How Long and Why?

Johannes W. J. Beentjes
Cees M. Koolstra
Nies Marseille
Tom H. A. van der Voort

This chapter discusses the amount of time children spend on various media and the reasons why they use these media. Unlike most previous studies on these issues, the present study includes interactive media (i.e., electronic games, PCs, and the Internet), which have recently gained much importance in children's lives. The general question of this chapter is whether the rise of interactive media has had substantial consequences for children's media time expenditure and the functions fulfilled by various media. How much time do children spend on interactive media in comparison with other media, and for which purposes do they use interactive media, again as compared to other media?

It is of particular interest to learn how much time children spend on interactive media in comparison with print media. Since the coming of television, the fear has been expressed that the traditional reading culture or word-oriented culture is being replaced by an image-oriented one (McLuhan, 1964). It has been pointed out that children are reading less and less, and television has received the blame. Although some early studies (Himmelweit, Oppenheim, & Vince, 1958; Schramm, Lyle, & Parker, 1961) suggested that the coming of television affected only children's comic book reading, later research has shown that television may also reduce children's book reading (for a review, see Beentjes & van der Voort, 1989; Koolstra & van der Voort, 1996). For present generations of children, there is a possibility that children's appetite for books is not only affected by their pleasant experiences with television but also by the gratifications fulfilled by interactive media. Of course, the cross-sectional data presented here are unfit to determine causal relationships between the amount of time spent on interactive media and the time children spend with print media (for a discussion of the methodological limitations of cross-sectional studies of children's media use, see Koolstra & van der Voort, 1996). However, the data collected in our cross-national study do permit conclusions about the amount of time today's generations of children devote to interactive media, and about the position these media occupy in children's leisure-time activities relative to print media. In addition, the time-use data on reading found in the present study may be compared with findings obtained from earlier research, which may lead to conclusions about historical changes in children's reading behavior.

Both time expenditure and functions fulfilled by media are related to three characteristics: children's age, gender, and the socioeconomic status (SES) of their parents. Age is important because of the cognitive and experiential developments that take place within the age range studied, especially during childhood. In addition, age, together with gender and SES, helps to structure media use because these factors determine which persons or subgroups in children's environment are likely to influence their dispositions towards media use (Muijs, 1997). Although the relationships between media use and children's age, gender, and parental SES have not been previously investigated in one comprehensive European study, there are relevant national research data. We review studies that assess the time spent on various media, whether by means of diaries or through direct time estimates, in order to extrapolate predictions about the relationship between media use and the three demographic variables.

TIME SPENT ON MEDIA

Several different studies in Europe and the United States investigated the amount of time spent on various media. These studies include diary studies in the United States (Comstock & Paik, 1991), Sweden (Rosengren & Windahl, 1989), and the Netherlands (van Lil, 1989; Beentjes, Koolstra, Marseille, & van der Voort, 1997), and time-estimate studies in Germany (Klingler & Groebel, 1994). All the studies show that by far the most time is spent on television viewing. Among adolescents, television viewing is often equaled or even surpassed by the time spent on listening to audio media as a secondary activity, that is, when listening to audio media is combined with other activities. In studies that did not incorporate interactive media, television and audio media are, in terms of time expenditure, found to be followed by print media (Klingler & Groebel, 1994; Rosengren & Windahl, 1989; van Lil, 1989). However, according to a recent study that included interactive media, the time spent on interactive media is about equal to the time spent on reading (Beentjes et al., 1997).

Age Trends

All studies show that television viewing increases up to the beginning of adolescence. This seems evident because as children grow older, they stay up longer and are interested in more programs. Data on development during adolescence are less unambiguous. According to some studies, television viewing decreases after the age of 11 (Rosengren & Windahl, 1989; Comstock & Paik, 1991), but in a Dutch study (Beentjes et al., 1997) and a Danish study (Fridberg, Drotner, Schulz-Joergerson, Nielsen, & Soerensen, 1997), television viewing continues to increase during adolescence. The latter two studies were conducted more recently: Perhaps television viewing was found to increase in these studies because in the 1990s the supply of program genres that attract adolescents (e.g., domestic soap operas, series about college and high-school students, and MTV) has greatly increased.

Although in many studies watching video is treated together with watching television, studies that consider the time spent on video watching separately report no age trend until early adolescence and an increase in the course of adolescence (Klingler & Groebel, 1994; Rosengren & Windahl, 1989). Listening to audio media increases somewhat during middle childhood (Klingler & Groebel, 1994), but the real increase appears to take place during adolescence when for many children listening to audio media becomes a frequent primary and even more frequent secondary leisure activity (Beentjes et al., 1997; Rosengren & Windahl, 1989; van Lil, 1995).

In all studies, reading is found to increase with age from the time that children learn to read until the beginning of adolescence (Beentjes et al., 1997; Comstock & Paik, 1991; Klingler & Groebel, 1994; van Lil, 1989). In the course of adolescence, reading increases as children get older in one study (Comstock & Paik, 1991), but reading does not increase with age in two other studies (Beentjes et al., 1997; van Lil, 1989). The two latter studies do show, however, that reading matter varies by age (Beentjes et al., 1997; van Lil, 1989). The time spent reading books remains about the same in all age groups, whereas the time spent reading comics increases somewhat up to the age of 11, followed by a slow decrease during adolescence. Finally, during adolescence, reading newspapers and magazines increases somewhat with age.

One study charted the relationship between interactive media and age (Beentjes et al., 1997). Playing electronic games increases with age to a peak around the age of 13, after which a slow decline takes place. PC use for other purposes than playing games increases steadily between 8 and 17 years.

Gender Differences

Although some studies fail to find gender differences in the time spent on various media, the differences that are found consistently point in the same direction. With respect to television and video viewing, some studies find no gender difference in time expenditure (Beentjes et al., 1997; Klingler & Groebel, 1994), but if differences are found, boys watch on average more television and video than girls do (Comstock & Paik, 1991; Roe, 1998; Rosengren & Windahl, 1989; van Lil, 1989).

According to most studies, girls spend more time listening to audio media than boys do (Klingler & Groebel, 1994; Roe, 1998; Rosengren & Windahl, 1989). One study did not find gender differences in listening to audio media, but this study registered only primary use of audio media (Beentjes et al., 1997), whereas audio media are usually used in combination with other activities.

Girls were found to spend more time on reading in several different studies (Beentjes et al., 1997; Klingler & Groebel, 1994; van Lil, 1989), but an American study found no gender difference in overall reading (Comstock & Paik, 1991). In studies that differentiate between various types of reading materials, however, gender differences are found. Girls read more books and magazines (Beentjes et al., 1997; Roe, 1998; Rosengren & Windahl, 1989; van Lil, 1989), whereas boys spend more time reading comics (Beentjes et al., 1997; Roe, 1998; van Lil, 1989).

Gender differences are also found in the time spent on interactive media. Boys spend more time playing electronic games (Beentjes et al., 1997; Roe, 1998) and using the PC for other purposes (Beentjes et al., 1997).

SES Trends

A Flemish study found that children from low SES homes spend more time watching television and video than do high SES children (Muijs, 1997). An identical SES trend was also found in other studies (Beentjes et al., 1997; Klingler & Groebel, 1994; van Lil, 1989).

With respect to audio media, opposing trends are found. In one study children from high SES homes were found to spend more time listening to audio media (Klingler & Groebel, 1994), whereas in other studies more time is spent listening to audio media by low SES children (van Lil, 1989). Finally, yet another study found no relationship between SES and listening to audio media (Beentjes et al., 1997).

High SES children are generally found to spend more time on reading than low SES children (Beentjes et al., 1997; Klingler & Groebel, 1994). In one Dutch study, no relationship between SES and overall reading was found, but high SES children spend more time reading newspapers and magazines, whereas the reading of books and comics is not affected by SES (van Lil,

1989). In a more recent Dutch study, however, the positive relationship between reading and SES was almost entirely attributable to the reading of books (Beentjes et al., 1997).

Two studies explored the relationship between the amount of time children spent on interactive media and SES (Beentjes et al., 1997; Muijs, 1997). In the Dutch study (Beentjes et al., 1997), no SES trends were found for playing electronic games or for the most frequent PC applications (making texts and drawing). However, high SES children were found to spend more time using Internet, e-mail, and CD-ROMs. In the Flemish study (Muijs, 1997), only the time spent on playing electronic games was assessed. In contrast to the Dutch study, an SES trend was found in the Flemish study: Lower SES children spend more time playing electronic games than do higher SES children.

USES OF MEDIA

Studies that compare possible uses of media for children have been conducted in the United Kingdom (Brown, 1976), Germany (Klingler & Groebel, 1994), and Switzerland (Bonfadelli, 1986). In addition, a cross-national European comparison was made between Belgium, the Netherlands, Spain, Germany, and Sweden (Greenberg & Li, 1994). In these studies children were asked to indicate which medium they would choose for various uses. Although a vast variety of media uses may be found in the literature (McQuail, 1992), the uses employed in studies with children can mostly be categorized under three headings: information, mood control, and entertainment. Results indicate that newspapers, magazines, books, and television are often chosen for informational purposes (Bonfadelli, 1986; Brown, 1976; Greenberg & Li, 1994), whereas television, audio media, and books are used for mood control and entertainment (Bonfadelli, 1986; Brown, 1976; Greenberg & Li, 1994; Klingler & Groebel, 1994). Generally, the media that fulfill entertaining or emotional functions are the media that are used most frequently, because these two motives for using media are by far the strongest in determining media choices (von Feilitzen, 1974).

Age Trends

The number of children who choose television for specific uses varies with age. Brown (1976) found that the number of children that choose television for informational purposes increases up until the beginning of adolescence but declines from the age of 15. For entertainment and mood control, two studies found an increase in the choice for television until the age of 10, followed by a decline (Bonfadelli, 1986; Brown, 1976), whereas one study did not find any age trends in the use of television for mood control (Klingler & Groebel, 1994).

When they are older, more children choose audio media for entertainment or mood control (Bonfadelli, 1986; Brown, 1976; Klingler & Groebel, 1994). Findings on books are less clear. Bonfadelli (1986) reported that books lose their overall functionality for an increasing number of children between the ages of 9 and 15. Brown (1976) did not find an age trend for books, but Klingler and Grocbcl (1994) showed an increase in the number of children that choose books for mood control.

Gender Differences

The use of media for informational purposes appears to be unrelated to gender (Brown, 1976). For entertainment and mood control, however, boys more often choose television, whereas girls more frequently prefer audio media and books (Brown, 1976; Klingler & Groebel, 1994).

SES Trends

Like gender, SES appears to be unrelated to media use for information (Brown, 1976), whereas media use for entertainment and mood regulation is SES-related: In one study, more low SES than high SES children choose both television and audio media for mood control purposes (Brown, 1976); in another study, no SES trends for television and audio media were found but higher SES children more often chose books than did lower SES children (Klingler & Groebel, 1994).

THE PRESENT STUDY

In the present study we investigate age trends, gender differences, and SES trends in media use by taking together the samples of the participating countries. Because of this aggregation, we will only find significant trends if the findings of the various countries are basically in mutual agreement. This conservative approach results in an overview of age, gender, and SES trends in which the role of incidental sample fluctuations has been minimized.

As a starting point for our analysis, we may extract some tentative predictions on both time expenditure and uses of media by rephrasing the most consistent findings from the previous research discussed so far. Our first set of expectations is related to the frequency of use, both in terms of time and in terms of purposes of various media. We would expect to find that television will be the most time-consuming medium. In terms of time expenditure, television will be followed, and in the course of adolescence surpassed, by listening to audio media. Findings from earlier research suggest that reading will come third, albeit at some distance. However, it is quite possible that the present study will show that the print media have been caught up with and passed by the interactive media. With respect to media uses, television will be the most frequently chosen medium for informational, entertainment, and mood control purposes. Books, too, will be frequently chosen for all three uses but less often than television. Listening to audio media will score high on mood control. Newspapers and magazines will be chosen for information.

The second set of predictions concerns age trends. Summarizing what was found regarding age trends, it seems opportune to make a distinction between middle childhood (6 to about 12 years) and adolescence (12 to about 17 years). During middle childhood, most media activities gradually take up more time. Previously, only for video viewing has no age trend been found; television viewing, listening to audio media, reading, playing electronic games, and using the PC for other purposes may all be expected to increase. During middle childhood, the number of children who choose television particularly for informational purposes will increase.

During adolescence no consistent age trends will be found for television viewing, overall reading, and reading books. Video viewing, listening to audio media, reading newspapers and magazines, and PC use for other purposes than playing, however, will increase during adolescence, whereas reading comics will decline. The playing of electronic games will also decline, but not before the age of 13. In the course of adolescence, the number of children who choose television for information will decline. Audio media will be chosen by more and more children for entertainment and mood control.

The third set of predictions focuses on gender. Girls will spend more time reading books and magazines, and listening to audio media, whereas boys will put more time into television and video viewing, reading comics, playing electronic games, and using the PC for other purposes than playing. More boys than girls will choose television for entertainment and mood control, whereas more girls than boys will choose audio media and books for these purposes.

Finally, some predictions may be made on the relationship of media use and SES. Low SES children will spend more time watching television and video, whereas high SES children will spend more time reading and using the PC for Internet, e-mail, and CD-ROMs. For entertainment and mood control, more higher than lower SES children will choose books.

RESULTS

Media Use

Percentage of Media Users. For each of the 11 countries that measured time use, Table 4.1 gives the percentage of children who use each of the ten types of media distinguished. In all of the countries, television is the medium that is universally used. The percentages of users of television vary from 98%

TABLE 4.1
Percentage of Users of Media by Country

						Country						
Medium	BE	CH	DE	DK	ES	FI	GB	IL	IT	NL	SE	Average
Television	100	99	100	98	100	99	100	100	99	99	100	99
Audio media	98	96	94	-	-	96	94	84	95	100	-	95
Video	92	85	89	90	90	94	79	76	89	96	95	89
Books	80	90	86	78	-	87	54	62	-	91	79	79
Magazines	87	79	82	82	-	74	64	56	70	92	85	78
Electronic games	62	74	71	76	68	90	66	64	-	89	81	74
Newspapers	68	66	61	65	-	82	33	68	-	71	89	67
Comics	87	67	56	69	-	85	24	22	-	82	73	63
PC (not for games)	60	60	48	67	56	89	37	46	44	76	76	60
Internet	13	21	13	59	26	66	16	31	18	20	65	32

to 100%. The audio media and video are also used by almost all children; in most of the countries, these media are used by more than 90% of the children.

In the majority of the countries, books, magazines, and electronic games are used by more than 70% of the children. The number of users of these three media is relatively high in the Netherlands, where about 90% of the children reportedly read books and magazines and play electronic games. In the United Kingdom and Israel, on the other hand, relatively few children use these three media (about 60%).

In most countries, newspapers and comics are read by more than 60% of the children. However, cross-national differences are huge: The number of newspaper readers varies from 33% (GB) to 89% (SE), and the number of comics readers varies from 22% (IS) to 87% (BE-vlg).

In the majority of countries, the number of children who use the PC (not for games) also is more than 60%, but there are countries (GB, DE, IS, IT) where fewer than half the children use the PC for purposes other than game playing. The Internet has the fewest number of users. Averaged over all countries, only 30% of the children were found to use the Internet, although in the Nordic countries (FI, SE, DK) some 60% of the children use the Internet.

For each of the 10 media distinguished, Table 4.2 subdivides users according to gender, age, and SES. Chi-square tests were used to establish whether there are significant differences in the frequency of media users between boys and girls, different age groups, and children from low, medium and high SES homes. Because thousands and thousands of children are involved in these analyses, there is a risk of finding significant differences that are so small that they are practically negligible. To omit such marginal findings, a highly conservative level of significance has been employed ($p < .0001$). In addition, the consistency (C) of gender, age, and SES related differences in media use across countries was established by calculating the percentage of countries where the differences found are similar to those found for all countries combined. If C is equal or approximates 100%, gender, age, or SES operates in similar ways across national contexts. If C is considerably lower, cross-national differences are discussed, that is, in cases where a plausible explanation is available.

Three media have a greater number of users among girls than among boys: audio media, and two print media (magazines and, in particular, books). However, there is one print medium that has a greater number of users among boys than among girls, namely comics. In addition, boys are overrepresented among the children who use interactive media (electronic games, PC [not for games], and the Internet).

The number of users of television and video is about equally high in the three age groups distinguished. For most media, the number of users increases as children grow older. With increasing age, there is a strong linear increase in the number of users of magazines, newspapers, and the Inter-

TABLE 4.2
Percentage of Users of Media by Gender, Age, and Socioeconomic Status (SES)

Medium	Gender			Age				SES			
	Boys	Girls	C^a	9-10	12-13	15-16	C^a	Low	Med	High	C^a
Television	99_a	100_a	-	99_a	100_a	100_a	-	100_a	99_a	100_a	-
Audio media	93_a	96_b	63	90_a	95_b	97_b	100	94_a	95_a	95_a	-
Video	89_a	88_a	-	86_a	90_b	89_b	-	87_a	88_a	89_a	-
Books	72_a	87_b	100	85_a	82_b	73_a	100	73_a	82_b	83_b	75
Magazines	73_a	83_b	100	60	82_b	88_c	100	76_a	78_a	79_a	-
Electronic games	83_b	65_a	100	73_a	79_b	69_c	80	74_a	75_a	74_a	-
Newspapers	68_a	67_a	-	44_a	70_b	84_c	100	64_a	68_a	71_a	-
Comics	71_b	62_a	88	70_a	70_b	61_a	88	60_a	69_b	71_b	88
PC (not for games)	62_b	56_a	90	48_a	61_b	65_b	80	50_b	62_b	70_c	70
Internet	37_b	24_a	100	14_a	32_b	41_c	90	25_a	30_a	37_b	90

Note. Means in the same row (per category) having no letter in common in their subscripts differ at $p < .0001$; C^a is the percentage of countries for which the gender-, age-, or SES-related difference in question is similar to that found for all countries combined.

net. The number of users of audio media and the PC (not for games) is greater among secondary school students (aged 12 to 13 and 15 to 16) than among the youngest age group. For three media, the number of users decreases after the beginning of the secondary school period, a phenomenon that applies to books, comics, and electronic games.

For most media, the number of users does not depend on children's SES. The number of users of books and comics is higher among children from medium and high SES homes than among children from low SES homes. The strongest SES-related differences are found for the more serious types of PC use. The number of users of the PC (not for games) and the Internet linearly increases with SES level.

Media Use

Time Spent on Media.   The data in Tables 4.3 through 4.10 represent figures based on the whole sample (i.e., users and nonusers combined) because this facilitates comparisons with previous findings. Note, however, that in cases where the percentage of users of a certain medium is low (as shown in Tables 4.1 and 4.2), the figure reported for the whole sample is considerably lower than that found for users only. The reader who is interested in the users-only figures can simply estimate this figure by multiplying the figure reported for the whole sample by 100% divided by the percentage of users (found in Table 4.1 or 4.2). Alternatively, the reader may look up users-only figures in Appendix C.

Television is not only universally used, it is also the medium to which children allot most time (see Table 4.3). Averaged across all countries, children spend a good 2 hours per day in front of the television set. The amount of time spent watching television is highest in the United Kingdom and Israel, where children on average spend almost 3 hours per day watching television. The amount of time devoted to television viewing is further increased by the fact that children spend about half an hour per day watching video. The audio media also attract considerable attention. On average, children spend about 1^{1}/$_{2}$ hours per day listening to audio media.

Electronic games are the most frequently used interactive media. On average, children devote about half an hour per day to playing electronic games. The more serious types of PC use (PC not for games, and the Internet) demand less time. On average, children spend about a quarter of an hour per day on the PC (not for games) and 5 minutes on the use of the Internet. Note, however, that users of the Internet spend about three times as much time on this medium. Most time on interactive media is spent in the Nordic countries (FI, SE, and DK): Whereas the average European child spends 52 minutes per day with interactive media, children in the Nordic countries devote some 73 minutes to these media. The relatively high

TABLE 4.3
Number of Minutes per Day Spent on Various Media by Country

Medium	Country											
	BE	CH	DE	DK	ES	FI	GB	IL	IT	NL	SE	Average
Television	140	112	133	153	138	144	160	160	108	112	135	136
Audio media	69	93	52	127	-	115	72	91	101	92	-	90
Electronic games	17	25	27	45	27	42	31	42	30	24	37	32
Video	27	25	17	44	29	35	31	40	24	16	42	30
Books	20	26	16	17	-	35	15	22	-	23	17	21
PC (not for games)	20	12	9	17	20	23	12	18	15	13	26	17
Comics	15	15	7	11	-	24	1	3	-	10	9	11
Magazines	12	10	10	11	-	8	8	9	-	11	11	10
Newspapers	6	7	7	5	-	9	4	15	-	5	9	7
Internet	2	3	1	10	4	8	2	9	3	1	13	5

Note. In France, the number of minutes per day spend on television, PC (not for games), and Internet were respectively, 91, 30, and 17 (data about other media were not available).

amount of time Nordic children spend on interactive media is partly due to the fact that the number of users of these media is highest in the Nordic countries. A second reason may be that Nordic children are more experienced in the use of interactive media, because the Nordic countries are early adopters of these media.

Books are the most heavily used print medium. Most time on book reading is spent in Finland (35 minutes per day). The high amount of time Finnish children spend on book reading is not due to more Finnish children reading at all, because the percentage of book readers is highest in Switzerland and the Netherlands (see Table 4.1). Apparently, the high amount of time Finnish children spend with interactive media does not prevent them from maintaining a strong appetite for books. In all countries combined, children spend on average about 20 minutes per day reading books. The other print media occupy less time. Children spend about 10 minutes per day each on magazines and comics and 7 minutes per day reading newspapers.

For each of the 10 media distinguished, Table 4.4 shows time expenditure for subgroups defined by gender, age, and SES. T tests have been used to establish whether there are significant differences in the time spent on each medium between boys and girls, different age groups, and children from low, medium and high SES homes. Again, a highly conservative level of significance was employed ($p < .0001$).

As shown in Table 4.4, in most countries the amount of time children devote to various media is related to children's gender. Only the amount of time spent on television is about equal for boys and girls. Compared with boys, in all countries ($C = 100$) girls spend more time listening to audio media and reading books, and in most countries ($C = 78$) girls also spend more time reading magazines. On the other hand, boys spend more time reading newspapers and especially comics, and they watch more video than do girls. In addition, compared with girls, boys devote considerably more time to the use of interactive media: the Internet, PC (not for games), and in particular, electronic games.

As children become older, the amount of time spent with media increases for most of the media. With increasing age, there is a linear increase in the amount of time children devote to audio media and newspapers. Compared with 9- to 10-year-olds, children in the two oldest age groups (12 to 13 and 15 to 16 years) spend more time on television, the PC (not for games), and magazines. In addition, the amount of time spent on the Internet is greater among the oldest age group than among 9- to 10-year-olds. However, three media attract most attention among younger children. The amount of time spent reading books and comics is greater among the two youngest age groups (9 to 10 and 12 to 13 years) than among the oldest age group (15 to 16 years). The amount of time spent on electronic games is at its highest level when children are 12 to 13 years old, and then decreases.

TABLE 4.4

Number of Minutes per Day Spent on Various Media by Gender, Age, and SES

Medium	Gender			Age				SES			
	Boys	Girls	C^a	9-10	12-13	15-16	C^a	Low	Med	High	C^v
Television	134_a	130_a	-	118_a	137_b	136_b	100	145_b	128_a	121_a	80
Audio media	73_a	98_b	100	48_a	78_b	120_c	100	94_b	85_a	86_a	-
Electronic games	47_b	14_a	100	29_{ab}	34_b	27_a	82	28_a	31_a	30_a	90
Video	33_b	25_a	91	30_a	30_a	27_a	-	31_b	27_{ab}	25_a	-
Books	15_b	28_b	100	25_b	24_a	16_a	100	19_a	23_a	25_a	90
PC (not for games)	23_b	11_a	100	11_a	17_b	21_b	91	11_a	16_{ab}	21_b	-
Comics	13_b	7_a	89	14_b	12_b	6_a	89	8_a	11_a	12_a	90
Magazines	9	11_b	78	6_a	11_b	11_b	100	10_a	10_a	10_a	-
Newspapers	9_b	7_a	78	3_a	7_b	11_c	100	7_a	10_a	8_a	-
Internet	7_b	3_a	100	3_a	5_{ab}	7_b	73	2_a	4_{ab}	6_b	70

Note. Denmark and France are not included. Means in the same row having no letter in common in their subscripts differ significantly at $p < .0001$; C^a is the percentage of countries for which the gender-, age-, or SES-related difference in question is similar to that found for all countries combined.

SES-related differences in time spent on media are confined to watching television and video and to the more serious types of PC use. Children from low SES homes spend more time watching television and video than do children from higher SES homes. Children from high SES homes, on the other hand, devote more time to the PC (not for games) and the Internet than do children from low SES homes.

Uses of Media

Excitement.   For each of eight countries, Table 4.5 gives the percentage of all children (i.e., not the percentage of users only) who choose a specific medium when they want excitement. With the exception of Spanish children, who most frequently choose audio media when they want excitement, children from all countries most frequently regard television and video as the media that are most apt to serve this purpose. Averaged over all countries, 45% of children think that television and video are best capable of providing excitement. In addition to Spanish children, Swiss children are also less likely to find television useful when they want excitement. Swiss children are more likely to turn to all of the print media, which may explain why they spend relatively more time on these media.

When children choose a medium for excitement, electronic games rank second, immediately followed by audio media and books. Each of these three media is chosen on average by about 10% of the children. However, the differences between countries are considerable. A striking outlier is the United Kingdom, where relatively many children (28%) choose electronic games for excitement and relatively few children (4%) choose books for the same purpose. Overall, only a tiny percentage (6%) chooses to spend time with the PC (i.e., PC not for games and the Internet) when they are looking for excitement. However, as far as Internet is concerned, this situation may be changing as the Internet diffuses more widely. Comics, magazines, and newspapers also are seldom seen as media that are fit to fulfill children's need for excitement.

Table 4.6 shows how the percentage of children who choose a medium for excitement varies with children's gender, age, and SES. Chi-square tests (Fisher's exact test) were used to establish the significance of differences on these three background variables ($p < .0001$). In comparison with boys, girls who want excitement are more likely to choose audio media, books, and magazines, three media on which girls usually spend more time than boys do. Compared with girls, boys are far more likely to choose electronic games for excitement, a difference that is associated with a tendency for boys to spend more time on this medium than do girls. Age-related differences in the choice of media for excitement parallel the amount of time different age groups spend on media. The three media to which younger children devote relatively more time (electronic games, comics, and books) are more frequently chosen for excitement

TABLE 4.5
Percentage of Respondents Using Media for "Excitement" by Country

				Country					
Medium	BE	CH	ES	FI	GB	IL	NL	SE	Average
Television & video	40	29	26	58	45	37	55	66	45
Electronic games	14	18	25	14	28	15	11	9	17
Audio media	15	12	31	4	13	29	3	6	14
Books	16	17	7	17	4	10	22	11	13
PC & Internet	6	12	6	4	4	6	4	6	6
Comics	5	7	3	3	1	1	3	1	3
Magazines	2	3	1	0	4	2	1	0	2
Newspapers	0	2	1	1	1	0	1	1	1

TABLE 4.6

Percentage of Respondents Using Media for "Excitement" by Gender, Age, and SES

Medium	Gender			Age				SES			
	Boys	Girls	C^a	9-10	12-13	15-16	C^a	Low	Med	High	C^a
Television & video	46_a	45_a	-	43_a	45_{ab}	50_b	38	47_a	42_a	48_a	-
Electronic games	25_b	8_a	100	19_a	18_{ab}	13_a	100	16_a	18_a	16_a	-
Books	7_a	19_b	100	17_b	13_b	8_a	88	13_a	14_a	16_a	-
Audio media	9_a	16_b	88	11_a	11_a	15_a	-	13_a	11_a	9_a	-
PC & Internet	7_a	6_a	-	4_a	7_b	9_b	38	5_a	7_a	7_a	-
Comics	4_a	3_a	-	6_b	3_a	2_a	88	4_a	5_a	3_a	-
Magazines	1_a	3_b	88	1_a	2_a	2_a	-	2_a	3_a	2_a	-
Newspapers	1_a	1_a	-	0_a	1_a	1_a	-	1_a	1_a	0_a	-

Note. Means in the same row having no letter in common in their subscripts differ significantly at $p < .0001$ (Fisher's exact Chi-square test). C^a is the percentage of countries for which the gender-, age-, or SES-related difference in question is similar to that found for all countries combined.

by the youngest age group than by the oldest children. The older age groups, on the other hand, more frequently choose the PC (not for games) and the Internet as a source of excitement than does the youngest age group.

The choice of media for excitement is unrelated to children's socioeconomic status. Hence, children from higher SES homes entertain views about the capability of media to generate excitement that are similar to those held by children from lower SES homes.

Avoidance of Boredom.   Television and video are not only most frequently used for excitement but also to help children to stop being bored (see Table 4.7). In each of the eight countries, television (including video) is most frequently chosen when children want to avoid boredom; on average, 40% of children choose television for this purpose. The next three media that are most frequently chosen to avoid boredom (electronic games, audio media, and books) also appear, though in a different order, in the Top Four list of media chosen for excitement. Electronic games and audio media, which are both chosen by about 20% of the children, are more frequently used to avoid boredom than books, which are chosen by about 10% of the children. Only tiny percentages of children choose other media to avoid boredom.

As shown in Table 4.8, there are three media that girls more frequently choose to avoid boredom than boys do, namely, television (including video), audio media, and books. On the other hand, more boys than girls choose electronic games to drive away boredom.

In most countries, the choice of media to avoid boredom is independent of children's age. Compared with the youngest age group, the oldest age group more often chooses television and video to stop being bored. Conversely, relative to the oldest age group, the youngest age group more frequently chooses books and comics to drive out boredom. The percentage of children choosing media to avoid boredom does not depend on children's socioeconomic status.

Learning.   When children want to learn about things, they most frequently choose print media (except for comics), the PC, and the Internet (see Table 4.9). In five of the eight countries, books are chosen most frequently as a medium for learning; averaged across all countries, 30% of the children choose books for this purpose. Interestingly, children in the Nordic countries (FI and SE) are the least likely to use books for learning, despite the fact that Finland in particular is the country where the amount of time spent on book reading is highest. Instead of books, high numbers of Finnish children turn to television for learning, which may be due to the very active and responsible public service tradition in this country. In Sweden, high numbers of children look to PCs and the Internet for learning, a finding that is consistent with the fact that these media are most frequently used in Sweden.

TABLE 4.7
Percentage of Respondents Using Media "To Stop Being Bored" by Country

	Country								
Medium	*BE*	*CH*	*ES*	*FI*	*GB*	*IL*	*NL*	*SE*	*Average*
Television & video	48	23	40	32	35	56	40	39	40
Electronic games	11	15	17	22	26	19	19	22	19
Audio media	20	20	20	22	19	8	20	18	18
Books	10	3	7	12	8	8	10	8	9
Comics	6	9	7	7	1	2	5	5	5
PC & Internet	3	10	5	2	4	3	2	5	4
Magazines	2	3	2	1	8	2	3	2	3
Newspapers	1	5	2	2	1	2	0	1	2

TABLE 4.8
Percentage of Respondents Using Media "To Stop Being Bored" by Gender, Age, and SES

Medium	Gender			Age				SES			
	Boys	Girls	C^a	9-10	12-13	15-16	C^a	Low	Med	High	C^a
Television & video	35_a	41_b	88	35_a	36_{ab}	42_b	75	35_a	36_a	41_a	-
Audio media	16_a	22_b	88	19_a	19_a	19_a	-	21_a	19_a	17_a	-
Electronic games	27_b	12_a	100	20_a	10_a	18_a	-	21_a	19_a	18_a	-
Books	6_a	12_b	100	12_b	8_{ab}	6_a	88	10_a	8_a	10_a	-
Comics	7_a	5_a	-	8_b	5_{ab}	3_a	100	4_a	6_a	7_a	-
PC & Internet	6_a	4_a	-	3_a	6_a	6_a	-	4_a	6_a	4_a	-
Magazines	3_a	4_a	-	2_a	3_a	4_a	-	5_a	3_a	2_a	-
Newspapers	2_a	2_a	-	2_a	3_a	2_a	-	1_a	3_a	2_a	-

Note. Means in the same row having no letter in common in their subscripts differ significantly at $p < .0001$ (Fisher's exact Chi-square test); C^a is the percentage of countries for which the gender-, age-, or SES-related difference in question is similar to that found for all countries combined.

TABLE 4.9
Percentage of Respondents Using Media for "Learning" by Country

| | Country | | | | | | | | |
Medium	BE	CH	ES	FI	GB	IL	NL	SE	Average
Books	29	30	48	21	36	29	29	14	30
PC & Internet	11	26	18	12	33	26	10	32	21
Television & video	30	7	10	33	12	15	13	17	17
Newspapers	9	13	7	19	14	19	28	17	16
Magazines	12	9	5	8	4	7	16	10	9
Audio media	7	8	6	4	1	4	4	4	5
Electronic games	2	4	4	2	1	1	0	4	2
Comics	1	3	2	2	0	0	0	2	1

The PC (not for games) and Internet rank second: About one fifth of all children see the PC and Internet as a suitable learning medium. About 15% of the children choose television and video as media for learning, and a similar percentage chooses newspapers. Only tiny percentages of children see audio media, electronic games, and comics as suitable media for learning.

In comparison with boys, girls are more likely to choose books for learning (see Table 4.10). Conversely, relative to girls, boys are more likely to choose television and video as media from which they can learn things. Compared with the two older age groups, children in the youngest age group (aged 9 to 10) more frequently choose books and electronic games as learning media. Relative to the youngest age group, the two older age groups (aged 12 to 13 and 15 to 16), on the other hand, tend to choose more frequently the PC (not for games), newspapers, and magazines as media from which one can learn things.

DISCUSSION

Time Expenditure

The proliferation of interactive media among European children has had substantial consequences for both their media time expenditure and their perception of media functionality. In terms of time expenditure, electronic games have conquered the third position behind television and audio media. The various print media take up less leisure time than electronic games. (Note that the inclusion of school reading might considerably boost the time spent on reading books overall). The third place of electronic games in leisure time expenditure was found across all age and SES groups. However, this finding mainly holds for boys only.

Among girls, electronic games rank fourth, because they spend twice as much time reading books as playing electronic games. The finding that girls are less attracted to electronic games might be attributed to the contents of most electronic games and the perception that the computer in all its disguises is a boy's thing (Beentjes, d'Haenens, van der Voort, & Koolstra, 1999; Sutton, 1991). This perception might in turn explain why girls spend less time than do boys on the PC for other purposes than games (see chapter 12).

Perceived Media Functionality

With respect to the perception of media functionality, both electronic games and other types of PC use have gained an important position. Electronic games rank second, behind television and video, when children indicate which medium they would choose for excitement or to stop being bored.

TABLE 4.10

Percentage of Respondents Using Media for "Learning" by Gender, Age, and SES

	Gender			Age				SES			
Medium	Boys	Girls	C^a	9-10	12-13	15-16	C^a	Low	Med	High	C^a
Books	24_a	33_b	75	37_c	28_b	22_a	88	32_a	26_a	28_a	–
PC & Internet	25_a	21_a	–	18_a	24_b	26_b	50	20_a	23_a	21_a	–
Television & video	18_b	13_a	88	17_a	14_a	16_a	–	15_a	15_a	19_a	–
Newspapers	15_a	16_a	–	9_a	17_b	20_b	100	18_a	17_a	15_a	–
Magazines	9_a	9_a	–	6_a	9_{ab}	10_b	–	8_a	10_a	9_a	–
Audio media	5_a	5_a	–	6_a	5_a	4_a	63	4_a	6_a	4_a	–
Electronic games	3_a	2_a	–	5_b	1_a	2_a	–	2_a	2_a	2_a	–
Comics	2_a	1_a	–	2_a	1_a	1_a	–	1_a	2_a	1_a	–

Note. Means in the same row having no letter in common in their subscripts differ significantly at $p < .0001$ (Fisher's exact Chi-square test) C^a is the percentage of countries for which the gender-, age-, or SES-related difference in question is similar to that found for all countries combined.

Closer inspection again shows a considerable gender difference in the perceived functionality of electronic games. Girls put electronic games fourth behind television, audio media, and books for excitement, and in joint third place with books behind television and audio media to fight boredom.

For all children and young people, the PC (including the Internet) is associated with learning about things. It comes second behind books but before television and newspapers. Interestingly, in the association of the PC with learning we find only slight gender differences. It seems that girls and boys both see the PC's functionality in relation to learning, despite the large gender difference in time expenditure.

Comparison With Previous Findings

Our findings deviate in some respects from previous findings. Unchanged is that television viewing is by far the most time-consuming media activity, followed by listening to audio media. In contrast with previous research, however, television viewing is not surpassed or equaled by listening to audio media during adolescence. Another deviation from previous studies is that we do not find a significant gender difference in television use, whereas in previous studies boys were found to spend more time watching television. Three reasons may explain these deviations from earlier research. First, today's adolescents have more opportunity for watching, in private if they want, because more adolescents than ever have a television in their own room (see chapter 3). Second, an increasing number of commercial television channels have successfully tried to please adolescent taste with spectacular, erotic, and sentimental programs, as this age group has considerable sums of money to spend. Finally, the introduction of music channels has changed the distinction between television viewing and music listening.

Most age trends in the present study conform to those found in earlier studies: Specifically, television viewing increases during childhood and remains at a steady level during adolescence, and listening to audio media increases through childhood and adolescence. Unlike in previous studies, however, reading books does not increase during childhood and in fact appears to decrease during adolescence, whereas in former research, book reading was found to increase during childhood and to remain at the same level during adolescence. Research conducted 4 decades ago even suggested that adolescents spent more time reading than did younger children (e.g., Himmelweit, Oppenheim, & Vince, 1958).

Decline in Reading Time.   The finding that adolescents spend less time than children reading books may be another indication that reading is on the retreat. In the Netherlands there are clear indications that young people are reading less and less (Knulst & Kraaykamp, 1996). Diary-based time-use studies showed that the percentage of leisure time Dutch adolescents (12- to 17-year-olds) spent reading books and other types of reading material has dramatically reduced between 1955 and 1990. In 1955, when only 1% or 2% of the Dutch households had a television set in the home, girls spent 20% of their free time reading, a figure that was reduced to less than 10% in 1990. For boys, the percentage of time spent leisure reading dropped from 22% (1955) to 6% (1990)! In the British case, Himmelweit et al. (1958) found that children whose parents did not own a television set read for an average of 17 minutes per day, a figure that is somewhat lower than the diary estimate of reading time (20 minutes per day) that the British team involved in the present study found for today's children in the United Kingdom (Livingstone & Bovill, 1999). On closer inspection, however, it would be erroneous to conclude that in the United Kingdom reading figures did not decline (or even increased) and have always been low. As Himmelweit et al. (1958, p. 322) pointed out, their diary estimate was an underestimate, partly because the diaries were kept in summer, when reading was likely to be less, and partly because it also excluded reading earlier in the day and after going to bed. According to Himmelweit and colleagues, it is quite possible that the true reading time was twice as high as the figure they found. Hence, there is a possibility that reading time has also declined in the United Kingdom.

Displacement Effects of Interactive Media.   As discussed previously, there are indications that the coming and rise of television has contributed to the decline in children's reading time, both in the Dutch case (Knulst, 1991; van der Voort, 1991; Koolstra & van der Voort, 1996) and in the British case (Belson, 1961; Himmelweit et al., 1958). Although the present cross-sectional study cannot provide causal evidence about possible displacement effects of interactive media on reading, there are some findings that, at the least, add fuel to the suspicion that the recent increase in the use of interactive media may have a negative effect on children's reading. In particular, there is a possibility that electronic games, which in terms of time expenditure have conquered a third place behind television and audio media, have had the effect of reducing the time children spend with reading. Because boys spend more than three times as much time on electronic games as girls do, and because boys are also far more likely to choose electronic games for excitement, boys in particular may be suspected of being liable to a possible displacement effect of electronic games on reading. Even if the increased use of electronic games has not affected children's reading time, it is certain that the time spent on audiovisual media overall has been increased by the introduction of electronic games. Thus, again especially for boys, the increased use of electronic games has enhanced the shift from a word-oriented to an image-oriented culture that was foreseen by McLuhan (1964).

It is doubtful, however, whether the more serious uses of computers (i.e., not for games) and the Internet have strengthened the leisure-time shift from a word-oriented to a visual culture. Even if the time spent on these media is directly at the expense of the time previously spent with print media, it cannot be said that reading is reduced, because both the Internet and other serious uses of the PC require a considerable amount of reading. In fact, if serious uses of PCs strongly increase in the years to come, one could even see PCs and the Internet as the occasion for a revival of word-oriented media, albeit on the screen rather than the printed page.

Finally, we may speculate whether interactive media will gradually take up more of children and young people's time and will be more strongly associated with various media functions. Brown (1976) reasoned that the introduction of a medium into a child's life may result in a functional reorientation in media use if the following conditions are met: The medium presents a wide range of suitable content; it provides the child with control over the selection of content; and it does not demand specialized knowledge or skills to be used. It goes without saying that computers and the Internet potentially may be used for a wide array of content, and they also give the child a strong control over the selection of content. Although hitherto, computers have involved some specialized skills, many children have now acquired these skills. Hence, computers and the Internet seem to meet all of the three demands posited by Brown (1976). It therefore may be expected that in the years to come, the diffusion of these media will speed up and so occupy more of children's time. In addition, it may be expected that interactive media will converge with other media, which could make the present distinction among media obsolete.

REFERENCES

Beentjes, J. W. J., d'Haenens, L., van der Voort, T. H. A., & Koolstra, C. M. (1999). Dutch and Flemish children and adolescents as users of interactive media. *Communications, 24*, 145–166.

Beentjes, J. W. J., Koolstra, C. M., Marseille, N., & van der Voort, T. H. A. (1997). *Waar blijft de tijd? De tijdsbesteding van kinderen en jongeren van 3 tot 17 jaar* [Where's the time gone? Time expenditure of children and young people aged 3–17]. Leiden, the Netherlands: Leiden University.

Beentjes, J. W. J., & van der Voort, T. H. A. (1989). TV and young people's reading behavior: A review of research. *European Journal of Communication, 4*, 51–77.

Belson, W. A. (1961). The effects of television on the reading and buying of newspapers and magazines. *Public Opinion Quarterly, 25*, 366–381.

Bonfadelli, H. (1986). Uses and functions of mass media for Swiss youth: An empirical study. *Gazette, 37*, 7–18.

Brown, J. R. (1976). Children's uses of television. In R. Brown (Ed.), *Children and television* (pp. 116–136). London: Collier MacMillan.

Comstock, G., & Paik, H. (1991). *Television and the American child.* San Diego, CA: Academic Press.

Fridberg, L., Drotner, K., Schulz-Joergerson, P., Nielsen, O., & Soerensen, A. S. (1997). *Mønstre i mangfoldigheden: De 15-18-åriges mediebrug i Danmark* [Unity in diversity: Media uses of 15- to 18-year-old Danes]. Copenhagen: Borgen.

Greenberg, B. S., & Li, H. (1994). *Young people and their orientation to the mass media: An international study.* East Lansing, MI: Michigan State University.

Himmelweit, H. T., Oppenheim, A. N., & Vince, P. (1958). *Television and the child.* London: Oxford University Press.

Klingler, W., & Groebel, J. (1994). *Kinder und Medien 1990* [Children and media 1990]. Baden-Baden: Nomos Verlagsgesellschaft.

Knulst, W. (1991). Is television substituting reading? Changes in media usage 1975–1985. *Poetics, 20,* 53–72.

Knulst, W., & Kraaykamp, G. (1996). *Leesgewoonten: Een halve eeuw onderzoek naar het lezen en zijn belagers* [Reading habits: Half a century of research on reading and its rivals]. The Hague, the Netherlands: Sociaal en Cultureel Planbureau.

Koolstra, C. M., & van der Voort, T. H. A. (1996). Longitudinal effects of television on children's leisure-time reading: A test of three explanatory models. *Human Communication Research, 23,* 4–35.

Livingstone, S., & Bovill, M. (1999). *Young people, new media.* London: London School of Economics and Political Science.

McLuhan, M. (1964). *Understanding media.* New York: Signet.

McQuail, D. (1992). *Media performance: Mass communication and the public interest.* London: Sage.

Muijs, R. D. (1997). *Self, school and media: A longitudinal study of media use, self-concept, school achievement and peer relations among primary school children.* Leuven, Belgium: Catholic University of Leuven.

Roe, K. (1998). Boys will be boys and girls will be girls: Changes in children's media use. *Communications, 23,* 5–25.

Rosengren, K. E., & Windahl, S. (1989). *Media matter: Television use in childhood and adolescence.* Norwood, NJ: Ablex.

Schramm, W., Lyle, J., & Parker, E. B. (1961). *Television in the lives of our children.* Stanford, CA: Stanford University Press.

Sutton, R. E. (1991). Equity and computers in the schools: A decade of research. *Review of Educational Research, 61,* 457–503.

van der Voort, T. H. A. (1991). Television and the decline of reading. *Poetics, 20,* 73–89.

van Lil, J. (1989). Media use by children and young people: A time-budget study. *European Broadcasting Union Review, 40,* 23–28.

von Feilitzen, C. (1974). The functions served by the media. In R. Brown (Ed.), *Children and television* (pp. 90–115). London: Collier MacMillan.

5

Media Use Styles Among the Young

Ulla Johnsson-Smaragdi

The introduction of a new medium has often caused fears that it will soon displace previous media or other leisure activities, especially in the lives of children. Himmelweit, Oppenheim, and Vince (1958) assumed that "children exercise choice in how much they view, and in the way they make time for viewing. They may drop a few activities completely, reduce them all proportionately, or reduce some more than others" (p. 3). Maletzke (1959) discussed similar questions in other studies from the same period. The issue of displacement has reappeared regularly over the years in discussions of the relation between different media activities, most notably between book reading and television viewing, but also regarding the relation between media and nonmedia activities (Broddason, 1996; Hincks & Balding, 1988; Johnsson-Smaragdi, 1983, 1986, 1994). In later years it appears again in connection with the fear that the increasing importance of moving images will eventually lead to higher levels of illiteracy or to a decline in overall book reading (McLuhan, 1964; Saxer, Langenbucher, & Fritz, 1989). Today Coffey and Stipp (1997), who examined in detail whether Internet users abandon the television set and prefer to surf the Internet, discussed it again.

The ideas underlying displacement are rather unclear, however (Mutz, Roberts, & van Vuuren, 1993). The commonly used hypothesis of a symmetrical, zero-sum relationship between time for one medium and time for other occupations is oversimplistic, and different empirical results are produced depending on the type of measure and the type of data that are compared.

The discussion of one medium displacing another is becoming increasingly difficult to grasp because a transformation is occurring in which the functions of old media are taken over by the functions of new media (see chapter 4). Rather, these developments are to be understood in terms of the process of differentiation and specialization that always happens when new things come into existence (Adoni, 1985; Johnsson-Smaragdi, 1986; van der Loo & van der Reijen, 1992). The discussion of displacement is further complicated by the fact that it relates to at least two different levels of reality—to the societal and cultural level and to the individual level—and a distinction is not always made between these two levels. Adoni (1985) discussed the interchangeability and coexistence of media and developed a model to describe their relation. The model, which can be applied at both the macro and the micro levels, discusses the degree to which media are interchangeable and one medium may take over the functions of another. If a medium is functionally equivalent (or superior) to another in certain respects or in certain situations, it may replace a former medium in these functions or situations.

On the societal macro level, no established older medium has so far been displaced or disappeared completely from the media scene. Some media, like radio and magazines, are gradually forced toward greater specialization in order to try to find their specific niche and thus keep at least part of their audience or to find new segments of potential users (Johnsson-Smaragdi, 1986; Smith, 1980). This does not contradict the fact that on the individual micro level, some users of new media may more or less replace the former media they have used, whereas other users add new media to their menu without ceasing to use older ones. With more media to choose among, with more diversified content, and with greater control of which media, what content, and of where and when to use them, individual preferences and lifestyles are becoming more important. There is now greater individual freedom and more opportunity to adopt a specific style of media use to suit one's preferences and circumstances (Johnsson-Smaragdi, 1994).

The main focus in this chapter is on individual styles of media use, already described in relation to television by Hasebrink (1997) and Krotz and Hasebrink (1998). These patterns are based on the assumption that it is the individual who constructs sense and meaning in the organization of his or her life, confined within the context of lifestyles and culture. On the other hand, an individual is not unique in his or her construction of reality. It is possible to identify particular types of media users, which may be compared both within and between cultures.

In the visions and debates concerning the future media society, old print and new digital media are often placed in opposition to one another, as if it were a matter of either/or and not a choice of both. An analysis of how different types of media are interwoven in actual use gives an indication of whether media use tends to be diversified or restrictive and for which groups of young people.

SPENDING TIME WITH MEDIA

As we saw in previous chapters, the new media are already becoming part of the everyday media environment among European children and adolescents. So far, the television set, the videocassette recorder (VCR), and audio media are still the most pervasive media for children and youth, and television continues to hold a dominant position in their media activities. Nevertheless, young people tend now to spend as much or more time on PCs, Internet, and electronic games as with print media (see chapter 4).

The question of using or not using a medium is, however, not entirely a matter of easy physical access, for instance, having it available at home. Physical accessibility somewhere is certainly a prerequisite for the use of a medium, but it is in no way sufficient. It is as much a matter of social, cultural, and psychological accessibility or attractiveness (Chaney, 1972; Johnsson-Smaragdi, 1983). These factors may be related to the degree of social acceptance of a medium in a specific culture, to the social context in which it is used, and to individual requirements, habits, and attitudes. It is important that government and policymakers have this in mind, if they are to develop appropriate policies for new media. In order to reduce inequality and perceived information gaps between social groups and individuals, it is not sufficient to reduce differences in access to a medium. It may be equally or more important to enhance the social and psychological attractiveness of a medium in order for it to be accepted and used.

As we saw in previous chapters, some among the young choose not to spend time with some media in leisure time, even when they do have physical access at home (see chapter 3). Either social and psychological barriers work against the medium and/or other available media are perceived as more attractive in that their functions are better in fulfilling the requirements of the young. Psychological barriers are likely to underlie those cases in which, even when accessible, a medium is excluded totally from the individual media menu. Using that medium seems not to be an option for these young people. In other words, we should recognize that freedom of choice is not only the freedom to do something, it is also freedom not to do it. Thus, the nonusers of a medium, or of specific contents, are interesting in that they provide evidence of the exercise of individual choice. In the "expectancy-value theory" (Palmgreen & Rayburn, 1985), the role of personal motivation for using a medium is acknowledged. Here, personal attitudes toward a medium are shaped both by past experiences and expected rewards and by personal preferences, leading to "the proposition that media use is accounted for by a combination of perception of benefits offered by the medium and the differential value attached to these benefits" (McQuail, 1994, p. 305).

Physical, social, and psychological barriers interact in complex ways in creating nonusers of different media. In the early phases of the diffusion of a new medium, these barriers may be high. To gain access to a medium by bringing it into the home, social (economic, cultural) and psychological hindrances have to be overcome. Early adopters of a medium probably have lower barriers than late adopters (Rogers, 1995), not least psychological ones.

Table 5.1 displays the proportion of young people in different countries claiming they spend *no leisure time at all* with either print, screen media, or ICT's (information and communication technologies), thus totally excluding one or several of these media from their menu. There are common features as well as marked differences in the proportion of nonusers between the countries. Most notably, there are very few not using television in any of the countries, the range only being between 0% to 5% nonusers. The video has the second lowest range, between 3% and 22% nonusers—the highest percentage in the United Kingdom and the lowest in Finland. This shows how commonly used these two media are, especially television, irrespective of country.

There are, though, also large differences between countries indicating that cultural and social factors are influencing the young in their media options and choices. The highest range in the proportion of nonusers is seen in the use of comics and newspapers, the range for comics being 4% to 76% and for newspapers 8% to 67%. In the United Kingdom, three quarters do not read comics and two thirds do not read a newspaper; in Finland and Sweden the percentages for newspapers is 8% to 9%. Books are used by an overwhelming majority (> 90%) of the young in Finland, Switzerland, and the Netherlands, whereas there are many young people not reading any books at all in the United Kingdom and Israel (46% and 34%). Thus a comparison between countries shows that the old print media tend to have the largest ranges in proportion of nonusers.

There are also marked differences in the proportion of nonusers of computers and the Internet. More than 90% of the young people in Finland, and about 80% in Sweden and the Netherlands, use a computer in leisure time for purposes other than playing games. At the other end of the range are the United Kingdom, Germany, Italy, and Israel, where half or more of the young people do not use computers in their leisure time. For the Internet, nonusers range between 31% and 86% of the young people. The largest proportion of Internet users is found in Sweden and Finland (69% and 68%) and least in Germany, the United Kingdom, Flanders, and Italy, where in 1997 only between 14% and 20% have used the Internet. These figures are probably changing rapidly, though, along with growing access to the Internet.

The proportion of nonusers of different media in different countries may tell us something about tendencies towards either inclusive and additive use

TABLE 5.1
Percentage of Nonusers of Different Media in Leisure Time Among Children and Adolescents (Aged 9-10, 12-13, and 15-16 Years) in Different Countries

	Print				Screen Entertainment			ICT	
	Book	Newspaper	Magazine	Comics	TV	Video	Games	PC (not for games)	Internet
BE-vlg	20	32	13	11	0	8	38	40	81
CH	8	30	17	21	2	9	20	35	70
DE	13	37	17	37	3	11	29	52	86
ES	15	42	23	34	1	7	28	40	68
FI	6	8	16	4	1	3	4	9	32
GB	46	67	37	76	5	22	34	63	84
IL	34	29	40	67	4	21	32	49	53
IT	17	14	7	33	1	8	25	51	80
NL	9	28	7	10	1	3	11	23	76
SE	15	9	13	16	1	3	12	18	31
Average	18	29	18	30	2	9	22	37	63

Note. The percentage for the Internet indicates those who have not used it themselves either in leisure time or in school. For Italy the sample only includes ages 12-13 and 15-16 years.

or exclusive and specialized use. In some countries, most notably in Finland, but also in Sweden and the Netherlands, the proportion of nonusers across all media is relatively low, whereas in the United Kingdom and Israel it is relatively high for most media. A low proportion of nonusers means that most of the young people use most of the media at least sometimes; a high proportion of nonusers means that large groups tend to avoid certain media altogether, suggesting more specialized uses of media in the United Kingdom and Israel, compared with the case in the Nordic countries and the Netherlands.

Of course, some nonusers do not have access to a medium at home, whereas others, although they have physical access, may be influenced by social and psychological factors not to include it in their personal media menu. Compared with access to print media, access to expensive ICTs at home is more likely to be influenced by the economic and cultural capital of the family and associated priorities. Also, it is clear that physical access to a medium, as well as its social and psychological attractiveness, influence use (see Table 5.2). For the five media (books, PCs, the Internet, video, and games consoles) included in Table 5.2, it makes a real difference if the medium is available at home, the proportion of nonusers being predictably greater if there is no home access. It is also evident, however, that though access at home matters, it is not sufficient in explaining use. Many young people do not use a medium even if it is present at home: They do not read books, do not use the PC or connect to the Internet, do not watch videos or play computer games even if the necessary equipment is available to them. This is a clear indication that either these media lack attractiveness, or they are in some way barred from using them. This is especially striking for computers, where in several countries, between 30% and 40% of those with home access do not use it, and for the Internet, where in Germany, the United Kingdom, and Flanders, half or more of those with home access still never use it. Apparently there are other barriers to overcome. There may be social (they are not allowed by their parents) or economic (too expensive to be connected) reasons for not using ICTs at home. There may also be more personal reasons—they have not yet become familiar with the medium, they do not see or value its benefits, they find other media are better in fulfilling their requirements, or they have used the medium earlier and past experiences did not fulfill their expectations.

Another indication that easy physical accessibility does not seem to be a necessary factor for using a medium is the fact that many young people use a medium even if it is not available at home. They still read books in their leisure time (borrowing them from school, from the library, or from friends), they watch the video and play games (probably in the homes of their friends), and they use the PC and the Internet (in libraries, in friends' homes, or in the parents' work place). In short, young people are finding means of overcoming the barrier of not having access at home when the social obstacles are low and the media are socially or psychologically attractive in their view. The practi-

TABLE 5.2

Percentage of Nonusers of Media Among Children and Adolescents (Aged 9-10, 12-13, and 15-16 Years) if (a) Home Access (b) No Home Access

	Book		PC		Internet		Video		Games	
	Home Access	No Home Access	Home Access	No Home Access	Home Access	No Home Access	Home Access	No Home Access	Home Access	No Home Access
BE-vlg	19	55	38	51	50	90	(2)	43	28	47
CH	6	31	16	43	45	80	4	24	12	26
DE	12	(32)	34	55	65	88	5	53	10	38
ES	14	(17)	28	42	16	79	(2)	19	14	45
FI	6	(8)	(3)	12	18	37	(1)	25	(2)	6
GB	42	63	40	74	54	86	20	37	20	59
IL	32	45	43	50	32	67	15	46	23	38
IT	15	43	22	64	24	87	4	41	11	36
NL	9	(50)	10	100	51	84	(1)	23	5	16
SE	14	33	12	19	10	42	1	21	7	22
Average	17	45	27	51	37	74	8	33	14	33

Note. % within brackets indicate that it is based on actual numbers from 10 or lower. These percentages are not included in the calculations of the total percentage.

119

Media access in home

		Yes	No
	Yes	1 Available and Desirable	3 Not available/ Desirable
Media Use	**No**	2 Available/ Not desirable	4 Not available and Not desirable

FIG. 5.1.   Typology: media access in home and media use.

cal obstacles may also vary between the countries. Sweden and Finland seem often to provide superior public access for children who do not have equipment at home. Different options created by combining the dimensions of access to, and use of, media may be visualized in a typology as in Fig. 5.1.

Two of the categories in the typology are of special interest: the second in which media are available at home, but where they are not desirable, and the third, in which media are not available at home but where they are desirable. For the second category, the medium seems to not be sufficiently socially or psychologically attractive; for the third, it is so attractive as to be used despite the obstacle that lack of home access may create. In Fig. 5.2 the proportion of users of five different media have been related to the categories of the typology.

Clearly, availability and use of media interact in different ways for different media. VCRs are almost always available and very desirable; books are very available and often desirable; electronic games are less available, but desirable; PCs are often not available but desirable; and the Internet is least available but desirable. Figure 5.2 suggests that if there is an interest in a medium, this can override the difficulty of not having easy home access. This is clearly evident for PCs and for games machines, which are used by many without home access. Some of the attractiveness of these media may stem precisely from their social use, in company with peers at one's own or another's house (see chapter 9). Conversely, if there is no interest in a medium, it is not used despite access: 15% of the young do not read books and 8% do not use the PC or connect to the Internet (6%) despite these media being available at home. They are selecting among available media, choosing the ones they perceive to be socially and psychologically attractive, and discarding those not perceived to be sufficiently desirable.

Access in home

Yes   *No*

Media use	

<table>
<tr><td colspan="2">1</td><td colspan="2">3</td></tr>
<tr><td>VCR:</td><td>81 %</td><td>PC:</td><td>36 %</td></tr>
<tr><td>Books:</td><td>77 %</td><td>Games:</td><td>34 %</td></tr>
<tr><td>Games:</td><td>45 %</td><td>Internet:</td><td>21 %</td></tr>
<tr><td>PC:</td><td>27 %</td><td>VCR:</td><td>10 %</td></tr>
<tr><td>Internet:</td><td>13 %</td><td>Books:</td><td>5 %</td></tr>
<tr><td colspan="2">2</td><td colspan="2">4</td></tr>
<tr><td>Books:</td><td>15 %</td><td>Internet:</td><td>60 %</td></tr>
<tr><td>PC:</td><td>8 %</td><td>PC:</td><td>29 %</td></tr>
<tr><td>Internet:</td><td>6 %</td><td>Games:</td><td>16 %</td></tr>
<tr><td>Games:</td><td>6 %</td><td>VCR:</td><td>4 %</td></tr>
<tr><td>VCR:</td><td>4 %</td><td>Books:</td><td>3 %</td></tr>
</table>

Yes corresponds to the upper row (cells 1 and 3); *No* corresponds to the lower row (cells 2 and 4).

FIG. 5.2. Percentage of children and adolescents using each of five media by access in home.

MEDIA USE STYLES ACROSS EUROPE

Identifying User Styles

If we consider both the different rates of diffusion of new media across Europe and their consequent differences in availability, together with differences in perceived attractiveness, a central question is how young people in different countries actually combine the media in their daily lives. Are there tendencies toward accumulation and additive use or toward replacement and specialization? When people add new media to their previous menu, they may either increase the total time spent with media or decrease time spent with one or several of the media used formerly, thus causing their media use style to become more inclusive. Or they may replace older media completely, or at least reduce their time with them considerably, causing their media use style to become more specialized and exclusive.

In order to trace changes over time, question of displacement should properly be addressed with longitudinal data. Studies of changes over time have, for instance, been central to the Swedish research project, The Media Panel Program (Johnsson-Smaragdi, 1992; Johnsson-Smaragdi & Jönsson, 2000; Rosengren, 1994; Rosengren & Windahl, 1989). With the present com-

parative data, we cannot directly investigate changes over time. Nonetheless, it is possible to compare proportion of users and amount of time spent
on various media, which indirectly may give indications of tendencies
towards displacement (see chapter 4).

The combination of different media into distinct media use styles was investigated in the comparative project by a series of cluster analyses, based on the
time-use variables for eight media used during leisure time across the whole
sample (i.e., users and nonusers). The media included in these analyses were
print[1] (books, newspapers, magazines, and comics), screen media (television,
video, and electronic games), and ICT (computers).[2] Music listening was not
included because not all countries asked sufficient questions to construct a
time index. Besides, music is often listen to in the background, while young
people are occupied with other activities, even media-related ones.

The cluster analyses[3] were carried out for boys and girls separately within the three age groups for the 10 different countries (i.e., 60 analyses in all).
On the basis of these analyses, it proved possible to assign all children to four
broad media use styles, of which two encompass further subgroupings.[4]
Table 5.3 shows, for each country, the proportion of children and adolescents
in the eight specific media use styles, which may be subsumed under four
broader headings. It should be emphasized that the percentage of adherents
to each user style in the 10 countries is better seen as an approximate estimate of the relative size of each user style and not as exact percentages, as
there is always an element of arbitrariness in cluster analysis.

The distinctive features of the media use styles are described in brief
next. The time-use profile for the eight user styles is described in more detail
in the following section.

Low Media Users.   Children and adolescents in this group do not spend
much time on media. They are primarily distinguished by their relatively low
consumption of television, though they watch much more television than
anything else. On the whole they tend to have a low and diversified pattern
of media use.

---

[1]Italy and Spain did not ask questions about time use for print. The cluster analyses for them
encompass thus only four media.

[2]The Internet was not included in the analyses forming the clusters because few actually use
the Internet, but it is included in the description of the clusters.

[3]The cluster analyses performed were the Quick cluster method with running means. In the
time indexes used, extreme values were first recoded.

[4]The result of a cluster analysis is sensitive both to the type of analysis performed and to
the status of the input variables used. In the analyses conducted here, both the original time
index and standardized versions of the input variables (with z-scores and with the original time
index recoded into groups from nonusers to high users) were tried out. It is also a matter of
judgment which number of clusters is deemed to give the best and most interpretable solution.
Solutions with different numbers of clusters turned out to be unexpectedly stable, though. The
big clusters largely remained; the small clusters more easily split up into other small ones.

TABLE 5.3
Media Use Styles Among Children and Adolescents (Aged 9-10, 12-13, and 15-16 Years) in 10 Countries (Percentages)

						Country					
Media Use Styles	*BE-vlg*	*CH*	*DE*	*ES*	*FI*	*GB*	*IL*	*IT*	*NL*	*SE*	*All*
Low use	47	54	41	54	20	27	38	51	49	37	44
Traditional	20	21	27	6	25	29	14	13	22	22	20
Specialists											
Television	22	15	20	31	28	26	32	26	20	18	23
Books	2	4	3	N/A	13	2	3	N/A	4	2	3
PC	1	-	-	2	-	2	-	2	2	2	1
PC & games	8	1	2	-	8	-	-	1	1	4	2
Screen fans											
TV & video	-	3	1	2	6	7	5	2	-	9	4
TV & games	-	2	5	4	-	7	8	4	3	6	4

Note. In Italy the data relate only to 12-13 and 15-16 year olds. Answers from adolescents both with and without home access to a medium are included in the analysis.

123

Traditional Media Users. In this group the media mix is fairly traditional and diversified. The *traditionalists* are low on new media and electronic
games and about average on other media. They resemble both the *low users*
and the *television specialists* in most of their media tastes, except for television. They spend more time on television, and slightly more on video, than
the *low users*, and they are distinctly lower on television, and slightly lower
on video than *television specialists*.

Specialists. This group encompasses four distinct subgroups, in each of
which one kind of medium tends to be used for considerably longer than the
average amount of time, whereas other media are used for average amounts
or less. Of the specialist groups, two concentrate on traditional media and
two on new media. The latter two resemble each other in many respects, but
there are also distinct differences.

- *Television specialists:* The young people in this group focus heavily on
  television, on average spending over 3.5 hours a day on it. They are low
  on books and on the new media (electronic games, PC, and the Internet), and average on the other print media and on video. They are by
  far the largest group of specialists and are found in all countries.
- *Book specialists:* In this group, the traditional book fans are found,
  spending about 1.5 hours a day on books. They also spend more than
  average amounts of time on other print media. They are lower than
  average both on screen media and on the new media. Despite this, they
  spend more time on television than on books (110 vs. 86 minutes a day
  on average). This group is also found in all countries.
- *PC specialists:* In this group, the new media users are found, specializing
  in computers and the Internet. They are also high on electronic games
  and books, but fairly low on television. It is a very small group still, and
  is found in only 6 out of the 10 countries.
- *PC and games specialists:* This group is also strongly focused on computers, electronic games, and the Internet. These young people also spend
  above average amounts of time on magazines and comics, but less than
  average on books, television, and video. The main difference between
  these two specialist groups lies in their relation to the print media.

Screen Entertainment Fans. This group focuses on combinations of
screen media and encompasses two subgroups, both of which are high on
television, but they differ in their relation to video and games.

- *Television and video:* Young people in this group spend large amounts of
  time on both television and video, but are low on games, computers,
  and books.

- *Television and games:* On average 2.5 hours a day is spent on electronic games and about as much on television. These young people are also relatively high on video and computers, but low on books.

Three of the eight media use styles—the low users, the traditionalists, and the television specialists—together encompass more than four fifths of the sample. The *low user* group is by far the largest, being double the size of the other two. The low users are found in all countries, among both boys and girls, and in all age groups, and this style of media use becomes more common with age. Only in Finland are there no low users among boys in the youngest and oldest age groups. The *traditional* media users and the *television specialists* each consist of about one fifth of the children. The *traditionalists* are slightly more prevalent among girls and among the younger children. This group is seldom found in Italy, Spain,[5] and Israel.

There is a considerable difference in size between these three groups and the other three specialist groups and two screen fan groups. Though the group of *book specialists* is small, it exists in all countries, being particularly large in Finland where there seems to be an established reading culture. The *book specialists* are commonly found among young teenage girls (12 to 13 years), being less prevalent among the youngest and the oldest as well as among boys.

Only a few among the young people can be described as *PC specialists.* They are found in only 6 out of the 10 countries, above all in the 12 to 13 year age group and more often among boys than girls. An exception is in Sweden, where PC specialists are found among girls in the two oldest age groups and in the youngest boys' group. The *PC and games specialists* group is most common in Belgium and Finland, where 8% of the young fit within this group, whereas in the United Kingdom, Israel, and Spain, it is not found at all. Combining game playing with either watching television or using the computer is almost exclusively done by boys. Only in the Netherlands and Spain is a small group of young teenage girls to be found who adopt either of these combinations. The screen fans, with the two subgroups *television and video* fans and *television and games* fans, together comprise less than 10% of the sample. These two groups are found in 8 of the 10 countries. The *television and games* combination is found almost exclusively among boys; girls tend to prefer *television and video,* though boys are also occasionally found in this user style. Both user styles are found in all age groups, though they tend to become more common with age.

---

[5]In Italy the 9- to 10-year-old age group is not included in the sample. The cluster analysis for Italy and Spain is also based on only four media, as there is no time index for the print media.

Time Spent on Media by User Style

Patterns of access across European countries were addressed in chapter 3, and chapter 4 presents broad outlines of time use, generally finding commonalities rather than differences. At the beginning of this chapter, it is shown that access does not always determine use, but that other factors also influence media use. These analyses are now followed up with a more detailed look, not at the overall time spent, but at the patterns of time spent through combining media in different ways. The focus here, thus, is on individual lifestyle choices (cf. Hendry, Shucksmith, Love, & Glendinning, 1993; Johansson, 1994; Johansson & Miegel, 1992). The eight media use styles identified in the cluster analysis differ as to the emphasis their young adherents assign to different media and media combinations. Each user style has its own distinct media and time use profile.

The questions asked when examining the profiles of each media use style are whether these tend mainly to be inclusive or exclusive—that is, if there are signs of accumulation or replacement of media—and whether there is any sign of rearrangement of media time. The amount of time spent on various media and the way the media are combined is central here. The proportion of users to nonusers may also give some indications as to whether some media tend to be dropped. To study replacement and/or the rearrangement of time properly would, of course, require longitudinal data. It is possible here, though, to compare the relative amount of time spent with different kinds of media across the eight media style groups. The discussion moves from universals (what is alike?) to particulars (what differs?).

An overview of the eight user styles is given in Table 5.4. This is a heuristic device to make the general points insofar as it presents the aggregated profile of the user styles across countries. This general picture is then complemented with the profile within each country for each of the user styles.

Low Use Media Style. The user style with the largest proportion of young adherents is the *low users* (see Table 5.3). Their media profile is characterized by a certain lack of interest in media as a leisure time activity, the average media time overall being only 2.5 hours a day (see Table 5.4). Although the time they spend with all media is lower than average, this is particularly the case for screen media and the new ICT media. Above all, they are distinguished by their low television consumption, though they still watch more television than anything else. For every single medium, there is a larger proportion of nonusers in this group than in the total group.

Comparing the time profile of the *low users* across countries, the overall commonalities are striking: In the main, the profiles do not differ much between countries (see Table 5.5). Slightly over an hour is spent on televi-

TABLE 5.4

Average Minutes per Day Spent With Media During Leisure Time in Eight Media Use Styles Among Children and Adolescents (Aged 9-10, 12-13, and 15-16 Years)

| | User Styles | | | | | | | | |
| | Specialists | | | | | Screen Fans | | | Total Group Average |
	Low Use	Traditional	TV	Books	PC	PC & Games	TV & Video	TV & Games	
Print	*38*	*39*	*39*	*119*	*53*	*49*	*45*	*42*	*25*
Books	16	16	14	86	27	14	13	13	20
Comics	7	8	8	11	7	11	15	11	9
Magazines	8	9	10	12	11	16	10	10	9
Newspapers	7	4	7	10	8	9	7	8	7
ICT	*12*	*13*	*13*	*14*	*150*	*124*	*21*	*35*	*22*
PC	9	10	10	11	122	105	12	25	17
Internet	3	3	3	3	28	19	9	10	4,8
Screen	*100*	*175*	*265*	*146*	*195*	*227*	*295*	*357*	*189*
Games	14	16	20	14	56	90	21	149	29
Video	17	21	27	21	30	21	104	39	28
Television	69	138	218	110	109	117	170	168	132
Total media use	150	227	317	279	398	400	361	434	256

Note. The estimate of minutes used includes all those belonging to a specific cluster, both users and nonusers of single media. The total group average is the average for single media, irrespective of the cluster belonging.

127

TABLE 5.5

Average Minutes per Day Spent With Media in Leisure Time Within the Low Media User Style

Media Use Style: Low Users

	BE-vlg	CH	DE	ES	FI	GB	IL	IT	NL	SE	Average
Print	40	40	35		35	22	48		44	40	38
Books	15	19	16	N/A	12	11	21	N/A	20	17	16
Comics	11	9	5	N/A	13	1	2	N/A	9	7	7
Magazines	8	6	8	N/A	6	7	8	N/A	10	8	8
Newspapers	6	6	6	N/A	4	3	17	N/A	5	8	7
ICT	12	9	5	15	13	6	22	11	12	22	12
PC	10	7	4	12	8	5	17	9	11	13	9
Internet	1.5	1.9	0.5	3.2	5.0	0.9	4.7	1.7	0.6	8.6	2.8
Screen	107	74	96	113	106	109	111	89	95	106	100
Games	7	11	14	16	9	14	17	19	15	16	14
Video	21	12	12	19	19	20	19	17	12	23	17
Television	79	51	70	78	78	75	75	53	68	67	69
Total media use	159	123	136	-	154	137	181	-	151	168	150

sion (although in Italy and Switzerland it is less than an hour), 10 to 20 minutes on video, games and books, 5 to 15 minutes on computers, and 5 to 10 minutes on magazines, newspapers, and comics. Only a couple of minutes are generally spent on the Internet, with the exception of Finland, Israel, and Sweden where *low users* spend 5 to 10 minutes on average.

However, the time profile of the *low users* in the 10 countries does differ in some respects. The *low users* spend least time with media in Switzerland, Germany, and the United Kingdom and most time in Israel, followed by Sweden. One key difference between these countries is that the young *low users* in Israel and Sweden spend relatively more time with the computer and with the Internet, whereas in the former three countries, they spend much less time with these media. In Israel, comparatively more time is also spent on books and newspapers. Bearing in mind their overall low media use, some of the main differences in the *low user* profile between countries may be summarized in the following way:

- In Israel they spend relatively more time on ICT media, books, and newspapers, being about average on screen media;
- In Sweden they spend more time on ICT, and on video, being average on other media;
- In the United Kingdom they are lower on ICT and print media, about average on screen media;
- In Switzerland ICT and screen media are less used; time with books is above average;
- In Germany little time is spent on ICT and video, other media being average;
- In Flanders and the Netherlands they spend average time on ICT. More time is spent on comics, television, and video in Flanders and more on books in the Netherlands;
- In Finland they are high on the Internet and on comics, low on games and newspapers.

Traditional Media Use Style. The *traditional* media use style encompasses about one fifth of children and adolescents. They can best be described as "average" and fairly traditional in their media use, neither using any media in excess nor neglecting any. They spend less time than average on the more recent media, like video, games, and ICTs, but also less on books and newspapers, while being average on television, magazines and comics. Their total media use time amounts to almost 4 hours a day (see Table 5.4). Most of this time is devoted to screen media and, in particular, to television viewing, which dominates their media menu. Only about 40 minutes are spent on print media and hardly a quarter of an hour on ICTs. They are very close to the *low users* in their overall media use profile, except in their television viewing, which is double the amount of the *low users*. Except for the new media, where there are more nonusers among the *traditionalists*, the proportion of nonusers is close to the average proportion in the total sample. The *traditional* users stick to the well-known, well-established media, which they generally use rather moderately.

The profile of the *traditional* users differs between countries as to which kind of media they emphasize (see Table 5.6). In Finland, Israel, and Sweden, the *traditionalists* are higher than their counterparts in other countries on ICTs (though compared with the total group they are average). These three countries differ with respect to which other media they use: In Israel and Sweden they are higher on screen media, in Finland on the print media. In Flanders, Germany, the United Kingdom, Spain, and the Netherlands, they are low on ICTs, particularly on the Internet. The *traditionalists* in Flanders, Spain, and Italy also spend less time on games.

Most of the young *traditionalists* in Finland, Sweden, and the Netherlands use computers. Only a minority (a quarter or less) in these countries does not use this medium. In Sweden, particularly, but to a lesser degree also in Finland, they also use the Internet. The great majority in these three countries also uses the various print media and even electronic games, except in Sweden. On the whole, therefore, the media use in these countries tend to be inclusive and additive. The situation is different, particularly in the United Kingdom, but also in Israel, which both tend to have a large proportion of nonusers of most media among the *traditionalists*. Large proportions of nonusers are most evident in the use of ICTs, especially in Germany, the United Kingdom, and Italy. Thus media use in these countries shows tendencies towards exclusion and specialized use.

Specialists.   Among the four specialist user groups, the *television specialists* are by far the largest group (see Table 5.3), with a total media use time amounting to more than 5 hours a day (see Table 5.4). They spend relatively little time on print media (especially on books), on electronic games, and on ICTs (about as much as the *low* and *traditional* users) and average time on video. Their preferred medium is television, on which they spend about 3.5 hours a day, thereby being the group devoting most time to this medium (Table 5.4).

More than one third of the *television specialists* do not read any books at all (the average for the total group being one quarter). There is, though, no significant correlation between amount of television viewing and amount of time spent on book reading among the *television specialists*. For most other media except comics, the proportion of users does not differ from the total group.

Comparing the *television specialist* time profile across countries, it appears their relation to print media, to ICT, and to other screen media differs (see Table 5.7).

TABLE 5.6.
Average Minutes per Day Spent With Media in Leisure Time Within the Traditional Media User Style

Media Use Style: Traditional

		BE-vlg	CH	DE	ES	FI	GB	IL	IT	NL	SE	Average
Print		34	43	31		52	24	35		43	42	39
	Books	12	22	11	N/A	23	11	13	N/A	18	14	16
	Comics	9	8	8	N/A	15	2	5	N/A	11	8	8
	Magazines	9	12	8	N/A	6	7	7	N/A	11	11	9
	Newspapers	4	6	4	N/A	8	4	10	N/A	3	9	4
ICT		7	13	5	10	18	7	22	9	12	21	13
	PC	7	10	5	9	13	7	17	7	11	13	10
	Internet	0.3	2.8	0.2	0.5	4.8	0.4	4.8	2.1	0.8	8.1	2.7
Screen		162	176	162	183	169	180	224	135	172	187	175
	Games	6	17	14	6	13	13	42	8	22	20	16
	Video	22	16	14	27	22	25	31	14	17	26	21
	Television	134	143	134	150	134	142	151	113	133	141	138
Total media use		203	237	198	-	239	211	281	-	227	250	227

TABLE 5.7

Average Minutes per Day Spent With Media in Leisure Time Within the Television Specialist Media User Style

		BE-vlg	CH	DE	ES	FI	GB	IL	IT	NL	SE	Average
						Media Use Style: Television Specialist						
Print		45	43	30		52	22	42		42	33	39
	Books	16	15	9	N/A	21	7	18	N/A	14	11	14
	Comics	13	11	5	N/A	15	1	1	N/A	10	8	8
	Magazines	12	11	10	N/A	8	8	8	N/A	12	7	10
	Newspapers	4	6	6	N/A	8	6	15	N/A	6	7	7
ICT		8	8	8	16	18	12	11	8	13	27	13
	PC	8	8	7	14	12	11	8	7	12	16	10
	Internet	0.1	1.0	1.0	1.8	5.6	0.5	3.4	1.3	0.8	10.8	2.6
Screen		267	295	264	259	260	276	284	242	244	260	265
	Games	9	26	23	19	20	17	15	23	21	23	20
	Video	26	24	16	26	33	25	38	30	21	32	27
	Television	232	245	225	214	207	234	231	189	202	205	218
Total media use		320	346	302	-	330	310	337	-	299	320	318

132

Findings can be summarized thus:

- In the United Kingdom and Germany *television specialists* are low on print media, especially books and comics, and on the Internet
- Finnish *television specialists* are, in contrast, high on books, comics, and the Internet
- Israeli *television specialists* are especially high on newspapers, but also on books and video, and low on comics and games
- In Sweden *television specialists* spend double the amount of time on ICTs relative to other countries. They are especially high on the Internet, but also on computers, being about average on other media
- *Television specialists* in Flanders, Switzerland, Italy, and the Netherlands are all low on the Internet. They are slightly above average on print media. Flanders and Switzerland differ in that the former is low and the latter is high on games.

Most characteristic of this group is their relatively high total media time, of which the major part is devoted to television viewing. Their high viewing time seems not to decrease time spent with other media a great deal; instead it increases the proportion of available leisure time spent on media. Young *television specialists* in both Sweden and Finland spend above average amounts of time on media, but they spend less time on television than the average for young people in this group. Furthermore, they are relatively high on both computers and the Internet. In both these Nordic countries, the proportion of nonusers is small, not exceeding one third of the population for any medium. The *television specialists* in these countries do not discard any medium en masse, but try out most media to a greater or lesser extent. The new media do not yet present severe competition to the highly preferred medium, but they are nonetheless finding their way into this media use style. The *television specialists* are to be found in all countries and among all age and gender groups.

The other three specialist groups, the established *book fans* and the recent *PC fans* and *PC and games fans*, are considerably smaller, only encompassing a small percentage of children and young people. The media profile of the *book fans* is of course dominated by their interest in books. Not surprisingly, many of the *book fans* also devote more time than average to other print media such as magazines, newspapers, and comics. However, they do not spend a lot of time on screen media, especially not on electronic games or on ICTs. The total media time for the *book fans* is an average of 4.5 hours a day.

The profile of *book fans* also differs between countries. Three rough profiles can be defined in terms of how they combine books with other media:

- In Flanders, Germany, and Switzerland, the *book fans* are notably *low* on both ICTs and on most screen media
- In Finland, Israel, and Sweden, they are comparatively *high* on both ICTs and on screen media in general
- In the United Kingdom and the Netherlands, they are *low* on ICTs (most notably on computers and on the Internet, respectively), but relatively *high* on screen media

Book fans are most often 12- to 13-year-old girls, even if they are also found among boys and among both younger and older age groups.

The *PC fans* and the *PC and games fans* resemble each other in many respects, but there are also significant differences in time use profiles between countries. They have therefore been kept as two distinct groups.

The media use profiles of the *PC fans* and the *PC and games fans* are characterized by their common interest in computers. The *PC fans* group is the smallest of the groups, and the figures have to be interpreted with caution. This group is found in only 5 out of 10 countries, whereas the PC and games fans are found in seven. The total media time for both these groups is well over 6.5 hours a day. They thus spend a considerable amount of time with media, not only on computers and the Internet but also on games. They are also above average on print media in general, but slightly lower on television (Table 5.4). Further, the proportion of users compared with nonusers tends to be above average for most media. Overall, therefore, more of this group spend more time on most media except television. This does not indicate a simple replacement of other media by the computer, but rather suggests an additive use of old and new media. However, some reallocation of time from television in favor of the PC seems to take place, together with a reallocation of some nonmedia time to media time.

These groups both favor the computer and the Internet, spending more time with these media than with television. The main difference is that the *PC fans* concentrate more on computers (for purposes other than games) and the Internet and less heavily on games, whereas the *PC and games fans* spend somewhat less time on computers and the Internet and more on games. Both spend slightly above average time on print in general, although *PC fans* favor books and *PC and games fans* favor magazines and comics and are rather low on books (Table 5.4).

The profiles of both the *PC fans* and the *PC and games fans* vary considerably between the countries. Figures must, however, be interpreted with caution because the number of individuals in each country group is small. The largest groups of *PC fans* are found in Sweden, Italy, Spain, and the United Kingdom and of *PC and games fans* in Sweden, Flanders, and Finland.

- The *PC fans* in Sweden spend 2 hours per day on the computer and another three quarters of an hour on the Internet, besides three quarters of an hour on games playing, they are about average in their television viewing (about 2.5 hours) and video viewing (half an hour) and also in their book reading (a quarter of an hour). The *PC and games fans* in Sweden are equally high on the Internet, even higher on the computer (well above 2.5 hours) and of course on games (1.5 hours), though lower on books (5 to 10 minutes) and television (2 hours).

- The *PC fans* in the United Kingdom and Italy spend a similar amount of time on the computer (some even more than in Sweden), but less time on the Internet: in the United Kingdom half an hour and in Italy a quarter of an hour. In both countries they spend about an hour playing games, being average on television and video viewing. In the United Kingdom this group also combines book reading with their interest in the computer, the Internet, and games. In Spain the *PC fans* concentrate heavily on the computer, spending about 2 hours with it, but are low on both the Internet and on all screen media, spending only 1.5 hours with all three of them.

- The *PC and games fans* in Finland spend more time on games than on the computer for other purposes, and in Flanders the opposite is the case. In both countries they spend only a few minutes on the Internet and they also spend little time with books. Their television and video viewing is about average.

In summary, it appears that not even these groups are generally replacing older media in favor of newer, although they seem to be reallocating some time from books, video, or television. Mainly these groups are adding to the total time spent on media, instead of using new media at the expense of other media-related leisure time activities.

Screen Entertainment. Under this heading, there are two user styles with a common interest in television, but favoring different combinations of screen media: the fans of *television and video* and of *television and games*. Both groups are small, each only encompassing a small percentage of children and young people. However, the total media time spent on all media is as high as 6 and 7 hours a day respectively, thus making them, together with the *PC fans*, the groups with the highest total daily media use. These two groups share a similar relation to print media, that is, they spend somewhat less time on books and somewhat more on comics and magazines, being average on newspapers.

The *television and video* fans spend over 4.5 hours a day in front of the television screen. They use computers and the Internet for only 20 minutes and read books less than the average young person, but spend more time on comics. Thirty-five percent of this group are nonreaders, compared to 23% on average (Table 5.4).

Comparing their time profiles across countries, it is evident that the time they spend with the screen differs. In Sweden, the United Kingdom, Israel, Finland, Spain, and Switzerland, they spend 5 to 5.5 hours a day on television and video, whereas in Germany and Italy they spend 3 to 3.5 hours a day. In no country do they spend over half an hour on games. The *television and video* fans in different countries also differ in their relation to computers and the Internet. In Sweden, Finland, and Italy, they are relatively high on both computers and Internet (above half an hour with computers and 10 to 15 minutes with Internet); in the other countries they use computers and the Internet less than average, being exceptionally low in Germany and Switzerland.

The fans of *television and games* are the highest media users of all the eight user groups. They spend more than 7 hours a day on media, of which almost 6 hours are devoted to the screen and in particular to television and games playing (Table 5.4). In contrast to the former group, they are only slightly above average on video viewing. This group also spends more than average time on computers and the Internet and about average time on print in general, though less time on books. The proportion of users to nonusers for most media does not deviate substantially from the proportion in the total group, although there are more who do not read books at all in this group (44% vs. 23%), and among those who do read, they are below average. In time spent, on the whole, there are no unambiguous signs here of a rearrangement of media time in this group; instead they tend to be adding new media to their total media time.

Across countries, the profiles of the *television and games* fans show some variation. The main difference is connected to the new ICT media. In Spain, Sweden, and Israel, they spend about 1 hour on ICT each day, whereas in the United Kingdom, Italy, and the Netherlands, they spend barely a quarter of an hour. Especially avid Internet users are the Israeli and Swedish television and games fans, with 20 to 30 minutes a day on average. In the United Kingdom this group is particularly low on all print media; in Switzerland they are higher than average on all print media. There is thus no uniform relation between time spent on screen entertainment media and print in general or books in particular.

REPLACEMENT, REARRANGEMENT OR ACCUMULATION OF MEDIA

As mentioned earlier in this chapter, media displacement is too often discussed in terms of symmetrical, zero-sum relationships, that is, more time for one medium means less time for another medium or for another activity.

In a simple sense this is, of course, true because the day has only a finite number of hours. However, this is also too simplistic an equation as there are many factors to consider besides time in relation to media use and media displacement, not to mention the fact that sometimes more than one medium may be used at any one time. The availability of media somewhere in the home is of course important, though it is not a sufficient factor to ensure use. To actually make use of an available medium, it must also be socially and/or psychologically attractive in the eyes of the user. Personal motivation, shaped both by past experiences and expected rewards, is thus of major importance. So too is the overall lifestyle of the individual and of the group(s) to which he or she belongs, whether or not temporarily. There are always some individuals and groups who seem to discard some media altogether, and the size of these groups varies depending on gender, and age, and on the culture in which they live.

A major concern in this chapter was not the use of single media but rather the patterns of time spent by combining media in different ways. Young people of today in Europe may be selective in their media use, favoring only certain media and discarding others, or they may combine different media, adding new ones to their individual menus. Through a series of cluster analyses, eight distinct media use styles, classified into four broader user styles, were identified. Some general conclusions may be noted:

- Television is still the dominant medium for *all* user types, both in terms of the number of users and the amount of time spent. Everyone, everywhere, watches television, and television viewing makes up the main part of his or her media time
- The largest group *par excellence* is the *low users*. The group contains large proportions of nonusers of individual media, and overall these young people spend little time with media
- The new ICTs are used within *all* user styles, though the proportions of users and the amount of time spent vary
- There are tendencies towards media accumulation. In countries where access to computers and/or the Internet is relatively high, such as Finland, Sweden, the Netherlands, and Israel, the new media are often combined with traditional print and screen media
- There seems also to be a concurrent trend towards increasing specialization in media use. The groups that specialize in computers, the Internet, and electronic games are still small, but are not insignificant. These groups may be growing fast as new media disperse to a majority of the population.
- Cases of pure displacement of media are rare, and instead we are witnessing instances of media specialization and combination. Media time

is rearranged, allocating time for new media to be included in the menu. The more specialized groups are the heaviest media users, and this is especially the case for groups whose specialization centers on the new media (see Table 5.4), indicating that they are expanding their total media time in order to make room for their interest in the new media, without much lessening of time spent with traditional media.

- There are tendencies pointing to an uneasy relationship between books and television in some countries; in other countries, these different kinds of media seems to go together quite well. Thus, slight indications of displacement from books to screen media, and also from television in favor of the PC, occur in some countries and in some user groups. Among *television specialists* as well as *television and video, television and games*, and *PC and games fans*, the number of book readers and the time devoted to books are below average.

The overall time profiles for the eight media use styles discussed here indicate that instances of simple media displacement are rare. Instead, we have seen instances of specialization of media use, reallocation of media time, and of additive media use. Single individuals may still displace certain media in favor of others, as the proportion of nonusers shows, but this is not the general tendency. Rather, distinct user styles are developing as new media become available and differentially accepted by children and young people across Europe. Interest gaps are a reality, and information and knowledge gaps may be a consequence. To counter this, it is necessary to make media not only available, but also desirable—and that is a political and cultural concern.

REFERENCES

Adoni, H. (1985). Media interchangeability and co-existence: Trends and changes in production, distribution and consumption patterns of the print media in the television era. *Libri, 35*(3), 202–217.

Broddason, T. (1996). *Television in time. Research images and empirical findings*. Lund studies in media and communication 2. Lund: Lund University Press.

Chaney, D. (1972). *Processes of mass communication*. London: MacMillan.

Coffey, S., & Stipp, H. (1997). The interactions between computer and television usage. *Journal of Advertising Research, 37*(2), 61–7.

Hasebrink, U. (1997). In search of patterns of individual media use. In U. Carlsson (Ed.), *Beyond media uses and effects* (pp. 99–112). Göteborg: Nordicom.

Hendry, L. B., Shucksmith, J., Love, J. G., & Glendinning, A. (1993). *Young people's leisure and lifestyles*. London and New York: Routledge.

Himmelweit, H. T., Oppenheim, A. N., & Vince, P. (1958). *Television and the child: An empirical study of the effect of television on the young*. London and New York: Oxford University Press.

Hincks, T., & Balding, J. W. (1988). On the relationship between television viewing time and book reading for pleasure: the self-reported behaviour of 11 to 16 year olds. *Reading, 22*(1), 40–50.

Johansson, T. (1994). Late modernity, consumer culture and lifestyles: Toward a cognitive-affective theory. In K. E. Rosengren (Ed.), *Media effects and beyond. Culture, socialization and lifestyles* (pp. 265–294). London and New York: Routledge.

Johansson, T., & Miegel, F. (1992). *Do the right thing. Lifestyle and identity in contemporary youth culture.* Stockholm: Almqvist & Wiksell International.

Johnsson-Smaragdi, U. (1983). *TV use and social interaction in adolescence. A longitudinal study.* Stockholm: Almqvist & Wiksell International.

Johnsson-Smaragdi, U. (1986). Tryckta kontra audiovisuella medier—konkurrens eller samexistens? [Printed versus audiovisual media—competition or coexistence?]. *Wahlgrenska stiftelsens rapportserie, 3.*

Johnsson-Smaragdi, U. (1992). Learning to watch television: Longitudinal LISREL models replicated. *Lund research papers in media and communication studies.* Report no. 5. Lund: Dept. of Sociology.

Johnsson-Smaragdi, U. (1994). Models of change and stability in adolescents' media use. In K. E. Rosengren (Ed.), *Media effects and beyond. Culture, socialization and lifestyles* (pp. 97–130). London and New York: Routledge.

Johnsson-Smaragdi, U., & Jönsson, A. (2000). *From a homogenous to a heterogeneous media world: Access and use of media among teenagers over three decades.*

Krotz, F., & Hasebrink, U. (1998). The analysis of people meter data: Individual patterns of viewing behavior of people with different cultural backgrounds. *Communications, 23*(2), 151–74.

Maletzke, G. (1959). *Fernsehen im Leben der Jugend* [TV in the life of adolescents]. Hamburg: Hans-Bredow-Institut.

McLuhan, M. (1964). *Understanding media. The extensions of man.* London and New York: Signet.

McQuail, D. (1994). *Mass communication theory. An introduction* (3rd ed.). London: Sage.

Mutz, D., Roberts, D. F., & van Vuuren, D. P. (1993). Reconsidering the displacement hypothesis. Television's influence on children's time use. *Communication Research, 20*(1), 51–75.

Palmgreen, P., & Rayburn, J. D. (1985). An expectancy-value approach to media gratifications. In K. E. Rosengren, L. A. Wenner, & P. Palmgreen (Eds.), *Media gratifications research* (pp. 61–72). Beverly Hills, CA: Sage.

Rogers, E. M. (1995). *Diffusion of innovations.* New York: Free Press.

Rosengren, K. E. (Ed.). (1994). *Media effects and beyond. Culture, socialization and lifestyles.* London and New York: Routledge.

Rosengren, K. E., & Windahl, S. (1989). *Media matter. TV use in childhood and adolescence.* Norwood, NJ: Ablex.

Saxer, U., Langenbucher, W. R., & Fritz, A. (1989). *Lesen in der moderne Gesellschaft* [Reading in the modern society]. Gutersloh: Bertelsmann.

Smith, A. (1980). *Goodbye Gutenberg. The newspaper revolution of the 1980's.* New York and Oxford: Oxford University Press.

van der Loo, H., & van der Reijen, W. (1992). *Modernisierung. Project und Paradox* [Modernization. Project and paradox]. Munich: dtv.

6

Media Genres
and Content Preferences

Carmelo Garitaonandia
Patxi Juaristi
José A. Oleaga

This chapter is devoted to the analysis of children's and young people's expressed preferences for television programs and electronic games. It therefore seeks to address the often neglected issue of media content, a theme that has emerged as important but has thus far remained implicit in this volume. Findings are based on the answers of children and teenagers from 12 European countries (DK, FI, BE-vlg, FR, DE, IT, NL, ES, SE, CH, GB) and from Israel who were asked to name their favorite television program and/or their favorite type of electronic game. In several of these countries, they were also invited to identify their main interest from a list of 14 topics and to name the media they considered best for following it up. On the basis of their replies, we are able to address the following intriguing questions:

- Does children's choice of favorite program and favorite type of electronic game reflect their more general interest in particular types of subject matter, or do the media generate their own distinctive set of interests?
- Do children follow their interests across several different media, or do they follow particular interests in relation to particular media?
- Do children's television preferences indicate an appetite for contents specifically produced for child or youth audiences?

In recent years, the programming strategy of generalist television channels in most European countries has seen the steady erosion of programming made especially for children and a parallel reduction in time slots dedicated to children's broadcasts (Blumler & Bitereyst, 1998). This programming policy is, of course, much more common in commercial television companies than among public service broadcasters. In the United Kingdom and the Nordic countries, for example, where the tradition of public service broadcasting is strong, there are still children's programs in after-school hours as well as educational programs aimed at children during the mornings. However, traditional time slots are under threat, and budgets for more expensive series are ever more difficult to secure, as even public service broadcasters come under pressure to maximize their audiences. Consequently, in many countries, programs made especially for children are likely to be limited on terrestrial television channels to cartoons around breakfast time during the week, and later in the morning at weekends (García Muñoz, 1997). As a result, in many European countries, unless the household subscribes to a multichannel network that has a children's channel, such as Cartoon Network, Disney Channel, Nickelodeon, etc. (see figures for number of subscribers to children's television channels in Table 1.4, chapter 1), it is almost impossible for a child to watch a children's program during the afternoon or evening. It follows that children in countries where satellite, cable, or digital television systems are widespread (see Fig. 1.1, chapter 1) have more opportunity to watch children's programs than children in countries with less developed systems. Otherwise, it is generally higher income families who are able to afford such channels for their children.

In justification of this trend, broadcasters point not only to the increasing provision of dedicated commercial channels for younger children, but also to the fact that audience figures for older children are often largest for adult, or family, programming rather than for dedicated children's programs. However, audience figures do not necessarily provide an accurate picture of children's preferences because in many cases the choice of programs offered to children is limited. In addition, we should not forget that much of their exposure to adults' programs is a direct result of viewing choices made by other members of their families (Huston & Wright, 1996). Given this context, can new insight be provided by our survey into children's perspectives on program preferences? Further, as the variety of media available to children in the home diversifies—and here we particularly focus on preferences for types of electronic games—how do content preferences for any one medium relate to those for other media?

FAVORITE TOPICS AND MEDIA CONSIDERED BEST FOR FOLLOWING THEM

When asked to select, from a list of 14 options, the topics of particular interest to them, children from different countries proved to have very similar tastes. Some small differences exist (see Table 6.1).[1] For example, sport is

---

[1]Topics listed were war, crime, comedy/humor, horror, animals/nature, adventure/action, romance, news, sci-fi, music, sport, stars (film/pop/television personalities), art/theatre, travel.

TABLE 6.1
Favorite Topics: Base All Children Age 9-10, 12-13, 15-16 (percentages)

Topics	DK	ES	FR	GB	IL	IT	SE	AV.
Sport	26	22	25	34	14	26	21	24
Music	15	14	22	15	16	21	18	17
Animals/Nature	9	17	6	9	7	5	9	9
Comedy/Humor	6	6	3	9	15	2	7	7
Adventure/Action	5	8	5	3	7	5	9	6
Horror	2	7	7	6	4	7	5	5
Stars (Film/Pop/TV)	9	8	2	6	6	2	4	5
Romance	6	2	8	1	5	8	6	5
Travel	4	2	9	3	1	8	5	3
Sci-Fi	2	3	4	4	6	4	4	4
War	3	2	1	2	6	2	2	3
Crime	1	1	1	1	3	3	1	2
News	3	1	2	0	2	3	1	2
Art/Theater	0	1	2	5	3	2	1	2
Other	7	5	2	0	6	2	7	4

Note. Figures in the last column represent an average of the percentages in 7 countries, when each is given equal weight.

most frequently chosen as an interest in the United Kingdom (34%), and least frequently in Israel (14%), compared with an average across countries of 24%. Music is rather more popular in France (22%, compared with an average across countries of 17%), animals/nature in Spain (17%, compared with an average of 9%) and comedy/humor in Israel (15%, compared with an average of 7%).

Overall, children's and young people's favorite topics are sport, music, and animals/nature, although there are also some who choose adventure/action and comedy/humor as their top preference. Moreover, their tastes concur regarding the topics that hold the least interest for them, namely, art/theater and news. In the case of news, children's lack of interest is perhaps unsurprising if one takes into account the findings of previous research that suggests that a sizeable minority of children (37% in the United States) feel frightened or upset by news stories on television (Cantor & Nathanson, 1996).

Interestingly, neither the socioeconomic status (SES) of the family nor the geographical location of the children's home (urban, suburban, or rural)

An additional "other" category was provided for those who wished to identify an interest not on the list, though few made use of this. Children in 7 countries (DK, FR, IS, IT, ES, SE, GB) were asked to name the *one* topic on the list that they were particularly interested in; these are included in Table 6.1. Children in Finland were allowed to identify three topics, and children in Germany and Switzerland could name as many as they wished. Data from these countries are not, therefore, included in the table, although findings are generally in line with those found in other countries.

influences children's interests in any of the countries surveyed. However, both age and gender are important. For example, we find a number of age-related trends common across countries:

- Interest in music and romance increases with age.
- The opposite occurs with the topics of adventure/action and animals/ nature; as boys and girls get older, interest in these topics declines.
- Interest in stars (film/pop/television personalities) and science fiction peaks between the ages of 12 and 13.
- By contrast, interest in sport is high and remains stable across age groups, as does the moderate level of interest in comedy/humor and the low interest in travel.

The influence of gender is particularly evident: Boys' interests are generally more uniform and more action-oriented, whereas those of girls are more diverse and more people-oriented. Above all, boys are interested in sport and adventure/action. They also show more interest than girls in science fiction, although even among boys, this is the favorite interest of only a few (7% to 8% of boys are interested compared with only 1% to 2% of girls). On the other hand, although music is the topic most likely to interest girls, they also like animals/nature, sport, stars (film/pop/television personalities), and romance. This said, it is important not to exaggerate these gender differences. Sport, for example, is liked by a significant number of girls, and some boys show a certain interest in music (see chapter 12).

When we focus more narrowly on the favorite topics of both genders within different age groups, the picture becomes clearer (see Table 6.2). Sport dominates the interests of boys at every age, followed some considerable way behind by adventure/action. At the ages of 9 and 10, animals/nature

TABLE 6.2
Favorite Topics by Age Within Gender

	Age 9-10		Age 12-13		Age 15-16	
Boys	Sport	27%	Sport	27%	Sport	28%
	Adventure	15%	Adventure	13%	Music	15%
	Animals	13%	Sci-FI	11%	Adventure	12%
	Comedy	8%	Comedy	11%	Sci-Fi	9%
	War	6%	Music	8%	Comedy	8%
Girls	Animals	26%	Music	20%	Music	26%
	Music	13%	Stars	13%	Romance	13%
	Stars	11%	Animals	12%	Sport	11%
	Sport	10%	Sport	11%	Comedy	8%
	Comedy	10%	Comedy	9%	Stars	8%

is almost as likely to be the main interest as adventure action. At 12 to 13 interest in animals/nature disappears, to be replaced in third position by interest in sci-fi and comedy. At this age, music is beginning to attract a minority. By the age of 15 or 16, music attracts sufficient number of boys to challenge adventure/action for second place.

The favorite topics of girls change more radically as they grow older, although the pattern of falling interest in animals/nature and rising interest in music is similar. Thus girls aged 9 and 10 are mostly interested in animals and nature. Smaller and roughly equal proportions like music, stars (film/pop/television personalities), sport, and comedy. Their preferences, however, change dramatically when they are 12 and 13. At this age, girls like music above all, whereas interest in animals or nature falls by half. The level of interest in stars (film/pop/television personalities), sport, and comedy remains relatively unchanged. When they get to 15 and 16 years of age, music continues to be the topic most often selected. Interest in stars drops and romance emerges as a favorite topic, although it is chosen by only marginally more than choose sport (Suess et al., 1998).

In order to summarize the most relevant findings, we carried out a Correspondence Analysis in which we related the children's and young people's favorite topics (selected from the 15 possibilities in Table 6.1) to their age and gender (a total of six groups). We obtained a two-dimensional space (see Fig. 6.1) that explains 92% of the variance and that graphically illustrates the different tastes of boys and girls in the three age groups.

It is noteworthy that masculine and feminine patterns are perfectly distinguishable within the topic preferences of boys and girls of different ages. The boys and their topics are situated on the left-hand side of Graph 1 (the negative part of factor 1); the girls and their topics are on the right-hand side (the positive part of this factor).

Among the girls, as already discussed, a greater range of interests is evident. Each age group is associated with a different topic: animals/nature for the 9- and 10-year-old girls, stars (film/pop/television personalities) and music for girls of 12 and 13, and music and romance for the girls of 15 and 16 years of age. The oldest girls also show some interest in travel and news. Boys' tastes are more homogenous: In all age groups, to a greater or lesser extent, boys like sport, adventure/action, science fiction, and war. Once again, only the oldest show some interest in news.

FOLLOWING UP INTERESTS THROUGH THE MEDIA

Having ascertained children's and teenagers' favorite topics, we next asked which out of 10 media they choose in order to follow up these interests. Are particular media, we wondered, associated with particular interests? Or,

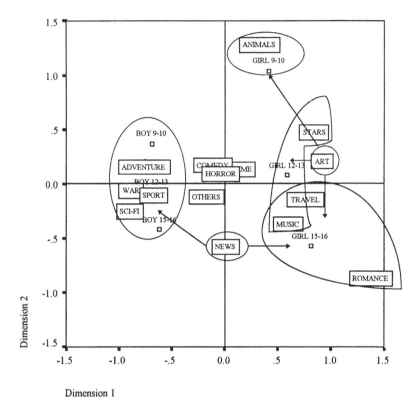

FIG. 6.1.   Correspondence Analysis: favorite topic according to age and gender.

conversely, is there any evidence that children follow their interests across a number of different media?

Although in each country only a few boys and girls express an interest in some of the 14 topics, and although many media are identified as useful for following these interests, some consistent patterns do emerge. Overall, boys and girls from the different European countries prefer the same media genres for following an interest in particular topics (see Table 6.3).

Television is the medium most commonly used to follow up any of the interests we asked about. This accords well with the fact that television and videos are seen as the best media when children want excitement or to stop being bored (see chapter 4) and with the finding that in many countries their own television set is what children would most like to receive as a birthday gift (see Table 3.11, chapter 3); (Sherman, 1966). Books are the second most popular medium used to follow interests in animals/nature, art/theater, travel, crime, and war, and the third most popular for romance and horror. On the other hand, electronic games, comics, and newspapers have a much more

TABLE 6.3
The Best Media for Following Particular Topics*

Favorite Topics	Best Media	Other Media
WAR	Television, Books	Video, Cinema, Newspapers
CRIME	Television, Books	Video, Cinema
COMEDY/HUMOR	Television, Cinema, Video	Books, Comics
HORROR	Television, Video, Books, Cinema	
ANIMALS/NATURE	Television, Books	Magazines, Video
ADVENTURE/ACTION	Television, Video, Cinema, Books, Electronic games	
ROMANCE	Television, Cinema, Books, Video, Magazines	
NEWS	Television, Newspapers, Magazines	Books
SCI-FI	Television, Video, Cinema, Rooks, Electronic games	
MUSIC	Television, Magazines	Video
SPORTS	Television, Newspapers, Magazines	
STARS (FILM, POP, TV)	Television, Magazines	Cinema, Video, Newspapers
ART & THEATER	Television, Books	Cinema, Newspapers, Magazines
TRAVEL	Television, Books, Magazines	Newspapers

Note. *Data from Belgium (Flanders) are not available.

limited use in this respect, and at present, CD-ROMs and the Internet are not widely used by children to follow their interests, as is corroborated by the very small numbers who say they would turn to them for excitement or to stop being bored (see chapter 4). There is, however, enough diversity to suggest that children do follow their interests across different types of media. As Table 6.3 demonstrates, no topic is associated with only one medium. Indeed, most media are considered useful for following up a number of different interests.

Once again we carried out Correspondence Analysis relating the 14 topics to the 10 media genres, and obtained a two-dimensional space that accounts for 74% of the total variance (see Fig. 6.2). What we most wish to draw attention to in this figure is the well-represented and central position occupied by television, which is considered to be the best medium for the enjoyment of the majority of topics.

Also of interest is the very different appeal of the four types of print media, which are situated in different quadrants. Comics (in the lower left-hand quadrant) are, unsurprisingly, almost exclusively associated with comedy/humor. Magazines are situated on the right-hand side of the figure and associated, to a greater or lesser degree, with stars (film/pop/television personalities), travel, music, romance, news, and sport. In the top left-hand quadrant, we find books linked with cinema and video, all media principally associated with romance, horror, comedy/humor, adventure/action, and science fiction. (Books are also associated with travel, and, together with all the media in this cluster, are used by those who are interested in the topic

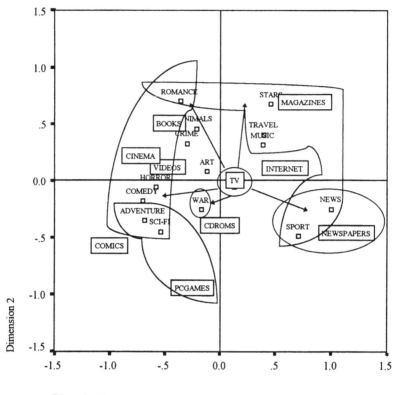

FIG. 6.2.   Correspondence Analysis: the best media for each topic.

of war.) Predictably, newspapers, in the bottom right-hand portion of the figure, are associated with news and sport.

The newer electronic media are not yet so strongly associated with any of
the interests we asked about, although electronic games are linked with
adventure/action and science fiction. Interestingly, despite the fact that most
children do not consider the Internet to be a good medium through which to
follow their favorite topics (presumably because of its limited availability as
yet), it is interesting to see that associations with stars (film/pop/television
personalities), music, and sport are already building up.

FAVORITE TELEVISION PROGRAMS

Focusing now on television, children and young people in six countries (FI,
DE, IL, ES, SE, CH, GB) were asked to name their favorite program. There
were two main issues that we hoped to address. First, do the genres identi-

fied as most popular reflect the interests identified at the general level in the previous section, or does television generate, or meet, its own rather different set of interests? Secondly, is there evidence that there is a demand for programs specifically made for children?

Findings showed that young people in the six countries studied have quite similar tastes. The largest single proportion of 6- to 7-year-old children in every country choose cartoons: They are most popular in Israel, where 81% nominate a cartoon and least popular in Sweden, where only 34% make such a choice. The favorite genres of European youngsters aged 9 or older are primarily narrative genres, such as soaps or other types of series or serial. Next come the somewhat less popular situation comedies and sports programs (see Table 6.4). There are, however, some interesting cross-cultural differences:

- British and German children and teenagers like sports programs more than do those from other countries.
- British, German, and Israeli children are particularly interested in soaps.
- Series are particularly popular in Sweden, whereas in Israel they are not greatly appreciated.
- Among children aged 9 or older, cartoons are most liked in Germany, Finland, and Spain.
- Spain is the only country in which children show a great interest in quizzes and family shows.

Many of these differences are likely to be attributable to differences in availability. For example, the highly popular national soaps in Germany (*Good Times, Bad Times*) and the United Kingdom (*EastEnders*) are certainly

TABLE 6.4
Favorite Television Genres: Base All Children Age 9-10, 12-13, and 15-16 (Percentages)

	CH	DE	ES	FI	GB	IL	SE	AV
Series/Other serial	23	12	21	29	13	12	43	22
Soap	10	27	7	21	29	37	19	21
Comedy/Sitcom	17	9	16	16	10	18	10	14
Sport	9	13	10	6	18	7	7	11
Cartoon	11	15	14	16	10	4	3	10
Sci-FI	5	8	1	5	7	9	6	6
Quiz/Family show	2	4	18	2	3	2	1	5
Music program	4	2	4	0	2	1	2	2
Wildlife/Animal program	5	1	2	1	3	1	2	2
News/Current Affairs Documentary	2	2	2	1	1	2	1	2
Magazine program	3	1	2	1	3	5	2	2
Films	7	6	3	3	2	2	3	4
Chat show	1	1	0	0	0	0	2	1
Other	0	0	1	0	0	3	1	1

responsible for the large number of nominations for soaps in those countries. In Israel, a number of Latin telenovelas, as well as American soaps, are available and highly popular with young viewers. In other cases, apparent differences may be due to discrepancies in coding decisions. For example, in Sweden, only programs that are broadcast everyday (like *Skilda världar* and *Vänner och fiender*) were coded as soaps, a definition that would have excluded most British soaps. Other similar but less frequently broadcast programs (such as *Rederiet* and *Tre Kronor*) were coded in the category series or serials. The very low figure recorded in Spain for soaps may also (at least in part) be an artefact of coding procedures. The very popular program *Family Doctor* has been coded as a situation comedy, although it also contains many soap-like features. Such "error" in coding in fact reflects real cross-national differences in the definitions of key genres such as the soap opera (Liebes & Livingstone, 1998) and so cannot be easily resolved.

Once again the SES of the family[2] and the geographical location of the home (urban/rural) have no discernible impact on children's program preferences, but age and gender do have an influence. The most striking differences are those between boys and girls, regardless of their national origin. European boys' preferences are similar, but different from those of European girls and, in turn, girls across Europe also share very similar tastes. European boys like cartoons when they are younger, and graduate to sports programs, series other than soaps, and comedy programs as they get older. Girls' interest in cartoons falls off dramatically after 7, and thereafter narrative (soaps or other series) predominates (see Table 6.5).

At no age does sport figure among the top five genres nominated by girls. Once again, however, it is important not to exaggerate this difference. After all, cartoons, series, and comedy appeal to both boys and girls, if to a different extent.

When we study program preference by age (see Table 6.5), we find that there are certain general tendencies that may be summarized as follows:

- Girls' preference for soaps peaks between the ages of 9 to 13.
- As children of both genders get older, they become less interested in cartoons.
- Interest in sport increases with age only in the case of boys; girls' comparative lack of interest in this topic remains stable.
- A taste for situation comedies increases with age, above all after the age of 9.
- Interest in series increases with age, although by the age of 15 this interest tends to decrease for boys.

---

[2]There is one noteworthy exception. In France, horror is the favorite genre of 17% (a truly exceptional percentage) of youngsters from families with low socioeconomic status.

TABLE 6.5
Genres of Favorite Television Program by Age Within Gender (Percentages)

	Age 6-7		Age 9-10		Age 12-13		Age 15-16	
Boys	Cartoon	63	Cartoon	23	Series	22	Sport	22
	Series	8	Series	20	Sport	17	Comedy	16
	Magazine	7	Sport	15	Comedy	15	Series	16
	Family Show	5	Comedy	12	Cartoon	11	Sci-Fi	12
	Comedy	4	Soap	10	Sci-Fi	9	Cartoon	8
Girls	Cartoon	48	Soap	29	Soap	35	Series	33
	Series	11	Series	25	Series	30	Soap	28
	Soap	10	Cartoon	13	Comedy	13	Comedy	14
	Family Show	10	Comedy	12	Music	4	Sci-Fi	5
	Magazine	7	Family Show	6	Sci-Fi	4	Music	4

There are some interesting national variations. For example, in Israel and Switzerland, interest in sport peaks between the ages of 9 and 13, although it remains stable after 9 in Sweden and actually increases among both boys and girls at 15 and 16 in the United Kingdom, Germany, Spain, and Finland. Similarly, the age at which boys' and girls' interest in series peaks varies between countries. Amongst 15- and 16-year-old German, Finnish, and Swedish boys, interest does not decrease as in other countries, and the figures for girls are even more disparate. The interest of Israeli girls in series increases linearly with age, whereas that of German and Spanish girls remains stable after 12 (at around 13% and 28% respectively). The pattern in the United Kingdom, Sweden, and Switzerland deviates most from the norm of increased interest with age. The youngest British girls are just as keen on series as the oldest, Swedish girls' interest decreases slightly in the teenage years, and Swiss girls of 12 and 13 are less interested (18%) than either 9- to 10- or 15- to 16-year-old girls (both with 25%).

These findings show that young people's general interests are reflected in their program choices. This is particularly true for boys, whose interest in both sport and sports programs is paramount. Girls' interest in personalities can also be seen as informing their choice of narrative genres such as soaps and other types of series and serials. Interestingly, however, teenage girls' preoccupation with music is not reflected in the numbers choosing music-based programs as their favorite. By the age of 15 or 16, such nominations account for only 4% of girls' choices overall.

At the beginning of this section, we asked about the demand for programs made specially for children. To address this, we classified programs according to whether they were made specifically for a child audience or for a family or adult audience. Findings (see Table 6.6) confirm that the great majority of all but the youngest children prefer adult or family-oriented programming (Alonso, Matilla, & Vazquez, 1995).

TABLE 6.6
Origin of Favorite Television Program (Percentages)

	CH	DE	ES	FI	GB	IL	SE
Age 6-7							
Children		82	60	72	68	84	64
Adult/family	n/a	18	40	29	32	16	35
Age 9-10							
Children	48	55	25	27	33	14	19
Adult/family	52	45	75	73	67	86	81
Age 12-13							
Children	14	19	13	13	12	5	3
Adult/family	86	81	87	87	88	95	97
Age 15-16							
Children	18	18	8	8	4	1	2
Adult/family	82	82	92	92	96	99	98

From 9 years old onwards, in all the countries (with the exception of German and Swiss children of 9 or 10 who continue to prefer children's programs), the overwhelming majority prefer programs aimed at adults. Moreover, where the youngest children have named a children's program, in the majority of cases (80%) these are cartoons. As children get older, narrative programs account for an increasingly large proportion of favorite children's programs. In short, although the youngest children prefer cartoons, as they grow older children rapidly develop a preference for family and adult programs over those made specifically for children. Those children's programs that remain successful tend to be narrative-based.

FAVORITE ELECTRONIC GAMES

Not only do children prefer television programs made primarily for adult audiences but also, as is commonly observed, both children and adults share similar interests in electronic games. This relatively new domain of media contents, therefore, enhances the overlap in children and adult leisure interests. So are the specific types of content preferred also similar across television and electronic games? For a profile of the heavy user, see Roe and Muijs (1998).

Once again there appear to be more similarities than differences across the children and teenagers from the European countries studied (see Table 6.7). The order of preference for these games is more or less common to all the countries studied: adventure games and fighting games rank highest (cf. Funk & Buchman, 1996). Next come sports games, games with cars or aircraft, then games in which you have to plan things, card/board/puzzle games, and finally, drawing/painting games. There are, however, a few cross-national differences worthy of mention. In Germany there is comparatively

TABLE 6.7
Favorite Type of Electronic Game (Percentages)

	BE (vlg)	CH	DE	DK	ES	FI	FR	GB	IL	NL	SE	AV
Adventure/quests	21	19	9	19	32	25	13	25	21	30	28	22
Fighting	19	12	19	18	12	26	19	17	19	24	21	19
Sports	14	17	16	13	21	12	29	28	20	10	13	18
Cars/aircraft	13	17	15	13	11	9	7	7	9	12	10	11
Card/Board/Puzzle	11	9	9	8	4	10	9	5	9	12	6	9
Where plan things	4	9	17	8	7	11	6	6	13	3	8	9
Drawing/Painting	8	7	3	5	6	5	11	6	3	6	5	6
Games that teach things	6	10	11	6	5	2	2	5	3	4	8	6
Fashion/Design	5	2	2	3	4	2	4	2	4	1	2	3

Note. *based on those age 9-10, 12-13, and 15-16 who play electronic games.

little interest in adventure/quest games, but considerably more than average interest in games where you have to plan things and games that teach you things. Swiss children are also more interested in educational games, although this remains a minority interest. In France and the United Kingdom, young people are particularly interested in sports games.

As expected, children who like watching sport on television also like playing electronic games concerned with sport. Similarly, children who like watching cartoons also like electronic games about fighting; this relationship is perhaps due to the fact that many cartoons, particularly Japanese cartoons, feature a high level of fighting.

As with television programs, the SES of the family bears no relation to children's preferences for electronic games. The major difference, as ever, lies between boys and girls. Their preferred games confirm that, as with television programs, boys' and girls' choices tend to reflect their general interests. Boys of all ages like fighting and sports games, although they also show interest in games with cars or aircraft and adventure games (see Table 6.8). Girls, on the other hand, prefer adventure games and those that involve a degree of quiet creativity, like drawing/painting or card/board/puzzle games. Boys also show an earlier interest than girls in games in which you have to plan things, although these games are by no means the ones they like best, whereas girls are more interested than boys in educational and fashion/design games.

Interests remain fairly stable for both boys and girls; however, there are some observable age trajectories in some of the less frequent choices. Interest in games where you have to plan things develops as children grow older, although it remains very much a minority interest. In general, girls, though not boys, are interested in drawing/painting games mainly up to the age of 10, but interest disappears after this age.

TABLE 6.8
Favorite Electronic Game by Age Within Gender (Percentages)

	Age 6-7		Age 9-10		Age 12-13		Age 15-16	
Boys	Fighting	29	Fighting	33	Fighting	27	Sport	27
	Adventure	24	Sport	20	Sport	25	Fighting	23
	Sport	16	Adventure	17	Adventure	17	Cars/aircraft	17
	Cars/aircraft	14	Cars/aircraft	11	Cars/aircraft	16	Adventure	15
	Teach you	6	Plan things	6	Plan things	9	Plan things	12
Girls	Adventure	35	Adventure	32	Adventure	36	Adventure	32
	Drawing	22	Drawing	16	Card/board	11	Card/board	21
	Teach you	11	Teach you	13	Fighting	10	Sport	10
	Card/board	8	Card/board	12	Drawing	9	Plan things	8
	Sport	7	Fighting	8	Sport	9	Fighting	8

Note. *At age 6-7 these figures are based on all children who play electronic games in BE-vlg, DE, ES, IS, NL, SE. At age 9-10 data are also available for GB, FI, CH. At age 12-13 an 15-16 the information is available for all countries so far mentioned and Italy.

In order to describe in the most accessible way the relation between electronic games and the gender and age of the children, we carried out another Correspondence Analysis. We obtained a two-dimensional space (Fig. 6.3, which shows 91% of the total variance) in which the tastes of boys and girls in each age group are reflected.

As in Fig. 6.1, which describes differences in interests between boys and girls of different ages, Fig. 6.3 clearly shows how tastes and preferences in video or computer games bear the stamp of the specialization and separation of the genders. Girls are situated on the left-hand side of the figure and are associated with "feminine games" such as card/board/puzzle games (15- to 16-year-olds), fashion/design, adventure and drawing/painting games (12- to 13-year-olds), and drawing/painting, adventure, and educational games (the under-12s). Boys, on the other hand, are situated on the right-hand side of the figure, where their choices show that on the whole, they are reproducing the traditional masculine roles of adult society. Those over 11 years old are associated with games in which you have to plan things, sports games, games with cars or aircraft, and fighting games. (The latter are most closely linked with 12- to 13-year-old boys.) The younger boys are associated with fighting games, sports games, and games with cars or aircraft.

CONCLUSIONS

The age and gender of the child have a crucial impact on interests and media preferences. On the other hand, the SES of the family and the geographical location of the home appear to have little influence on interests

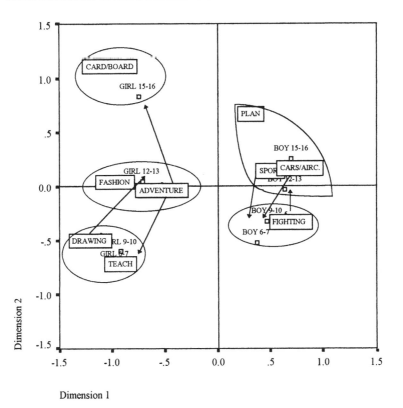

FIG. 6.3. Correspondence Analysis: favorite electronic game according to age and gender.

and preferences, although of course these do affect children and young people's access to media, especially to new media, at home. Once age and gender are taken into account, similarities in tastes among children and teenagers from different countries greatly outnumber differences. Although cross-national differences in content preferences are minor, above all it is gender that discriminates (Roe, 1998). Our findings suggest that the socialization processes responsible for the development of gender roles are remarkably consistent across Europe and that these largely account for the observed differences in media preferences (see chapter 12). In general terms, we conclude that in all countries, with only minor variations, boys are interested in sport and oriented toward action, whereas girls love music and are more interested in personalities and relationships. Girls' interests change as they grow up (from animals to music and people), but both little boys and male teenagers share a continued strong interest in sport. These gender-related interests are reflected in the television programs and electronic games children and young people particularly enjoy. Boys, when they are younger, love cartoons with their fast-action rough and tumble. Later, sports programs become their main interest. Similarly fighting or sports games are their favorite type of electronic game. Girls prefer narrative programs on television (soaps and series) and electronic games with a narrative thread (adventure/quests). Cartoons interest a substantial proportion of only the very youngest group.

Although such differences are very real, they should not be exaggerated. Among all but the youngest boys, substantial minorities enjoy narrative programs on television, and at all ages, sport is amongst the top five interests listed by girls. On the basis of such findings, it is clear that children's preferences for television programs or electronic games cannot be seen as primarily media-led. Children and young people choose programs and games that are in line with their general interests and then may be seen to follow those interests across different media.

However, children and young people choose their favorite programs and their games from the set of possibilities available to them. It also needs to be acknowledged that broadcasters and the media industry exert a powerful influence on children's choices in terms of the provision they make both in television programming and electronic game design. There is, for example, growing concern about the dominance of animation in children's programming (see Blumler & Biltereyst, 1998). Yet although there is clear evidence of the overwhelming popularity of cartoons among the youngest children, our findings show that after the age of 7, cartoons are the favorites of an ever decreasing minority of children, and although we have found that both boys and girls by the age of 9 or 10 generally prefer adult or family programs, there are some indications of an appetite among older children for series or serials aimed at their age group. The enormous popularity of national soaps among children in those countries where these are available also indicates that young people are likely to respond well to narrative programs made in their own countries and reflecting their own culture when these are provided. In view of the overwhelming importance of television in young people's lives—children around Europe spend on average over 2 hours a day watching television (see chapter 4)—a wider range of quality children's programming is surely desirable and, our research suggests, is likely to be welcomed by children as well as their parents. However, the resultant audience ratings may increasingly be insufficient on their own to justify such productions in economic terms. It is also clear that audiences for children's programs face tough competition from programs made for adult/family audiences and from other media, particularly screen media.

REFERENCES

Alonso, M., Matilla L., & Vazquez, M. (1005). *Toloniños públicos. Toloniños privados* [Tellychildren (public and private)]. Madrid: Ediciones de la Torre.

Blumler, J. G., & Biltereyst, D. (1998). *The integrity and erosion of public television for children: A pan-European survey*. Research monograph sponsored by the Center for Media Education, the Broadcasting Standards Commission, the European Institute for the Media and the EBU.

Cantor, J., & Nathanson, A. I. (1996, Fall). Children's fright reactions to television news. *Journal of Communication, 46*(4), 139–152.

Fisher, S. (1994). Identifying video game addiction in children and adolescents. *Addictive Behaviors, 19*(5), 545–553.

Funk, J. B., & Buchman, D. D. (1996, Spring). Playing violent and computer games and adolescent self concept. *Journal of Communication, 46*(2), 19–32.

García Muñoz, Nuria (1997). *Los hábitos del niño frente al televisor en el hogar* [Children's home-viewing habits]. *Journal of Communication Studies ZER, 3*, 67–81.

Huston, A. C., & Wright, J. C. (1996). Television and socialization in young children. In T. M. MacBeth (Ed.), *Tuning in to young viewers* (pp. 37–60). Thousand Oaks, CA: Sage.

Liebes, T., & Livingstone, S. (1998). European soap operas: the diversification of a genre. *European Journal of Communication, 13*(2), 147–180.

Roe, K. (1998, March). Boys will be boys and girls will be girls: changes in children's media use. *European Journal of Communication, 23*(1), 5–25.

Roe, K., & Muijs, D. (1998). Children and computer games: a profile of the heavy user. *European Journal of Communication, 13*(2), 181–200.

Sherman, S. (1996, November–December). A set of one's own: TV sets in the children's bedroom. *Journal of Advertising Research, 36*(6), RC9–RC12.

Suess, D., Suoninen, A., Garitaonandia, C., Juaristi, P., Koikkalainen, R., & Oleaga, J. A. (1998). Media use and relationships of children and teenagers with their peer groups. *European Journal of Communication, 13*(4), 521–538.

CONTEXTS OF YOUTH
AND CHILDHOOD

7

Media at Home: Domestic Interactions and Regulation

Dominique Pasquier

Media have close links with family life: There is a wealth of research evidence that, after the stage of early adoption by media "pioneers," their economic future depends on successful integration into domestic routines. Hoggart's (1957) seminal study of the working classes and mass entertainment showed how popular newspapers relate to the daily life and values of the people for whom they are produced. Frith (1983) and Moores (1988) discussed how integration of radio has gone through an evolving process of domestication, and Bausinger (1984) or Silverstone and Hirsch (1992) demonstrated the same for other information technologies. Other recent studies in telecommunications stressed the major role the telephone plays in the regulation of intergenerational relationships (Segalen, 1999) and how much its use depends on family composition and evolves with the life cycle—in particular, whether or not users are in a couple relationship (Smoreda & Licoppe, 1997). Studies with an historical focus remind us that forms of domestic integration are heavily influenced also by differential modes of appropriation in different social settings. For example, in working-class rural settings, reading books aloud during family evenings remained a collective activity long after reading had evolved into a lonely, silent practice in bourgeois settings (Chartier, 1996).

Television has been the focus of many such analyses. Spigel and Mann (1992) studied the spatial integration of television sets in middle-class American homes in the 1950s, and showed how much this disrupted existing family patterns of interaction. Other researchers noted that television viewing, at its beginning, used to be more ritualized and open to nonfamily members than it is at present (Bourdon, 1995; Levy, 1999), though, as Dayan and Katz (1992) showed, those old patterns of viewing may be reactivated for special media events. In the 1980s, the research focus shifted as researchers became more and more interested in television reception in the domestic context. Morley (1992) drew attention to how patterns of television viewing reflect and express power relations between men and women, and between parents and children. In contrast, Lull (1990) stressed television's positive influence on family members' day-to-day interactions. Such studies point to a double process: television viewing is shaped by family routines, but at the same time, it is changing them.[1] For example, British mothers interviewed in the late 1950s about the main changes produced by television agreed on the fact that it kept husbands from going out to public places and prevented children from escaping domestic surveillance (Himmelweit, Oppenheim, & Vince, 1958). In their interviews with British parents 40 years later, Livingstone and Bovill (1999) reported the same discourse about television as a safe alternative to the dangers of life outside the home. In summary, there is a considerable body of evidence to suggest that media increase the attractiveness of home as a place of leisure and reshape the social organization of family life.

Compared to television, however, little attention has been paid so far to the integration of domestic computers and television-linked games consoles into family dynamics. Most studies focus on issues outside the domestic sphere, such as access to knowledge, modes of learning, or social networking. Consequently, we lack precise research on the effect of domestic computers on existing domestic arrangements and relationships to other media. In this chapter, we seek to remedy these omissions. First we focus on differential family interactions around an old screen medium, television, compared with those around new digital technologies, such as computers or game consoles. We then examine the ways in which, as media access at home expands and attitudes to parental authority evolve, parental guidance and control of media use are being transformed.

TELEVISION AND PERSONAL COMPUTERS WITHIN FAMILY DYNAMICS

Historically, the domestic career of computers has not followed the pattern set by television. All social classes quickly acquired television sets and since its very beginning, television has been part of collective family life, integrated into intergenerational exchanges and into interactions between the

---

[1]The latter process is well exemplified in Behl's (1988) description of the transformation of domestic routines in rural Indian families.

genders. In the case of the domestic computer, we have already seen how ownership is still mostly a middle-class phenomenon in the majority of countries (see chapter 3). Moreover, interest in, and talk about computers is overwhelmingly more common among boys than among girls (see chapters 3, 4, and 12). Interestingly, our survey shows that such gender-related differences are as marked in countries where domestic computers have been widely available for several years (Northern Europe and the Netherlands) as they are in countries, such as France and the United Kingdom, where ownership of a computer is still largely the prerogative of families of high and middle socioeconomic status (SES).

We should not, therefore, think of social inequalities around computers as merely an economic problem of access. They are also the result of cultural patterns. The example of the telephone illustrates how democratization of access does not necessarily mean democratization of use. In all countries, most families now have a telephone (see chapter 3), but, as the survey shows, it is used less often by lower class children. Undoubtedly, this is in part a problem of cost, but it probably also reflects an historically inherited situation. Traditionally, blue collar male social networks were based on casual meetings in public places outside the home, whereas "bourgeois" families quickly adopted the phone as a means of organizing and controlling social relations and invitations (Goldthorpe et al., 1969). Confidence and competence with respect to computers similarly require abilities that are ultimately dependent on wider socialization processes. They are strongly linked to gender expectations and depend on cultural capital in Bourdieu's sense of the word (Bourdieu, 1979): knowledge of English and fluency in reading and writing, as well as access to a social network of other users. The majority of higher SES parents acquire these through education and professional position, but in low SES families, the lack of such skills and advantages acts as an impediment to ordinary uses of the new media.

Television

Our survey shows striking differences between the ways in which television and computers have been integrated into domestic life. Although many families now own a number of different sets that may be watched independently, television appears to remain a major focus for family interaction. When we ask which activities, media- and nonmedia-related, children most often share with their parents, watching television together is the top of the list in every country.

As seen in Table 7.1, most children also say they watch their favorite television program with other members of their family. Even in Germany, where the largest proportion of children report viewing alone, two thirds watch in the company of others, generally family members. Interestingly, although,

TABLE 7.1
"Who Do You Usually Watch Your Favorite Television Program With?": (Percentage Naming
Base: All Who Have Named Favorite Program)

	BE (vlg)	DE	DK	ES	FI	FR	GB	IL	NL*	SE
Watch alone	11	35	19	16	27	24	24	28	17	20
Watch with:										
mother	53	30	41	39	26	27	33	17	37	42
father	38	18	36	28	17	22	26	12	4	29
sister	38	23	32	24	28	34	28	31	19	30
brother	44	21	34	30	26	34	30	30	18	31
friends	19	19	42	8	21	12	6	19	3	37
others	10	2	10	9	3	4	2	5	2	10

Note. *In the Netherlands children were restricted to one of the 7 options. In all other countries, those who did not usually watch alone were allowed to name more than one other person they usually watched with.

together with music, television is the main topic of discussion with friends (see chapter 9 and Pasquier, 1996, 1999), coviewing with them is a rather unusual practice, except in Denmark and Sweden, countries where the peer culture of children is particularly well developed (see chapters 8 and 9). With the exception of Israel, mothers appear to be central characters in coviewing practices, although watching with a sibling is almost as common. Watching television with the mother appears to be more frequent among girls and older adolescents than with boys and younger children. This probably reflects the fact that coviewing has more to do with watching programs that both enjoy than with mothers monitoring their young children's television diet. It is also more usual in lower SES families, where parents themselves are likely to watch more (see Livingstone & Bovill, 1999).

Qualitative observations and interviews confirm that this incorporation of television into the routines of daily life is more complete in lower SES families. In such homes, the television set is more often switched on when children come home from school (see Livingstone & Bovill, 1999, Ch.10, p. 9), and children are more likely to do their homework and eat evening meals in front of the television (Schwartz, 1990). Families often say they have developed habits and enjoyable rituals linked to specific programs, such as watching game shows or serials before or while preparing the evening meal, gathering in the evening around series or films, or letting younger children watch Sunday morning cartoons in their parents' bed. By comparison, in high SES families, television viewing is more selective: The set is turned on for particular programs, rather than left more or less permanently switched on as it often is in low SES families. Of course, parents and children in higher SES families also chat about television and watch programs together, but parts of family life are more zealously guarded from its encroachment. In particular, such parents express the wish to share other cultural interests and activities with their children, such as playing or listening to music or reading books (Jouët & Pasquier, 1999).

Computers and Games Machines

With computers, whether used for games or other purposes, we observe a very different pattern. As seen in Table 7.2, electronic games are much more likely to be played alone; if they are played with someone else, this is almost never a parent and very seldom a sister. Thus, playing electronic games is a more solitary, male activity than watching television; it is also more peer-than family-oriented.

Other questions in the survey confirm that computers introduce a different form of sociability inside the home. For example, a large number of children say they chat sometimes about television with their mothers and fathers—from a third to two thirds do so, depending on the country. Far fewer chat about computers—one fifth on average with mothers, somewhat fewer with fathers. Interestingly, we note that chatting about television with parents is more frequent among girls than boys, as is chatting about the telephone. Conversely, boys chat more often about computers. Answers to another question—"Who knows most about computers in your family?"—confirm the gender effect. Mothers and sisters are very seldom considered as the most competent persons. We should oppose this to the much higher

TABLE 7.2
"Who Do You Usually Play Electronic Games With?": (Percentage Naming Base: All Who Play)

	BE (vlg)	DE	ES	FI	FR	GB*	IL	NL**	SE
Play alone	37	43	26	46	30	45	40	64	28
Play with:									
mother	4	5	9	1	6	3	4	2	5
father	9	9	13	3	13	7	6	3	8
sister	15	9	16	7	27	10	17	6	14
brother	27	15	31	16	54	20	28	12	28
friends	27	40	40	31	50	29	31	12	58
others	11	16	16	2	9	2	7	2	10

Note. *The British sample does not include the youngest children aged 6 to 7.
**In the Netherlands children were restricted to one of the 7 options. In all other countries, those who did not usually play alone were allowed to name more than one other person they usually played with.

degree of competence accredited to fathers. They are named by a third to a half of children as those who know most about computers in the family. Of course, using a computer requires a greater degree of focused attention than watching television, which may partly explain why fewer mothers, who generally have more household duties than fathers, use them at home. This may change with technological innovations and the development of uses that require less close attention being paid to the machine. However, so far there is little reason to believe that such developments will erase the strong differences in social patterns of interactions around television and the computer. The referent adults for television are mothers; for computers they are fathers, although fathers play this guidance role much more often in higher SES families than they do in low SES ones, as seen in Table 7.3.

Qualitative data substantiate the claim that modes of domestication of computers also differ from one social setting to the other. In lower SES families, many parents are anxious to provide access to a computer at home because of its educational potential. They are usually disappointed when they find out that children mainly use it for playing games, and that other uses can require fairly regular expenditure on new equipment. This problem can occur in high SES families, too, but usually fathers, who are more likely to use computers themselves, have the necessary expertise to encourage their children to make more diversified use of the computer. It may be claimed, therefore, that in lower SES families, computers have a high symbolic status but marginal utility. They are not integrated into collective life at home: It is very significant that, in most countries, low SES children appear to have more private access to a computer in their own bedroom and that they name themselves more often as the person most knowledgeable about

TABLE 7.3
"Who Knows Most About Computers in Your Family?" by SES (Percentage Naming)

	Self		Mother		Father		Sister		Brother	
	High	Low	High	Low	High	Low	High	Low	High	Low
BE (vlg)	28	23	9	13	29	34	5	4	16	12
CH	19	16	4	7	46	25	4	5	13	10
DE	16	13	7	23	50	33	1	3	12	8
DK	19	27	8	6	40	24	2	3	14	13
FI	23	30	7	11	45	21	2	4	17	19
FR	12	20	6	6	46	16	2	10	14	16
GB	15	31	13	10	55	22	1	7	15	21
IL	25	36	6	3	23	16	7	7	22	21
NL	9	25	11	11	66	34	2	5	8	17
SE	27	37	5	12	42	23	2	2	19	14

Note. Figures for the medium level of SES are omitted from this table.

computers in the family.[2] At home their use of computers is likely to be solitary and such skills as they acquire self-taught, and because at school they are more likely to be surrounded by other children who have little or no practice with computers, evolution toward social equality may be expected to be slow.

In view of the importance of fathers as referent adults for computer use, it is interesting to consider the case of the growing number of children living in single-parent families (90% of whom in our study live with their mothers). How does the absence of a father affect the way media are used and integrated into these children's lives? In the countries presently studied, children living with only one of their parents represent a small but significant percentage of the whole sample (14%).[3] There are, however, large differences between countries, with, at the two extremes, only 9% of children living in a single-parent family in Germany compared to 25% in Sweden.[4] Comparison with the national statistics in chapter 1, Table 1.2 suggests that single parents are therefore considerably underrepresented in our German sample and a little overrepresented in the Swedish sample. Furthermore, this group in our sample is skewed demographically in other ways. Children living with only one parent are more often girls than boys (with a 10-point difference), more often teenagers than younger children (except in Germany), and more often from lower than from higher SES families (except in Flanders). As many as four in every five children in such families are from the low SES group in the United Kingdom and Germany. Unfortunately, our sample is not large enough to allow us to separate out the effects of such different economic circumstances and demographic profiles. We must therefore note that our findings should be approached with caution, as any observed differences between children living in single-parent and two-parent families may be influenced by gender, age, or SES differences, rather than absence of a father per se.

First, some differences appear concerning the availability of equipment. On the one hand, children in single-parent families are less likely to have access to a computer at home (50% vs. 62%). On the other, when they do have a computer at home, it is more likely to be located in their own bedroom (see Table 7.4). We already know that lower SES families in general are less likely to have a computer in the home, and we may suppose that the bedroom location is due, at least in part, to less frequent use of computers by mothers. However, it may also indicate that single mothers are particularly anxious to provide their children with the advantage of experience with

---

[2]For a discussion of privatization, individualization, and bedroom culture, see chapter 8.

[3]The question was not asked in Denmark. For more statistics about marriage, divorce, and single-parent households, see Eurostat Data in chapter 1, Table 1.3.

[4]These disparities are clearly due to different cultural and social patterns about family norms that cannot be studied here.

TABLE 7.4
Percentage of Children Who Have a Television or Computer in Their Own Room
(Base: All Children With a Television or Computer Somewhere in the Home)

	TV Set in Bedroom		PC in Bedroom	
	Single-Parent	Two-Parent	Single-Parent	Two-Parent
BE (vlg)	34	24	20	19
CH	23	13	34	25
DE	38	41	50	37
ES	36	28	43	33
FI	38	38	54	32
GB	64	64	31	11
IL	43	35	60	44
SE	50	47	43	31

computers. We do not notice such a consistent difference concerning television sets in the bedroom, although here, too, children from single-parent families, considering their financial disadvantage, are better equipped than we might have expected.

When it comes to time spent using different media, the data do not indicate that children in single-parent families differ from those living with both parents. Although they do spend less time reading books, this is probably due to lower SES rather than to family composition. However, if we investigate the family context of media use, several differences appear. First, unsurprisingly, there is a very unequal balance between fathers' and mothers' role in media life at home. Compared with children living with both parents, children from single-parent families are much less likely to watch their favorite television program or play electronic games with their fathers; they are also less likely ever to chat with their fathers about different media. Some of these children may not see their father any more, and in all cases fathers are not a daily presence in their lives, which explains these large differences. However, we may also make the hypothesis that time spent with fathers during holidays or weekends is less oriented than everyday life toward consumption or discussion of media (for example, outside activities or visits to the father's family or friends may be more frequent). Clearly, when media are not framed in the day-to-day life of children, they appear to be less central in relationships with family members.

In the younger age band (ages 6 to 7), the lack of links with father as a media interlocutor or co-user is associated with more frequent watching of the favorite television program alone. In the two older age bands, the absence of fathers is linked with watching more often with friends. Interestingly, in most countries, for children living in single-parent families, friends appear to be more significant companions for playing electronic games and for watching television than siblings. This is probably a consequence of single-parent families seldom being large families, but it is also possible that mothers compensate for a reduced family by being more tolerant to peer sociality at home.

Judgments about computer literacy among family members also show interesting differences. Single parents' children far less frequently designate their father as the most competent person in the family, and more often think that their mothers or themselves are the ones who know most. In some countries the gap is very large: In Germany, for example, 30% of children in single-parent families name their mother as the one who knows most about computers and only 9% name their father. In families where children live with both parents, only 10% name mothers whereas 44% name fathers. This shows that the absence of the father affects not only the possibility of shared use, which is obvious, but also the image of fathers and of males in general as referent persons for computer use.

This brief look into single-parent families shows that on several points—access to media and amount of use—similarities with two-parent families are more striking than differences. However, the trends we noted when every-day domestic experience with media is not routinely linked to interaction with fathers and the adult male world suggest that further investigation of the differences due to family composition would be very interesting. Future research should deal with samples large enough to reflect a diversity of family situations (single mothers, divorced mothers, recomposed families), and a range of cultural and financial backgrounds (educational level of parents and economic status of the family) in order to tease out how relationships to media differ when they are not embedded within daily patterns of interaction with a parent of each gender.

CHANGING PATTERNS OF PARENTAL AUTHORITY

Part of the interaction in the family about media deals with rules and restrictions, laid down mainly by parents and sometimes by older siblings (see Pasquier et al., 1998). In our international survey, children were asked if their mother or father sometimes said they could or could not use a medium.[5] Tables 7.5 and 7.6 show two major trends, common to all countries:

---

[5]Answers to these questions confirm that, from the child's perspective, parental control of the use of computers at home is comparatively weak. Other studies that compare parents and children's evaluations in the same families have shown that children report less control than parents do (Livingstone & Bovill, 1999; Australian Broadcasting Authority, 1994; Buckingham, 1996). However, our study focuses on comparisons among different media, which should be unaffected by this tendency.

TABLE 7.5
"Does Your Mother Sometimes Say When You Can or Can't Do the Following Things?"
Percentage Agreement (Base: All With Medium Somewhere in Home)

	BE (vlg)	CH	DE	ES	FI	GB	IL	SE
Watch television/videos	67	44	43	59	35	39	41	30
Make a phone call	33	35	29	51	29	54	33	24
Use/play on a PC	39	27	16	46	19	33	29	15
Listen to music	24	11	5	39	3	18	21	11
Read books (not for school)	9	6	6	36	2	7	14	7
None of these	NA	18	22	12	40	12	28	37

TABLE 7.6
"Does Your Father Sometimes Say When You Can or Can't Do the Following Things?"
Percentage Agreement (Base: All With Medium Somewhere in Home)

	BE (vlg)	CH	DE	ES	FI	GB	IL	SE
Watch television/videos	56	37	30	53	26	33	34	25
Make a phone call	20	26	16	43	21	44	27	19
Use/play on a PC	26	30	25	45	15	31	25	15
Listen to music	16	9	3	34	4	14	21	11
Read books (not for school)	8	5	3	31	1	7	10	6
None of these	NA	20	35	17	57	23	32	45

- Television and the telephone are the media most likely to be controlled by both parents and in almost all countries. Control of the use of computers appears to be much weaker.
- Mothers usually control media use more than fathers, *except* for computer use.

Control of media use is also linked, at least in part, to amount of use as well as the social desirability of the activity. Thus boys, who spend more time with and are more interested in computers, appear to be somewhat more likely than girls to be told when they can and cannot use them. Similarly, girls are more likely than boys to be told when they can use the telephone. There is, on the other hand, no major gender difference when it comes to the most common media activities, such as watching television or listening to music, and none with respect to reading books, which the vast majority of parents wish to encourage. The main impact of age is that control decreases as the child grows up. The youngest age group is the most restricted. SES has different effects depending on the medium and the country. In the majority of countries, but not in all, parents in high SES families are more likely than those in low SES families to control television viewing. This is particularly likely to be the case in the United Kingdom, France, Switzerland, and Finland. British mothers, if they come from high SES families, also appear to control the use of computers much more than those from low SES backgrounds. Telephone use by children, on the other hand, is more likely to be controlled in lower SES families in several countries, especially in Finland, the United Kingdom, and Israel.

Qualitative data gathered in different countries give us more insight into forms of media control. The topic was easy to discuss in interviews with both parents and children. Talking about media rules is a way of talking about the role and importance media have within the home. It involves moral judgments both about media and about family life, and so it is also a discourse about ideals. Media rules are both a good illustration of the larger stakes that underlie interactions around media, and an expression of day-to-day oppositions, conflicts, or alliances among the different members of the family unit.

Public debate and press campaigns usually focus on control regarding content, that is, restrictions put on programs judged too violent or too sexually explicit. This concern was voiced in interviews with parents, but very often emerges as a "third person perception." In other words, parents acknowledge the problem of violence or sex in television programs or electronic games but think this is more likely to affect other children rather than their own. The topic of unsuitable programs is therefore high on the public agenda, but not so visible at the level of the family. In everyday life at home, control of unsuitable contents is usually seen as a problem only with younger children, mostly under 10 (Livingstone & Bovill, 1999). The main focus of daily conflict around media is more on the amount of television viewing or computer game playing, and interference with other activities like sleep or homework, rather than on the content of specific programs. Media rules at home are, therefore, usually concerned with competition for use of the best television set, disputes (often between siblings) about the choice of what to watch, or the competing claims of homework or housework over media use.

We propose several hypotheses about the reasons underlying this trend toward a more lax control of media use. First, the drastic increase in the number of channels due to digital technology makes it very difficult to control (or even know about) all contents. This drives many parents to adopt a selective attitude to content control. They do not try to check every program, but may ban specific programs that have been the focus of press campaigns labeling them as violent or vulgar (see Maigret, 1999, for a discussion of Japanese Mangas and Pasquier, 1999, for series). Second, the parents we interviewed belong to a generation born with television. They are aware that watching some violent programs in their own childhood did not lead them to be especially violent themselves. For them, contrary to their own parents, television is a taken-for-granted domestic technology (see Bertrand, 1999). Last, but not least, this greater lenience in controlling content is probably an expression, among other things, of changing patterns of parental authority. As sociologists of the family point out, nowadays children's duty is less to obey than to succeed at school, and decisions in families have been democratized toward cooperation between parents and children. This last trend would certainly help to explain why parental control of media has moved from restricting access to unsuitable content toward limiting time taken away from activities that might improve school performance, like homework and sleep. It might also explain why there are fewer restrictions on computers (and on books, of course) compared to television. For all parents, the former are media that provide competencies needed at school and in later professional life.

Is control efficient? Apparently not. Children who say their use of television and telephone is controlled are as likely as other children to be heavy users of both media. Of course, their media access may be controlled *because* they are heavy users and we cannot, therefore, conclude that control does not work. However, in the qualitative phase of the study, interviews with parents reflect the feeling that control is more and more difficult to impose. A Swedish mother confesses that because she does not trust her children to do their homework instead of watching television when she is still at work, she puts the television cable in her purse when she leaves in the morning, only to discover that her children have borrowed a cable from the neighbors and the set is still hot when she gets home! A British mother tells us she locks the television set in a closet to make sure it will not be overused while she is away from home. Other parents report hiding games machine controls in a different place every day. Most parents have stories to tell about children finding new ways of escaping restrictions: rewinding a video tape to watch it twice, pretending to read a book in bed with a small radio hidden under the sheets, switching television channels when parents pop into their bedrooms, using a borrowed remote control when their own has been confiscated, etc. This day-to-day struggle with rules leads some parents to refuse any purchase of a game console, or of a second television set. These are not likely to be located in the main room and will therefore be harder to control.

Interviews with children about parental control give other insights. First, we discovered that children are very familiar with their parents' arguments about the necessity of controlling media use, which they can repeat verbatim. They may say that "watching too much television is bad for your eyes," that "it is more interesting to read than to play electronic games," or that "violent movies can give you nightmares." Girls are particularly likely to express the adults' point of view. Yet in general, children's actual behavior is very far from being in line with such beliefs. Children know how their parents want them to behave with media at home, and they know it very early. In the French study, some 6-year-olds are perfectly able to explain what they are allowed to watch or do, at which times, for how long, and even in which room of the house. Of course, they also tell us they are very good at not following those rules, or at least trying not to follow them. Breaking media rules is one of the favorite sports, especially of younger children. If parents' discourse about media rules is a discourse about education, children's discourse about media rules is a discourse about autonomy. The stakes are clear: Doing forbidden things, or not following the rules exactly, is a way of showing that you are grown up. From the children's point of view, rules are for younger kids, not for themselves. So just as with parents, children think that media's harmful effects apply to others, not themselves ("Of course my younger sister should not watch it, it would scare her," explains an 8-year-old fan of Batman cartoons). In the interviews, children happily describe strategies they themselves have developed to avoid parental control. Many have already watched television programs they are not supposed to have watched, peeping through a half-closed door, or when parents were away. They tell how they succeed in avoiding bedtime restrictions by negotiating with their father for an extra half-hour to watch the end of a program, when they know their mother would not agree. Children are very good at exploiting any disagreement between their parents about the rules: They know which parent is the stricter (usually the mother, as our data show) and negotiate with the other one. Others have even said that they go to watch disapproved programs at their grandparents' home. The game with media rules, for a child, is a way of learning more about the adult world, and the backstage of parents' roles.

Thus, it seems evident that traditional forms of media control have been weakened in most families. This is in part due to the fact that the parents of the children we surveyed were born into media-rich homes and as a result are not prone to many of the anxieties felt by earlier generations of parents. Television, hi-fi, and the telephone were an integral part of their own childhood and they have learned to live with them. Of course, they may still use television as a reward or a punishment, as it was used in the 1950s (Himmelweit, Oppenheim, & Vince, 1958), but more often it is a shared conversational resource. As far as parental control is concerned, talking to children about television appears to be a more important form of guidance than imposing restrictions on viewing (Livingstone & Bovill, 1999). In most families, the problem is now less about control than about finding a balance between other duties and media, and about protecting family members' need for privacy—not a simple task in an ever-growing domestic media environment.

DISCUSSION

Our survey points to major changes in family interactions around media. Meyrowitz (1985) showed how electronic media have undermined parents' authority over children. Radio and television to an even larger extent challenge adults' abilities to control children's progression to knowledge. With television, home is no longer a place where parents may prevent children from knowing too much about the adult world. Our findings suggest that new media weaken the traditional power relations between parents and children even further. Paradoxically, learning to use new media puts parents at the greater disadvantage. Children encountered digital innovations before their parents, reversing traditional status hierarchy. Moreover, they have developed a routine attitude to these media that the previous generation is unable to have. For children, computers are fun; for parents they are socially important. This is a major divergence, resulting in fundamental differences in attitudes toward new media. Of course, the situation we observe today is at a transitional stage: Most of the next generation of parents will be computer literate. Moreover, the expansion of the Internet may lead to more diversified use of the computer at home, which will attract both parents and children.

However, we should be aware that gender differences with respect to the new media appear to be strongly entrenched and that this may result in fathers playing a more active role than they have done in the past with respect to media in the home. Since the introduction of domestic media, mothers have played the more important part in connecting them to family culture and history. Research on the telephone shows that once in a couple relationship, men usually delegate to their wives the charge of maintaining wider family links by telephone, even with their own mothers (Segalen, 1999; Smoreda & Licoppe, 1997). Similarly, men take photographs, but women take care of photograph albums. Our survey showed the major role mothers play in discussions with children about television, books, and music. However, computers and games machines appear to escape the traditional mediation of the mother between media and family life. They encourage interactions that are rarely intergenerational and, when they are, they are mostly linked to the father. As such, their introduction into the home may provoke an interesting rebalancing of family dynamics, giving a more active part to the fathers in media guidance at home. However, we should acknowledge that these new links with fathers are strongly gender-segregated, and sons benefit much more often from them than daughters do. Television was a medium that operated gender segregation mainly through the types of programs watched (Morley, 1986). Family members of both genders view, but mothers and daughters gather more around serials, whereas fathers and sons do so around sport or action programming. With new media, the segregation does not operate through content as much as it operates through access. Fathers, especially in high SES families, know more about and use computers more often than mothers do. The discrepancy is less important between brothers and sisters, but is still significant. In the feminine domestic sphere, television and the telephone still play the major part. In the masculine domestic sphere, electronic games and computers serve more and more as markers of gender identity: In many families (especially lower SES ones), they are specifically male territory. As Drotner (1999) warned, women are becoming the janitors of media of the past. With this in mind, the situation of children living with their mother only becomes of considerable interest. As we saw, those children tend not to develop links with their father about media, nor do they perceive fathers as knowing most in the family about computers. This is likely to have interesting repercussions for their future socialization to new media. Lacking a male role model, are children necessarily disadvantaged, or does this situation hold some advantages for girls in particular? More research is needed to discover which of these alternative scenarios is likely to be the more influential.

The second major trend we observe is the reconfiguration of the balance between family and peer relationships around media, a trend clearly linked to the previous one. Television appears to be a major focus for family patterns of interaction: It is often watched and talked about with other family members. On the other hand, computers and games machines are commonly used in a number of different locations. The majority of children have used the Internet outside the home, they often go to play electronic games in their friends' houses, and they use computers at school. Digital media are thus much more often connected to peer relations than they are to family life. Most parents' lack of skills is certainly one reason why this occurs: They cannot usually give the necessary help to improve performance with computers. Again, girls appear to be the main losers in this new configuration. Social cooperative networks around digital media are largely male, and it is hard for girls to enter them, which explains why they play electronic games much less often with friends than boys do. Besides playing with their brothers—who are often reluctant to do so—they have few possible partners whether at home or outside. Like their mothers, daughters stick to more traditional media, based either on interpersonal relations, like the telephone, or linked to emotional intensity, like listening to music or reading novels. American feminists consider this situation to be prejudicial to girls' future opportunities in the labor market (Cassel & Jenkins, 1998). Others are less pessimistic. First, as Drotner (1999) reminded us, female resistance to computers is due more to a lack of interest in electronic games than to reluctance to use the computer per se, and the development of the Internet may reduce gender differences in the future. Moreover, there is no proof that interpersonal communicative skills, a particularly feminine competence, will be less important in social life in the future than technical competence with machines. We are probably heading toward more gender-segregated domestic media uses, but the advantages of being on one side or on the other are not clear.

It does, however, seem proven that if media in the past led to more time being spent at home and more interaction occurring between family members, the new computer-based technologies are nowadays operating the reverse process. They are fostering new forms of peer sociability within the home that may have an effect on media regulation by parents and on collective uses within the family. New patterns of interaction within the family, with more distinct territories marked according to gender and to age, seem likely to emerge. It will be a task for future research to analyze in detail how such changes affect family life and media use.

REFERENCES

Australian Broadcasting Authority (1994). *Cool or gross. Children's attitudes to violence, kissing and swearing on television* (monograph 4). Sydney: Australian Broadcasting Authority.

Bausinger, H. (1984). Media technology and everyday life. *Media Culture and Society, 6*(4), 343–351.

Behl, N. (1988). Equalizing status: Television and tradition in an Indian village. In J. Lull (Ed.), *World families watch television.* Newbury Park, CA: Sage.

Bertrand, G. (1999). Pratiques télévisuelles dans la famille et processus de décision [Decision processes in television domestic uses]. *Réseaux, n°92/93,* 315–343.

Bourdieu, P. (1979). *La distinction. Critique sociale du judgment.* [Distinction. A social critique of the judgment of taste]. Paris: Les Éditions de Minuit.

Bourdon, J. (1995). Le flash et le papier peint, mémoires de télévision [Flash or wallpaper? Television memories]. In J. P. Eskenazi (Ed.), *La télévision et ses téléspectateurs.* Paris: l'Harmattan.

Buckingham, D. (1996). *Moving images. Understanding children's emotional responses to television.* Manchester: Manchester University Press.

Cassel, J., & Jenkins, H. (1998). *From Barbie to Mortal Kombat. Gender and computer games.* Boston: MIT Press.

Chartier, R. (1996). *Culture écrite et société* [Print culture and society]. Paris: Albin Michel.

Chartier, R. (1998). *Au bord de la falaise, l'histoire entre certitudes et inquiétude* [History between certitudes and anxiety]. Paris: Albin Michel.

Dayan, D., & Katz, E. (1992). *Media events. The live broadcasting of history.* Cambridge, MA: Harvard University Press.

Drotner, K. (1999). Netsurfers and game navigators: New media and youthful leisure cultures in Denmark. *The French Journal of Communication, 7*(1), 83–108.

Frith, S. (1983). The pleasure of the hearth. In J. Donald (Ed.), *Formations of pleasure.* London: Routledge.

Goldthorpe, J., Lockwood, D., Bechhofer, F., & Platt, J. (1969). *The affluent worker in the class structure.* London: Cambridge University Press.

Himmelweit, H., Oppenheim, A. N., & Vince, P. (1958). *Television and the child: An empirical study of the effect of television on the young.* London: Oxford University Press.

Hoggart, R. (1957). *The uses of literacy. Aspects of working class life with special reference to publications and entertainment.* London: Chatto and Windus.

Jouët, J., & Pasquier, D. (1999). Youth and screen culture: National survey on 6–17 years old. *The French Journal of Communication, 7*(1), 29–58.

Levy, M. F. (Ed.). (1999). *La télévision dans la République. Les années 50* [Television in the Republic: The 1950s]. Paris: Ed. Complexe.

Livingstone, S., & Bovill, M. (1999). *Young people, new media.* An LSE Report, available from http://psych.lse.ac.uk/young_people.

Lull, J. (1990). *Inside family viewing. Ethnographic research on television's audience.* London: Routledge.

Maigret, E. (1999). Le jeu de l'âge et des générations: culture BD et esprit Manga [The plot of age and generations: Comics culture and Manga spirit]. *Réseaux, n°92/93*, 241–260.

Meyrowitz, J. (1985). *No sense of place. The impact of electronic media on social behavior.* Oxford: Oxford University Press.

Moores, S. (1988). The box on the dresser: Memories of early radio. *Media Culture and Society, 10*(1), 23–41.

Morley, D. (1986). *Family television. Cultural power and domestic leisure.* London: Comedia/Routledge.

Morley, D. (1992). *Television audiences and cultural studies.* London: Routledge.

Pasquier, D. (1996). Teen series reception: Television, adolescence and culture of feelings. *Childhood, 3*(3), 351–375.

Pasquier, D. (1999). *La culture des sentiments. L'expérience télévisuelle des adolescents* [The culture of feelings. Adolescents' television experience]. Paris: Ed de la Maison des Sciences de l'Homme.

Pasquier, D., Buzzi, C., d'Haenens, L., & Sjöberg, U. (1998). Family lifestyles and media use patterns. An analysis of domestic media among Flemish, French, Italian and Swedish children and teenagers. *European Journal of Communication, 13*(4), 503–519.

Schwartz, O. (1990). *Le monde privé des ouvriers, hommes et femmes du Nord* [Workers' private world, men and women in northern France]. Paris: PUF.

Segalen, M. (1999). Téléphone et culture familiale [Telephone and family culture]. *Réseaux n°96*, 16–44.

Silverstone, R., & Hirsch, E. (Eds.). (1992). *Consuming technologies: Media and information in domestic spaces.* London: Routledge.

Smoreda, Z., & Licoppe, C. (1997). *Effets du cycle de vie et des réseaux de sociabilité sur la téléphonie* [Life cycles' and social networks' effects on telephone uses]. Paris: Report CNET.

Spigel, L., & Mann, D. (Eds.). (1992). *Private screenings. Television and the female consumer.* Minneapolis: University of Minnesota Press.

8

Bedroom Culture
and the Privatization of Media Use

Moira Bovill
Sonia Livingstone

WHAT IS "BEDROOM CULTURE"?

In the second half of the 20th century, growing affluence, changing patterns of family interaction, reduction in family size, the emergence of youth culture, and the consumer power of the youth market have all combined to make children's bedrooms increasingly important as sites of leisure and learning. It is common nowadays for young people in Europe to have their own bedroom and for its furnishings to reflect their individual tastes and interests. Surveys in five countries in our project (CH, DE, FI, GB, IL) show that even among 6- to 7-year-olds, more than half (56%) do not have to share a bedroom. As expected, the figures are higher for older children: two thirds (69%) of 9- to 10-year-olds have their own room, and more than three quarters of 12- to 13-year-olds (77%) and 15- to 16-year-olds (82%).[1]

European children's bedrooms are, furthermore, increasingly well equipped with media (see chapter 3). Alongside the more traditional books and radios, many young people now have a television set, video recorder, TV-linked games machine, or PC in their room. To many children across Europe and North America (see Annenberg Public Policy Center, 1999), this media-rich *bedroom culture* represents a vital yet taken-for-granted aspect of their daily lives that significantly enriches the variety of leisure opportunities open

---

[1]Throughout this chapter, such figures represent the average across countries, weighting each country equally, and do not represent an average of individuals (see chapter 2).

to them. From a commercial viewpoint, these developments represent a new opportunity for targeted advertising and marketing, as the media-rich child's bedroom is both a site of reception for commercial messages and a location for the display and use of leisure goods. For their parents, therefore, there may be implications in terms of family communication and media regulation. In this chapter, we ask how bedroom culture intersects with children's and young people's media culture in general (Buckingham, 1993).

Accounts of children's use of their bedrooms focus on the bedroom as a site for the consumption and display of consumer goods or as a private social space where young people can express and experiment with a sense of personal identity. Thus, in terms of the four key theoretical concepts outlined in chapter 1, the emphasis has been on processes of *consumerism* and *individualization*. In the United Kingdom, the few early sociological accounts that draw attention to a "culture of the bedroom" point to its connections with teenage consumer culture, particularly that of girls (see Frith, 1978; McRobbie & Garber, 1976), emphasizing how teenage girls' search for personal identity through self-presentation and the development of "taste" has been led, exploited even, by powerful commercial interests in the fashion and music industries.

More recent research on bedroom culture placed increasing emphasis on the role of the media. Bjurström and Fornäs (1993) described how mediated consumer images provide the raw materials with which young people creatively construct "their" style. Similarly, studies of the domestic appropriation of media (Silverstone & Hirsch, 1992) showed how media products, like other consumer goods, are used to express individual and collective styles that, in turn, function as identity markers. Steele and Brown (1994) noted that "for many teens, the bedroom is a safe, private space in which experimentation with possible selves can be conducted"; what is notable about today's adolescents is that this safe, private space is increasingly also a media-rich space. Thus Bachmair (1991), when arguing that the bedroom is much more than a social context for media use, traced how the meanings inscribed in the arrangement of the bedroom also serve to frame and guide the interpretation of the texts transmitted by the media. The sign on the door ("Parents, keep out!"), the pop star posters on the wall, the collection of Disney mementos, and the program on the television screen combine as one fluid "text," highly individual but drawing heavily on a shared, commercialized peer culture.

Although the academic research literature remains sketchy, it suggests that across Europe the teenager's bedroom is where media and identity intersect: In this space, media technology and content are appropriated by young people to sustain and express their sense of who they are. This new leisure site raises a variety of questions for both family life and children's media use. "Bedroom culture" implies that children and young people spend significant proportions of their leisure time at home with the mass media, increasingly screen media, in their own private space rather than communal or family space. This provokes concerns about children leading increasingly isolated lives, and about parents' ability to regulate and monitor media use.[2] In raising some familiar but strongly felt fears about the privatization of children's and young people's lives, as well as more optimistic visions of opportunities for privacy and individual self-fulfillment, the notion of bedroom culture is in many ways suggestive of the new opportunities and dangers that arise under conditions of late modernity (see chapter 1). To address these issues, we take as our starting point the following simple but intriguing questions:

- How much time do children and young people spend in their bedrooms?
- How does personal ownership of media relate to time spent in the bedroom?
- Is time spent in the bedroom contributing to a pattern of social isolation?
- How does bedroom culture affect parents' media monitoring and regulation?
- In sum, what is the experience and significance of media use in the bedroom?

Our 12-nation cross-cultural project gives us a unique perspective from which to address such questions. As in previous chapters, we are interested in identifying both similarities and differences in children's and young people's leisure opportunities and experiences. On the one hand, bedroom culture appears very much a European and North American phenomenon, dependent on a high degree of modernization and wealth. This would lead us to expect cross-cultural similarities, given similar patterns of age and gender development. On the other hand, we may find differences between countries as a result of different cultural conditions or technological provision (see chapter 1). For example, we may ask where media-rich bedroom culture is more developed. Is it in the United Kingdom, because of its relatively stronger screen-oriented culture?[3] Or in Finland, Denmark, Sweden, Switzerland, and the Netherlands, ranked among the top ten in preparedness for the networked society by the World Economic Forum (1996)? Spain, Italy, and France, on the other hand, are

---

[2]For example, in a report from the American Academy of Paediatrics (*Paediatrics, 1999*), the committee chair, Miriam Baron, wrote, "Bedrooms should be a sanctuary, a place where kids can reflect on what happened that day, where they can sit down and read a book" (*The Times*, August 5, 1999).

[3]The UK emerges as screen-oriented from the present research, as shown through the comparatively small numbers of children with their own books and large numbers with their own screen media (chapter 3), as well as through the greater time spent watching television (chapter 4). By contrast, we may identify Switzerland and the Netherlands as more print-oriented cultures, where more children own books and fewer own televisions or VCRs.

cited as relatively low on all new technologies (see chapter 1) and, in terms of cultural conditions, have more traditional family relations. The Netherlands and the Nordic countries also form a distinct grouping in terms of their more egalitarian gender politics and antiauthoritarian approach to child-rearing: These conditions, too, may have implications for bedroom culture.

TIME SPENT BY EUROPEAN CHILDREN AND YOUNG PEOPLE IN THEIR BEDROOMS

How do young people in Europe divide their free time at home between their own private space and communal family space?[4] In our survey, we asked about the proportion of waking time at home that they spend in their own room. The results confirm that European children and young people spend sizable proportions of leisure time at home in their own rooms (and, perhaps surprisingly, sharing a bedroom makes little difference at any age to the proportion of time spent in it).

By the time they are 15 or 16, the majority of young people in Europe say they spend at least half of their waking time at home in their bedrooms (see Table 8.1). Young people vary in their use of the bedroom, of course, and we thus find demographic patterns that hold true across most countries. Teenagers are more likely than younger children to spend time in their own rooms and girls tend to spend a greater proportion of their time there than boys. The socioeconomic status (SES) of the family, although affecting media provision in the home (see chapter 3), makes no consistent overall difference to time spent in the bedroom.

However, there are also considerable differences across countries. Most striking is the comparatively small percentage of Dutch children of either gender, or any age, who spend half or more of their waking time in their own rooms, whereas the percentages in Germany and Flanders are among the highest. How can we account for such variation?

---

[4]Note that time spent at home outside the bedroom is not necessarily time spent with parents. For example, as the majority of Finnish mothers as well as fathers work, Finnish children spend a fair amount of time in the home alone, and so need not restrict themselves to their own rooms to secure privacy. Note also that asking about the proportion of waking time at home spent in one's own room does not tell us about the number of hours spent in the bedroom. Children in different countries spend differing proportions of their overall leisure time indoors as opposed to outdoors: thus apparently similar replies of "about half of the time," etc. may represent very different number of hours or minutes. For example, children in Nordic countries have more freedom to go out (see chapter 9), whereas a third of British parents tell us that their children spend "very little" or "none" of their free time outside the family home or garden. This is likely to mean that in absolute terms, British children spend more time in their own rooms than Finnish or Swedish children, despite indications to the contrary in Table 8.1. Moreover, the issue is further complicated by differences in school hours. In the United Kingdom and France, even the youngest children are in school until after 3 p.m., whereas children in most other countries have afternoons free.

TABLE 8.1
Percentage Claiming to Spend Half or More of Waking Time at Home in Own Room,
Age by Gender

	BE (vlg)	CH	DE	ES	FI	GB	IL	IT	NL	SE	AV
Age 6-7											
Boys	50		59	40	49	31	47		10	53	42
Girls	58	N/A	62	29	56	37	53	N/A	15	62	47
All	53		61	35	52	34	50		13	57	44
Age 9-10											
Boys	55		49	37	39	31	51		16	47	41
Girls	65	N/A	67	37	54	47	67	N/A	20	57	52
All	60		57	37	46	40	60		18	53	46
Age 12-13											
Boys	78	48	59	48	39	43	46	50	23	49	48
Girls	74	71	67	52	60	49	62	71	48	56	61
All	75	60	63	49	50	46	54	61	36	53	55
Age 15-16											
Boys	69	65	75	64	51	52	48	55	43	52	57
Girls	63	74	67	61	62	65	68	68	42	57	63
All	67	70	72	62	56	59	60	63	42	55	61

Note. bold $p < 0.001$; underline $p < 0.01$; italics $p < 0.05$.

One explanation for both the observed gender differences and cross-national variations in time spent in the bedroom focuses on the attractions of the media available in the bedroom. Hence, we expected to find increased use of the bedroom as a leisure space, together with a lessening of gender differences, in countries where bedroom culture is more screen-centered, more high-tech, and hence more boy-friendly. For although bedroom culture was identified as predominantly feminine by McRobbie and Garber (1976), these authors were writing in the 1970s when British bedrooms at least contained music and magazines, traditionally "girls'" media, but few or no screen media. However, our findings do not offer much support for the idea that new media encourage young people to retreat to their rooms. For example, British children generally spend only average amounts of time in their own rooms, despite the fact that they are particularly likely to own screen media (chapter 3). Conversely, as previously noted, German boys as well as girls spend a comparatively large proportion of leisure time in the bedroom, although they own comparatively few screen media. Furthermore, in Israel and the Nordic countries, older children are no more likely than younger ones to spend time in their own rooms, despite having more of the newest technologies (PCs with CD-ROM drive, Internet connections) as well as television sets and video recorders in their bedrooms. More generally, Table 8.1 does not show any greater gender differences in activities in those countries where there are relatively fewer media in the bedrooms. Clearly, then, there are no easy conclusions to be drawn that relate the degree of national diffusion of media to the growth of bedroom culture.

However, previous research also offers another explanation for the difference in boys' and girls' attachment to bedroom culture, and this explanation also might apply differently in different cultures. Frith (1978) located bedroom culture within gendered power relations in the home. Thus, he pointed out that girls are relatively more restricted to the home because parents exercise more control over them than boys and because they are assigned tasks in the home whereas boys generally are not. McRobbie and Garber (1976), on the other hand, following sociological accounts of American teenage culture, offered an explanation in terms of friendship styles. Teenage girls, they suggested, tend to have one best friend or a small group of close friends who can be easily accommodated in the bedroom. Boys' peer groups, by contrast, are typically larger and their culture encourages an escape from the home and family into the street or café. Does this hold true for European children today? If there are cross-national differences in the friendship styles of boys and girls, can this help to explain why girls spend more time in their bedrooms?

Several decades on, our European research largely confirms that boys are more likely than girls to spend their free time with a group of friends, whereas girls are more likely than boys to spend it with family members or one best friend (see Table 8.2).

TABLE 8.2
Who Mostly Spend Free Time With, by Gender (All Age 6-7, 9-10, 12-13, and 15-16)

	BE (vlg)	CH	DE	DK	ES	FI	FR	GB	IL	NL	SE	AV
Boys												
On my own	8	_10_	6	13	9	11	16	**6**	_12_	9	11	9
Group of friends	35	_44_	36	42	40	57	36	**44**	_43_	45	64	44
One best friend	15	_21_	29	12	_12_	16	22	**22**	_23_	27	14	19
Family	42	_25_	29	31	39	17	25	**29**	_21_	_19_	12	26
Girls												
On my own	7	_10_	5	7	5	10	13	**3**	_7_	6	10	8
Group of friends	29	_34_	27	41	39	48	26	**33**	_36_	39	58	37
One best friend	21	_25_	38	15	_14_	21	30	**27**	_28_	30	16	24
Family	43	_32_	30	36	_42_	21	30	**37**	_29_	25	16	31

Note. bold $p < 0.001$; underline $p < 0.01$; italics $p < 0.05$.

Once again, although there are noteworthy differences between countries in friendship patterns, these bear no consistent relation to differences in proportion of time spent in the bedroom. Only in the two Nordic countries do we find the expected pattern: Swedish and Finnish teenagers are overwhelmingly most likely to spend their free time with a group of friends and, as expected, they also spend a smaller proportion of their free time in their own rooms. On the other hand, German and Dutch boys are more likely than those in other countries to spend time mostly with one best friend, yet in Germany the highest percentage, and in the Netherlands the lowest, spend half or more of their waking time at home in the bedroom.[5] Similarly, in Spain and Flanders, boys as well as girls are particularly likely to spend time with the family. Yet in Flanders, above-average numbers of boys spend half or more of their leisure time at home in the bedroom, whereas in Spain relatively few do so before the age of 15.

MORE MEDIA IN THE BEDROOM, MORE TIME SPENT THERE?

The discussion so far attempts to relate patterns of time spent in the bedroom to national variations in domestic media provision. Here we examine the possibility of a direct link on an individual basis between personal media and time spent away from the family. In short, how does having more or fewer media in the bedroom relate to time spent there? Having an often costly medium in one's own room suggests some interest in it, and so one might expect young people to spend longer where it is located.

In general, there is an association between the number of media, particularly screen media, that teenagers have in their bedrooms and the proportion of time they spend there: for 12- to 13- and, especially, 15- to 16-year olds, having more media is correlated with spending more time in the bedroom.[6] Again, too, gender makes a difference. Time spent by boys and girls in their

---

[5]German and Dutch boys are more likely than those in other countries to spend time mostly with one best friend, yet in Germany the highest percentage, and in the Netherlands the lowest, spend half or more of their waking time at home in the bedroom. This may partly be due to a practical limitation. The Netherlands has the greatest population density of any country in the sample and so Dutch homes have small rooms, making them possibly less attractive as leisure locations (Eurostat Yearbook, 1997). Similarly, in Spain and Flanders, boys as well as girls are particularly likely to spend time with the family. Yet in Flanders, above-average numbers of boys spend half or more of their leisure time at home in the bedroom, whereas in Spain relatively few do so before the age of 15.

[6]This claim was tested using Spearman correlations between total number of media, total number of screen media, and proportion of time spent in the bedroom, and was significant ($p < 0.05$) in most cases. However, as our four-point measure of time spent in the bedroom is broadbrush, this association can only be seen as indicative.

own rooms is associated with different media, although television is a major attraction for both (see also chapters 3, 4, and 12). For example, among 9- to 10-year old boys, having a TV-linked games machine is most closely associated with time spent in the bedroom, whereas for older boys, the link with having their own PC with a CD-ROM drive is dominant. For girls, on the other hand, having their own television set is most closely associated with time spent in the bedroom at all ages, and having a radio at age 12 to 13 and a telephone at the age of 15 to 16 are the next most important factors.[7]

We explored this further and asked whether children and young people who have books, television, a TV-linked games machine, radio or hi-fi, or a PC in their own rooms spend more time using these media than those who have access to family-owned media only. Generally speaking, we find that in each country, those who own media personally report spending more time using them (see Table 8.3).[8]

Although some differences are comparatively small, the overall picture is unequivocal. Amongst 9- to 10-year-olds, having screen media (television, games machine, or PC) in the bedroom is associated with the greatest increase in time spent. Among older children, being able to play music in their own room makes the most difference, although having a television set remains important, particularly among those aged 12 to 13.

Once again, cultural factors seem to matter, as different media are salient in different countries. For example, in Germany and the United Kingdom, having a television in the bedroom is likely to be associated with the most sizable difference in time spent. In Germany, where ownership of a set is comparatively rare and school starts early, this is particularly the case for weekend viewing, whereas in the United Kingdom, where ownership is high and bedtimes later, average weekday viewing is most affected. In Finland and Sweden, countries that lead in diffusion of Information Technology, personal ownership of a PC is associated with particularly large increases in the amount of time spent with PCs (see Table 8.3).

Our surveys provided us with more detailed information about use in the bedroom of television and the PC in particular. For example, of those with their own television set, about one in five in all four age groups say they usually watch television in their own rooms in the morning and, among secondary school age children, about half usually watch there in the evening (see Table 8.4).

---

[7]Spearman correlations between time spent in the bedroom and personal ownership of these media, although positive and significant, are very small in all cases. The highest are correlations of 0.13 between time spent in the bedroom and owning a games machine for 9- to 10-year-old boys ($p < 0.001$) and owning a PC with a CD-ROM drive for 15- to 16-year-old boys ($p < 0.001$).

[8]The time measure used here is not minutes per day averaged over a week but minutes per day where the medium is used.

TABLE 8.3
Differences (+ or –) in Minutes Use per Day if Have Medium in Bedroom

	CH	DE	ES	FI	GB	IL	IT	NL	SE
Age 9-10									
Television	**+26**	**+30**	-7	+26	+27	+8		**+28**	+18
on weekdays	+27	+24	-15	+25	+36	+8		+31	+18
at weekends	+25	+45	+12	+30	+3	+7	**n.a.**	+22	+18
Games machine	n.a.	+12	**+60**	n.a.	+1	+25		+12	**+30**
PC	+24	+6	+4	**+56**	+11	**+48**		+8	+17
Music	+13	+29	n.a.	+39	+14	+4		n.a.	n.a.
Books	+11	+8	n.a.	+23	+12	-37		+2	+11
Age 12-13									
Television	**+25**	+27	**+23**	+6	**+39**	+21	+10	**+22**	+29
on weekdays	+23	+30	+25	+7	+44	+23	+8	+29	+30
at weekends	+30	+21	+18	+5	+25	+17	+16	+3	+27
Games machine	n.a.	**+33**	+17	n.a.	+15	+13	+1	-5	+10
PC	+18	+23	+1	+34	+5	+22	+40	+10	**+52**
Music	+20	+4	n.a.	**+56**	+42	**+54**	**+47**	n.a.	n.a.
Books	+12	+12	n.a.	+32	+7	+40	n.a.	+17	+28
Age 15-16									
Television	+53	**+44**	+15	+12	+39	+20	+26	+10	+14
on weekdays	+62	+49	+19	+13	+39	+21	+31	+7	+18
at weekends	+30	+33	+6	+11	+38	+19	+12	+18	+3
Games machine	n.a.	+13	+9	n.a.	+32	+35	+6	+12	+18
PC	+12	+30	**+24**	+37	+8	+23	+34	+12	**+34**
Music	**+95**	+27	n.a.	**+86**	**+88**	**+59**	**+48**	n.a.	n.a.
Books	+32	+23	n.a.	+33	+21	+22	n.a.	**+42**	+36

Note. Figures in bold indicate the largest differences, by age band for each country.

Among children (6 to 7 and 9 to 10), fewer than one in five watch television in their bedroom in the morning and a third do so when they get home from school. Over a quarter of 6- to 7-year-olds watch there in the early evening, as do nearly two in five 9- to 10-year-olds. Similarly, only one in eight 6- to 7-year-olds and nearly a quarter of 9- to 10-year-olds watch in television in their own rooms after 9:00 in the evening.

However, there is considerable variation across countries, consistent with the picture in Table 8.1. Dutch children who have their own sets generally show least interest in watching them, whereas Israeli children are particularly likely to make use of them after they come home from school and late into the evening: Three quarters of Israeli secondary school children with their own set say they usually watch it after 9:00 in the evening.

TABLE 8.4
Percentage of Those With TV in Own Room Usually Watching There at Different Times of Day

	BE (vlg)	DE	ES	FI	GB	NL	IL	IT	SE	AV
Age 12-13										
Before school	9	10	21	14	15	21	22	16	16	16
When get home	30	35	49	35	32	12	67	56	34	39
Early evening	55	46	39	52	39	37	78	58	55	51
After 9 pm	46	20	56	58	32	20	76	66	51	47
Age 15-16										
Before school	3	11	9	15	13	14	22	9	14	14
When get home	22	30	44	33	36	17	52	56	30	36
Early evening	38	45	30	38	41	27	57	44	40	40
After 9 pm	51	49	63	63	52	34	76	72	65	58

Note. These data are for teenagers only as in most countries too few children have their own set.

Our data show particularly interesting trends in children's and young people's use of the PC in the bedroom. Contrary to what we might expect, having one's own PC, compared with having access to one elsewhere in the home, is generally associated with more "serious" computing activities and does not seem to encourage greater games use. In Israel, for example, 9- to 10-year-olds with their own PC, compared with those with access to a PC elsewhere at home, spend half or more of their time with the PC doing homework (43%, compared with 17%). In Spain, 15- to 16-year-olds with their own PC are more likely (48% compared with 32% of those without their own PC) to use it for looking up information on CD-ROMs. In Sweden, such children are more likely to use their PC for looking up information on CD-ROMs (42% compared with 24%), programming (28% compared with 9%) and e-mail (26% compared with 14%).

We conclude that across Europe, having a media-rich bedroom is associated with greater use of the bedroom. Whether a media-rich bedroom actually encourages children and young people to spend more time there, or whether those inclined to spend time alone also tend to acquire more media goods, is a question we cannot resolve without a longitudinal study. However, we also see that, for boys and girls at different ages, different media attract. For boys, computer-related technologies are more important; as girls grow older their interest in communication, music, and narrative helps to explain why ownership of the telephone, radio, and television emerge as predictors of time spent in their bedroom.

ARE MEDIA CONTRIBUTING TO A PATTERN
OF SOCIAL ISOLATION FOR CHILDREN?

There is a negative association between spending time in the bedroom and spending free time with family and a positive association with mostly spending free time alone. Although this might seem to support the notion that the media-rich bedroom encourages social isolation, as is commonly feared by parents and by the media themselves, there are difficulties in drawing causal conclusions from these correlations. Clearly, there are many factors operating within families that lead some children to prefer spending time in company, whereas others choose more solitary occupations, and spending time in either living room or bedroom represents the most obvious way to manage such preferences. Although in our project we sought to investigate some of these factors, we found, perhaps unsurprisingly, that they are not readily amenable to investigation through a survey. However, our more qualitative work certainly leads us to question the negative connotations of leisure time spent "alone," as often implied by the moral panics that surround the changing media environment (Buckingham, 1993).

Here then, we explore the social contexts of media use while remaining neutral about the value of being either alone or with others (see also chapter 7). Putting to one side the intractable question of causality, we focus here on the social context in which children and young people watch their favorite television program or play computer games, as for both of these activities there is often an element of choice, and our qualitative work suggests such choices are particularly exercised for favorite programs and game playing.

The survey findings show that, overall, those with a television set in the bedroom are more likely to watch their favorite program alone; this is particularly the case for teenagers (see Table 8.5). By contrast, although it is generally much more common to play computer games alone than it is to watch a favorite television program alone (see chapter 7), having one's own games machine or PC makes comparatively little difference to the social contexts of use. In fact, for the two older age groups, in some countries the tendency is for children to be less likely to play alone if they have their own PC or games machine.

However, the most striking finding is the difference between countries in the numbers of children and young people watching television or playing computer games alone, regardless of media in the bedroom. In Spain, having their own television makes little difference to children's behavior and fewer than one in five at any age watch alone. In Germany, on the other hand, two in every five of those who have their own set watch their favorite program alone at the age of 9 or 10 and this figure rises to almost half at the age when television viewing is most popular, 12 to 13. Because rather more German than Spanish children have their own televisions (see chapter 3, Table 3.1) it may be that

TABLE 8.5
Percentage of Children and Young People Watching Favorite Television Program and Playing
Computer Games Alone, by Whether or Not Have Medium in Bedroom

	BE (vlg)	DE	ES	FI	GB	IL	IT	NL	SE
Age 6-7									
Watching fav. prog. alone if have . . .									
TV set in bedroom	29	25	18	27	25	42		n/a	26
no TV set in bedroom	13	34	20	20	18	34			28
Playing alone if have . . .							n/a		
PC or games machine in bedroom	29	41	23	55	n/a	54		64	60
no PC or games machine in bedroom	39	31	16	39		42		62	47
Age 9-10									
Watching fav. prog. alone if have . . .									
TV set in bedroom	18	40	17	28	18	31		n/a	15
no TV set in bedroom	8	24	15	14	5	22			9
Playing alone if have . . .							n/a		
PC or games machine in bedroom	27	44	37	48	49	47		63	20
no PC or games machine in bedroom	41	38	26	45	45	38		59	23
Age 12-13									
Watching fav. prog. alone if have . . .									
TV set in bedroom	**23**	48	18	39	31	29	n/a	n/a	28
no TV set in bedroom	**6**	35	14	22	16	21			13
Playing alone if have . . .									
PC or games machine in bedroom	**18**	39	25	45	46	41	63	65	19
no PC or games machine in bedroom	**41**	44	21	50	41	33	61	63	26
Age 15-16									
Watching fav. prog. alone if have . . .									
TV set in bedroom	**17**	43	17	42	38	36	n/a	n/a	25
no TV set in bedroom	**8**	26	13	28	18	20			20
Playing alone if have . . .									
PC or games machine in bedroom	41	52	24	51	48	41	56	67	23
no PC or games machine in bedroom	37	46	33	48	40	36	61	71	32

Note. bold *p* < 0.001; underline *p* < 0.01; italics *p* < 0.05.

media ownership per se leads to a more established culture of solitary view-ing. However, fewer Spanish than German children play computer games alone, even though many more Spanish children compared with German chil-dren have their own TV-linked games machines and just as many have their own PCs (see chapter 3, Table 3.6 and Table 3.7). This suggests that wider cul-tural factors lead family life in Spain to remain largely communal, whereas in

Germany the individualization processes associated with late modernity are further advanced and "living together separately" (Flichy, 1995) is becoming a more common occurrence (see chapter 1). Similarly, at 12 to 13 almost two thirds of Italian and Dutch children who have their own TV-linked games machine (60% and 64% respectively) usually play alone. In Sweden fewer than one in five play alone. Yet far more Swedish children have their own TV-linked games machine (see chapter 3, Table 3.6). Because computer games are most often played with siblings or friends (see chapter 7), we speculate that the low incidence of playing (and indeed watching) alone in Sweden can be related to larger family size (see chapter 1, Table 1.2) and the high proportion of children spending most of their time in friendship groups (see Table 8.2). Conversely, the fact that so many Italian children play alone may be partially explicable in terms of the low birthrates in that country. Such findings suggest that, although having media in the bedroom is likely to encourage young people to spend time alone with media, demographic factors and social practices rooted in the culture of the country are at least as important.

However, having media in the bedroom may affect the social context of media use in other ways. Particularly, given that the living room generally remains a communal space for the family, a media-rich bedroom opens up a new space in which to share media not with family but with friends. Thus we may ask whether having screen media in one's own bedroom influences children's choice of viewing companion or game-playing partner. In some of the countries surveyed (FI, BE-vlg, DE, IL, SE, GB), those children who said they usually watched television or played computer games with someone else were asked with whom they usually used these media. The findings suggest that, at least for teenagers, media in the bedroom may be encouraging social contacts outside the family circle, rather than encouraging them to spend more time alone. Overall, 12- to 13- and 15- to 16-year-olds are more likely to watch television and play computer games with friends if they have their own television or TV-linked games machine or PC.[9] There is no comparable effect for younger children, however, who presumably have less control over invitations to friends and are more likely to share a bedroom with younger siblings.

DOES TIME SPENT IN THE BEDROOM REDUCE PARENTAL INVOLVEMENT IN MEDIA REGULATION?

Qualitative interviews in different countries identified similar parental concerns about children's media use. Television is seen as taking up valuable time that could be spent more profitably on other activities (see chapter 7).

---

[9]80% of 15- to 16-year-olds with their own PC or TV-linked games machine usually play games with a friend, compared with only 62 % of those who share access to such media ($p < 0.001$). Similarly, 49% of 15- to 16-year-olds with a television set in their own room watch with friends, compared with only 36% of those who watch on a communal set ($p < 0.001$).

There are also concerns about the violent and possibly addictive nature of computer games, as well as worries about the Internet and the child's access to pornography and other unsuitable materials. The growth in media-rich bedrooms fuels these fears by making domestic regulation of media more difficult in practical terms.

In the United Kingdom, twice as many parents (35% compared with 17%) think it a bad thing for a child to have a television set in his or her bedroom as consider it a good thing (Livingstone & Bovill, 1999). Views are even more negative in Germany (Krotz, Hasebrink, Lindemann, Reimann, & Rischkau, 1999). In general, the younger the child and the higher the social grade of the family, the more negative are parents' reactions. However, personal owner-ship by children of media may also be seen in terms of the positive aims par-ents have for their children, namely encouraging their autonomy as well as offering benefits for parents themselves in terms of privacy and choice: thus, even disapproving parents consent.[10]

Our qualitative work suggests that, in practice, few families apply rules about media strictly, especially for teenagers (see chapter 7). The reasons are numerous. Television in particular is so well integrated into family life that it appears less a matter of rules and more one of family habits. Busy par-ents often lack the energy to insist on rules. As the Israeli qualitative work shows, parents are physically and emotionally exhausted and often go to bed before their children. Among those aged 12 or older, children often report viewing television late into the night without parents' awareness or supervision (Lemish, personal communication, 1999). Also typical are the findings from the United Kingdom that although expressing reservations about the effects of media on children in general, parents are often less con-cerned for their own child, whom they trust to have enough common sense not to be unduly influenced. In general, our impression is that family rules about media use are fairly relaxed, and are typically less salient to children than they are to their parents. For example, one middle-class British father claimed confidently, "We censor television. We draw the line usually at the 9 o'clock watershed," while in another room talking to another interviewer, his sons (aged 13 and 10) painted a very different picture regarding the use of their own television set:

Int: Do they have lots of rules that you go along with or do they not have
       rules?

M: No, not really rules.

Int: Rules about what time you have got to go to bed?

S: Yes, well.

---

[10]In the UK 20% of parents who think it a bad thing nevertheless provide their child with their own set (Livingstone & Bovill, 1999).

M: They tell us to go up at about 9.30 or 10 or something, and then we just watch TV until they come up and tell us to switch it off.

S: They shout at you and tell you to turn it off.

Int: When do they tell you to do that?

M: At about 11, 11.30.

This excerpt illustrates what has been termed *restrictive mediation* of television by parents (Bybee, Robinson, & Turow, 1982; van der Voort, Nikken, & Vooijs, 1992), in contrast to more positive mediation, most notably conversational guidance during or after viewing. To explore children's perceptions of these strategies more systematically, in our survey we asked them whether their parents told them when they could or could not use certain media (restrictive mediation) or chatted with them about these media (conversational guidance). In general, we find that most mediation strategies are practiced more by mothers than fathers (see chapter 7). For television, parents are more likely to use restrictive strategies to control when younger children may watch, but in most countries they are just as likely to talk to older children as younger ones about their viewing. Both restrictions and positive mediation are considerably less common for the PC than for television in all countries. However, does having media in the bedroom make a difference? Are parents less likely to regulate television viewing and/or use of the PC if the child has a television set or a PC of his or her own?

We find that in the case of younger children, parental mediation is largely unaffected by the location of the media. In most countries, parents of younger children are just as likely to control access to television and the PC and to talk about them if their children have these media in their own rooms, as opposed to having access only elsewhere in the home. It appears that at this age children are still keen to spend time with their families, and bedroom culture is less established. As we saw (see Table 8.5), only in the United Kingdom do we find a slightly larger proportion of younger children watching alone if they have their own set.

However, for older children, location does matter, though this depends on the medium (see Table 8.6).

Access to television, according to children over the age of 11, is more controlled if located in a communal rather than a private space. Teenagers who have their own set are significantly less likely to say that their parents tell them when they can or cannot watch (in CH, DE, FI, SE, GB). Family chat about television is less affected, but where there is a difference (in DE, GB, and IL), parents are more likely to talk if children do not have the opportunity to watch in their own rooms. The pattern is very different for the PC. Here among teenagers it is more common to be told when they can or cannot use the PC (for games or other more serious purposes) if they do have their own com-

TABLE 8.6
Percentage of Parents Who Say When Children Can or Can't Watch, and Who Chat About
Television/Videos or Use the PC (for Games or Other Uses), by Whether or Not Child has Medium
in Bedroom (Base: all aged 12-13 and 15-16)

	BE (vlg)	CH	DE	ES	FI	GB	IL	SE
Television/Videos								
Mother says when can/can't watch								
TV in bedroom	61	**12**	<u>22</u>	52	<u>13</u>	27	33	<u>19</u>
TV elsewhere only	59	**40**	<u>33</u>	52	<u>28</u>	44	25	<u>29</u>
Father says when can/can't watch								
TV in bedroom	44	**8**	<u>15</u>	44	7	25	27	18
TV elsewhere only	50	**34**	<u>28</u>	49	*15*	40	21	21
Mother chats about watching								
TV in bedroom	93	41	<u>57</u>	45	66	47	27	35
TV elsewhere only	89	44	<u>72</u>	38	60	58	*39*	37
Father chats about watching								
TV in bedroom	75	35	48	40	52	37	23	34
TV elsewhere only	73	41	55	40	49	46	27	29
PC (for games or other use)								
Mother says when can/can't use PC								
PC in bedroom	46	13	11	**49**	*16*	21	<u>25</u>	*15*
PC elsewhere only	35	20	13	**26**	*9*	25	<u>12</u>	*9*
Father says when can/can't use PC								
PC in bedroom	*34*	**7**	12	**46**	11	17	18	<u>16</u>
PC elsewhere only	*21*	**22**	14	**27**	6	23	15	<u>9</u>
Mother chats about using PC								
PC in bedroom	*53*	<u>30</u>	36	*26*	37	29	26	*23*
PC elsewhere only	*40*	<u>17</u>	28	*18*	17	*16*	16	*16*
Father chats about using PC								
PC in bedroom	<u>61</u>	**44**	34	*33*	45	35	30	<u>35</u>
PC elsewhere only	<u>43</u>	**26**	26	*23*	27	36	20	<u>24</u>

Note. bold $p < 0.001$; underline $p < 0.01$; italics $p < 0.05$.

puter (in ES, FI, IL, and SE).[11] Control over access is highest in Spain, where
media regulation of all types by both fathers and mothers is particularly common (see chapter 7). Similarly, for positive mediation, parents are also more
likely to talk about using the PC if their child has one in his or her own room.

---

[11]The only exception is Switzerland, where fathers are more likely to restrict use of the PC
if their child uses a family PC.

In summary, television, the family medium, almost universally found in the living room, is more regulated in that location. The PC, which as yet has a less well-established place in the home, and which, when not in the child's room, tends to be located in less private areas such as spare rooms, hallways, or parents' bedrooms, attracts more parental control and comment when the child has his or her own. Possibly when children watch television in a communal room, parental mediation is more common because it functions both to regulate the child's viewing and to preserve parents' access and privacy. Parents' regulation of the PC is much less likely to involve such dual motivation, as parental leisure is less likely to be disturbed by PC use because of its less central location in the home. As a result, mediation may be more closely linked to the child's own behavior, particularly as parents are often uncertain yet regarding the kinds of activities and contents to which children may have access through the PC.

WHAT IS THE EXPERIENCE AND SIGNIFICANCE OF MEDIA USE IN THE BEDROOM?

In sociohistorical terms, the media-rich bedroom is new in the lives of European children and their parents. In the 1950s, Himmelweit, Oppenheim, and Vince (1958) were preoccupied with the arrival of the single television set in the home, and in McRobbie and Garber's (1976) identification of bedroom culture, the television (far less the computer) played no role. Even in Morley's (1986) study of family television, the analysis is centered on the struggles of multi-person households to share "the television set." However, as rooms (or people) rather than the home (or the household) increasingly become the unit for acquisition of screen media, today's parents cannot rely on their own childhood experiences to guide them in managing the spatial and temporal structures of domestic and family life. Rather, they must figure out for their own household how to accommodate, regulate, and enjoy the plethora of media goods now widely available. This they generally do together with their children as part of a sometimes cooperative, sometimes conflictual negotiation, within a broader context that pits a discourse of new opportunities and consumer choice against one of parental duties to manage appropriately the social development of their children.

Our research established that a sizable proportion of children's and young people's time at home is spent in the privacy of their own rooms and that, if these rooms are media-rich, young people spend even longer there. From the parents' perspective, regulation of their children's media use is made more difficult by the development of a media-rich bedroom culture. We also noted that different media encourage different social practices.

Television is still, in most countries, a family medium (chapter 7), and fewer than a quarter (23%) of young people usually watch their favorite program alone. However, the future trajectory for television seems to be toward increasingly solitary use: Children are more likely to watch alone if they have their own set and therefore the choice to do so (Table 8.5). On the other hand, although almost twice as many (43%) already play computer games alone, there is no indication that this will increase if more children acquire their own PCs or games machines: The tendency is, if anything, toward more social uses. In particular, it seems that computer game playing is an important peer activity that encourages contact with friends (see chapters 7 and 9).

Although these general trends hold cross-culturally, it also appears that, as far as bedroom culture is concerned, different national cultures are likely to encourage rather different outcomes. Certain cultures may be more tolerant of, or more predisposing toward, leisure time spent alone, and this may have consequences for the development of bedroom culture, regardless of media provision. For example, Swiss teenagers spend a more-than-average proportion of their time in their own rooms, whereas Finnish teenagers spend less than average (Table 8.1), even though Swiss children own fewer televisions or PCs (see chapter 3, Tables 3.1 and 3.7) and spend less time on these media (see chapter 4). For Finnish children, the opposite is the case. This cultural difference is confirmed by the finding that, among 15- to 16-year-olds, only about 40% of Finns prefer to watch television or play computer games by themselves, compared with 60% of Swiss teenagers who prefer to watch television alone and 68% who prefer to play computer games alone.

Whether the development of bedroom culture is seen as a matter for interest or concern differs markedly across countries. Both tabloid and broadsheet press reaction to the British report, *Young People, New Media* (Livingstone & Bovill, 1999), a report that encompassed many aspects of children's and young people's media uses, focused almost exclusively on bedroom culture as problematic.[12] In Israel, on the other hand, no comparable national concern has emerged, even though by their own account Israeli children and young people spend a greater proportion of their leisure time in their own rooms than do British children, with a concomitant reduction in family viewing. Similarly, in the Nordic countries, although younger children in particular spend a considerable proportion of their free time at home in their bedrooms (Table 8.1), researchers encountered little concern about this among parents. This may be explained in terms of national antiauthoritarian patterns of child-rearing in Nordic countries, where independence and compar-

---

[12]Typical headlines read "The rise of bedroom culture spells trouble for our children" (Whittam Smith, 3/22/99) and "The youngsters with no life beyond the bedroom" (Alleyne, 3/19/99).

TABLE 8.7
Percentage Children and Young People Saying There Is Enough for Someone Their Age to do in the Area Where They live, by Age

Ages	BE (vlg)	CH	DE	DK	ES	FI	FR	GB	NL	IL	SE
6-7	49	88	n/a	n/a	n/a	84	78	n/a	86	69	n/a
9-10	50	67	60	69	75	76	75	57	74	85	73
12-13	50	76	59	61	90	43	63	30	52	74	50
15-16	44	63	54	66	91	34	47	17	47	47	30

atively unrestricted access to leisure opportunities outside the home are regarded as important (Suoninen, personal communication, 1999).[13]

In our research in the United Kingdom, we attributed the considerable amount of time (5 hours per day on average) spent by British children with the media to the combination of an increasingly personalized media environment in the home, a relative lack of things for children and young people to do in the area where they live, and parental fears for their safety outside the home (Livingstone & Bovill, 1999). British parents' fears may not be entirely unfounded. Home Office statistics (1994), reporting on child victims of crime, report twice as many cases of gross indecency with a child in 1992 compared with 1983 and a fourfold increase in the number of child abductions. Our survey showed that British children, compared with others in Europe, are the most likely to say that there is not enough for someone their age to do in the area where they live (Table 8.7).[14]

In short, we suggest that the meaning of bedroom culture in individual countries depends on the leisure context in which it develops: The boundary of the bedroom door is ultimately less important than the boundary of the front door.

Beyond cross-national differences, we may also identify cultural differences between parents and children, for there is certainly a difference between parents' and children's perspectives on bedroom culture. To parents, the media-rich bedroom represents both a refuge from the dangers of the streets and, on the other hand, a threat to family relationships and "constructive" leisure activities. To children, it is more important for providing a

---

[13]As our survey confirms, in every age group Finnish and Swedish children spend more days a week with friends and going out to clubs. Finnish children also spend up to twice as much time as British children simply "playing or messing about" outdoors.

[14]Matthews (1998) confirmed that only 33% of British children and young people say they find plenty of things to do locally, whereas 65% claim to be bored in their spare time. In addition, 82% claim they prefer being outside to being indoors, but the streets are perceived by half as fearful places.

unique space in which they can express their identity, experiment with their individuality, exercise personal control, and manage—through both connection and distance—their relations with family and friends.

The qualitative interviews confirm the growing importance of the bedroom for European children of all ages. Before the age of 9 or 10, most children are comparatively uninterested, although parents may try to encourage use of the bedroom as a play space in order to secure a modicum of privacy and quiet for themselves. On the other hand, escape from troublesome siblings can be an attraction for those who do not have to share a room. Here one exasperated British 7-year-old talks of trying to watch his favorite television program with his 5-year-old brother:

> J: I can't hardly see the TV, he goes zoom, zoom, zoom, he's whizzing around, I can't even hear what it's saying.
>
> Int.:   Right, so does that annoy you a bit?
>
> J: Yes, and then when I get really angry I have to, what I have to do is climb down—this makes me really mad—switch it off.

By the early teens, bedrooms are increasingly valued not just for practical reasons but also to support a developing sense of identity and lifestyle. The bedroom provides a flexible social space in which young people can experience their growing independence from family life, becoming either a haven of privacy or a social area in which to entertain friends. In tune with the account offered by McRobbie and Garber (1976), this 16-year-old, British girl describes how her bedroom expresses not only her sense of style, but also her sense of who she is, and, as befits a teenager's bedroom in the 1990s, the media play a key role:

> R: Well I've made it my own. It's got all my—I'm very into musicals, like West End things and er I've got all the posters and leaflets all over my wall. You can hardly see the wallpaper. And my CD player. I've always got music on. That's what I usually do—I just sit in there and listen to music. Or I sometimes watch telly if Mum's watching something I don't want to watch . . . whenever my friends come over we just usually go round and listen to music and talk and watch television.
>
> Int: Why are you in there rather than in the living room watching television?
>
> R: Well, usually because my Mum's down there. Don't want her listening to what I'm talking about . . . Um well I suppose, boys.
>
> Int: So your bedroom's quite a private place in fact?
>
> R: Yes. My personality's expressed.

To conclude, media-rich bedroom culture can contribute to the shifting of the boundary between public and private spaces in several ways. Within the home, the multiplication of personally owned media may facilitate children's use of individual, privatized space, as opposed to communal family space. However, such a relatively privatized bedroom culture is also developing because of the perceived failures of a more public, outdoor leisure culture (in terms of access, cost, variety, etc). At the same time, the nature of such private space within the home may be transformed as the media-rich bedroom increasingly becomes the focus of peer activity, and as the media themselves, through their contents, bring the outside world indoors. Although these general trends are apparent, we also identified some cross-national variations in bedroom culture. It remains to be seen how far national differences in culture, in family life, and in young people's access to public spaces and facilities will affect the future balance of outdoor versus indoor, social versus solitary, or family- versus peer-oriented leisure activities in young people's lives. What is clear is that the media—particularly screen media—are playing an increasingly significant role within the more indoor, more solitary, more peer-oriented space of the bedroom.

REFERENCES

Alleyn, R. (1999). The youngsters with no life beyond the bedroom. In *Daily Mail*, Friday, March 19th, p. 19.

Annenberg Public Policy Center (1999). *Media in the Home 1999: The fourth annual survey of parents and children*. The Annenberg Public Policy Center, Survey Series no. 5. Washington: The University of Pennsylvania, Annenberg Public Policy Center.

Bachmair, B. (1991). *Reconstructions of family systems in a media-negotiated world—the social and interpretative functions of TV*. Fourth International Television Studies Conference, London.

Bjurström, E., & Fornäs, J. (1993). Ungdomskultur I Sverige. In U. Himmelstrand & G. Svensson (Eds.), *Sverige—vardag och struktur. Sociologer beskriver det svenska samhallet* [Sweden—everyday life and structure. Sociologists describe Swedish society] (2nd ed., pp. 433–460). Sodertalje: Norsteds.

Buckingham, D. (1993). *Reading audiences; Young people and the media*. Manchester: Manchester University Press.

Bybee, C., Robinson, D., & Turow, J. (1982). Determinants of parental guidance of children's television viewing for a special subgroup: Mass media scholars. *Journal of Broadcasting, 26,* 697–710.

Eurostat (1997). *Eurostat yearbook—a statistical eye on Europe 1986–1996*. Luxembourg: Office for Official Publications of the European Communities.

Flichy, P. (1995). *Dynamics of modern communication: the shaping and impact of new communication technologies*. London: Sage.

Frith, S. (1978). *Sociology of rock*. London: Constable.

Himmelweit, H. T., Oppenheim, A. N., & Vince, P. (1958). *Television and the child; An empirical study of the effect of television on the young*. London and New York: Oxford University Press.

Home Office (1994). Children as victims of crime, by type of crime 1983 and 1992 (i.e. abductions and gross indecency). In *Central Statistical Office—Special Focus on Children 1994*. London: Government Publications.

Krotz, F., Hasebrink, U., Lindemann, T., Reimann, F., & Rischkau, E. (1999). *Neue und alte Medien im Alltag von Kindern und Jugendlichen. Deutsche Teilergebnisse einer europäischen Studie*. Hamburg: Hans-Bredow-Institut.

Livingstone, S., & Bovill, M. (1999). *Young people, new media.* An LSE Report, available from http://psych.lse.ac.uk/young_people.

Matthews, H. (1998). Research briefing on *Children and young people's views on and use of the street.* Children 5–16 Research Programme. Centre for the Social Study of Childhood. University of Hull.

McRobbie, A., & Garber, J. (1976). Girls and subcultures. In S. Hall & T. Jefferson (Eds.), *Resistance through rituals: Youth subcultures in post-war Britain.* Essex, England: Hutchinson University Library.

Morley, D. (1986). *Family television: Cultural power and domestic leisure.* London: Comedia.

Silverstone, R., & Hirsh, E. (Eds.) (1992). *Consuming technologies: Media and information in domestic spaces.* London and New York: Routledge.

Steele, J. R., & Brown, J. D. (1994). Studying media in the context of everyday life. *Journal of Youth Adolescence, 24*(5), 551–576.

van der Voort, T. H. A., Nikken, P., & Vooijs, M. W. (1992). Determinants of parental guidance of children's television viewing: A Dutch replication study. *Journal of Broadcasting and Electronic Media, 36,* 61–74.

Whittam Smith, A. (1999). The rise of 'bedroom culture' spells trouble for our children. In *The Independent,* The Monday Review, 22nd March.

World Economic Forum (1996). *Global Competitiveness Report 1996.* Geneva.

9

The Role of Media
in Peer Group Relations

Annikka Suoninen

Media research has often focused on the family as a natural unit of media consumption for the obvious reason that media equipment is often situated at home and media are used in domestic situations. In studies with this focus, media and media use were found to have several social functions in family life (see Lull, 1990; Morley, 1986; Silverstone, 1994). The role of the peer group in young people's media consumption and reception has been relatively little studied, even though they are both considered to be central socialization agents.[1] The peer group can be seen both to have an impact on media choices and to play an important role in the media reception process (for example, Buckingham 1993; Hodge & Tripp, 1986; Kytömäki, 1999).

In this chapter I look at how media are connected to interaction with friends—both inside and outside home—in the lives of European children and teenagers.[2] I concentrate on four major themes that came out from the qualitative interviews: how media are used together with peers, how media offer common topics for interaction, how media equipment and media products

---

[1]Norwegian sociologist Ivar Frønes (1987) considered "communicative competence" as being the main social competence in the information society—and that both peer group and media play a central role in creating and practicing this competence.

[2]This chapter is based on quantitative survey data from all 12 countries as well as qualitative interviews from six of the nine countries where qualitative material was collected (all Finnish qualitative material and selected extracts from British, Israeli, Spanish, Swedish, and Swiss interviews). "Children" are those in the study aged 6 to 7 and 9 to 10; "teenagers" are aged 12 to 13 and 15 to 16.

serve as status symbols, and what the role is of media in (re)creating youth cultures.

USING MEDIA TOGETHER WITH PEERS

The frequency of using media together with peers differs considerably from one country to another and according to the type of media, as well as to the age and gender of the youngsters. Notwithstanding the possibility of cross-cultural differences, one thing is common to all countries: Practically all children and teenagers prefer the company of friends to the company of media. Media can, however, be used to fill the gap if the child is lonely; they may also act as a friend by offering social contact in the form of parasocial interaction. Of course, using media with friends can also be a pleasurable activity—either as a sort of symbolic play, a way of "having a good time," or simply because friends share the same interests and tastes.

> – I don't think I have ever actually watched television with my friends. If there are friends round we usually chat or something, but you can always watch television.
> – You watch television mostly when you are alone, when there are no friends round.
> – Yes, exactly.
> – If there is nothing to do, then it is usually television or the computer . . .
>
> (12- to 13-year-old Swedish boys)

In some countries, using media with friends is a common everyday activity, whereas in other countries it mainly takes place during weekends or holidays. These cultural differences might be explained by the amount of leisure time spent with friends: Rare moments are not spent on media.

In order to understand the relative importance of the peer group in different cultures, the European countries studied were divided into three groups by using those survey questions that measured the amount of personal freedom of the child: how much children and teenagers spend their leisure time with family or friends, how common it is for parents to place restrictions on going out, and whether children and teenagers think that they have enough freedom to go out when they want. According to these variables, Flanders, Spain, France, and Italy could be classified as traditional family-oriented cultures: In these countries more than half of the children and one fifth of the teenagers spend their free time mostly with family, in most families there are restrictions about going out, and youngsters feel that they do not have enough freedom to go out when they want. By contrast Finland, Sweden, Netherlands, and Denmark could be labeled as peer-oriented cultures, for fewer than one third of the children and only some 10% of the teenagers spend their leisure time mostly with their family, there are fewer restrictions about going out even for young children, and youngsters themselves think that they have enough freedom. Israel, Germany, the United Kingdom, and Switzerland could be seen to represent a moderate family-oriented culture: In these countries children are quite family-oriented (but less so than in traditional family-oriented cultures) but the teenagers are quite peer-oriented (but less so than in peer-oriented cultures).

These differences in family culture and child-rearing practices may prove useful in explaining the variations observed in the amount of media use with friends:[3] The more personal freedom and unsupervised leisure time children and youth have, the more they spend time outside home and with their friends and the more they also use media together with their friends.[4] These cultural differences came out clearly in our study on the role of media in peer relationships of Finnish, Spanish, and Swiss children and teenagers (see Süss et al., 1998): In Finland, children and teenagers had more personal freedom and used media together with their peers more than in Spain or Switzerland. This is, however, a question that needs more detailed analysis of both quantitative and qualitative data, as well as including the macrolevel analysis of the societies.

Several media-related reasons can explain why some media are used among peers more than others. Some media are better suited to shared pleasure: Reading is a typically private activity, whereas screen media are easier to share. The number of users may also affect the media content itself: A television program is basically the same whether it is viewed alone or with someone else, but the whole "plot line" of a computer game changes if it is played against a living partner instead of a machine. Broadcast media can only be used at scheduled times; other media can be used whenever it is comfortable. Some media are tied to a certain place simply because of the

---

[3]The relationships between "personal freedom," "family culture," and "child-rearing practices" are, however, very complicated (as is the very meaning of these words). The complicated picture includes elements such as (the history of) women's role in the labor force, the role of family and society in childcare, the threats (both real and assumed) that children meet outside home, as well as community planning (for example, traffic planning and the way schools are situated). The "child-rearing practices" of any one country cannot be properly understood without a good knowledge of the infrastructure and history of that country. In some societies, children are presumed able to take care of themselves from a younger age than in others, and these children are therefore given more personal freedom and responsibility.

[4]The relationship between "personal freedom" (for example, how common it is to have restrictions about going out in the family and whether youngsters felt that they had enough freedom) and the amount of time spent with friends (whether youngsters spend their free time mostly alone, with friends, or with family) was so clear that the "family culture" types could be classified by using these variables. At least in the case of watching favorite television programs with friends, the relationship between "family culture" and using media together with friends is clear.

size of the required equipment, whereas other media may be carried around. Communicative media like telephone and Internet chat groups require a different story again, as the very essence of these is to use them with somebody. Next I concentrate on those media that are quite widely used with peers, namely television and video, computer games, and communicative media. Listening to music is discussed later on in this chapter in relation to fan cultures.

Watching Television and Video

Television is by far the most important medium for children and teenagers throughout Europe. Practically everyone has access to television and it is used almost daily. Television is, however, very much a domestic medium and most television viewing takes place either alone or with family members (see chapter 7, and Pasquier, Buzzi, d'Haenens, & Sjöberg, 1998). Favorite television programs are, however, quite often also viewed with a friend (see Table 9.1).

Viewing one's favorite program with a friend increases with age, and cross-national differences are largest among 9- to 10-year-olds; in peer-oriented cultures (SE, FI, DK), more than one quarter of children often watch their favorite program with a friend, but in traditional family-oriented cultures (FR, ES) less than 10% of the children do so.[5]

Watching one's favorite program can be seen, however, to differ from a "common" viewing situation; it comes out clearly from the Finnish qualitative interviews that young people prefer to watch their favorite program either alone or with friends (but not with the family). This observation is supported by the qualitative and quantitative data from other countries. Those youngsters who have a television set in their own room (and therefore presumably have more freedom in choosing their viewing company) watch their favorite program both alone[6] and with their friends[7] more often than those who do not have a personal television set.

---

[5]The United Kingdom and Flanders seem to be an exception to this rule: very few British children often watch their favorite program with a friend, whereas Flanders (which otherwise seems to be a very traditional, family-oriented culture) ranks in the "moderate" group together with Germany and Israel.

[6]This difference was statistically significant ($p < 0.001$) for both girls and boys, and for the three older age groups. The difference was statistically significant ($p < 0.001$) in the United Kingdom, Finland, Flanders, Germany, and Sweden and statistically almost significant ($p < 0.05$) in Israel, but no difference was found in Spain.

[7]This difference was statistically significant ($p < 0.001$) for both girls and boys and for the 15- to 16-year-olds. The difference was statistically significant ($p < 0.001$) in Finland, Flanders, and Sweden and statistically almost significant ($p < 0.05$) in Germany and Israel, but no difference was found in Spain and the difference was statistically nonsignificant in the United Kingdom.

TABLE 9.1
Percentage Within Country and Age Group Watching Favorite Television Program, "Usually"
With a Friend (Multiple Choices for Viewing Company Accepted)

Country*				Age Group	
	6-7	9-10	12-13	15-16	All Ages
BE (vlg)	4	12	19	32	19
DE	16	15	14	30	19
DK	15	26	49	51	34
ES	3	7	8	11	8
FI	8	29	36	35	27
FR	4	7	13	23	12
GB	5	3	6	9	6
IL	11	11	24	34	21
SE	11	35	43	50	39
Average	9	16	24	31	21

Note. *Question not asked in Netherlands and asked in different format in Italy and Switzerland.

Unlike television, videos can be used at the most convenient time (and place), and watching videos with friends is both a common and an important activity. In most of the countries, at least a quarter of all youngsters—and more than a third of the 15- to 16-year-olds—"sometimes" go to their friend's house particularly to watch videos. This percentage is even higher for those without a video recorder at home (see Table 9.2).

In countries like Finland where youngsters have free time on their own in the afternoons, videos are often watched during these afternoon hours. In countries like Spain where children do not have that much unsupervised leisure time during the week, videos are more often watched during the weekend (see Süss et al., 1998). Teenagers may also arrange special "video nights" when they may watch several video films together in a nonstop fashion. These video nights can also be part of the deviant youth culture when youth want to make a clear distinction from a sophisticated adult taste by watching together "rubbish" and/or films that are certainly not approved by their parents and teachers—violent action, slasher movies, horror, and pornography (see, for example, Bolin, 1994).

Int: When you think about watching a video what's the atmosphere, . . .

L: Terror!

[Laughter]

Int: Terror, are you into horror videos?

L: Aye.

Int: Tell me about it. You know, do you like being terrified?

TABLE 9.2
Percentage of Youngsters (over 9 years old) Going Round to a Friend's House Especially to Use
Media That Cannot be Used at Home (All, and Those With No Access to Particular Media
at Home)

Country*	Watching Cable/Satellite Channels		Watching Video		Playing Electronic Games		Using Computer, not for games		Using Internet	
	All	No Access	All	No Access	All	No Access	All	No Access	All	No Access
BE (vlg)	12	-	40	43	35	21	23	30	10	9
CH	9	9	30	37	26	15	12	15	7	7
DE	8	17	25	36	32	30	9	10	9	8
DK	7	-	22	-	21	-	14	-	8	-
ES	20	21	-	-	36	38	13	20	10	10
FR	14	-	44	-	39	-	20	-	6	-
GB	24	33	42	49	44	39	23	28	7	7
IL	14	34	13	33	38	55	22	33	25	29
IT**	22	22	22	55	32	42	26	37	31	32
NL	7	-	26	29	31	24	15	28	6	6
SE	14	21	12	35	23	25	14	17	19	25
Average	14	22	28	40	32	32	17	24	13	15

Note. *Questions not asked in Finland. **Only teenagers.

A: Yes.

Int: Well why?

A: Because like you and your pals and that and you're all like screaming and
      that, you just get a laugh.

L: Turn the lights off-

[Laughter]

Int: So when you watch a video is it normally alone, or with other people?

D: With other people.

A: You get too scared when you watch it by yourself.

(9- to 10-year-old British girls)

Electronic Games

Compared with television, electronic games are used with peers much more
often; with a few exceptions, friends are the most commonly mentioned
company for playing electronic games[8] (see also Table 7.2 in chapter 7). The

---

[8]Only the 6- to 7-year olds in Israel and the three younger age groups in Flanders usually play
games with a family member more often than with friends.

proportion of those who play games usually with their friends increases with age for both boys and girls, and more boys than girls say that they play usually with their friends (this is still the case when only those who do play electronic games are considered).[9]

There are, however, different ways of playing electronic games together with friends. For the youngest children, playing games with other people usually means sharing the same machine: Children give advice to each other and take turns to play. This is also the most common way to learn how to use the games machine or the computer. Older and more experienced players, however, want to concentrate in peace on their own performance, but they also find it more interesting and challenging to play with or against a living person rather than with a machine.[10] Boys especially are often quite ambitious in their playing, and they are ready to spend a lot of time and effort in improving their playing skills, which are then tested and ranked with friends (see Suoninen, 2001).

-      And driving games you can play with a friend.
-      And then also with a modem . . .
-      Yes, those shoot 'em 'up –games . . .
Int: With whom?
-      With someone who has a modem, too.
-      In theory you can play it with anyone you like . . .
-      I've also played *Diablo* in the *Virtual Center*
Int: Where?
-      In the *Virtual Center*. It is a place where you can go and play through the local area network. There are about 14 computers in the network.

                                                                         (13-year-old Finnish boys)

It is as common to visit friends in order to play electronic games as it is to watch videos, in some countries even more common (see Table 9.2). There is a clear difference between boys and girls: 44% of boys and 20% of girls sometimes go to their friend's house especially to play electronic games.[11] Surprisingly, when taking into consideration the availability of

---

[9]This gender difference is, however, statistically significant ($p < 0.001$) only in the United Kingdom, Germany, and Sweden.

[10]There are several ways of playing electronic games with/against another person: on the same games machine/computer with several control pads/joysticks; hot seat games on the same computer (i.e., where two or more players take turns in playing against each other); with two computers that are connected by cable in the same location; with two computers connected with a modem; or with several computers connected through the Internet or a local area network.

[11]This difference remains even when looking only at those youngsters who play electronic games: 45% of those boys and 21% of those girls who play electronic games sometimes go to a friend's house especially to do this.

games machines and computers at home,[12] it turns out that going to a friend's house to play games is most common among those boys who have their own games console, but not a computer, at home, rather than among those boys who have no access to a games machine at home. It seems that these players are searching for challenges they cannot meet with their consoles and therefore they go to a friend's house to play electronic games.

> The video-console is already old-fashioned. We've got one at home, but we don't use it much. Now we play computer games. Video-consoles are for younger children up to 12 years, because after that age you get bored to death with them.
>
> (15-year-old Spanish boy)

Communicative Media

If electronic games are especially part of boys' culture, telephone is definitely part of (teenage) girls' culture (see also chapter 12 in this book). Boys and younger girls use the telephone mainly for short calls to make arrangements with friends or family. Teenage girls, however, have endless and rather repetitive phone calls with their friends. This kind of "girl-talk" begins gradually from the age of 9 or 10, and hanging between childhood and youth can take interesting forms; for example, a group of Finnish 10-year-old girls told how they used to play with *My Little Ponies* on the phone with each other.

The telephone is considered to be both intimate and distant enough; some things are easier to talk about and some confessions easier to make on the telephone than face to face. Girls want to make their private calls—naturally—in privacy; if they have no phone in their own room (or cannot take a cordless phone there) and they have no personal mobile phone, either, girls may prefer to make their phone calls outside home.

> Every evening I go to a public telephone cabin to call my friends with my Calling Card . . . Here I'm not disturbed by my parents. They complain if I use the telephone too long, and I don't want them to listen to me when I talk to my friends about problems I have with my boyfriend.
>
> (15-year-old Swiss girl)

Teenage girls have also adopted other communicative media eagerly: They are very interested in mobile phones, and e-mail and on-line chats are among the most popular uses of computers and the Internet among girls.

---

[12]Boys were divided into four groups: those with no access to any kind of games machine at home, those who had both games console and computer at home, and those who had one but not the other.

Telephone and e-mail are for contacting friends, whereas chat groups are used for meeting new people: Internet Relay Chat (IRC) is considered to be a more relaxed way to make contacts, and usually the next phase in a relationship is e-mailing. These new friends met in cyberspace may either remain as virtual friendships (though these may nevertheless be quite warm and intimate relationships) or they may lead to real life contacts.[13]

> It is so easy to start to talk to people . . . When I've sometimes tried to talk with a guy about something more deeply, then . . . Well, it's quite difficult when you are face to face with each other. But in IRC it is really easy.
>
> (15-year-old Finnish girl)

MEDIA-RELATED TALK AND PLAY

Talking about media and media contents is clearly the most important way in which media affect peer group relationships. Swapping media with friends also plays an important role in peer group relationships; these exchange networks are a very effective and cheap way of gaining access to a broader variety of media products. These networks might, however, also play a role in peer group power games, as media products may not be swapped with everyone, at least without a decent "payback."

Television and Video

Television is by far the most commonly discussed medium among children and youth in general (see Table 9.3): 74% of teenagers and 57% of children talk about television with their friends.[14]

The proportion of those who talk about television increases with age,[15] but there is no clear gender difference. Popular television programs are sort of "joint cultural heritage": Everyone knows them, they reach everyone at the same time and therefore they serve well as common topics for talk.[16] Television related talk can take several forms: Sometimes a group of peers may go through a particularly amusing or interesting film almost scene by

---

[13]It is not at all unusual to go visit keypals (e-mail pen pals) in different cities or even plan an Inter Rail trip in order to meet foreign keypals.

[14]These figures are based on information from five countries: the United Kingdom, Finland, Germany, Israel, and Italy.

[15]In the United Kingdom, Finland, and Israel, this difference was statistically significant ($p < 0.001$). In Germany and Italy the peak was with 12- to 13-year-olds.

[16]Finnish folklorist Julkunen (1989) called children's media tradition (stories, talking, plays, etc.) *medialore* and he saw it as a very functional way of connecting children and youth and offering common topics for interaction. This is not only typical of youth culture as adults, too, use television as a common topic for talk in working places (see Hobson, 1989; Montonen, 1993).

TABLE 9.3
Percentage of Children and Teenagers Who Talk About Media With Their Friends

Country	Television		Video		Music		Books		Magazines		Games	
	Child	Teen	Child	Teen	Child	Teen	Child	Teen	Child	Teen	Child	Teen
DE	56	59	20	22	13	30	8	9	3	11	16	30
FI	52	73	37	43	34	63	27	21	8	22	58	39
GB	50	71	26	39	29	60	18	10	18	38	29	32
IL	69	84	41	47	41	74	47	31	37	28	62	43
IT	-	85	-	71	-	75	-	45	-	50	-	54
Average	57	74	31	44	29	60	25	23	17	30	41	40

scene, and sometimes it may be necessary to know certain phrases and "inside jokes" taken from a popular television program in order to understand and participate in the peer talk. Television programs may also provide a background to more "philosophical" discussions:

Int: If you are talking about *X-files*, what are you saying?
-      What has happened in the show.
-      Everything.
-      What we think actually happens and such.
Int: Whether it would be possible to happen in reality?
-      It can like happen that someone sees something odd and then they want to make other people believe it, too.
-      And you always have to figure out the end [of each episode] yourself. So we talk about how everyone thinks that the story ended.

(15- to 16-year-old Swedish boys)

Television-related talk is indeed quite often "bigger than television" insofar as television programs are used as background for discussions about real life situations and problems, things that are either present in the everyday life of the youngsters or probably will become part of their lives in the near future (see Kytömäki, 1999; Livingstone & Bovill, 1999).[17]

Among the younger children, television-related talk quite often takes the form of play, for young children develop media-related role-plays with each other. Television-related play can, in fact, be seen as an important part of children's reception process: Following viewing, the stories are rewritten, reinterpreted, and even recreated (see Hodge & Tripp, 1987). This play can take its models directly from popular cartoons or other television programs, but sometimes the origins are less than obvious (at least for the "unsophisticated" eye) as children mix elements from different media as well as real life and create their own variations.

Media talk and play, like media content, are loaded with intertextual and intermedial references. Popular media texts and media characters are often surrounded by *supersystems*,[18] and the same figures and the same story are available in several different forms. In fact, the whole world of popular culture relies greatly on genre knowledge, as well as on knowledge of certain

---

[17]These kinds of discussion can be classified as both *communication facilitation* or *social learning* in Lull's (1980) categories of the social uses of television, and they are often found also in the interaction between children and parents.

[18]This is a concept taken from Kinder (1991). She used *supersystem* to refer to a "product line" of commercial media products, where the different members of the "family" (for example, television series, film, video games, comics, books, toys, clothes, etc.) are so closely connected to each other that it is sometimes almost impossible to say which is the "original" one.

key texts that are then repeated and varied over and over again across different types of media (see Fiske, 1987).[19]

Television's universality is also evident from the fact that a much smaller percentage of youngsters talk about videos than television with their friends (see Table 9.3). Videos are, however, swapped with friends very often: One quarter of children and half of teenagers swap videos with their friends (see Table 9.4). Interestingly enough, in some groups it is more common to swap videos than to talk about their contents!

Books and Electronic Games

Books play a very different role in peer relationships in different countries depending mainly on the popularity of book reading in each country. Books are hardly discussed at all in the United Kingdom and Germany, whereas their relative importance is particularly clear for Finnish, Israeli, and Italian girls, for whom books are one of the most common media-related topics of talk (Table 9.3). Books (and magazines, too) are especially important in girls' peer culture. Girls also swap books much more often than boys: An average of 43% of teenage girls but only 18% of teenage boys swap books with their friends.[20] The importance of books is not, however, only connected to age and gender, but varies heavily from one interest group to another. For example, fewer boys who are especially interested in sports and more boys who are especially interested in science fiction talk about books with their friends.[21]

Games, on the other hand, are definitely a part of boys' culture (see also chapter 12). Games are the second most common topic of talk with friends among boys, and in Finland they are the number one topic. Boys also talk about computers in general (i.e., not specifically for game use) more than girls do, but not to the same extent that they talk about games. Boys also swap games with each other a lot,[22] and they may create exchange networks that do not necessarily rely on close personal friendship but rather on mutu-

---

[19]In my own previous study of young Finnish children's television use, I found that when children were asked to retell a story from their favorite television programs, the stories were usually "metastories" of these programs rather than stories from any particular episode. Even 3- to 4-year-old children could show a very sophisticated knowledge of, for example, genre conventions and production techniques (Suoninen, 1993).

[20]Book swapping is not necessarily a good indicator of the role of books in peer culture, however, as the importance of public libraries varies heavily from one country to another. For example, book swapping is least common in Denmark and Finland, but in these countries there are most library loans per inhabitant (see *UNESCO Statistical Yearbook,* 1998). In fact, the Netherlands is the only country that ranks above average in both library loans (according to UNESCO) and book swapping—and France is the only country that ranks below average in both.

[21]Both differences are statistically significant ($p < 0.01$).

[22]An average of 45% of all boys and 56% of teenage boys swap games with their friends (compared with 13% and 16% among girls).

TABLE 9.4
Percentage Swapping Media With Their Friends

Country	Books		Magazines		Music, CDs, Tapes		Games		Videos	
	Children	Teens	Children	Teens	Children	Teens	Children	Teens	Children	Teens
BE (vlg)	27	45	11	38	16	76	24	54	45	59
CH	19	39	3	19	16	72	12	34	21	52
DE	25	29	9	21	21	56	11	32	16	30
DK	7	12	4	14	11	71	16	27	22	57
ES	24	36	7	22	12	67	18	34	40	50
FI	-	18	-	11	-	56	-	32	-	46
FR	11	22	5	31	9	60	16	30	14	45
GB	20	20	7	31	9	56	16	34	22	42
IL	29	33	14	9	21	72	16	35	29	52
IT	-	43	-	27	-	74	-	39	-	68
NL	21	33	8	34	17	68	19	41	29	39
SE	13	25	2	15	16	61	16	28	17	54
Average	20	30	7	23	15	66	15	34	26	50

al interest. Interestingly, one may be able to "pay back" the exchanged games in the form of tutorial hints and help.

There are, however, many different kinds of computer- and game-related talk. First, youngsters talk about both hardware and software. Second, the function of the talk may resemble a discussion or tutorial (or something in between). Third, these discussions may take place either during the actual use situation or elsewhere. This plurality of types of talking is particularly typical for game- and computer-related talk, as other types of media talk are mostly about the media content and usually take place after use.

> - It [what you say about electronic games] depends on whom you are talking with. Usually we play games and use the computer together. But I have a couple, two, three friends that are more into computers. With them I can talk about the technology itself.
> Int: What do you talk about?
> - Mostly about the new products that have come out. And problems we have with the computer.
> Int: What kind of new products do you mean?
> - If there are new processors, for example, or some more special parts, then we can talk about that.
>
> (15-year-old Swedish boy)

MEDIA PRODUCTS AND MEDIA EQUIPMENT AS STATUS OBJECTS

Children and teenagers are very well aware of the status values connected to certain goods: that it is important to own some objects because everyone else has them, too, or that having certain things that are not so common but are highly valued can gain one appreciation from peers. For younger children, toys and clothes are most the typical media-related status objects; in the case of teenagers, however, status is often connected to more expensive products like computers or mobile phones.

Clothes, toys, CDs, games, and other minor objects come into and go out of style, but media equipment has a somewhat different kind of life-cycle: It retains at least part of its use value after the "status boom." Some new and rare media equipment might even convey "negative status" (at least in the eyes of girls) because people having this equipment are considered to be ridiculous "posers."

> G: I just do not like mobile telephones because they are just a waste of money
> R: They go like this, they're crossing the road -
> G: Yes, hello, can you hear me —

R: - and they get knocked down.

T: And then they get hit over by a bus.

(12- to 13-year-old British boys)

When youngsters gradually become aware of the practical advantages of having this equipment, these gadgets become desirable, and when this equipment becomes more common, it loses its status value.

-   Well, that seventh-grade [13-year-old] boy always keeps his mobile with his coat open so that everyone can see that he has one . . .
-   Yes. Really posing with it. But I think that's really stupid as most people have mobiles. So it's really stupid to try to pose with one.

(15-year-old Finnish girls)

The value attached to certain media technology can be seen from what children and teenagers wish to get as a birthday present (see also chapter 3). Among boys, games machines and computers are of special value:[23] If there is no computer or games machine at home, they wish to have one; if there is already one at home, they wish to have a personal one; if they only have a games machine, they wish to have a computer; if they already have a computer, they wish to have a bigger and better one; if they already have a good computer, they wish to have an Internet link.

For girls, no such "pan-European hit product" can be located. If there is not a computer available at home, many girls wish to have a computer for a birthday present.[24] However, if they already have access to a computer, they prefer other things to computers: Younger girls often want to have music players; older girls (who usually have stereos in their room) place value on a personal television set or possibly an Internet link. In some countries a personal mobile phone is very highly valued among teenage girls: About 15% of Israeli, Italian, and Swedish and one quarter of British teenage girls without a personal mobile phone wished to have one as a birthday present. In Finland almost half of those teenage girls who did not have a mobile phone wanted to have one.[25]

---

[23]Only German boys appreciate a personal television set more than a computer or games machine. The majority of those German boys who had neither personal television set or access to a games machine wanted to have a television as a birthday present. In all other countries, those boys without a personal television set nonetheless preferred a computer or games machine as birthday present.

[24]Although Flemish, German, and Swedish girls prefer a personal television set to a computer or games machine.

[25]And Finnish teenagers—both girls and boys—did get their mobile phones. There was a real "mobile explosion" among Finnish teenagers during the winter 1997–1998, a few months after collecting data for this study. Nowadays almost all Finnish teenagers have their own mobiles, and they are much more common than, for example, personal television sets or personal telephones.

FAN CULTURES

Listening to music—and talking about it—plays a very important role in the lives of teenagers. They have music on most of the time and it creates a constant background noise for other activities both in and outside home. Furthermore, 60% of the teenagers in the United Kingdom, Finland, Germany, Israel, and Italy talk about music with their friends (see Table 9.3): which artist, disc, or video is good or bad, whether the new CDs are worth buying, and who is the most gorgeous of all the pop stars. Music CDs and tapes are also the most common exchange items among teenagers—only British and Finnish boys swap games rather more than music CDs or tapes (see Table 9.4).

Traditional fan cultures are often born around a certain music style or artist, but they may penetrate the whole sphere of life and create rather solid subcultures. Although belonging to specific fan cultures is nowadays more common among younger adolescents, older teenagers often appreciate a more individual identity and style. This kind of "patchwork identity" and "shuttling" between subcultures is typical for the postmodern culture in general when "independent subjects" (Bauman, 1992) do their "identity work" (Ziehe, 1991).

> I'm a Homeboy. I wear these extra large clothes. And I'm a Raver, because I like techno. And I'm a sportsman. I don't have any idol.
>
> (15-year-old Swiss boy)

In a qualitative study of the role of media in peer relationships of Finnish, Spanish, and Swiss children and teenagers (see Süss et al., 1998), some differences in the cultural timing in the relationship to fan cultures were found.[26] It seemed that fan cultures—with a strong commitment to a certain youth group—are of particular importance at the stage when children are gaining more independence from their parents and are moving toward youth cultures and building up an individual identity. These three countries represent the three different types of family cultures sketched in this article (Spain is a traditional family-oriented culture, Switzerland a moderate family-oriented culture, and Finland a peer-oriented culture), but the connection between personal freedom and timing of fan cultures is not always so straightforward when taking a broader European perspective.

CONCLUSION

Young children's lives are more or less centered on the home and family. Their actual media uses take place within the family context and friends are of importance to the media reception process only afterward, mostly

---

[26]Fan cultures seemed to be of special importance for 9- to 10-year-olds in Finland, 12- to 13-year-olds in Switzerland, and 15- to 16-year-olds in Spain.

through role-plays that have their origins in media culture. Television (and videos) are the most important media for young children, but when computers and games machines find their way into their homes, games gain a more central role in their lives, especially among boys. The most popular media contents and media characters cross media boundaries and are typically available in television, video, books, comics, and games. All kinds of commercial products—for example, toys and clothes—connected to these supersystems serve as status symbols for children.

When children grow up, they become more peer-oriented and start to use media more with their friends and outside home. At what age this happens depends considerably on the culture: Peer culture is already quite important for 6- to 7-year-olds in Nordic countries, whereas in countries with more traditional family values, even teenagers might be very family-oriented. Television is still the most important medium for older children and teenagers. The relative importance of other media changes more when children grow up: For example, comics are replaced by magazines, and children become more and more interested in popular music.

From the point of view of peer group relationships, there are clear gender differences in the importance of certain types of media (see also chapter 12). Girls are more into music and communicative media (telephone, e-mail, and chat groups) than boys. Also, books are a part of girls' culture in those countries where youngsters read to any noticeable degree. As girls usually mature younger than boys do, they also get interested in "youth media," like music, a few years younger.

However, electronic games are probably the most gendered part of children's and, especially, teenagers' media culture. Compared with girls, boys play these games more, play with their friends more, visit their friends' houses in order to play games more, talk about games with their friends more, swap games with their friends more, and are more keen on owning new games machines and computers. Also, it seems that the bigger the relative importance of game culture in a country, the bigger the gender differences,[27] as most girls do not seem to get interested in electronic games even if they are available[28] (see also chapter 12).

Ever since of the rise of youth culture in the 1950s, youth has been seen in terms of subcultures. The role of the media in youth culture was thought of as spreading knowledge of innovation and fashion and providing role-models; youth culture—at least, that connected with media contents—has

---

[27]See, for example, the gender differences in time spent playing electronic games presented in chapter 4, Table 4.4 of this book: The gender gap widens when the time spent playing electronic games increases.

[28]Several reasons for girls' lack of interest in games can be found, but one major reason is that most games are currently designed for boys and represent the "male" genres of popular culture (see Suoninen, 2001; Cassell & Jenkins, 1998).

also been quite consumer-oriented. However, this kind of traditional view of youth and youth culture is not necessarily relevant to the late-modern youth of the 1990s. There is a plurality of subcultures and subgroups available, but actually only a few young people identify themselves—or want to be identified—with any one of them.

Somewhat typical for the 1990s, media-related youth culture is that the importance of fan cultures has moved to younger age groups whereas older teenagers tend to put more emphasis on building up an individual identity than on relying on any particular subculture. Individual media choices and media preferences play an important part in this identity work when young people build their own personal spheres of life. Furthermore, the role and meaning of *peer culture* has changed insofar as belonging to any one subculture is no longer total and exclusive; rather, a person can belong to and identify with several subcultures and several peer groups—some real life and some only virtual—simultaneously.

REFERENCES

Bauman, Z. (1992). *Intimations of postmodernity*. London: Routledge.

Bolin, G. (1994). Beware! Rubbish! Popular culture and strategies of distinction. *Young, 2*(1), 33–49.

Buckingham, D. (1993). *Children talking television*. Basingstoke, England: Falmer Press.

Cassell, J., & Jenkins, H. (Eds.) (1998). *From Barbie to Mortal Kombat: Gender and computer games*. Cambridge, MA: The MIT Press.

Fiske, J. (1987). *Television culture*. London: Routledge.

Frønes, I. (1987). Den tapte barndommen—eller den nye [The lost childhood—or the new one]. In I. Frønes (Ed.), *Mediabarn. Barnet-bildene-ordene og teknologien* [Mediachildren. Children-pictures-words and technology] (pp. 10–29). Oslo: Gyldental Norsk forlag.

Hobson, D. (1989). Soap operas at work. In E. Seiter, H. Borchers, G. Kreutzner, & E.-M. Warth (Eds.), *Remote control: Television, audiences and cultural power* (pp. 150–167). London: Routledge.

Hodge, B., & Tripp, D. (1987). *Children and television: A semiotic approach*. Cambridge: Polity Press.

Julkunen, E. (1989). Lasten ja nuorten joukkotiedotusperinne [Children's and youth's media tradition]. In J. Pöysä (Ed.), *Betoni kukkii. Kirjoituksia nykyperinteestä* [Concrete blooms. Essays on contemporary traditions] (pp. 49–63). Helsinki: Suomalaisen Kirjallisuuden Seura.

Kinder, M. (1991). *Playing with power in movies, television and video games*. Berkeley: University of California Press.

Kytömäki, J. (1999). *Täytyy kattoo, jos saa kattoo. Sosiaalipsykologisia näkökulmia varhaisnuorten televisiokokemuksiin* [You got to watch if you get to watch. Social psychologist perspectives on television experiences of young teens]. Social psychological studies 1. Helsinki: University of Helsinki, Department of Social Psychology.

Livingstone, S., & Bovill, M. (1999). Young people new media. *Report of the Research Project, Children, Young People and the Changing Media Environment*. London: London School of Economics and Political Science.

Lull, J. (1980). The social uses of television. *Human Communication Research, 6*(3), 197–209.

Lull, J. (1990). *Inside family viewing: Ethnographic research on television's audiences*. St. Ives, England: Routledge.

Montonen, M. (1993), Workplace discussions about television. In E. Vainikkala (Ed.), *Cultural study of reception*. Publications of the Research Unit for Contemporary Culture no 38. Jyväskylä, Finland: University of Jyväskylä.

Morley, D. (1986). *Family television: Cultural power and domestic leisure*. London: Comedia.

Pasquier, D., Buzzi, C., d'Haenens, L., & Sjöberg, U. (1998). Family lifestyles and media use patterns. An analysis of domestic media among Flemish, French, Italian and Swedish children and teenagers. *European Journal of Communication, 13*(4), 503–519.

Silverstone, R. (1994). *Television and everyday life*. London: Routledge.

Suoninen, A. (1993). *Televisio lasten elämässä* [Television in the lives of children]. Publications of the Research Unit for Contemporary Culture no 37. Jyväskylä, Finland: University of Jyväskylä.

Suoninen, A. (2001). Se pieni ero pelikellojen helinässä. Katsovatko pojat Quake-Quake-Maahan? [Boys, girls and computer games. Lost boys and the new Never-Never-Land?]. In E. Huhtamo & S. Kangas (Eds.), *Mariosofia—elektronisten pelien kulttuuri* [Mariosophy—The culture of electronic games]. Helsinki, Finland: Gaudeamus. In press.

Süss, D., Suoninen, A., Garitaonandia, C., Juaristi, P., Koikkalainen, R., & Oleaga, J. A. (1998). Media use and the relationships of children and teenagers with their peer groups. A study of Finnish, Spanish and Swiss cases. *European Journal of Communication, 13*(4), 521–538.

UNESCO Statistical Yearbook. (1998). Paris: UNESCO & Bernan Press.

Ziehe, T. (1991). *Uusi nuoriso. Epätavanomaisen oppimisen puolustus* [New youth. Apology for unconventional learning]. Tampere, Finland: Vastapaino. (The German original is published in T. Ziehe and H. Stubenrauch, *Plädoyer für ungewöhnliches Lernen. Idéen zur Jugendsituation*).

10

Computers and the Internet in School: Closing the Knowledge Gap?

Daniel Süss

This chapter focuses on the integration of new electronic media, such as computers and the Internet, in the schools of the 12 European countries investigated in this project.[1] The provision of new media in schools has the potential to compensate for uneven access in the home. This potential is not always realized, however, because many schools are still oriented to a print media culture and have some way to go to integrate audiovisual or electronic media in learning. This delay in media integration is caused not only by financial restrictions of the schools, but to a large extent by skeptical attitudes of teachers and education administrators toward audiovisual and electronic media (Postman, 1985, 1994, 1996).

A major aim of school is to provide basic cultural competencies to every pupil in society. In an information society, this means not only to be able to read, write, and calculate, but also to become media literate (Doelker, 1989; Potter, 1998). This includes old media like television but particularly new media like the computer and the Internet (Masterman, 1985, 1996). In the 1970s, television was integrated into school as a learning aid and as a subject of analysis. In the 1980s, the video was adopted, and in the 1990s, computers followed. In 1996, a campaign was launched in the United States to connect

---

[1]Qualitative material is integrated from interviews with children, parents, and teachers in the United Kingdom and Sweden (countries with a rather high proportion of computer and Internet in school) and Switzerland (a country with a rather low integration of new media in school). Many thanks to the British and Swedish team for providing me with their interview material. See also Livingstone and Bovill (1999).

all schools to the Internet. At "Netdays," schools started to cooperate with business enterprises and parents to obtain easy access to the information highway. In 1997, similar campaigns were adopted in various countries around the world.[2] Such political campaigns often stop at the level of providing access to new media. However, being connected to the Internet does not necessarily mean that schools use the computer and the Internet regularly and in a reasonable way. Media literacy means more than having access and not being afraid of technology (Butts, 1992; Hart, 1998; Issing, 1987). It means using new media in a way that provides advantages over other forms of learning and being critical and conscious of the impacts of the media itself. Therefore, media education in schools should involve helping young people to reflect on their use of new media at home in their leisure time and understand the influence of new media on society. However, educational strategies to integrate new media across the school curriculum are still very vague (Schorb, 1992) and research on this topic is limited to pilot projects (e.g., Bertelsmann Stiftung, 1998; Deckers, 1997; Diener, Dönhoff, Rieks, & Weigend, 1998).

A few countries, such as the United Kingdom, have Media Studies as a school subject. This means teaching students about media as well as with media. In contrast, most countries teach media as part of traditional school subjects such as language, history, or arts. In most cases, media are only explicitly taught in special interdisciplinary courses for 1 or 2 weeks per year. In a broader sense, media education means using media for other educational purposes in the most beneficial way. This chapter focuses on the use of new media in school, rather than on an evaluation of concepts of media education.[3] However, at the end of the chapter, we draw some conclusions for educational policy.

We asked children aged 6 to 16 years old in our European study if they used computers and the Internet in school, to what extent, and for what kind of purposes. We compare these data across the 12 countries to find out which countries are early adopters or late adopters of new media in school (see chapter 3 for a parallel analysis of the diffusion of new media in the home). We ask about the attitudes of young people toward new media and get their perspectives on the future role of new media, and we also want to know if the use of computers at school is more influential for the develop-

---

[2]Worldwide activities are documented under the following Internet addresses: Europe: www.netdays.org USA: www.netday.org Japan: www.netday.or.jp Australia: www.netdayoz.edu.au

[3]Concepts of media education and practices in schools in different European countries are investigated in a new project 1999–2001, coordinated by Andrew Hart, University of Southampton, with the participation of Flanders, Finland, France, Germany, Greece, Hungary, Norway, Russia, Slovenia, Spain, Switzerland, and the United Kingdom. See also Hart and Benson (1993) or Hart and Hicks (1999). For further information on the Euromedia Project, see www.soton.ac.uk/~mec/MECWEB/Researchpage.htm

ment of computer literacy than the use of computers at home. Finally, we want to know if there is a relationship between computer use at school and attitudes toward school.

These questions are important because if computer use develops first in the home and the schools only follow slowly, then social inequalities will increase and working class children will become further disadvantaged. A similar gap in provision could develop between different countries. Importantly, these gaps may not only be a question of finances but a question of priorities in the political agenda. Education of the population is the most important resource for an information society, and the integration of new media in schools reflects the value that is given to this in the countries investigated. From an academic point of view, the comparison of computer use at home and in school informs socioecological studies of media environments (Baacke, Sander, & Vollbrecht, 1990). Are the mechanisms of media use and media valuation the same for children at home and in school? Are gender and social class differences in media access and usage in the home reproduced in the school environment? Is the knowledge gap between these groups increased or decreased by access at school (Bonfadelli, 1994; Winterhoff-Spurk, 1999)? With these questions as a framework, we now examine the data on the use of new media in schools across our European sample.

COMPUTER USE IN SCHOOL: DIFFERENT CONCEPTS OF INTEGRATION

An average[4] of about 60% of the young people in the 12 countries told us that they use computers in school (see Table 10.1). The leading countries, with 80% or more, are the United Kingdom, Denmark, Sweden, and the Netherlands. This is consistent with the classification of these countries as societies that focus on new technologies (see chapter 1). Spain and Germany are at the bottom of the list with fewer than 40% using computers in school. In most of the countries, boys and girls have equal access to computers in school and there is no difference between the social classes. This is very different from the picture for computer access at home, where gender and social class influence access (see chapter 3). In the United Kingdom, Denmark, and the Netherlands, students of every age have a similar amount of access to computers, whereas in other countries like Spain, Germany, and Switzerland, access is much higher for older students than for younger ones.

---

[4]We refer to the average of the national averages, rather than to an average of the whole aggregated data set. The national data sets are representative for their country, but the aggregated data are not representative for all Europe.

TABLE 10.1
Percentage Using Computer in School (All Respondents, Age Bands 6-7 Years, 9-10 Years,
12-13 Years, 15-16 Years, $N = 10842$)

| | All | Gender | | Age | | | | SES | | |
Country		Boy	Girl	6-7	9-10	12-13	15-16	High	Med	Low
GB	87	89	86	85	90	95	80	87	86	88
DK	84	85	83	81	73	87	96	85	84	80
SE	82	85	79	44	82	93	86	78	81	84
NL	80	83	76	80	89	85	65	73	80	82
FI	74	79	70	34	86	87	91	75	72	76
IL	60	60	60	42	61	80	57	56	51	81
IT	58	63	61	-	-	57	58	53	60	62
FR	51	52	51	28	44	71	59	50	52	49
CH	48	49	47	-	31	44	66	50	49	41
BE (vlg)	45	48	42	28	21	35	74	51	38	45
ES	37	42	31	1	34	48	57	-	-	-
DE	29	32	25	6	10	38	54	28	28	25
Average of the averages	61	63	59	43	56	68	70	62	62	65

Note. Base: all 12 European countries.

These results reflect three different underlying models of how to integrate computers in school. In the first model, information technologies (IT) and other new media are introduced in the first grade of primary school (the United Kingdom, Denmark, and the Netherlands). In the second model, IT is introduced from the age of 12 years or 15 years, but achieves a high percentage of use in secondary school classes (Flanders, France, and Switzerland). The last model introduces IT late and stays at a comparatively low level until the end of school (Germany, Italy, and Spain). We have to take into consideration that adoption of IT is generally increasing and that, in time, more and more countries will have broader diffusion of new technologies across the age range.

Even in the United Kingdom, however, the country with the highest levels of adoption in schools, many teachers are still using computers in a limited way, as the following quote from a teacher in a British primary school shows:

> It is difficult to bring them (computers) into the classroom. I mean they are supposed to be part of the curriculum and they are supposed to be in use and children are supposed to have equal access to them, but I was talking to other teachers and it is difficult. I mean the management of the computers is really hard and we are all really busy.

Across our 12 European countries, an average of 41% of the students reported that at least some of the computers at their school are equipped with a CD-ROM drive. In this respect, we find large differences between the countries. More than 50% of the students in Sweden, the United Kingdom, and Finland have access to a CD-ROM machine in school and 25% or fewer in Flanders, Spain, and the Netherlands. These data may not be very precise, because in some countries more than 30% of the students did not know if the computers in school have CD-ROM drives, but their responses indicate at least that they have not yet used one.

Even if students have access to computers, computer use in school is not a very frequent activity (see Table 10.2) In all the countries, children report using computers about once or twice a week in school, with no difference in gender, age, or social class. This means that even in countries where computers are available for most students, as in the United Kingdom, teachers do not integrate them into lessons very often.

If we examine those who do use a computer at school, there is no tendency for older students to use computers more frequently than younger students. However, if we look across all students, the older the students get, the higher the proportion of students who use computers at school (see Table 10.3). Interestingly, even the Nordic countries, which have the highest percentage of children using computers in schools, have the same frequencies of use as other countries (once or twice a week).

The Computer as Typewriter and Games Machine

Computers can be used in many ways to enhance the learning process. (Gill, 1996). In the countries investigated here, the computer is used most as a typewriter (59%), for games (34%), and for drawing and math (30%). Least frequent are uses that depend on multimedia or the Internet: 13% use the Internet, 9% CD-ROM, and 6% e-mail. There are clear differences between countries in the uses of new media (see Table 10.4), with the United Kingdom leading in many forms of computer use in school.

TABLE 10.2
Overview of the Computer Use in European Schools in Percentages
(Computer Users Only, $N = 5213$)

How often do you use computers in school?	Average All Ages	Age 6-7	Age 9-10	Age 12-13	Age 15-16
Less than once a month	18	16	18	19	19
About once a month	14	15	18	13	12
About once a week	42	42	39	47	39
2 or 3 days a week	21	16	19	19	24
4 or 5 days a week	6	10	6	3	6

Note. 10 countries. Data from Denmark and France not available in common database.

TABLE 10.3
How Often Do You Use Computers in School?
(Users Only; N = 6393)

Country	All	Gender		Age				SES		
		Boy	Girl	6-7	9-10	12-13	15-16	High	Med	Low
IL	1.6	1.7	1.5	1.7	1.9	1.4	1.4	1.5	1.7	1.6
BE (vlg)	1.4	1.6	1.4	2.0	0.9	0.5	1.8	1.3	1.8	1.5
GB	1.4	1.5	1.4	1.6	1.1	1.2	1.8	1.4	1.4	1.5
ES	1.4	1.5	1.3	0.1	1.5	1.5	1.4	-	-	-
SE	1.3	1.4	1.1	1.0	1.2	1.2	1.4	1.2	1.2	1.3
DE	1.2	1.2	1.1	0.6	1.1	0.8	0.7	0.9	0.8	0.9
NL	1.1	1.2	1.1	1.2	1.3	1.2	0.9	1.0	1.1	1.2
FI	1.0	1.1	0.9	0.7	1.0	0.9	1.3	1.1	0.9	1.0
CH	1.0	1.1	0.9	-	0.9	0.9	1.1	1.0	0.9	1.2
IT*	1.0	0.9	1.0	-	-	0.8	1.0	0.6	1.0	1.3
DK	0.9	1.1	0.6	1.1	0.8	0.8	0.7	0.9	0.8	0.9
Average of the averages	1.2	1.3	1.1	1.1	1.2	1.1	1.3	1.1	1.2	1.3

4-5 days a week	4.5	about once a month	0.25
2-3 days a week	2.5	less than once a month	0.1
about once a week	1		

*Age groups 12-13 and 15-16 only in Italian sample; French data not available.

TABLE 10.4
Percentage   Using the Internet in School (Based on All Respondents, Four Age Bands; N = 7041)

Country	All	Gender		Age				SES		
		Boy	Girl	6-7	9-10	12-13	15-16	High	Med	Low
SE	36	38	34	3	13	37	59	32	39	34
FI	34	33	35	1	14	45	59	33	35	34
DK	22	28	17	1	7	33	47	24	20	20
CH	11	15	7	-	-	1	18	25	10	3
IL	7	8	6	6	3	9	9	8	8	5
DE	7	8	7	0	0	3	12	3	3	10
NL	6	8	3	1	2	7	13	7	5	5
GB	5	6	4	0	1	6	12	7	4	4
ES	1	1	1	0	1	2	1	-	-	-
E (vlg)	1	1	1	0	0	0	1	1	0	2
FR	1	1	1	-	-	2	2	3	0	2
Average of the averages	12	13	11	1	5	13	21	14	12	12

Note. 11 European countries; Italian data not available.

226

Computers can be used either in a more playful or in a more serious way. The younger children are, the more they mention playing games on computers in school; the older they are, the more they use computers for different and more complex activities like programming. There are variations across countries in allowing (IL and NL) or disallowing (CH, DE, BE-vlg) children to play electronic games. Playing games in school means both using "learning games" (edutainment) and just playing on the computer to fill time. Using the Internet for participating in chat groups is often forbidden to the students, as is illustrated in the following quote from a 16-year old Swedish girl, although the educational potential of this use for practicing English conversation appears not to be valued by the teachers: "We are not allowed to chat and such things on the Internet. I think that we should be allowed to do that, as one is learning English."

The initial rationale for the introduction of computers into schools in the 1980s was that children would learn programming skills. Subsequently, most schools stopped teaching programming and instead used existing programs for writing, drawing, etc. Some countries (like Germany, Flanders, and Spain),[5] with a comparatively low percentage of students who use computers in school, still have an old-fashioned approach to teaching programming. Other countries (e.g., the Nordic countries), with a high percentage of computer use and modern multimedia equipment in schools, very seldom teach programming. The use of computers in math seems to be of special importance for children aged 9 to 10 years old. This may be connected to edutainment software to train basic mathematical operations. For example, 15- to 16-year-old students mainly use database programs and spreadsheets. About half of the computer-using students of this age group in the United Kingdom, Spain, and Switzerland mentioned this use. In the Nordic countries and in Israel, this kind of use is not very common. Drawing with computers is an activity that starts with the 6- to 7-year-olds, if they have computers in school. The United Kingdom and Israel especially have a high proportion of the youngest children who use computers for drawing.

The Nordic countries are innovative users of the Internet in school, with a considerable difference of average Internet use compared to all the other European countries. In most countries, use of the Internet is only worth mentioning at the age group of 12 to 16 years.

The United Kingdom and Finland stand out for many forms of computer use, whereas Flanders shows the lowest figures for several forms of computer usage (see Table 10.5). This is again consistent with computer use in the adult population in these countries.

---

[5]To be able to construct a computer program is a qualification that is useful only for specialists nowadays, as computers are considered as a tool to be used as "plug and play" technology. Above all, there is no sense for primary school children to learn programming.

TABLE 10.5
Computer Activities in School Based on All Who Use a Computer in School ($N = 4459$)

Ability (in percentages)	Average of the Sample	Country With Highest Average	Percentage in Country With Highest Average	Country With Lowest Average	Percentage in Country With Lowest Average
Writing on the computer	59	GB	75	BE (vlg)	35
Playing games	34	IL	62	BE (vlg) and CH	16
Drawing/Design	29	GB	50	BE (vlg)	17
Using PC for math	28	NL	53	CH and IL	16
Using PC for database	20	GB	34	FI and IL	11
Using the Internet	13	FI	42	BE (vlg)	1
Programming	18	DE	34	SE	6
Using CD-ROM	9	GB	27	ES	3
E-mail	6	FI	17	BE (vlg) and ES	1

Note. 10 European countries; Danish and French data not available.

PLACES AND FUNCTIONS OF COMPUTER USE

The following quote from a 16-year-old Swiss boy shows that even when computers are available—in this case, in his bedroom—they may be used only rarely for schoolwork.

> If we have to write a presentation for the school, I write it on the PC. But this happens maybe once in two months. ... As I'm a group-leader in the boy scouts, I write the schedule for the children on the PC, this happens about once a month.... Sometimes, when we don't know what else to do, my friends and I play games on my computer.

We asked children and young people how much they used computers at home for homework and for playing games. Not surprisingly, computers at home are used more frequently for playing games and less for doing homework. An interesting finding is that in some countries with a high percentage of computer use in school, like the Netherlands, Finland, and Sweden, computers are used for homework only for a small part of home usage time. In other countries with a relatively low percentage of computer use in school, computers are used more frequently for homework, but still less than half of the time. In a comparative analysis of qualitative interviews from Finland, Spain, and Switzerland (Süss et al., 1998), we found that the organization of access to computers in schools may be very different in the European countries. In Finland computer rooms in schools are open after school hours, and students are free to use computers and the Internet without supervision of teachers. Importantly, this system allows children to practice their computer skills and do homework on the computer even if they do not have a computer at home. This is not the case in many other countries. In Switzerland and Spain, computer rooms in schools are only open to students during lessons with the guidance of their teacher, and most schools have no independent Internet access for students. This produces a higher influence of social class on the possibility of developing computer competency, because more children of higher social classes have a computer at home or even in their room and have Internet access at home (see chapter 3). The following quote from an interview with a 15-year-old Swiss girl illustrates how access to the computer room in schools may be restricted:

> We are not allowed to use a PC on our own for homework or other things in school, because we have not yet accomplished the computer-science course. But we follow a course in typewriting, where we write texts on a computer, but this does not allow us to use the computer room. Maybe we would have the possibility to use the Internet in the school library, but I never tried to figure out if this is true.

In the United Kingdom, after-school computer clubs, where available, make possible a more independent use of the school's IT facilities by its pupils.

ATTITUDES TOWARD COMPUTERS AND COMPUTER COURSES

We presented the young people with some statements concerning the value and influence of new media and asked them if they agree or disagree. We then looked at the difference in the answers of children who use a computer at home or not and of students who use computers in school or not. In most cases, young people with access to or use of computers agreed more with the positive judgments on computers and they disagreed more with the negative ones. This may be interpreted as an example of cognitive dissonance (Festinger, 1957): If one is not able to use computers, one will be more likely to think that this is not important. The social pressure to be computer literate is increasing in all sectors of the Information Society. A 15-year-old Swiss boy, whose father is a farmer and who wants to become a farmer himself, showed little interest in the computer and explained that for a Swiss farmer it is not very important to use computers. This would be different in the United States, he explained, where projects are done to steer tractors with a computer from the house, but with the small pieces of land in Switzerland, he expects that this will never be the case there. He admitted, however, that his father and mother use the computer for bookkeeping, calculations, and for writing letters.

I don't like to work with the computer, but I know that one should be able to do this. I wouldn't like to learn a profession, in which I would be forced to sit in front of the screen the whole day long. For an hour or so it is OK, but not for longer.

Students who use computers at home and in school have the most positive attitudes toward computers and are most confident about their computer literacy. In the United Kingdom, children who use computers only in school are more convinced that "people get left behind, if they don't know about computers" than children who use computers at home only (see Table 10.6). In most countries, attitudes toward computers are similar for children who use computers only at home or only in school. Children generally agreed that "school should teach you more about computers" (see Table 10.7). However, there are differences in the levels of perceived importance of teaching computing in school. In Italy and the Netherlands, children who only use computers at home think that school should teach more about computers, but in some other countries, children who use computers at home and in school or only in school want more computer courses. Children who do not use computers at all are the least interested in computer courses. Possible explanations may be that children who never used computers may be afraid of them or just do not know the benefits of computers for learning in school. Children who use computers just at home use them mainly for playing games, and they may fear that the teaching of computing at school will force them to do more serious computer work.

TABLE 10.6
Percentage of Children Saying They Think "People Get Left Behind" by Usage of Computers at Home or in School ($N = 6548$)

	Location of Computer Usage			
Country	Neither at School or home	In School Only	In School and at Home	At Home Only
CH	16	39	34	31
DE	31	51	65	49
ES	27	36	36	33
GB	47	54	61	44
IL	23	32	27	30
IT	32	31	43	42
NL	29	41	44	48
SE	29	39	48	35
Average of averages	29	40	45	39

Note. Base: 8 European countries; data from Flanders, Denmark, Finland, France not available.

TABLE 10.7
Percentage of Children Saying They Think "School Should Teach Them More About Computers"
by Usage of Computers at Home or in School ($N = 3619$)

Country	Location of Computer Usage			
	Neither at School or home	In School Only	In School and at Home	At Home Only
CH	52	66	68	61
DE	50	72	80	71
IL	42	53	62	58
IT	76	85	78	85
NL	50	50	47	69
Average of averages	54	65	67	69

Note. Base: 5 European countries; data from the other 7 countries not available.

Unimaginative attitudes toward the use of computers appear not to be limited to today's teachers. Even young people who want to become teachers are sometimes unaware of new concepts of media-integrated learning strategies. For example, a 16-year-old Swiss girl, who wants to become a teacher, talked in an interview about the use of computers as a teacher in school: "If I have to prepare an examination for the students or some kind of test, the computer may be helpful and I will need some computer competency. But otherwise I don't see any sensible use for the computer in school."

A similar pattern emerges in responses to questions about personal competence and enthusiasm toward computers (see Table 10.8).[6] Children who use computers at home and in school are most confident about computers and think of themselves as having high levels of computer competency. Children who do not use computers at all are least confident, although 44% of them feel comfortable using computers. Looking at the average of the whole European sample, we see that 67% of the children who use computers only in school feel comfortable with them and 77% of children with computer use only at home feel comfortable with them. 14% of the European children have computer use neither at home nor in school. Of these "underprivileged" children, 23% do not feel comfortable, 35% are unsure, but still 42% feel comfortable with computers: "I don't really like them [computers]. I don't really know much about them, so I'm scared I'm going to break them" (15–16-year

---

[6]In the evaluation of the results, we realized that this question might have been understood in different ways. Some children may have referred to GameBoys and other games-computers, whereas others may have referred only to personal computers (as was our intention). For this reason, the results should be interpreted with caution.

TABLE 10.8
Percentage of Children Saying "They Feel Comfortable Using a Computer" by Usage of
Computers at Home or in School ($N = 6339$)

| | Location of Computer Usage | | | |
Country	Neither at School or home	In School Only	In School and at Home	At Home Only
CH	38	59	72	65
DE	15	67	94	86
ES	46	75	90	89
GB	72	95	94	90
IL	56	79	91	86
IT	25	49	71	66
NL	40	50	53	52
SE	63	80	91	85
Average of averages	44	69	82	77

Note. Base: 8 European countries; data from Flanders, Denmark, Finland, France not available.

old British girl, working class). Of the 41% "highly privileged" children in the European sample with computer use at home and in school, only 8% do not feel comfortable with computers, 13% are unsure, and 79% feel comfortable.

In most countries, children feel more comfortable using computers if they use them at home only than if they use them in school only. For some children, the place for learning about computers is mainly at home and with peers, as for example for the Swedish girl cited here:

Int: Do you think that you are learning much about computers in school?

G: I learn at home!

Int: Is there a difference between those who can't use a computer and those who are good at it?

G: Yes, for those who are good at it, they have it easy, like Peter in our class. He is the best at computers in our class, and he is using it much more, because I don't really know how to turn it on, and not many do so. It's more him, who can do it, who turns it on.

(9-year-old Swedish girl)

Qualitative interviews with adolescents in Switzerland showed that some students take voluntary computer science courses in school, because they think it will "look good" on their applications for apprenticeships, even if they do not learn new competencies in these courses. The 16-year-old Swiss girl cited in the following quote has her own PC in her bedroom and she uses it for writing texts for school and applications, but mostly for playing games. She considers her computer literacy as mediocre:

> All of us are bored in the computer science course in school. It would be an interesting subject, but the teacher makes it all boring. So we are really happy that the course takes place only every second week. It is a voluntary course. I applied to it because this is general knowledge. It looks good, if one has accomplished this course. Even if one knows already everything in advance.

To some extent the excitement or boredom in computer courses is influenced by children's view of school computers. Working class children are often satisfied with the equipment, as it is better than their computers at home, if they have one at all. For middle-class children, it is often different, as they are well equipped with the latest technology at home. Consider the following group discussion that took place in the computer room of a secondary school:

Int: Are there lots of computers? I see there are lots in this room, but are they used in the school?
S: Yeah.
E: These computers are crap.
A: There are about three good computers and that's about it.
S: They're all rubbish, like kiddies' computers . . .

(12–13-year old British girls).

In the countries where a higher proportion of children feel comfortable with computers, they also think computers are more exciting. British youngsters were the most enthusiastic (83%) and Dutch youngsters the least (39%), with an average of 60% across 10 countries. Of course, excitement is related to newness: The more computers are taken for granted in all environments, the less exciting they are, unless they are of the best technical standard. At the same time, more and more people should feel comfortable using computers; otherwise it would be alarming for the educational and political system.

ATTITUDES TO SCHOOL AND THE USE OF NEW MEDIA

In most countries, younger children like going to school more than older children, and in all countries, girls like school more than boys. There are no differences between social classes. Overall, the relationships between teachers and students seem to be good for the vast majority of young people. Most of the children in Europe like going to school, with an average between "sometimes" and "usually" (see Table 10.9). There are slight differences among the

TABLE 10.9
Attitudes Toward School by Age Group: Percentage of Pupils "Usually Feeling Like This . . ."

Usually feeling like this . . .	6-7 Years	9-10 Years	12-13 Years	15-16 Years	Average (all age bands)
"I like going to school."	56	42	31	27	34
"I get on well with most of my teachers."	68	61	57	50	58
"I am bored in class."	4	14	20	24	19
"After the weekend I hate going back to school."	11	32	46	45	38

Note. Base for all questions: Respondents from 10 European countries. Not all questions are given to all age bands in every country. Number of respondents varies from 3894 to 7566.

countries. Children like going to school best in Denmark, Sweden, and the Netherlands and they least like going to school in Flanders and Germany.

We looked at the relationship between using computers in school and liking going to school. There is a very small significant correlation between these two variables in the 9- to 10- and 12- to 13-year-old children. If children of these ages use computers in school quite frequently, they like going to school more often than children who use computers very seldom or never. However, other variables such as having good relationships with the teachers seem to be much more important (see Table 10.10). Our data do not allow us to give a more precise picture of how the relationship between liking school and the availability of computers will develop, but it gives some clues to follow in further projects. Young students may be motivated if they get the chance to learn with new media in school. This may be particularly worth noting for the countries that have hitherto only integrated new media in classes for older students. Starting off young pupils in computers may have positive effects on general attitudes to school.[7]

ON THE WAY TO NEW MEDIA LITERACY

In some respects, schools already compensate for uneven access to new media. There are much fewer gaps between girls and boys and between children from different social classes at schools than in homes (see chapters 3 and 4). However, "learning" is still most strongly associated with using print media by both teachers and pupils in most countries (see Table 4.9 in chap-

---

[7]In Switzerland for example, a pilot project started in 1998 with the integration of computer use, English lessons, and new teaching concepts from first grade of primary school on in the region of Zurich (project 21).

TABLE 10.10
Spearman Correlations of Liking School With Other Variables

	Correlation of degree of liking going to school with . . .	
Age bands:	Frequency of computer use in school	Feeling like: "I get on well with most of my teachers."
6-7 years	.056 n.s	.604
9-10 years	.082	.317
12-13 years	.104	.366
15-16 years	-.033 n.s.	.415
Gender		
Boys (9-13 years)	.093	.363
Girls (9-13 years)	.090	.311

Note. Underlines = correlation is significant at the 0.01 level; n.s. = not significant. Base: 10 European countries; Danish and French data not available.

ter 4). There are some differences between the countries in terms of the perceived value of new media to learning. In the Nordic countries, audiovisual media are well accepted as useful for learning processes, whereas in countries like Switzerland and Spain, this is rarely the case. The following quote from a 15-year-old Swedish girl illustrates a successful integration of different media in the learning process at school and the development of a critical awareness of the need to check the credibility of sources, whether they come from old or new media:

Int: Are the teachers encouraging you to use the Internet?

Girl: Yes, they do. We are usually getting some hours to our disposal . . . Well, now you can either go to the library or those who want may go to the computer room and use the Internet to see if you find anything . . . Most of them use the Internet.

Int: What does your teacher say about the Internet?

Girl: Just that it is another source.

Int: Do they teach you to be critical?

Girl: Yes, but we also have to be that with books or articles in the newspapers. I think it is good to be a little critical, checking if it is really so.

Observations and interviews in a private computer camp in Switzerland showed a new style of learning environment that seems to be very much liked by children because of its difference from school (Süss, 1998). Children can learn all kinds of computer techniques, use the Internet, and even play the latest virtual reality games with head-mounted display and cyber mouse. Part of the time they play games, and part of the time they can choose computer courses at different levels. Because of the relatively high cost of such courses, the participants in these camps are mostly from families with a high socioeconomic status. The media equipment of these children at home is far above average and their computer literacy gets strong support, so that when they go back to school after vacations, they are a bigger challenge to their teachers and their underprivileged colleagues than before.

Examples from a Swiss manual for media education may indicate possible ways for schools to enhance computer literacy of the students, in the sense of learning more than just knowing how to "plug and play" (see Fröhlich, Ramseier, & Walter, 1994, p. 75). Electronic games may not just be played in school, but may also be a subject of analysis. Students may bring their electronic games to class and demonstrate them, and the specific experience of the game is discussed in class. Students may go to supermarkets and computer shops, analyze the range of available games, and report it in the lesson. The informal market of sharing games in the peer group may be described and discussed. Electronic games can be analyzed systematically by using criteria such as: What kind of activities lead the player to success? (Shooting, killing, being smart, having fast reactions, etc.) What are the consequences of making mistakes? How close is the plot of the game to situations in real life? Are there any games that could be played without computers? Children can compare the prices, games manuals, and advertising for different games. They could try to invent their own games, report their experiences with electronic games or other computer use at home and in other places, and discuss their opinion on possible positive or negative influences on them. Older students try to find out what kind of youth groups (age, gender, social grade, and educational level) are fans of certain genres of electronic games and their motivations. Students produce a newsletter with their recommendations of good electronic games (Fröhlich et al., 1994, p. 108).

This is just one example of how new media could be integrated in school, not just as a learning tool or to pass the time, but as a school subject in its own right that can help children and young people become aware of the role of media in their life and of the potential positive and negative uses and effects in the context of learning processes as well as work and leisure time. We are not yet clear on the benefits of game playing—is entertainment just fun? Aufenanger (1999) argued that electronic games should be integrated in school because of their potential for cognitive learning, and stressed the value of the ethical, social, and political aspects that can be discussed with students in the context of the games' stories, characters, and strategies for winning. Using the broadest possible range of computer applications, including electronic games, may also result in young people having more positive attitudes toward computer use. As discussed in detail in chapter 11, the motivation to use computers is likely to be increased if young people not only consider them to be important tools for their future professional lives, but if they also associate them with enjoyment.

CONCLUSIONS

About 60% of European youngsters use computers in school. Most children like learning with and about computers in school. The feeling of competency is highest when children use computers in both school and at home. However, even 42% of those without access at school or home feel comfortable using computers. In the schools of the 12 countries, we can find different forms of computer use: more playful or more serious, more varied or more limited. The Internet and e-mail is still very rarely used in schools, with the exception of a few countries like Finland. The political discourse of "Netdays" and "Webteaching" was not yet an integral part of school in Europe in 1997.[8] In interviews, children complain about old-fashioned computers in school or teachers without sufficient computer skills. Some teachers, on the other hand, fear the development of "cut-and-paste" attitudes among students if they allow them to use the Internet for creating papers or essays, as 12–13-year-old Swedish boys explained in the interview:

> We are not allowed to get anything from the Internet, at least not when we are writing. We may write by hand, writing down various facts. (. . .) They think we should write by hand all the time. If we ask if we can use the computer, they say: 'No! But you have such a nice handwriting.' (. . .) One teacher usually says that we first have to write a draft by hand, when we want to use the computer.

The pace of technological development in the private sphere of the home is much faster than in the public sphere of the school. Teachers are not yet prepared enough to teach computer and Internet competencies and to deal with the social aspects of new media. Allowing children to use the computer rooms on their own would be desirable but it can create problematic situations. Some children use the Internet in school to search for pornography, and boys are mobbing girls with dirty jokes in the computer room of the school (Bingham, Holloway, & Valentine, 1998).

---

[8]It is obvious that we refer to a very dynamic process here. That is, in some countries the diffusion of the Internet has increased dramatically since our data collection. We can just give a report of the state at the end of 1997, and this may be useful as a point of comparison for future reports.

Gender differences in the approach toward computers and in computer literacy may be illustrated by the following quotes:

> I'm really bored in the computer-science course in school, because I already know a lot about computers. The course-group is divided into two groups, the weak ones, these are all the girls in our class, and the strong ones, these are all the boys. But unfortunately our group of boys is not supported or challenged enough in this course. The aims of the course are to provide basic knowledge about computer use. After the course one is only able to write texts on a computer. For the girls the course seems to be even too difficult. And the boys are bored, because we know everything already. At home, I like programming, I know Office 97 very well. I have integrated a 64-Bit-Soundcard into my PC, so I can watch television on my PC now. Sometimes I use programs for image processing and I help my colleagues to make a nicer layout of their papers.

> (16-year-old Swiss boy)

> Int: Is it often the case, that when you are using the computer in the class, that certain boys fix everything?
>
> Girl: Yes, because if you can't do anything, you don't call for the teacher, you call for that person (a boy from the class).
>
> Int: So the pupils know to handle the computers better than the teachers?
>
> Girl: Yes, especially the boys in the class, they are very good.

> (15-year-old Swedish girl).

Some teachers try to solve problems between girls and boys with segregated IT courses, groups, or classes (Livingstone & Bovill, 1999). This seems to alleviate boys' dominating behavior toward girls. School administrators try to solve these problems by integrating filter software. A better strategy might be to teach children how to use media in a responsible way; this should be the main aim of media education.

Media education is a mandatory part of the core curriculum in only a few countries. In most countries, students depend on the initiatives of teachers who are media enthusiasts. There are often only a few courses of media education provided during initial training and in-service courses for teachers (Butts, 1992; Sobiech, 1997).

New media literacy is—for some students—achieved thanks not to courses in school but in spite of these courses. Students with computer access at home and a lot of experience and support from parents or friends are "bored to death" in these courses, whereas other students feel the same courses are too demanding. This increasing gap in the knowledge of students (and teachers) demands a new approach to media and computer science courses in schools. Furthermore, it may encourage a new kind of relationship between students and teachers. Some of the students know more about certain programs than their teachers, but taking these students as partners in the learning process could productively use this, as for example tutors for students with less advanced competencies. This could be an opportunity for a democratization process in school in the same way that Pasquier describes for families (see chapter 7).

Like national cultures, families, and bedrooms, schools can be media-rich or media-poor. As we have seen, however, media are not only simply absent or present. In some countries new media are used in more diverse ways (mainly in the United Kingdom, the Nordic countries, and the Netherlands) and in other countries they are used in a more limited way. Like persons or groups, institutions such as schools can be early or late adopters of new media, and innovation can be fast or slow. Children from high SES families are in the "fast lane" of the Information Society because they can use educational resources from outside school. If we look at the ITC expenditure per inhabitant (see chapter 1), we see that some countries with high rates (like Switzerland as No. 1) are far from leading in the integration of new media in schools. This is a challenge for the educational system in Europe, and our findings indicate that schools in some countries still need more support to face this problem successfully.

Some countries are still in the phase of providing schools with PCs or laptops or with connecting schools to the Internet. Others are already a step ahead and support creative use of new media with initiatives like "Web Site Awards for schools and colleges" (for example, the United Kingdom in 1999). Countries with a tradition of a competitive system for schools, like the United Kingdom, where schools are evaluated and publicly positioned in a ranking system, are more likely to rapidly enhance the use of new media in school than countries with a noncompetitive system of state schools like Switzerland. In the latter group of countries, the education policy should support schools with specific profiles. Innovative media use should be one of these profiles for schools, not only for colleges but also for all kinds of schools from kindergarten up to universities.

Further research should evaluate schools with media integrated curricula and give feedback on their development. As the development of media and IT does not stand still, we will have to observe continuously the diffusion of new media (interactive television, portable wireless Internet devices, electronic books, and virtual reality head gear) and document their use in home and school. Only with continuous research and development projects in children's media use and media education is it possible to close the knowledge gap between "digital haves" and "digital have-nots."

REFERENCES

Aufenanger, S. (1999). Computer- und Videospiele—in die Schule! [Computer- and videogames—to the school!]. *Computer und Unterricht. Anregungen und Materialien für das Lernen in der Informationsgesellschaft, 36*, 6–10. [Computer and instruction. Ideas and materials for learning processes in the Information Society].

Baacke, D., Sander, U., & Vollbrecht, R. (1990). *Lebenswelten sind Medienwelten* [Environments of daily life are media environments]. Opladen: Leske und Budrich.

Bertelsmann Stiftung. (Ed.). (1998). *Computer, Internet, Multimedia—Potentiale für Schule und Unterricht. Ergebnisse einer Schul-Evaluation* [Computer, the Internet, multimedia—Potentials for school and teaching. Results of an evaluation project]. Gütersloh: Verlag Bertelsmann Stiftung.

Bingham, N., Holloway, S., & Valentine, G. (1998, March 5–6). *"At Home" or "Off Limits"?—Differences amongst children's experiences on-line and their implications for an inclusive "Information Society."* Paper presented at the Children & Social Exclusion Conference. Centre for the Study of Childhood. Hull University, Hull, England.

Bonfadelli, H. (1994). *Die Wissenskluft-Perspektive* [The knowledge gap perspective]. Konstanz: Oelschläger.

Butts, D. (1992). Strategies for media education. In C. Bazalgette, E. Bevort, & J. Savino (Eds.), *New directions. Media education worldwide* (pp. 224–229). London: British Film Institute.

Deckers, J. (1997). *Nutzung des Internet in der Schule. Eine Einführung* [The use of the Internet in school. An introduction]. Gütersloh: Verlag Bertelsmann Stiftung.

Diener, U., Dönhoff, H.-U., Rieks, K.-E., & Weigend, M. (1998). *Neue Medien im Unterricht—Vorbild USA? Bericht von einer Studienreise in verschiedene Schulen der USA* [New media in teaching—USA as a model? Report from travel to different schools in USA]. Gütersloh: Verlag Bertelsmann Stiftung.

Doelker, C. (1989). *Kulturtechnik Fernsehen. Analyse eines Mediums* [Watching television as a cultural skill. Analysis of a medium]. Stuttgart: Klett-Cotta.

Festinger, L. (1957). *A theory of cognitive dissonance*. Stanford, CA: Stanford University Press.

Fröhlich, A., Ramseier, E., & Walter, R. (1994). *Medienpädagogik. Wegleitung für alle Schulstufen* [Media education. Manual for all school levels]. Liestal: Verlag des Kantons Basel-Landschaft.

Gill, T. (Ed.). (1996). *Electronic children. How children are responding to the information revolution*. London: National Children's Bureau.

Hart, A. (Ed.). (1998). *Teaching the media. International perspectives*. Mahwah, NJ: Lawrence Erlbaum Associates.

Hart, A., & Benson, T. (1993). *Media in the classroom. English teachers teaching media*. Southampton: Report from the School of Education.

Hart, A., & Hicks, A. (1999). *Teaching media in English. Summary report*. Southampton: Report from the Research and Graduate School of Education.

Issing, L. J. (Ed.). (1987). *Medienpädagogik im Informationszeitalter* [Media education in the information age]. Weinheim: Deutscher Studienverlag.

Livingstone, S., & Bovill, M. (1999). *Young people—new media*. Report of the research project "Children, young people and the changing media environment." London: London School of Economics and Political Science.

Masterman, L. (1985). *Teaching the media*. London: Routledge.

Masterman, L. (1996). Media education worldwide: Objectives, values and superhighways. *Africa Media Review, 10*, 2, 37–51.

Postman, N. (1985). *Amusing ourselves to death. Public discourse in the age of show business*. New York: Viking-Penguin.

Postman, N. (1994). *The disappearance of childhood*. New York: Viking-Penguin.

Postman, N. (1996). *The end of education. Redefining the value of school*. New York: Viking-Penguin.

Potter, J. W. (1998). *Media literacy.* Thousand Oaks, CA: Sage Publications.

Schorb, B. (Ed.). (1992). *Medienerziehung in Europa. Auf dem Weg zu einer europäischen Medienkultur* [Media education in Europe. Towards a European culture of media]. München: KoPad Verlag.

Sobiech, D. (1997). *Theorie und Praxis der Medienerziehung im Vergleich. Eine Analyse von Konzepten, Strukturen und Bedingungen* [Theory and practice of media education in comparison. An analysis of concepts, structures and conditions]. München: KoPäd.

Süss, D. (1998). Kinder im Sog virtueller Realitäten [Children in the wake of virtual reality]. In P. Hugger (Ed.), *Kind sein in der Schweiz* [Childhood in Switzerland] (pp. 435–440). Zürich: Offizin.

Süss, D., Suoninen, A., Garitaonandia, C., Juaristi, P., Koikkalainen, R., & Oleaga, J. (1998): Media Use and the relationships of children and teenagers with their peer group. A study of Finnish, Spanish and Swiss cases. *European Journal of Communication. Special Issue, 13*(4), 521–538.

Winterhoff-Spurk, P. (1999). Von der Wissenskluft zur medialen Klassengesellschaft [From the knowledge gap to the media related class society]. In Gesellschaft für Medienpädagogik und Kommunikationskultur (Ed.), *Mediengesellschaft–Neue Klassengesellschaft?* [Media Society–new class society?] (pp. 28–43). Bielefeld: GMK-Rundbrief, 42.

EMERGING THEMES

11

Who Are the New Media Users?

Friedrich Krotz
Uwe Hasebrink

WHAT IS "NEW"?

Whenever media technologies start their diffusion process, they are discussed as *the new media*. Accordingly, there has to be a concept of *the old media* that might be displaced or at least change their former social functions (see chapter 5). Thus, thinking in terms of old and new media is a familiar aspect of media-related discourse. As a rule, this kind of discourse also includes the concept of *new media users*. The (often implicit) argument here is that the new media are not used as just another, more comfortable means to serve certain functions in everyday life, but that they are linked to new functions, to new patterns of social and cultural behavior, and finally, to new identities (Turkle, 1995). Although it is not yet possible at this stage of the diffusion process of today's new media to evaluate this strong hypothesis, this chapter aims to provide empirical evidence with regard to the question of how far the so-called new media are actually new in functional terms and what place they occupy in young people's media environment.

Because qualifying some media as new and others as old means making a distinction that is not at all unambiguous, we first try to clarify the notion of *new* in the context of our study.

At any given time, some media are regarded as new: television in the 1950s and 1960s, video in the 1970s, cable and satellite broadcasting in the 1980s. Within the context of this study, all computer-based applications and services are regarded as new. The *new media* are thus not necessarily those that were technically invented most recently, but rather those that recently experienced a fast first phase of diffusion or for which opinion leaders expect such a fast diffusion to begin very soon. Thus, the *new media* is a social construct that partly reflects the communication-related concerns and hopes of a culture at a given time.

This construct aggregates quite different meanings. Although for some people the new media are still unknown or in the realms of science fiction, others have already gotten used to them. Thus, although the notion of new media might refer to exactly the same technology and content, their social meaning and hence the quality of their newness may be very different for different groups. One important point here is whether people have lived in an environment without the new media and thus can judge whether new media technologies or contents are different from what they knew before. For many of today's children and young people, who grow up with computers and the Internet, these media are not new; they do not know a life without them. Of course, they understand that their parents, other adults, and the public discourse qualify these everyday tools as something new and important for the future. It is in this context that we must understand the specific relation between children and their parents as it evolves with regard to computers and computer literacy (see Tapscott, 1998, and chapter 7).

Taking the pragmatic definition of new media as computer-based digital media as a starting point, a first answer to the question, "Who are the new media users?" would simply be "all those making use of new media." As was shown in previous chapters, computer-based media have attained quite an important place in children's and young people's lives, so that computers are used by almost all children and young people—at least sometimes and for some purposes. Thus, in general and certainly in the long term, it is unlikely that we could identify a specific group of users of digital media to be called the new media users, because more or less all children and young people would be included (see e.g., Fidler, 1997; Negroponte, 1995).

In order to deal with our question more properly, we have to reflect on the process of diffusion of any new media. How do the new media diffuse into society and the everyday lives of children and young people? Which conditions influence this diffusion process? What are the core purposes for which the new media are used and what is their relationship to the old media (see chapter 5)? Which consequences do different paths of diffusion have for society in general and children in particular? In what follows, we first briefly discuss the concept of diffusion. Then we present a stepwise approach to identifying different paths of diffusion. Starting with patterns of access to computers, findings are presented regarding patterns of computer use and attitudes toward computers. Finally, we discuss this empirical evidence with regard to the future diffusion of computers and computer-mediated communication.

DIFFUSION AS A CONSTRUCTIVE PROCESS

Assuming that more or less all children and adolescents will use computers in the near future, the data collected in our study can be seen as providing a snapshot of a certain stage of the diffusion process of digital media in Europe. According to a mechanistic model, diffusion could be defined in terms of technical equipment with a built-in social or cultural function. Then the process of diffusion would be just a question of the quantitative distribution of the new equipment. However, although new media usually start their diffusion as just a technological option, as basic hardware and basic software, the matter is more complex. How this option is put into practice, for which purposes it is used, is defined by those who make use of the new tools, by consumer demand, by marketing strategies, by enthusiasts who develop enhanced hardware and software, and by critics who impose certain limitations on development (see Rogers, 1986, 1995). This collective network of actions gradually leads to a general image of the new technology that refers to general expectations about what can and should be done with the new medium. Thus, the diffusion process is a qualitative and constructive process.

It is by this process only that a new technological option is culturally and socially defined as a medium. Several researchers, although of different theoretical backgrounds, emphasized this difference between technological options and culturally and socially contextualized media. Kubicek, Schmid, and Wagner (1997) differentiate between "first order media" as technical options, which are transformed into "second order media." Through this transformation process, media are "cultivated" (Rammert, 1996) and a specific media "disposition" is developed (Hickethier, 1993). Similarly, Höflich (1998), with reference to Goffman (1976) talks of the "framing" of computer technologies.

In this chapter, we are less interested in quantitative measures of how many people have access to or use the new media (see chapter 3). A more challenging question is to analyze how digital technologies are appropriated within everyday practices and thus which kind of medium is constructed as a result.

In order to answer this question, we cannot speak of today's new media in general. Instead, we have to understand personal computers (PC) and the practices associated with them as one innovation, and computer mediated communication (CMC), the most important being the Internet today, as another innovation.[1] It is obvious that CMC depends on access and use of computers, and it is likely that in the future, children and young people will

---

[1]Of course, today's "new" digital media include further important features (e.g., the cellular phone or Tamagotchis). However, in the following we confine ourselves to PC and CMC in order to develop our argument as clearly as possible.

not differentiate them. However, for 1997, the time of our survey, it is important to differentiate between these innovations because they had reached a different stage of diffusion—the computer was clearly the older new medium than was the Internet.

Taking the Internet as an example, we can understand each country involved in our study as a social and cultural system in which diffusion gradually takes place and has reached a certain stage in 1997. Table 11.1 shows how many children and young people have used the Internet in the different countries. A simple interpretation of the results in terms of diffusion theory would take the differences with regard to Internet use as indicators for the countries being positioned in different phases of a regular and linear process of diffusion. For example, one could conclude that, in 1997, Sweden and Finland had reached a far more advanced phase within this process than Germany, and that in some years, Germany might be where Sweden was in 1997. For several reasons, however, the diffusion process of new media is unlikely to follow the same linear path in different societies and cultures and in different practices of everyday life.

One indicator for different diffusion processes is the difference with regard to age. Although there is a clear linear trend across countries (with the exception of Flanders) according to which the use of the Internet is more widespread in the older age groups, in some countries this age effect is particularly strong. For example, Germany has by far the lowest figures for the three younger age groups, but among the 15- and 16-year-old adolescents, use of the Internet comes closer to the standards set by the other countries. Differences like this might be interpreted as cultural differences in the social construction of the new medium: In Germany, the Internet seems to be linked with becom-

TABLE 11.1
Percentage of Young People Who Have Used the Internet

Country (n_{total})	Total	6-7 Years	9-10 Years	12-13 Years	15-16 Years	Male	Female
SE (1230)	66	29	46	75	86	71	61
FI (753)	55	15	45	73	86	63	47
IL (759)	37	19	31	43	53	43	31
ES (693)	29	7	28	30	34	35	23
CH (1049)	**26	n.a.	11	25	40	**33	**20
IT (763)	*20	n.a.	n.a.	19	21	*26	*15
NL (893)	17	1	10	22	33	23	10
BE vlg (570)	14	6	7	20	17	19	9
GB (869)	13	1	8	18	23	16	9
DE (829)	11	0	2	11	28	15	6

Note. In % of total; basis: age bands 6-7, 9-10, 12-13, and 15-16 years. *Age bands 12-13 and 15-16 years only. **Age bands 9-10, 12-13, 15-16 years only.

ing adult, whereas in Spain, Italy, Flanders, and the United Kingdom, the increase in the use of the Internet from age group 12 to 13 to age group 15 to 16 is lower, thus the medium seems to be less focused on a specific age group and its specific purposes for using it.

In order to understand better the paths by which new media are integrated within social and cultural practices, and so are constructed as new media, we have to examine more closely the patterns of use observed in different countries.

THE SENSE OF PLACE: INSTITUTIONAL
AND PRIVATE PATHS TOWARD NEW MEDIA USE

With regard to the diffusion of PCs and CMC, there are at least two main channels: school and family (see chapters 10 and 7). We refer to these two channels as the public or institutional one on the one hand and the private one on the other hand. Our study provides clear evidence that there are substantial differences between countries as to whether young people get access to computers and the Internet at school or at home. These paths depend on political, cultural, and economic factors.

Here it has to be emphasized that for the age group we are interested in, we cannot directly apply the models of diffusion as discussed in the literature (e.g., Jäckel, 1990; Rogers, 1995). Children and young people can decide only to a limited extent whether they buy a new piece of technical equipment. Such media are expensive and in addition are rather complicated to use. Thus, when they become interested in new technologies, young people have to rely significantly on their parents or other adults, who usually are themselves not too familiar with the new options and thus might not support the diffusion process even if children are intrinsically motivated to use computers. On the other hand, many politicians, teachers, and even parents strongly emphasize the importance of media education and computer skills. This might create a kind of extrinsic motivation to use new media and as such support diffusion. As a consequence, whether children or young people become early adopters of new media strongly depends on their parents, their school, and their social and cultural environment.

Against this background, we begin our analysis of different paths of diffusion with the very basic question of where young people get access to computers and the Internet. The first column in Table 11.2 summarizes the results discussed in chapter 3 with regard to access to computers at home. In face of the considerable differences among countries in terms of computer access, we would expect similar differences when it comes to the question of computer use. However, the picture presented in Table 11.2 is not at all clear. Although there is a trend indicating that young people in the four big-

TABLE 11.2
Access to PC at Home and Frequency of Computer Use in School Versus at Home

| | | | | PC used . . . | | |
Country (n)	Access to PC at Home	No PC Use at all	Only at School	School at Least as Often as at Home	More Often at Home	Only at Home
BE (vlg) (592)	94	25	16	14	14	31
NL (889)	84	6	24	24	31	15
IL (817)	74	12	14	12	33	28
FI (753)	70	12	18	12	43	15
SE (1291)	66	7	26	21	35	11
CH (1125)	61	18	11	13	23	35
ES (927)	54	32	16	8	14	31
IT (789)*	53	16	20	11	25	28
DE (815)	51	41	10	6	12	30
GB (688)	50	7	48	18	22	5

Note. In % of total, row percentages; basis: age bands 6-7, 9-10, 12-13, and 15-16 years.
*Age bands 12-13 and 15-16 years only.

ger countries, which have only low access to computers at home, are more likely not to use the PC at all, there are notable exceptions. British children belong to those with the most widespread computer use, whereas quite a lot of Flemish children do not use the PC although there is a computer at home. There is also no systematic association between computer access at home and the most common location for using the computer. In some countries (e.g., CH, IT, IL, FI), more than 50% use the computer more often at home than at school. In the United Kingdom, the opposite is true; here "the institutional way" appears to be favored, with more than half of the respondents saying they use the computer more often in school than at home. Sweden and the Netherlands also seem to provide many opportunities to use computers in school.

Another result shown in Table 11.2 is that computer use at home is generally more attractive (or available) than at school. The comparison between those groups who definitely can use both options, because they combine computer use at school and at home, shows that the group of those who use the computer more often at home than at school is bigger than the group who uses the computer at least as often at school as at home; the only exception here is Flanders.

These results underline the fact that there is no common pattern of diffusion across the countries. Whereas in some countries the computer is something that is closely linked to school, in other countries it is mainly used at home in leisure time.

The same is true with regard to the places where young people have contact with the Internet (see Table 11.3). With the exception of Israel, contact with the Internet in schools and libraries is closely correlated with the overall distribution of this medium (see chapter 1). For other places—at home, at the parents' workplace, and at a friend's house—there is no correlation with the overall distribution at all. Countries differ with regard to the relative importance of the places where young people have access to the Internet. Whereas in Sweden and Finland, school is by far the most important place (in terms of broad access), in Italy, Spain, and Israel, most young people have contact with the Internet at home. For all countries, Internet use at a friend's house plays quite a role; in Flanders, Germany, Israel, and Switzerland, this is the most common way to access the Internet. Cybercafés seem to be used mainly in those countries, which seem to have the least developed public infrastructure (e.g., in schools, libraries) and at the same time the lowest figures of Internet use. These results point to the important role of public support for new technologies within the process of diffusion.

With regard to the public path to new technologies, the difference between access in schools and access in other public places has to be emphasized: According to results presented in chapter 7, many parents experience difficulties with new technologies, being not always sure how to use them and how to integrate them into their lives. The resulting competence gap between parents and children was discussed by, among others, Tapscott (1998) as a growing generation gap, which might pose a serious challenge for the future. After all, providing access to PCs and CMC in schools means providing access for children only, whereas public libraries also offer access for the older generation. Thus, the differences between countries (see Table 11.3) in how and where teenagers gain contact with the Internet has implications for age-based stratifications within the so-called information societies.

The results in Table 11.3 suggest that it is very likely that differences in the kind of access to new media are linked to different functional approaches to these media. Having contact with a certain medium in a school context only should lead to a rather instrumental and learning-oriented attitude, whereas using the same medium at home or at a friend's house should link it with more entertaining and exploratory functions. The following section discusses this hypothesis.

PATTERNS OF NEW MEDIA USE:
PLAYING AND WORKING

One characteristic of today's new media technologies is their multifunctionality—computers can be used for very different purposes. Thus, in order to understand different paths of diffusion and different conceptions of what the

TABLE 11.3
Where Do Teenagers Have Contact With or Use the Internet?

	SE	FI	IL	CH	ES	NL	GB	DE	BE	IT
(a) adolescents using/watching the Internet (% of total)	94	91	80	65	57	53	46	39	37	52
(b) adolescents using/watching the Internet at specific places										
as a % of those who do use it (see row a)										
At home	33	24	38	26	30	n.a.	n.a.	20	25	20
At parents' workplace	13	11	13	15	16	n.a.	n.a.	8	15	13
At a friend's house	40	36	53	39	11	n.a.	n.a.	42	43	51
In school	61	73	15	21	14	n.a.	n.a.	19	2	6
At a cybercafé	6	n.a.	1	10	8	n.a.	n.a.	14	14	12
In a library	22	51	10	8	26	n.a.	n.a.	3	8	7
At other places	8	4	9	n.a.	23	n.a.	n.a.	15	18	9

(a) Percentage of teenagers (age bands 12-13 and 15-16 years) having used the Internet or at least watched somebody else using the Internet.
(b) Percentage of teenagers according to row a who had contact with or used the Internet at the respective place.

new media mean to young people, we have to look in more detail at what young people are actually doing with these almost universal tools. Table 11.4 shows for which purposes children and young people use a computer, separately for uses at home and at school. The figures in Table 11.4 are based on those respondents only who claimed to use computers at both home and school. Playing games and writing are the most popular options, whereas the majority does not yet use the on-line applications like the Internet or e-mail. What is important here is the comparison between use at school and at home. Clearly, playing games is the leading purpose at home, with writing and drawing following. At school, writing is the most common option, followed by playing games. Mathematics and database are the only options used more often at school; for Internet and e-mail the figures for school and home use are very similar.

The multifunctionality of computers varies depending on country, age, and gender. Table 11.5 shows the average number of applications used by the different groups. As a rule, computer use at school is focused on a smaller spectrum of applications than at home. Both at home and school, the range of applications increases by age—with the remarkable exception of Israel where younger children use a wider spectrum of applications than young people of 15 and 16 years. The gender differences are small: Only for computer use at home do boys in some countries use significantly more applications than girls, whereas at school, no gender difference is to be observed.

The results in Tables 11.4 and 11.5 show plausible differences between the range and kind of computer applications at home and at school, reflecting the different meaning given to the computer in these different contexts. However, these differences are not very strict, indicating that we cannot

TABLE 11.4
Which of These Things Do You Use a Computer in School or at Home For?

	N	At School or at Home	At School	At Home
Playing games	3525	88	36	86
Writing	3515	82	62	67
Drawing/design	3519	53	28	43
Maths/Number work	3516	34	29	14
Looking up info on CD-ROMS	3424	30	12	23
Internet	3433	28	19	16
Database/Spreadsheets	3364	26	21	12
Programming	3401	24	15	15
Email	3428	14	7	8

Note. In % of all respondents—6 to 7 years—who use the computer both at school and at home; all countries except Italy; bases differ as a consequence of some countries leaving out some of the items and of more or less missing values.

TABLE 11.5
Average Number of Computer Applications Used at School and at Home

			Computer Use at School				
		Age Groups				Gender	
Country	Total	6-7	9-10	12-13	15-16	Boys	Girls
BE (vlg)	1.7	1.1	1.1	1.7	1.9	*1.7*	*1.8*
CH	2.0	n.a.	1.6	1.5	2.4	*2.1*	*1.9*
DE	2.2	1.3	2.2	2.0	2.5	*2.3*	*2.2*
ES	2.2	1.0	2.6	2.2	2.1	*3.0*	*2.7*
FI	2.3	1.8	2.0	2.2	2.8	*2.2*	*2.4*
GB	2.7	2.3	2.4	3.1	3.1	*2.8*	*2.7*
IL	2.3	3.0	2.3	2.3	1.9	*2.2*	*2.4*
NL	2.4	1.8	2.0	3.1	2.9	*2.5*	*2.4*
SE	2.5	2.1	2.4	2.4	2.7	*2.5*	*2.5*
Total	2.4	2.1	2.2	2.4	2.5	*2.4*	*2.4*

			Computer Use at Home				
		Age Groups				Gender	
Country	Total	6-7	9-10	12-13	15-16	Boys	Girls
BE (vlg)	2.2	1.7	1.7	2.4	2.4	2.3	2.0
CH	2.7	1.4	2.3	2.9	2.9	2.8	2.5
DE	2.4	1.6	1.9	2.5	2.7	2.4	2.3
ES	2.9	1.6	2.9	3.4	3.0	3.0	2.8
FI	2.5	*2.4*	*2.3*	2.6	*2.6*	2.5	*2.5*
GB	2.7	2.1	2.5	2.9	3.0	3.0	2.4
IL	3.1	3.6	3.1	3.0	2.7	*3.2*	*3.0*
NL	3.0	2.3	3.0	3.3	3.1	3.2	2.8
SE	2.8	2.1	2.6	2.9	3.1	3.0	2.7
Total	2.7	2.4	2.5	2.9	2.9	2.9	2.6

Note. In % of those who use computers and reported at least one application; only age bands 6-7, 9-10, 12-13, and 15-16 years; all significance at $p < .01$ unless in italics.

speak of two separate media—the "computer-at-school" and the "computer-at-home." Instead, most of the functions and applications are to be observed in both contexts. This might be due to two trends that seem to affect the distribution of computers in recent years. First, teachers increasingly understand computers not only as a tool for specialized pupils or "freaks" or just for specific applications like maths or programming. Rather, they see it also as a companion for most of their pupils who use it for a lot of purposes (cf. Turkle, 1995), and therefore they are beginning to integrate applications like games, simulations, or communication into their didactical repertoire. Second, parents intentionally support their children in using computers for instrumental purposes because they are concerned about an appropriate education for the challenges of the information society, as quoted in many political speeches and programs.

The findings presented so far, which rely on the quality and quantity of computer applications, underline the variety of diffusion paths the new media technologies take into the lives of young children. In a next step, we go beyond the range of applications and consider how motivational patterns may be linked to specific ways of using the computer.

ATTITUDES TOWARD NEW MEDIA: INTRINSIC AND EXTRINSIC MOTIVATION

Different patterns of use should be related to different attitudes toward the new media. In the questionnaire used within the comparative study, we tried to cover two attitudinal perspectives. First, some items referred to the public debate on the importance of computer skills as a crucial qualification for the information society. The participants of the survey were asked to respond to the two following statements: (A1) Do you think that people will get left behind if they don't know about computers? and (A2) Do you think that it is more important for young people to understand computers than for their parents? Second, two items covered the participants' own view, their affective attitude toward the computer: (B1) Do you think that computers are exciting? and (B2) Are you comfortable using a computer?[2]

We chose a straightforward means of exploring attitudinal patterns by defining five groups on the basis of the answers to those four questions:[3]

1. *Low Motivation*: This group includes children and young people who did not explicitly agree to any of the four items or at least were unsure about them.
2. *Moderate Motivation*: Here we observed no determined agreement or disagreement to any of the items.
3. *Extrinsic Motivation*: These young people clearly agreed that for their future life, computers will be very important ("yes" for items A1/A2). On the other hand, they do not feel comfortable when using the computer (B2) and they do not find computers exciting (B1).

---

[2]Answer categories were "yes," "don't know," and "no" respectively.

[3]These questions were not included in the Finnish and British surveys. In the Dutch and Flemish survey, no "unsure" answer category was allowed, which might affect the results in Table 11.6.

4. *Intrinsic Motivation*: As an analogue to the previous pattern, this group is characterized by a positive affective attitude (B1/B2) without emphasizing that computers might be important in an instrumental way (A1/A2).

5. *Full Motivation*: Finally, this group combines the two motivational dimensions; they like computers (items B1/B2) and at the same time they believe computers to be important tools for their lives (items A1/A2).

Table 11.6 provides an overview of the distribution of these motivational patterns in the countries and by age and gender. In total, the largest group is that which has been qualified as *intrinsic motivation*, that is, those who like computers and do not explicitly emphasize that they are important in an instrumental sense. The smallest group is made up by those who show the opposite pattern, called *extrinsic motivation*. Because of the methods used, one cannot simply interpret this difference as suggesting that extrinsic motives might be less important for the diffusion process, as the relative size

TABLE 11.6
Patterns of Motivation Toward Computers by Country, Age Group, and Gender

	Low Motivation	Moderate Motivation	Extrinsic Motivation	Intrinsic Motivation	Full Motivation
Total (*n* = 7686)	22	24	8	34	13
BE-vlg (*n* = 935)	23	11	14	30	23
DE (*n* = 808)	11	23	7	33	27
IL (*n* = 833)	23	30	7	32	7
IT (*n* = 1347)*	18	30	13	29	11
NL (*n* = 685)	45	14	15	17	10
ES (*n* = 866)	26	27	2	43	2
SE (*n* = 1557)	16	26	5	41	13
CH (*n* = 654)	18	26	4	43	9
6-7 years (*n* = 805)	22	34	5	30	10
9-10 years (*n* = 1035)	24	30	6	32	9
12-13 years (*n* = 1964)	21	21	7	39	12
15-16 years (*n* = 2180)	21	21	9	34	8
Boys (*n* = 3802)	16	21	8	38	18
Girls (*n* = 3873)	27	27	9	30	8
SES high (*n* = 1655)	21	19	11	32	17
SES low (*n* = 1412)	25	25	9	30	12

Note. Row percentages are based on all respondents for the attitudinal question, across all age bands. These figures have been rounded (hence some rows add to more than 100%).
   *12-17 years only.

of these groups is a consequence of the procedure for constructing the groups. However, when we compare the distribution of these groups in different countries and age groups, there are some notable differences.

The *full motivation* pattern is most widespread among German young people, which contrasts with all those results throughout our study that demonstrate the comparatively low access and use figures in Germany. A possible explanation would be that because of the early stage of diffusion of new media, young people in Germany are still more excited about these new options, whereas their colleagues from the Netherlands, for example, for whom the computer has become an everyday tool, are much more "cool" toward the computer or they may have developed a more extrinsic motivation. Another reasonable explanation might be that in Germany, new technologies—in the time of the survey—have been the focus of considerable marketing, in which positive attitudes are regarded as more important than actual use in everyday lives. However, it must be emphasized that the interpretation of these country-by-country comparisons can only be tentative, and problems of meaning and translation exist, particularly for attitude measurement.

This problem should be less severe for the analysis by age groups and gender, because here we aggregate over countries (see Table 11.6). The figures for the age bands indicate that extrinsic motivation becomes increasingly important as the young people grow older: the extrinsic motivation and full motivation groups are more common among teenagers. Whereas there is a constant group of low motivated young people across all age bands, the moderate motivation becomes less in the older groups, as young people seem to develop stronger and more concrete motivations with age. Here it is interesting that the intrinsic motivation pattern has its peak among the 12- to 13-year-olds, whereas the extrinsic motivation continues to grow. Table 11.6 shows clear gender differences as well. The first three groups are overrepresented among girls, whereas the two groups characterized by intrinsic motivation are stronger among boys. Finally, the results for the influence of SES indicate that both intrinsic and extrinsic motivations are more widespread among the better-off young people.

How are these motivational patterns linked to the different means of access and use of the new media? The answer to this question leads us to a more comprehensive picture of the different paths of the diffusion process. Table 11.7 shows under which circumstances the five motivational patterns occur. In general, the two groups characterized by an intrinsic motivation have better access to computers and use them far more often. As a rule, they have access to a computer at home, often in their own bedroom. They are more likely to use a computer at home and, overall, use computers at least once a week for games as well as not for games, as well as having greater access to the Internet.

TABLE 11.7
Patterns of Motivation in Different Contexts of Access and Use

	Low Motivation	Moderate Motivation	Extrinsic Motivation	Intrinsic Motivation	Full Motivation
	n = 1617	n = 1803	n = 626	n = 2573	n = 968
Access to computer at home					
PC in bedroom	13	19	20	29	38
PC somewhere else	51	40	48	45	44
No PC at home	37	42	32	26	18
Regular use (at least once a week) of computers for games and for work ("not for games")					
Work and games	24	26	27	49	56
Only work	8	9	10	9	9
Only games	24	29	25	23	19
None of it	44	36	39	19	16
Computer use at home and at school					
Only at home	25	27	26	30	31
More often at home	17	20	22	32	39
At least as often at school	17	15	21	15	11
Only at school	19	18	17	15	11
No PC use at all	22	20	15	8	6
"Have you used/or watched somebody using/or heard of the Internet?"					
Used it myself	20	23	24	41	42
Watched using it	25	24	20	22	18
Never used (watched) it	41	24	45	27	29
Never heard of it	14	19	11	11	11

Note. Column percentages; basis: all respondents of the questions involved, all age bands.

Compared to these highly motivated groups, the extrinsic pattern is very close to the lower motivation groups, but there is a trend toward a rather work- and school-oriented use of the computer. The results of the moderate motivation pattern reflect the fact that this group is the youngest one and has the lowest SES (see Table 11.6). Such moderate motivation may thus result from the fact that these young people most often live in households without a PC and many of them use the computer only for games.

As a final step in examining different patterns of integrating new media to young people's lives, we consider what children and young people told us in the survey regarding which medium is seen as most appropriate to meet particular needs. As shown in chapter 4, in general, television is by far the most preferred option when it comes to "excitement," and we find this to be the case for all five motivational groups. However, for both groups characterized by intrinsic motivation, electronic games are given the second place. By contrast, these games are ranked fifth or sixth among the extrinsic group and the low motivation group—behind reading books, watching videos, and making a phone call. For learning, books are still the most preferred medium overall. However, for the full motivation group, books rank behind television and the Internet. Here again, we find indicators for different conceptions of PCs and CMC among young people, suggesting that there are indeed different types of new media users.

CONCLUSIONS

Who are the new media users? In this chapter, we argued that the idea of a linear process of diffusion, in which children and young people as well as adults gradually gain contact with computers and computer-mediated communication and as such become "new media users," does not seem to be appropriate to understand the current changes in children's and young people's media environment. Instead, we proposed that one should think in terms of different paths of innovation leading to different conceptions of the particular new media. It is a specific feature of these media that they bring together formerly separated media and merge them with new communicative options—the process called *convergence*—and this may occur in various ways. As a consequence, these media technologies are able to offer a wide range of communication possibilities, and—depending on the general path of development a society has chosen—there are different ways of defining the place of these media and the role they might play in the everyday lives of children and young people.

Insofar as the computer is introduced by school and other societal institutions, the new medium is constructed according to institutional criteria—as a tool for learning, as something of which teachers and parents approve and that is seen as important for the future in the so-called information society. The same is true with regard to the Internet. Insofar as the Internet is being introduced by school and other societal institutions, it is mostly understood as a medium of information or a medium with which to learn to communicate about information.

On the other hand, insofar as new media are introduced by private households and their use depends on the actual interests and purposes of children, computers today are introduced as games machines, particularly for boys. From a parent's perspective, which as a rule is rather skeptical about games, computers may be preferred to games consoles, because computers allow for other applications and thus provide a better opportunity for other purposes to become more important.

In this chapter, we provided empirical evidence for different conceptions of new media and for the emergence of different types of new media users. These are characterized by specific patterns of access to technological options, range of applications and services used, purposes of use, and attitudes and motivation underlying the use of computers. In doing this, we hoped to overcome some oversimplifications typical of much public and political discourse. In short, there is no such thing as "the" new media and consequently we will not find "the" new media user. The new technological options are culturally and socially transformed into institutional structures and everyday practices. This transformation process takes place according to the specific conditions of cultures, political frameworks, concrete social situations, and individual dispositions. Therefore, the direction and the results of this process may be very different between countries as well as between social groups within and across countries.

When it comes to the question of what we can learn from the empirical evidence provided by this comparative survey, we must emphasize that we are dealing with a snapshot taken during a process of rapid development. Due to differences in population, politics, economy, and culture discussed in chapter 1, the development of new media is not occurring simultaneously across Europe. With regard to the general, globally influenced trends in the technology and economy of new media, our snapshot of the European situation in 1997 shows that different countries have reached different stages of this development. Further, and particularly in this chapter, it became obvious that below the level of the general trends, there are quite different paths of diffusion of new technologies and different conceptions of new media between the European countries and between social groups within the countries. We end by discussing our findings in light of some general theses concerning the role of new media in the lives of children and young people.

First, this role is influenced by an economic perspective. The introduction and diffusion of digital media is first of all an economically motivated process. Politicians view information and communication technologies as a top priority with regard to the future of European economy (see Bangemann, 1994). With this political support, the paths of diffusion of new media are heavily influenced by an economic model according to which everybody is becoming an individual entrepreneur for her or his own interests, being electronically connected within a global cyber-economy. This ideal of the information society, as outlined in many programmatic documents, has become part of parents' attitudes toward computers and CMC and is becoming an increasingly important part of the curricula of educational institutions at all levels. With regard to the role of new media, this economic perspective seems to lead to substantial changes in European media and communications systems: Concepts like public service, pluralism, and diversity, and fundamental distinctions such as that between information and entertainment, will become less important. Instead, media and communication will be linked to economic parameters, to efficiency, and to shareholder value.

Second, computers and CMC will play an increasingly important role in the process of socialization. Children and young people socialize themselves by using computers, particularly by playing games. The computer is not just a tool for calculations, but rather a means to express oneself, to simulate different realities, to experiment with one's ideas (Turkle, 1995). This might widen the range of communicative options and diversity, and at the same time support a general trend toward individualization within an electronically mediated global space of communication (Krotz, 1995).

Third, the different paths of new media's diffusion into the everyday lives of young people, as illustrated in this chapter, produce different patterns of competency gaps and inequalities between and within the cultures and societies analyzed in our project. How, in practice, children and young people realize the new communicative possibilities and develop new communicative skills and social practices depends on several conditions. When investigating media access and/or ownership in the child's bedroom, gender, age and, in most countries, SES all turned out to be strong predictors of PC ownership (see chapter 3). Here, the discussion on knowledge gaps (Bonfadelli, 1994) and competence gaps (Kubicek et al., 1998) is relevant: These may become more and more important in European societies in the future. There is some evidence that schools can play an important role in providing access to new media (see chapter 10), thereby encouraging the development of individual competence in computer use. At the same time, the data strongly support the thesis that in the future, the relative importance of computer use at home will grow because the school systems do not as yet seem to be able to keep pace with the development of new hardware and software in the digital world. Thus, it is unlikely that new media access through schools will reduce existing social inequalities by itself. Therefore, it is a task of European societies and governments to create conditions that can help to develop cultural practices and competencies related to new media that allow all groups of the population to fulfil their communicative needs, whether or not these can be fulfilled by CMC. Then the new media users will be as diverse and pluralistic as our European cultures and societies are.

REFERENCES

Bangemann, M. (1994). *Europe and the Global Information Society: Recommendations to the European Council Prepared by Members of the High-Level Group on the Information Society.* Brussels: European Council.

Bonfadelli, H. (1994). *Die Wissenskluft-Perspektive* [In the perspective of the knowledge gap thesis]. Konstanz: UVK & Oelschlaeger.

Fidler, R. (1997). *Mediamorphosis. Understanding new media.* Thousand Oaks, CA: Pine Forge.

Goffman, E. M. (1976). *Frame analysis* (3rd ed.). Cambridge, MA: Harvard University Press.

Hickethier, K. (1993). Dispositiv Fernsehen. Programm und Programmstrukturen in der Bundesrepublik Deutschland [Dispositiv Television. Patterns of Programming in Germany]. In K. Hickethier (Ed.), *Geschichte des Fernsehens in der Bundesrepublik Deutschland* [The history of television in the Federal Republic of Germany] (Vol. 1, pp. 171–244). München: Fink.

Höflich, J. R. (1998). Computerrahmen und Kommunikation [Communication framed by the computer]. In E. Prommer & G. Vowe (Eds.), *Computervermittelte Kommunikation. Öffentlichkeit im Wandel* [Computer mediated communication: The changing public sphere] (pp. 141–176). Konstanz: UVK Medien.

Jäckel, M. (1990). *Reaktionen auf das Kabelfernsehen. Kommunikationswissenschaftliche Erklärungen zur Ausbreitung eines neuen Mediums* [Consequences of cable TV: Explanations about the distribution of a new media by communication research]. München: Reinhard Fischer.

Krotz, F. (1995). Elektronisch mediatisierte Kommunikation. Überlegungen zu einer Konzeption einiger zukünftiger Forschungsfelder der Kommunikationswissenschaft [Electronically mediated communication: Some proposals about how to do research in some new areas of communication research]. *Rundfunk und Fernsehen 43,* 445–462.

Krotz, F. (1999). Kinder und Medien, Eltern und soziale Beziehungen [Children and the media, their parents and their social relations]. *TV diskurs 10,* 60–66.

Kubicek, H., Schmid, U., & Wagner, H. (1997). *Bürgerinformation durch "neue" Medien? Analysen zur Etablierung elektronischer Informationssysteme im Alltag* [Information for citizens by new media? Studies about electronical Information systems in the everyday of the people]. Opladen: Westdeutscher Verlag.

Kubicek, H. et al. (Eds.). (1998). *Jahrbuch für Telekommunikation und Gesellschaft* [Yearbook telecommunication and society]. Bremen: R. v. Decker's Verlag.

Negroponte, N. (1995). *Being digital.* New York: Knopf.

Rammert, W. (1996). Mit dem Computer zu Hause in den "digitalen Alltag"? Vision und Wirklichkeit privater Computernutzung [With the PC at home into the "digital life"? Visions from and reality of private computer use]. In J. Tauss, J. Kollbeck, & J. Mönikes (Eds.), *Deutschlands Weg in die Informationsgesellschaft* [The path of Germany into information society] (pp. 311–336). Baden-Baden: Nomos.

Rogers, E. M. (1986). *Communication technology. The new media in society.* New York: Free Press.

Rogers, E. M. (1995). *Diffusion of innovations* (4th ed.). New York: Free Press

Tapscott, D. (1998). *Growing up digital: The rise of the net generation.* New York: McGraw Hill.

Turkle, S. (1995). *Life on the screen. Identity in the age of the Internet.* New York: Simon & Schuster.

12

Gendered Media Meanings
and Uses

Dafna Lemish
Tamar Liebes
Vered Seidmann

Although cognitive–developmental approaches in communication and cultural studies have revealed much about the effects of age on children's consumption and comprehension of media, we still know very little about the effect of gender. Feminist theories of differences between boys and girls introduced the distinction between sex and gender to differentiate the sociocultural meanings (masculinity and femininity) from the base of biological sex differences (male and female) on which they are erected. Gender differences are assumed to be constructed through complex processes such as socialization, cultivation, and psychological development. It is our purpose in this chapter to examine boys' and girls' interactions with media in order to further understanding of how these are involved in the process of gender development. Do media, for example, play a different role in the lives of girls and boys? Do girls use media for different purposes than boys? Are there gender differences in the meanings associated with the various media? Which gender differences are universal and which culturally bounded? The purpose of this chapter is to address these issues by highlighting relevant findings from our comparative work on children in the changing media environment. In the following pages we examine—and, when appropriate, challenge—some of the conventional wisdom regarding gender differences in the place of media in children's and young people's lives. We also place media use in the context of gender differences in attitudes to technology, peer and family relationships, and social values and aspirations.

Many previous studies on children and media point to gender differences along expected traditional divisions. In Sweden, Rosengren and Windahl

(1989) found that boys aged 6 to15 watch television more than girls, listen more to radio, go more often to the cinema, and read more comics, whereas girls read more books and magazines than boys and, as they get older, also listen more to music. Boys are shown to have a preference for sports and nature programs, and girls for music and children's programs. Films, serials, and detective stories, on the other hand, are equally liked by boys and girls. In a study of Flemish children, tellingly entitled "Boys will be boys and girls will be girls," Roe (1998) found substantial gender differences in patterns of media use that increase with age. Here, too, boys devote more time to electronic games, whereas girls read more and listen more to music. Roe concluded, ". . . it is perhaps not too much of an exaggeration to say that, in this period of their lives, boys and girls increasingly inhabit different media worlds" (p. 23).

Similarly, in a host of studies on musical preferences and adolescent tastes, gender emerged as a central variable. Girls are shown to prefer pop music, and to use it for social purposes, such as dancing, whereas boys are drawn more to nonmainstream music genres such as hard rock, heavy metal, and fringe (Christenson & Peterson, 1988; Christenson & Roberts, 1998; Fine, Mortimer, & Roberts, 1990; Frith, 1983; Roe, 1990). Idolization of pop stars was also found to be more prevalent among girls, with a dramatic shift to preferring female singers during adolescence (Raviv, Bar-Tal, Raviv, & Ben Horin, 1996).

Hoffner (1996) in the United States also found significant gender differences in identification with television characters. Hoffner's data suggested that physical strength and activity level predicts boys' desire to resemble role models, whereas physical attractiveness predicts identification for girls (and boys to a lesser extent); indeed, attractiveness is the sole determinant of girls' identification with favorite female characters. A further finding that, on the whole, children between second and sixth grade prefer same-sex characters, provides further support for the argument that children are attracted to gender-appropriate contents and role models. Interestingly, however, although this is valid for almost all of the boys, it holds true for just a little more than half of the girls. One possible explanation, according to Hoffner, is the prevalence of male characters on television in terms of both quantity and diversity of characters. Other research emphasized the influence of broadcast industry attitudes toward young audiences. Based on in-depth interviews with key decision makers in television programming, Jordan and Woodward (1998) suggested that broadcasters prefer to direct their programs at boys rather than at girls or at mixed audiences for three reasons. They assume that boys control viewing habits in the home, that girls will watch boys' programs but not the other way around, and that boys are more susceptible to persuasive messages of commercials.

Such research suggests that the industry's growing attention to gender differences in children's and youth culture is fueled by economic interest in the marketing potential of specialized young audiences. It also confirms Inness' view (1998) that in most societies, girls are doubly marginalized by their age and gender, and their voice is often lost in accounts of boys' lives. However, growing girls, in particular, are now the target of many advertisers and marketers, who seek to draw them as early as possible into the uneasy feminine world where the Holy Grail of an "improved" self is sought through a continuous cycle of consumption. In addition, the contribution of feminist theory to communication and cultural studies in general, as well as to studies of children and media, has resulted in a new sensitivity to the effects of gender and a new emphasis on the female experience.

For example, several recent analyses, largely inspired by the Harvard Project on the Psychology of Women and Girls' Development (Brown & Gilligan, 1992; Gilligan, 1982; Pipher, 1995) argued that young girls are taught self-effacement by the culture around them. They are encouraged to direct their emotional and physical resources to the attainment of unrealistic expectations (such as the constant disciplining of the body in order to ensure physical perfection) in order to gain peer acceptance. Another rich line of recent research attempted to examine girls' reception of mediated texts and the role these texts play in the construction of identity and femininity (see for example, Buckingham, 1993a; Currie, 1997; Douglas, 1994; Frazer, 1987; Lemish, 1998; Lewis, 1990; Mazzerella & Pecora, 1999; Peterson, 1987). Taken as a whole, these studies suggested more optimistically that girl audiences are self-conscious and reflexive in their approach to popular media texts. It is presumed that through these texts, girls struggle with and resist the ideological workings of patriarchal and capitalist hegemony and at the same time, find themselves located within it. This approach, reinforced recently by Brown (1998), perceives girls as active meaning makers, in constant search of alternatives for empowerment. Yet, a number of the same writers warn us against rushing to celebrate the symbolic creativity of audiences and their potential political liberation by media (Buckingham, 1993b). Girls may be active constructors of possibly oppositional media meanings, but are still constrained by their own cultural milieu (Lemish, 1998).

Interestingly, inverting the earlier gender bias toward the study of male experience, very little similar research has been done on boys' culture and their reception of popular texts. An interesting exception is Maigret's (1999) study of French boys' perceptions of the psychological dimensions of the super-hero in comics. He concluded that this medium, far from reproducing traditional forms, serves as a means for learning a new and complex masculine identity. Comics, he argued, encourage male readers to reflect on their identity, and provide an opportunity to test a host of values, including those traditionally described as feminine. In the United Kingdom, on the other hand, boys who took part in focus groups about popular television programs (Buckingham, 1993b) found considerable difficulty in handling the self-exposure demanded by the discussion. They employed a number of different strategies to avoid talking about their personal and emotional reactions or about their viewing pleasures, adopting, for example, a mocking and condemnatory stance toward a soap opera and a family situation comedy that they nevertheless watched and presumably enjoyed.

Previous research has, therefore, amply demonstrated that gender is a complex cultural and social product. In this chapter, our discussion of gender is grounded in the cultural contexts of 12 very different countries, where gender roles are conceived and practiced in various ways. Our findings are based on both qualitative and quantitative research in these countries (see chapter 2) and give equal emphasis to the experience of boys and girls. We have data not only about media consumption and interpretation, but also about attitudes to technology, family and peer relationships, social values, and self-image. The purpose of this chapter is to pull together findings described in earlier chapters in this volume, as well as to provide additional insights, in order to present an integrative picture of gender-related issues. Our discussion of gender differences thus addresses key questions related to gender differences on the personal level—Are girls less technologically oriented than boys? Do boys and girls have different media-related content interests?—as well as those concerned with social contexts—Are girls more socially oriented? Do boys and girls occupy a different place at home?—and gendered perceptions and attitudes—Do boys and girls hold different perceptions of themselves and their futures?

Our cross-national perspective allows us to explore which, if any, of the gender differences we observe are universal and which are culturally specific. The discovery of universals will allow us to explore further the overall processes of gender construction. However, if we find national differences that color these processes in unique, contextualized ways, this will suggest which aspects of gender roles are culturally constructed and therefore potentially most responsive to social change. Findings will therefore, we hope, provide us with a clearer understanding of the gendered context of media consumption and meaning making for young people growing up in Europe today.

RESEARCH FINDINGS

Gendered Technological Orientations

Patterns of availability, use, and access to media in our cross-cultural data suggest that, universally, boys are more technologically oriented than girls. On the whole, boys' bedrooms are more high-tech than girls' bedrooms: Boys are more likely to have television sets, cable or satellite access, video recorders and television-linked games machines, computers and Internet connections. Girls, on the other hand, are more likely to report having a shelf of books in their bedrooms (see chapter 3, Tables 3.1 to 3.9). There is also a tendency for girls to be somewhat more likely than boys to have hi-fis and personal stereos.[1]

The picture sharpens when we consider not only availability of media in the child's room, but the actual use of media in the home in general (see chapter 4, Table 4.4). Interestingly, television is not only the most dominant medium in the lives of children and adolescents in terms of time spent; its appeal also transcends gender. Although boys are somewhat more likely to have a television set in their rooms, there is little difference in the amount of daily television viewing of boys and girls. With the single exception of Switzerland, where boys on average watch for about a quarter of an hour more per day, boys and girls watch similar amounts of television.

However, clear differences emerge between boys and girls of all ages in the great majority of countries, confirming that boys are attracted to "new" media, whereas the familiar "old" media have a greater following among girls. Time devoted to "serious" computer use and the Internet is twice as high, and the time spent on electronic games three times as high, for boys compared with girls. As one 15-year-old Swedish girl commented, "I have never met a girl who is really into computers." On the other hand, in the great majority of countries, girls spend more time reading than boys do. Reading preferences also differ: Girls read books and magazines, whereas boys are more likely to read comics and newspapers. These differing patterns of usage tend to become more marked as children get older.

These differences are also visible when we ask which medium children would like as a birthday gift: Girls are most likely to choose a television set, whereas boys prefer a computer or related accessories (see chapter 3, Table 3.11). Similarly, when asked to specify the medium that they would miss most (see chapter 3, Table 3.10), boys are more likely to name a technologically sophisticated medium such as the PC or a television-linked games machine, whereas older media such as the radio, telephone, or books figure more highly for girls.

It is important, however, not to lose sight of the fact that considerable numbers of girls use new media, whereas the majority of boys also use traditional media. Overall, in our 12 countries, almost all boys listen to music and around three quarters read books at least sometimes. Similarly, two thirds of girls play electronic games and read newspapers, and a quarter use the Internet (see chapter 4, Table 4.2).

---

[1]Overall, two thirds of girls (65%) have a hi-fi in their own room and the same percentage own a personal stereo; among boys, the figure in both cases is 60%, a small but statistically significant difference.

Gendered Content Interests

All in all, our quantitative data, reinforced by children's own accounts in the qualitative interviews, suggest that boys and girls have different interests and that these in turn are related to gendered preferences for particular media content (see chapter 6). Boys have a stronger interest in sports and in action and adventure generally (see Table 6.2). This was found to be the case for the three higher age bands in all participating countries in this analysis (the question was not posed to the youngest children). This influences their choice of television programs, electronic games, reading material, and video rentals, as well as affecting musical taste. "Boys play those awful shoot'em up games," as one 13-year-old Finnish girl noted scornfully. "Maybe girls play computer too, but different games. Pac-man," suggested one 16-year-old Israeli boy. "Most of the games today are violent battles and all this nonsense. Girls, especially those I know who are with us, don't like that so much . . ." continued his friend. Asked about their favorite television program, the youngest boys favor cartoons, typically rich in rough-and-tumble action; sports programs are clear favorites for those who are older.

Girls, on the other hand, have a clear interest in human relationships, particularly romance and friendships (see chapter 6, Table 6.2). Music and celebrities figure among their top five interests in each of the three age groups; interest in animals or wildlife falls after the age of 13, to be replaced by a growing interest in romance. Once again, these interests are not medium-specific but are followed across different media. Thus girls' engrossment in reading often centers on romantic plots, sex and beauty advice, and stories on the private lives of their idolized celebrities. They are heavier consumers of pop music, mostly expressing romantic love and longing. As we noted, many girls also play electronic games, but they prefer adventure games with a narrative plot, drawing, and graphics, or more old-fashioned card or board games, rather than the fighting or sports-based games that boys prefer (see chapter 6, Table 6.8). On television, at all ages girls are particularly interested in soap operas and other types of serials. On the Internet, girls mostly seek the chat groups or the personal websites of their favorite celebrities, This account by a 12-year-old Danish girl is typical:

> It was when I liked the Spice Girls we logged onto the Internet and surfed to find the Spice Girls, and we were allowed to print it out; but then we also found—because I have been very interested in design—we found some Calvin Klein designs, because I wanted some inspiration, you see, because at that time I used to make designs . . .

Further, for girls, so it seems, whatever the medium, the interest in relationships dominates. Listen to how one enthusiastic 14-year-old English girl described the personal and immediate nature of email: "It feels though you're actually talking to them in a way, that's the way I feel, you get really excited, like quick—send it, waiting for them to write back."

Children themselves recognize these differences and have their own theories about them. As two 13-year-old Finnish girls explained:

> Maybe boys just want to show off, I don't know . . . They always only talk about electronic games with their friends and how they have beaten someone in some game.

> And they can't, I think, really concentrate on reading a book. If it doesn't start happening a lot right on the first page.

The greater competitiveness of boys and their need for action is a recurring theme. A 14-year-old Israeli boy offered a similar, if less dismissive, and rather more sophisticated, explanation for boys' lack of interest in soap operas:

> . . . boys are less patient [than girls]. Soap operas—it goes on and on, the episode continues. You are all the time in suspense. Boys don't like those kinds of things. Boys like it when an episode ends . . . in the same episode it ends. And there is an ending. And soap operas—it continues afterwards. Boys don't have the energy to watch the same program every day.

Interestingly, this explanation—boys like narrative closure and girls like openness—echoes that given in the literature on soap operas (see Allen, 1985).

As young people enter adolescence, they seem to develop a growing awareness of such gender stereotypes (see Pasquier, 1999). As one French boy commented about the popular teenage soap, *Helen and the Boys*, "I hate this series because it is too sexual. I prefer *Code Quantum* [action/adventure series]. In *Helen and the Boys* they kiss all the time. My mother and sister watch it—it is for females." Here two Israeli sisters, aged 15 and 17, commented on the differences:

A: I noticed that boys don't like those romantic movies where a boy meets with . .

Int: They don't?

B: They don't like those series . . . soap operas.

A: Soap operas they don't like, and also all those love movies, and the emotional movies. If it is an emotional movie they shy away from it.

However, here again, it is important to stress that there are similarities as well as differences. Thus the two Israeli sisters continued their discussion of boys' and girls' program preferences:

B: But comedies and . . .

A: they <boys> also like.

B: and suspense and such things . . .

Int: What about *The X Files*, for example?

B: Everybody.

A: Boys too.

This reminds us that television series figure among the top five choices of boys as well as girls and that comedy programs enjoy increasing popularity with both genders as they grow older. Similarly, girls also enjoy sport, although it comes much further down in their hierarchy of interests.

More girls, however, seem to be attracted to typically male genres than vice versa. As one 11-year-old Israeli girl put it, "Today there isn't this thing of one thing for boys and one for girls. In the past only boys played soccer, today there are girls who like to play soccer."

In this way, equality between the genders can be perceived by adolescents as a form of female adjustment to male interests. Thus a British teenage boy, responding to the idea that computers are for boys, objected by saying, "That's a bit sexist because girls play computers and all." This conclusion supports both the industry's assumption that girls will watch boys' programs but not the other way around, as well as the general feminist literature that suggests that women do not abandon their traditional female responsibilities and interests, but just incorporate into them new typically male ones.

On the other hand, we also found some contrary indications. These 13-year-old Scottish boys talked enviously of girls' lifestyle magazines:

A: There's no boys' magazines that's what really sickens me. The boys' ones, the magazines for boys are all on a specific thing like football or cars . . . . you never get this thing for boys that are like the ones that the girls get. It's like giving you information about—like street-wise and so on, sort of thing. Street cred.

Int: Do you think you would like a magazine like that for boys?

B: Aye.

A: Aye. Lasses or something in it.

Gendered Styles of Sociability

Boys and girls socialize in different ways, which may be expected to have repercussions for media use. For example, in five countries (DE, FI, GB, IL, and IT), we asked how often children and young people played or "messed about" outside the home. Answers showed that boys are significantly more likely than girls to do so almost every day (41% compared with 31%). Interestingly, boys are in general also more satisfied with what is available for them to do in the area where they live—overall, 63% feel this way compared with only 56% of girls (see chapter 8). They are also somewhat more likely to say they have enough freedom to go out when they want to (75% compared with 69%). With the notable exception of the Nordic countries (see chapter 8), boys' and girls' friendship styles are also distinct, although when asked about the frequency of time spent with friends, differences are negligible. When children are asked whom they mostly spend their free time with, clear differences emerge (see chapter 8, Table 8.2). Although both boys and girls put friends first and family in a significantly lower second place, girls are more family-oriented. They are also more likely to report spending time with one best friend, whereas boys mostly spend their free time with a group of friends.

Our data suggest that gender influences how media are integrated within these rather different social networks. For example, teenagers in five countries (FI, DE, GB, IL, and IT) were asked which media they talked about with their friends. Not surprisingly, answers show that they talk about those media that interest them most. As a result, we find that girls talk more than boys do about listening to music (70% vs. 54%), phoning someone (50% vs. 30%), reading books (35% vs. 16%) or magazines (38% vs. 26%), and listening to the radio (26% vs. 19%). Boys, on the other hand, talk more than girls about playing electronic games (61% vs. 23%), using a computer, not for games (28% vs. 16%), and reading comics (17% vs. 11%). In four countries (FI, DE, IL, and IT), teenagers were also asked if they talked to friends about using the Internet. Once again, boys' greater interest in new media is evident: overall, 26% compared with only 20% of girls talked about it with friends.

Similarly, girls are more likely than boys to swap music CDs and tapes, books and magazines; boys are more likely than girls to swap electronic games and comics (see chapter 9). In addition, computers, including games and CD-ROM usage and the Internet, provide reasons for boys to visit their friends' houses. In contrast to the isolated, asocial "computer nerd" image, we found that children often use a computer with friends: 44% of all the boys in our study and 20% of all the girls report visiting a friend to play electronic games (see chapter 9).

Another stereotype weakly confirmed is that girls not only talk on the phone more than boys, but also do so for different reasons. Boys' talk is more exclusively goal-oriented, whereas girls tend to talk more for the social contact. In Finland, Germany, Israel, and the United Kingdom, children were asked to identify, out of a list of six possible alternatives, which one they used the telephone for most often. Overall, 55% of boys report that they use the phone most commonly to make arrangements, but only 31% of girls endorse this reason. On the other hand, 49% of girls, compared with only 26% of boys, report that their most common use of the phone is to chat with friends. As one 12-year-old Israeli girl confirmed, "Sometimes I used to call friends, and we would just be silent! The most important thing is to listen, to hold the phone. To talk, to tell about what happened today." However, given theories of the nature of gendered talk, where women's conversational goal is presumed to be to maintain closeness whereas men use language more pragmatically (see, for example, Tannen, 1990), the size of these differences is surprisingly low. As is evident from the following illustrations, girls, too, use the phone pragmatically in addition to relationally. When a 7-year-old English girl was asked about what she talks about, the words just tumbled out:

> We talk about school, we talk about math and we talk about if we like each other, we talk about if we're still going to see each other, talk about if we're going to die before the other one does and all that. We talk about when do you want to come over to my house, what time do you want to stay, when do you want to have lunch, when do you want to have tea and dinner and when do you want to do some drawing. Oh yes—and when do you want to play out the front on the bikes and when you want to watch a video and when you want to watch television or when you want to play a math game, when you want to read.

Social use of media, so it seems, corresponds to the gendered style of private use of media described earlier. Boys and girls share with their friends the same activities they like doing when they are by themselves. Girls exhibit a preference for more intimate relationships with a best friend, sharing inner thoughts in the privacy of their bedrooms or talking on the phone. They are more inclined to spend time with their peers listening to music, talking, handling objects—such as collectibles, souvenirs of stars, fashion items, or jewelry. Going out with friends often means spending time at the mall window-shopping or plainly killing time. Boys on the other hand, spend more time with their friends in front of the computer, or outdoors. Boys, so it seems, have a stronger preference for group-bonding—playing sports, exploring the streets and public places. Even playing the computer in the privacy of their homes operates as a legitimate opportunity for getting together and engaging in typical male bonding behaviors, such as loud shouting, back-slapping, grabbing the mouse, etc. (see Drotner, 1999). These differences were often expressed in the qualitative interviews. Here, for example, are the views of an 11-year-old boy in England:

> Boys I know don't like to spend their life in their bedroom. And I don't even know a boy that does. See, I know of a boy that kind of does, 'cause he likes, whenever he's not doing anything, he likes to just go to his room listen to loads of music and play on his laptop computer, and that's it. He doesn't spend his life in there, as much as her [his 16-year-old sister].

Interestingly, our interviews with teenagers confirm that when they are in mixed company, or with a boy friend, girls tend to follow boys' interests but not vice versa. The following excerpt from a focus group interview with four 13-year-old Finnish girls illustrates this point:

Int: If you rent videos together, what kind of videos do you watch?

A: Horror or something.

B: Usually horror.

C: At least if we are with guys.

D: Sometimes it is just us girls, then it is romance.

Int: You mean, when you are only a group of girls?

A: Then we usually choose some tearjerker. But if we are with guys then it must be horror.

B: 'Cos guys don't like those.

Similarly, while playing the computer in mixed groups, many of the girls seem to make an effort to adapt to boys' interests, as reported in one Israeli focus group with 16-year-olds:

A: I do play the computer. It's not something I do like a dork . . . when I am at his place we play the computer so I play too.

B: I play computers, all kinds. When we are at his place we play computers, motorcycles.

Although girls are making an effort to please the boys by incorporating their interests in joint activities, boys do not seem to reciprocate. Boys in our interviews did not report giving in to their female friends' interests or negotiating shared activities.

Gendered Patterns of Family Relationships and Media Use

In our surveys, we paid particular attention to mothers' and fathers' supervision of children's access to media and whether or not they talked to their children about media. Finland and Sweden stood out as having the lowest supervision rates, and across all countries generally girls were more heavily supervised than boys (see chapter 7). Significant gender differences for parental supervision were found for two media: both mothers and fathers limit their sons' computer time more than their daughters'[2] and their daugh-

---

[2]25% of fathers and 27% of mothers say when their sons can or cannot use the PC, compared with only 18% and 19% respectively similarly controlling their daughter's PC access ($p < 0.001$).

ters' telephone use more than their sons'.[3] This is of course not surprising, given our prior discussion of the gendered nature of media use. Both parents also tend to be somewhat stricter with their daughters regarding freedom to go outside.[4] This may be a contributing factor to girls' tendency to spend less time outdoors than boys, and may be related to both parents' and daughters' developing awareness of the safety problems that public spaces pose for growing girls.

There are also gender differences regarding topics of conversation between parents and their sons and daughters. Both parents talk more to their children about media that interest them—to their sons about computers and to their daughters about the telephone.[5] Mothers are on the whole more likely to chat to their children about most things and also to talk to daughters more than sons about music, books, and going out.[6] Differences are, however, fairly modest.

Media, so it seems, serve as a means of gendering of familial relationships. An Israeli family interview reveals the dynamics of the gender bonds and processes of socialization within the family. A 19-year-old girl with a 10-year-old sister explained how their relationship with their mother is cemented by shared interest in reading:

> All three of us read many books . . . our ties are usually through the books that she [little sister] reads. It's our childhood memories. . . . [our brother reads different types of adventure books] but with her, there is this pleasure of initiating her into the classics. I read it because my mother read it. My mother gave it to me, because her mother gave it to her. She comes to me and says: "I finished the book. Recommend something to me." Like this. So I take something out of the library that she hasn't read and I say: "Here is something I read when I was your age" and then I say: "Take it!" and then she reads it.

Masculine culture also thrives within the domestic space. An older male—father, brother, cousin, parents' friend—often serves as a role model and initiates the young boy into the computer world by letting him watch, includ-

---

[3]30% of fathers and 40% of mothers say when their daughter can or cannot use the telephone, compared with only 23% and 30% respectively who similarly control their son's access to the telephone.

[4]45% of fathers and 55% of mothers control when their daughters go out, compared with 40% and 48% respectively who control when their sons go out.

[5]36% of fathers and 29% of mothers chat to their son about computers, compared with only 27% and 18% respectively who talk to their daughters about them. Similarly, 28% of fathers and 44% of mothers chat to their daughter about the telephone, compared with only 24% and 34% respectively who chat to their son about it.

[6]32% chat about music to their daughters and only 27% chat to their sons about it: 36% chat to their daughters about reading books, and only 29% chat to their sons about them: 55% chat to their daughters about going out and only 46% chat to their sons.

ing him in the interaction, and providing information. Qualitative research also suggests that sons prefer to talk with their fathers about computers (see chapter 7), as one 12-year-old Swedish boy described enthusiastically, "I have so much to tell, as I don't see him very often, so I become almost anxious, so we usually talk about such things [the Internet]."

Same-gender activities are therefore typical in the family setting: Fathers will watch a ball game with their sons, or work on the computer with them; mothers and daughters will watch a family drama or a soap opera together, or browse through the same magazines. It seems that gender lines divide the family space in the same way that they segment children's culture. Our survey does not provide data regarding the status allocation of the feminine versus the masculine space. However, in this context it is important to remember that boys' bedrooms are better equipped, even with gender-free technologies such as television sets and video recorders, hinting possibly at a tendency for parents to prioritize sons, or for boys to be more demanding.

Overall, however, it is interesting to note that those few parents who refrain from talking to their children about media or from restricting their media use in any way do so regardless of their gender. There are also no differences between girls' and boys' reporting of the frequency of family activities such as having meals, watching television, or playing games with their parents or generally getting along well with them. Similarly, no gender differences were found regarding children's perceptions of their parents' attitudes toward their physical appearance, choice of friends, or desire for them to succeed in life.

Gendered Social Values and Self-Image

A number of questions in the survey attempted to tackle children's and young people's perceptions of themselves and of society and its values and their own future aspirations. The assumption underlying this inquiry is that these characteristics are a result of continual interaction between each boy and girl and the environment in which they grow up, which includes family, peers, school, neighborhood, and the media (Johnsson-Smaragdi & Jönsson, 1994). Not surprisingly, gender differences emerge here as well.

Answers to questions about personal characteristics showed that boys and girls are equally likely to report getting bored, having difficulty making new friends, and feeling awkward around other people. However, teenage girls, our data suggest, are more cautious than boys about expressing self-confidence and in praising themselves. They "worry about things" more than boys[7] and

---

[7]Teenagers were asked in the survey how often they worried about things. Overall, two thirds of boys (65%) said they worried "at least sometimes," compared with four in every five girls (79%).

are less likely to agree that they usually "like being the way I am."[8] They are also somewhat less likely to agree that they "feel confident about myself and my abilities."[9] A link was made by Johnsson-Smaragdi and Jönsson (1994) between television viewing and such differences in self-esteem. High television consumption for boys during childhood was found to be related to more positive self-esteem at the age of 21, whereas for the girls, the reverse was true. One possible explanation points to the nature of their content preferences. Boys are heavier consumers of genres such a sports and action/adventure series that show active, higher status male characters who are in control of themselves and others. Girls, on the other hand, are heavier consumers of genres (such as soaps and series or magazines that highlight romance) that define women through their relationships with men.

We also asked children to choose, from a number of alternatives, which characteristic was most likely to make someone their age popular: The list included wearing the right clothes, being good-looking, having money to spend, being helpful/kind, having the latest things, having a good sense of humor, doing well at school, being good at sport, being honest, and "being yourself/natural." Although boys and girls do not differ significantly in their evaluation of those traits, boys do tend to attach more importance to having money to spend and being good at sports, whereas girls value being yourself/natural. This difference sharpens when we consider the findings from a question that required participants to choose, from the same list, the most important thing for being popular. The personality traits of being yourself, being helpful/kind, and being honest were highest for girls in most countries. As one 13-year-old British girl responded to the interviewer's question about fitting in socially, "No, just be myself, man. Can't take me for what I am, then don't take me at all. I think there's a bit of pressure with clothes and trainers and all that you know . . ." Less consistent were the results for the boys, who made a variety of choices in the different countries.

In a further set of questions, children were asked to pick the one asset they thought would be most important to them in the future. The list included good looks, a happy family life, lots of money, lots of friends, an interesting job, and a good education. In all the participating countries, a happy family life was rated by far the highest of all; however, it was named more often by girls (ranging from 24% to 50% for the boys in the various countries, and from 31% to 61% for the girls). As a whole, girls express a deeper need to spend time with family members. As one Swedish 16-year-old commented, "I don't like to watch alone, I like to watch with the whole family. It is much

---

[8]Only half of girls (49%) compared with two thirds of boys (64%) say this.

[9]Teenagers in seven countries (BE-vlg, CH, DE, FI, IL, IT, and NL) were asked how often they felt confident about themselves and their abilities: 55% of boys, but only 45% of girls said this was usually the case.

more fun. You only live once .... brothers and sisters, parents, we joke around and stuff, watching films and series too."

Boys, on the other hand, consistently rated "lots of money" more highly than girls did (ranging across countries from 4% to 34% for boys, and from 1% to 18% for girls). However, it should be noted that a similar question asking for the least important asset revealed that for both boys and girls "lots of money" (together with "good looks") is graded lowest for future importance.

What can we make of these findings? In many ways, they reinforce our previous discussion. Clearly, girls are more family-oriented than boys and place higher value on traits that are relational, such as being helpful/kind, being honest, and being yourself. However, along with these relational traits, we also find indications that girls, too, have an interest in self-improvement. When asked which three things will be most important when they grow up, just as for boys, an interesting job and a good education are their second and third choices after a happy family life. Such expectations and aspirations may be compared with the finding that girls are less concerned with their looks and with having lots of money than one might have expected. Similarly, the qualitative interviews revealed that girls today assume they will have a career of some sort, in addition to getting married and having children (which they take for granted). In theory, the variety of professions available to them seems wide, although there are practical restrictions, as one middle-class 14-year-old Israeli girl confided:

> I am interested in art, but . . . there isn't much of a future as a painter. Because only one in a hundred really makes it. So I thought of something else in the same area. I thought about fashion design, because I like clothes and there is a need for designs and it interests me. There are many other things that interest me, such as archeology or being a spy or something, but that's a dream.

Boys, on the other hand, express more self-confidence and have more diverse aspirations. They choose sports significantly more than girls and are more likely to consider money to be one of the three most important goals to achieve when they grow up. However, although boys rate good looks, having the right clothes, and having the latest things as highly as do girls, neither rate these more traditionally feminine values particularly highly.

DISCUSSION

Our analysis of the data supports two seemingly opposing conclusions. First, we may conclude that boys and girls in Europe differ in their access to media, patterns of use, and content preferences as well as in the social practices and meanings they attach to them. Boys are more technologically oriented; girls are more likely to listen to music and read. Boys prefer the genres of action/adventure and sports; girls prefer human relationships and romance. Boys hang out more with groups of friends outdoors or at their computers; girls spend more time with a best friend in the intimacy of their own rooms. Boys' culture is game dominated. Girls' culture is all about relationships and talk. Parents reinforce these trends by their own gendered behavior: Boys and fathers share similar interests in sports and computers, girls and mothers share similar interests in human relationships. In short, the study does confirm traditional gender differences. Interestingly, it is the girls who are more reflexive about these differences and willing to discuss them openly. They often position themselves and their female culture as superior to that of boys, and are quick to criticize and put down boys' culture as aggressive, childish, and plain "stupid."

At the same time, we can easily arrive at a very different conclusion, as many of the differences we noted are rather small, if nevertheless statistically significant. Many girls as well as boys play outdoors and many boys as well as girls read books. Some girls show a strong interest in computer technologies, including the Internet. Some like sport and electronic games that feature action and adventure. Yes, fewer girls than boys have such tastes, but nevertheless, girls too are exploring and engaging in the new media environment. Boys, for their part, are now retreating more into their bedrooms, once a female territory, to play electronic games with friends and siblings. As one 12-year-old Israeli girl explained, "I don't think there is a difference [between boys and girls]. I think there is a difference in the same way that there is a difference also between girls and girls. There are different interests." A few exchanges later, her 12-year-old friend reinforced the same idea:

> I don't think that this is at all related to boys or girls. It is the type of personality! There are those who are interested and those who like . . . I don't know what . . . to sing, to exercise. It's the kind of personality.

The equalizing role television may be playing in this process provides us with insights into these changes. Boys and girls watch television, both intensively and extensively, in similar amounts. This is a change from previous research that suggested that boys are heavier television viewers. One possible explanation draws on the expansion of viewing alternatives through cable and satellite channels, which currently provide girls with a wider selection of attractive programs to suit their interests. In addition, the social world presented on the television screen has been changing. Although far from being a just world of equal opportunities, television nevertheless offers girls today a greater variety of role models that show independent women in positions of power, with successful careers.

However, boys and girls continue to have very different content interests. Genre preferences cross generational gaps—girls watch the same programs as their sisters and mothers, creating a feminine commonality of interests; boys watch the same programs as their brothers and fathers, guarding their own masculine space at home. It may be that it is not so much the media technologies themselves that create the gender segregation as it is the contents and meanings these technologies offer, as well as the contexts of their consumption. When girls are offered attractive options for them, they too use the computer, visit Internet chat rooms, and play outdoors.

The interpretation that attributes differences to content rather than to media may be specifically observed in the case of the computer. There are possibly many factors contributing to the image of computers as a sphere dominated by men. The computer market, similarly to the broadcast one, has neglected to cater to girls' specific interests and needs. In addition, parents seem to be less inclined to encourage their girls to experiment with computers. Other research has also found that household practices (such as giving boys priority over computer use, negative role models provided by mothers, boys' superior networking with other computer users, etc.) strengthen gender segregation in relation to computer use (Wheelock, 1992). This relatively unchallenged assumption, that computer playing requires technological skills for which boys are better socialized, is deeply rooted in the historical perception of technology as essentially masculine. A social analysis of technology from a feminist perspective (Cockburn, 1992) suggested that technology is much more than hardware—it is also a process of production and consumption, a form of knowledge, a site of gender and racial domination as well as of a power struggle. Gender relations in the household and its characteristic division of labor shape the way technologies—including leisure technologies such as computers—are adapted and used domestically.

Interestingly, we were not able to find cultural differences associated with different social and political contexts (e.g., in the status of women) between countries or groups of countries. For example, we expected to find that children growing up in the Nordic countries in our study (Sweden, Finland, and Denmark, where women are much more visible in positions of power in the public sphere) would exhibit less gendered media uses. This was not the case. Neither were we successful in creating subsets of countries (using both statistical tests and the typology offered in chapter 1) along gender-related criteria. In some cases, even the contrary can be said to hold true. For example, the French data document a much smaller gender gap in computer use than in Finland. One possible interpretation suggests that as the use of a new technology becomes widespread and routinized, the gender differences sharpen and become more evident. This seems to hold true both across countries (i.e., computers are much more accessible in Finland than in France) and along age lines (i.e., the older the children, the more evident the gender differences are).

In way of a tentative conclusion, we would like to speculate about our findings and ask whether we have a new story to tell. On one hand, the new media environment seems to reinforce a traditionally gendered youth culture as well as gendered domestic lifestyles. At the same time, however, many girls in our study seem to be impelled nowadays to explore traditional gender boundaries and to step into the so-called male territory of new technologies and related genre interests. The development, then, is asymmetrical: girls are increasingly showing an interest in traditionally masculine genres whereas boys continue to show little interest in feminine genres. Our data do not allow us to determine whether this trend reflects boys' higher control over and mastery of media technologies, girls' continuing growing sensitivity to the advantageous position that boys hold in our society, or indeed a fundamental change in girls' interests and needs. The possibility of such a change may be a genuine indication of the shrinking of the gender gap and the incorporation of girls in a seemingly unisex, but rather masculine, world of mediated popular culture.

How do we view this change? Whether we see it as good or bad news depends on what kind of feminism we believe in. On one hand, feminists criticize soaps and romances as stories allowing girls and young women to escape into fantasies of unachievable romantic longing, implying salvation by the right man and an obsessive occupation with good looks. Others have pointed to the latent subversive potential in these genres for the women who follow them (Ang, 1985; Radway, 1984). Would these authors defend romance and melodrama with regard to girls who are still growing up and have the potential to develop their own social identities, different from those of their mothers? If not, should the alternative be the adoption of masculine genres? Here feminism itself divides into those who believe that in order to have equal status women should be incorporated in the target-oriented, ambitious, masculine world of action, and those who believe in preserving women's cultural specificities in the realm of relationships, emotions, and caring (van Zoonen, 1994). Even if one belongs to the second camp, it would still have to be proved that feminine genres genuinely cater to these sensibilities. Another way of looking at feminine and masculine genres is to see both as keeping the same feminine stereotypes, with soaps positioning the women frontstage (rather than backstage) as the flip side of the masculine genres.

The decision as to whether we would wish for girls to join the media world of boys is further complicated by the issue of reception. Whereas our study tells us about patterns of media use and about content preferences, it tells us less about the meaning these have for girls and boys. For example, do girls who watch the boys' genres identify with the women in the shows or move toward identifying with the masculine heroes?

The differential socialization process involved in the construction of female versus male identity is a complicated one, involving central agents such as the family, school, peer culture, and the media. The result of this process, argued Maccoby (1988), is that boys and girls, on the average, develop somewhat different personality traits, skills, and activity preferences. Media consumption, we suggest, is both a means and an end to the process of gender construction: Media contribute to the cultivation of values, social norms, and expectations that, in their turn, help shape children's self-evaluation and aspirations. Simultaneously, self-perception and socialization pressures shape the construction of gender-appropriate interests and behaviors related to media consumption. Either way, girls and boys are probably adapting their media behaviors to the changing perception of their own position in society and to their own interests and needs. Only the future will show whether the picture presented in these pages is indeed one of a moment in a process of transition toward a less gender-segregated youth culture.

REFERENCES

Allen, R. C. (1985). *Speaking of soap operas.* Chapel Hill, NC: University of North Carolina Press.

Ang, I. (1985). *Watching Dallas: Soap opera and the melodramtaic imagination.* London: Methuen.

Brown, L. M. (1998). *Raising their voices.* Cambridge, MA: Harvard University Press.

Brown, L. M., & Gilligan, C. (1992). *Meeting at the crossroads.* Cambridge, MA: Harvard University Press.

Buckingham, D. (Ed.). (1993a). *Reading audiences: Young people and the media.* Manchester, England: Manchester University Press.

Buckingham, D. (1993b). *Children talking television: The making of television literacy.* London: The Falmer Press.

Christenson, P. G., & Peterson, J. B. (1988). Genre and gender in the structure of music preferences. *Communication Research, 15*(3), 282–301.

Christenson, P. G., & Roberts, D. F. (1998). *It's not only rock & roll: Popular music in the lives of adolescents.* Cresskill, NJ: Hampton Press.

Cockburn, C. (1992). The circuit of technology: Gender, identity and power. In R. Silverstone & E. Hirsch (Eds.), *Consuming technologies: Media and information in domestic spaces* (pp. 32–47). London: Routledge.

Currie, D. H. (1997). Decoding femininity: Advertisements and their teenage readers. *Gender & Society, 11*(4), 453–477.

Douglas, S. J. (1994). *Where the girls are: Growing up female with the mass media.* New York: Penguin Books.

Drotner, K. (1999). Netsurfers and game navigators: New media and youthful leisure cultures in Denmark. *Reseaux; French Sociology Review, 7*(1), 83–108.

Fine, G. A., Mortimer, J. T., & Roberts, D. F. (1990). Leisure, work and the media. In S. S. Feldman & G. Elliott (Eds.), *At the threshold: The developing adolescent* (pp. 225–254). Cambridge, MA: Harvard University Press.

Frazer, E. (1987). Teenage girls reading Jackie. *Media, Culture & Society, 9,* 407–425.

Frith, S. (1983). *Sound effects: Youth, leisure, and the politics of Rock 'n Roll.* London: Constable.

Gilligan, C. (1982). *In a different voice.* Cambridge, MA: Harvard University Press.

Hoffner, C. (1996). Children's wishful identification and para-social interaction with favorite television characters. *Journal of Broadcasting and Electronic Media, 40,* 389–402.

Inness, S. A. (Ed.). (1998). *Millennium girls: Today's girls around the world.* New York: Rowman & Littlefield.

Johnsson-Smaragdi, U., & Jönsson, A. (1994). Self-evaluation in an ecological perspective: Neighbourhood, family and peers, schooling and media use. In K. E. Rosengren (Ed.), *Media effects and beyond* (pp. 150–182). London: Routledge.

Jordan, A. B., & Woodward, E. H. (1998). Growing pains: Children's television in the new regulatory environment. *Annals, AAPSS, 557,* 83–95.

Lemish, D. (1998). Spice Girls' talk: A case study in the development of gendered identity. In S. A. Inness (Ed.), *Millennium girls: Today's girls around the world* (pp. 145–167). New York: Rowman & Littlefield.

Lewis, L. A. (1990). Consumer girl culture: How music video appeals to girls. In M. E. Brown (Ed.), *Television and women's culture: The politics of the popular* (pp. 89–101). Newbury Park, CA: Sage.

Maccoby, E. E. (1988). Gender as a social category. *Developmental Psychology, 24*(6), 755–765.

Maigret, E. (1999). Strange grew up with me: Sentimentality and masculinity in readers of Superhero comics. *Reseaux; French Sociology Review, 7*(1), 5–27.

Mazzerella, S., & Pecora, N. (1999). (Eds.) *Growing up girls: Popular culture and the construction of identity.* New York: Peter Lang.

Pasquier, D. (1999). *La culture des sentiments* [The culture of sentiments]. Paris: Ed de la MSH.

Peterson, E. E. (1987). Media consumption and girls who want to have fun. *Critical Studies in Mass Communication, 4*(1), 37–50.

Pipher, M. (1995). *Reviving Ophelia.* New York: Ballantine.

Radway, J. (1984). *Reading the romance: Women, patriarchy, and popular literature.* Chapel Hill, NC: University of North Carolina Press.

Raviv, A., Bar-Tal, D., Raviv, A., & Ben Horin, A. (1996). Adolescent idolization of pop singers: Causes, expressions, and reliance. *Journal of Youth and Adolescence, 25*(5), 631–750.

Roe, K. (1990). Adolescents music use: A structural-cultural approach. In K. Roe & U. Carlsson (Eds.), *Popular music research: An anthology from Nordicom-Sweden* (pp. 41–52). Gotberg, Sweden: Nordicom.

Roe, K. (1998). 'Boys will be boys and girls will be girls': Changes in children's media use. *Communications. The European Journal of Communication Research, 23*(1), 5–25.

Rosengren, K. E., & Windahl, S. (1989). *Media matter: TV use in childhood and adolescence.* Norwood, NJ: Ablex.

Tannen, D. (1990). *You just don't understand: Women and men in conversation.* New York: William Morrow, Ballantine.

van Zoonen, L. (1994). *Feminist media studies.* London: Sage.

Wheelock, J. (1992). Personal computers, gender and an institutional model of the household. In R. Silverstone & E. Hirsch (Eds.), *Consuming technologies: Media and information in domestic spaces* (pp. 97–112). London: Routledge.

13

Global Media Through
Youthful Eyes

Kirsten Drotner

As was demonstrated throughout this book, the media today operate as pervasive, yet often imperceptible, elements in the everyday cultures of children and young people. For example, television is a stable companion after school hours, music is a mood creator, and electronic games may be catalysts for meeting friends. In very concrete terms, the media help structure time and space for their users, just as their various genres, formats, and social uses serve as symbolic means of meaning making and interpretation for the young. What may be termed the thorough mediation of contemporary juvenile culture means that the often complex constellation of media has become fundamental in the formation of the cultural identities of children and young people.

The enormous expansion of media for domestic uses that we witnessed over the last 2 decades has been accompanied by an unrivalled globalization of media economy, production, and distribution. Thus, today, the mediated formation of children's cultural identities is played out against ongoing and often contradictory revisions of received notions of both actual, geographical and virtual, symbolic boundaries. These processes have led to public debates and scholarly speculation concerning the position and possible futures of national identities, cultural traditions, and established media institutions in the face of increasingly global media developments. In a European context, the clearest political evidence of these debates is the European Union Parliament's legal disputes in defining media production either as a form of culture in need of national protection, or as an industry that is subject to the free flow of commodities, including mediated commodities from overseas, that is, the United States.

Taking these important, adult questions as a point of departure, this chapter focuses on analyzing media globalization from the young users' perspective. The overarching issue is whether or not children and young people of today see themselves as belonging to a global—or at least transnational—community of media users and, by implication, a global, perhaps homogenized, culture. This general issue is tackled by seeking to answer more specific, empirical questions. Do European youngsters prefer domestic or foreign media output, and what do they consider to be the respective markers of the "domestic" and the "foreign"? Are certain genres, and even certain media, associated with domestic output, whereas others are associated with foreign output? If so, what are the implications for the young audiences' interpretations of these genres and/or media? Also, the question of linguistic norms is analyzed: is English assuming a position as the lingua franca for European youngsters, and if so, what role do the media play in this? Last, but not least, what part does the Internet play in the articulation of global cultural identities? The chapter closes by framing these empirical questions within a media-centered and a child-centered perspective; first, by discussing ways in which a generational perspective may enhance more nuanced theories of citizenship and public service media, and second by discussing ways in which the globalized mediation of juvenile culture necessitates revaluations of basic social and cultural competences in education.

THE MEDIA GO GLOBAL

In the many, recent theorizings on globalization, it is a bone of intellectual contention whether globalization is a consequence or a cause of modernity (Giddens, 1990; Wallerstein, 1991), whether the concept describes a recent, indeed postmodern, development (Bhabha, 1990; Hall, 1992; Harvey, 1989), or whether it is also a premodern phenomenon characterizing, among others, ancient civilizations (Friedman, 1994; Robertson, 1992). Equally, disagreement can be found in definitions of globalization as being either an economic and political phenomenon (Luke, 1989; Wallerstein, 1991) or a cultural process (Friedman, 1994; Hall, 1992).

Few scholars, however, dispute that the media play a vital role in contemporary processes of globalization. Combined developments in media technology, economic frames of production and distribution, together with new modes of reception have served to change the international media landscape quite dramatically over the last 2 decades. In many ways, the inception of CNN in 1980 and of MTV a year later are indicators of these changes: In technological terms, these new channels pioneered transnational satellite television, and in economic terms they became harbingers of a progressively commodified and globalized corporate media production that is often based on genre concepts originating in the United States. In terms of programming, CNN and MTV signaled an increasing emphasis on narrowcasting that, in terms of reception, created more segmentation of audiences across traditional geographical borders.

In Europe, these changes were accompanied and augmented by a concomitant deregulation of national media institutions—television, radio, and to some degree also, film. Traditionally, these institutions are closely linked both formally and informally to public service ideals with their underlying notions of geographically defined citizenship, equity of access, quality of output, and a homogeneous conception of cultures and populations. Conversely, transnational media are traditionally associated with commercial production of news, fiction, and easy entertainment, and with notions of consumerism that cut across divisions of gender, age, and ethnicity.

The combined forces of globalization, commodification, and deregulation of the international media landscape served to rekindle recurrent public and scholarly debates about the perceived threats facing national cultures, languages, and identities. In much of Europe, as elsewhere, such debates have latched on to very old discussions about media panics (Barker & Petley, 1997; Drotner, 1992) and more recent debates about cultural imperialism, a term that usually implies the cultural hegemony of the United States (Schiller, 1969, 1989). In the 1990s, the rapid take-up of computer-based media in general and the Internet in particular served both to radicalize these debates and to change their focus: The debates can no longer be limited to single media as has previously been the case, and Internet communication almost defies regulatory measures that were previously applied on a national and transnational scale in order to counteract perceived threats to cultural institutions and identities.

MEDIA STUDIES GO GLOBAL

Within media studies, the concept of globalization, or transnational media, is often analyzed in terms of media production and/or political economy of communication.[1] Here, two discursive perspectives prevail. On one hand, in the more recent theorizings of cultural imperialism, globalization is under-

---

[1]In media studies, the term *transnational media* (or transnational media corporation) tends to be applied in institutional or organizational analyses, whereas the term *globalization* often refers to overall media developments and their societal consequences. In the following, the two terms are used interchangeably.

stood in modernist terms as a mutually exclusive dichotomy (Jensen, 1990). Transnational, corporate channels such as CNN and MTV, and transnational genres such as the soap opera, are seen in opposition to the output of national, or indeed local, media and genres—an opposition that within a European context resonates with the distinction between public service and commercial media. On the other hand, from a postmodern perspective, globalization is understood in terms of processes of flow, as transcendence of physical borders and mental boundaries—a transcendence that foregrounds processes of diaspora and heterogeneous identity formations. In both modernist and postmodern theories, two divergent trajectories may be discerned. On one hand, a note of cultural optimism stresses the new possibilities in globalization processes of reaching beyond narrow local and national confines to create dialogues that enhance mutual expression of, and respect for, multiculturalism and civic rights, thereby ultimately advancing social change (Demers, 1999; Gershon, 1997; McChesney, 1997). On the other hand, a note of cultural pessimism focuses either on the dangers of social and cultural atomization (also termed Balkanization) or, conversely, on a cultural assimilation to the United States and its economic and cultural standards (Frèches, 1986; Garnham, 1990; Turkle, 1995).

With their focus on processes of production and/or media politics, few modernist and postmodernist media theories of globalization involve systematic, empirical studies of media users. Those that do tend to focus on a single medium (notably television) or a single genre (notably news) and harbor a tacit understanding of the users as adult and often male viewers (Jensen, 1998; Lull, 1988). However, these theoretical priorities on a single medium and adult viewers in issues of mediated globalization are severely challenged with the advent of the new digital techonologies, notably the Internet and cell phones, both of which are mainly developed within a commercial framework.

First, by going beyond mass-mediated forms of communication through facilitating person-to-person, two-way, and (almost) simultaneous forms of communication that transcend spatial borders and create virtual presences, these new technologies serve to question received notions of where the global and the local are actually located. Second, by blurring traditional boundaries between processes of production and reception, the new technologies question modernist notions within media globalization of receivers as more or less passive objects of transnational media output, just as the commercial frameworks of these technologies serve to undermine some postmodernist eulogies of a power-free global village. Third, and most importantly in the present context, by having children and young people among their avid users, the Internet and cell phones serve to foreground issues of generation in the context of mediated processes of globalization.

THE YOUTHFUL MEDIA LANDSCAPE

Contemporary media globalization has vital consequences for production, programming, and reception. In general, the increase in global media production and distribution is as much, if not more, geared toward leisure pursuits as toward occupational or educational purposes. This means that the reception (and increasingly also the production) of transnational media output is situated within the more informal networks of family and peers, and within rather flexible private and public arenas of interest such as bedrooms, sports clubs, cultural venues, and libraries. Thus, in structural terms, global media output situates children and young people at a vantage point of individual and collective maneuvering, while in symbolic terms, it signals leisure and the liberties of having a good time.

In television, transnational output now often means narrowcasting with Cartoon Network, Nickelodeon, and MTV catering to discrete age bands. Because these channels are all commercial, their narrowcasting means niche marketing, and children with money to spend are rapidly assuming a position as lucrative consumers, a position that was initially reserved for adults and, from the 1950s and 1960s on, also for adolescents.

Within a European perspective, this new position challenges the focal role traditionally accorded the young in public service institutions. Here, all children are addressed as citizens-to-be, which means a more or less explicit educational or pedagogical objective in programming. With their aims of universal access, public service producers cater to all children, but do so with a view to their respective positions as adult citizens. Conversely, commercial producers target the well-off, but do so irrespective of divisions of nationality, gender, age, and ethnicity (Drotner, 1999a). As the development of MTV demonstrates, this means that in practice, transnational media corporations often address older boys first, in order subsequently to maximize an audience across age and gender. Because most European children and young people have access to both public service and commercial media, they encounter different forms of address and have to negotiate these in their social uses of the media.

The combined developments in transnational media production also influence programming. Traditionally, certain media formats have been more open to export than others, and these divisions have often, if not always, been dependent on language. Obvious examples of exportable media genres are audiovisual and print fiction, music, and electronic games. Conversely, newspapers, television news, and most radio programs have tended to be more confined to operating within national or local boundaries in many European countries, a situation reinforced by the strong public service tradition in radio and television production.

However, satellite television, video recorders, and, more recently, the Internet are rapidly transforming this picture. For example, groups of Swedish fans may exchange videos with their Italian counterparts located through the Internet, thus creating symbolic sites of particularistic similarity and identification that transgress actual borders as well as universalist claims to a common European identity (Bolin, 1998).[2] Also, as first seen with the television series, *The X-Files*, producers now shape their output partly through interaction with fans over the Internet. The low-budget horror film, *The Blair Witch Project* shows how the Internet can also be used as a lever of marketing (Drotner, 1999a). These virtual, interpretive communities transcend and supplement geographically located interpretive communities and may thus serve to question perceived homogeneities in national cultures.

Moreover, we see a generational blurring in modes of address across various types of media. More informal modes of address that in the 1920s originated, for example, in juvenile weeklies in several countries, were subsequently introduced into commercial radio and television programs aimed at adolescents in the 1960s. These are currently being introduced into mainstream programming for adults also in many types of public service programs such as talk shows and national news (Langer, 1998; Livingstone & Lunt, 1996). Conversely, highly popular genres such as soaps, that originated in the United States as adult women's fare, have been refashioned to cater to a supposedly well-heeled adolescent audience across national boundaries. These symbolic blurrings of generational boundaries in programming create new hybrid modes of address that serve to bridge former oppositions between commercial and public service media output. A general youthfulness is assuming symbolic supremacy in much media output, leaving many older children and young people in a position where they seek out new ways of marking cultural distinctions.

In terms of reception, other chapters in this book (see especially chapter 6) made it clear that children's and young people's media uses are lodged within and depend on a range of social and genre-specific preferences. This means that, in general, young audiences go by contents and use, not by formalities of production in their choice of media: They care more about what is on offer for which uses than about the national origin of a particular text. This does not imply, however, that origin of production is not recognized or plays no part in their choices, as we shall see, but it does mean that our framework of interpretation must take the users' media priorities for content into consideration.

---

[2]The advancement of transnational interpretive communities shaped by means of video recorders and the Internet is not limited to older children and young people, but may also be seen, for example, with immigrant adults who use videos and satellite television to create and uphold (perceived) symbolic links to their countries of origin, thus creating so-called diaspora cultures in their new homelands (Kolar-Panov, 1997).

Moreover, depending on age, children's and young people's media uses are often more wide-ranging than many adults' reception modes. Most adults read, listen to the radio and CDs, watch television or film, and use the computer or cell phone either on an individual basis or in small groups such as with their spouses or families. Naturally, children and young people obey similar patterns. However, in addition, older children and adolescents use media as part of more collective forms of interaction, such as watching videos or playing electronic games with a group of friends, or swapping cassettes or magazines at school or in the sports ground (see also chapter 9). This pattern of mediated interaction is an important analytical backdrop to understanding the more recent creation of transnational, virtual (fan) cultures previously mentioned.

In empirical terms, these combined trends in youthful media production, programming, and reception indicate the complexities involved in describing and seeking to analyze global media developments within an age-sensitive perspective. In both actual and symbolic terms, children and young people are often situated differently from adults in the mediated cultures of today, a position that should caution against using empirical results from adults to make inferences about juveniles and vice versa. In theoretical terms, the trends signal the importance of paying analytical attention to what Swedish anthropologist Hannerz termed "the entire media landscape" on a global scale, rather than singling out a particular medium or a particular dimension of mediation—be it production, programming, or reception (Hannerz, 1990). Although that description cannot do justice to the complexities and contradictions found in this landscape, it draws on the general trends found in analyzing the media developments in the 12 European countries that took part in the research described in this book, and its "holistic aim" should be borne in mind when we now turn to detailing the empirical analysis of media globalization found in our study.

NATIONAL AND INTERNATIONAL MEDIA PREFERENCES

Because television is the most time-consuming of the media analyzed in this book, it is natural to take television as our empirical point of departure in this chapter. When analyzing the origin of favorite television programs for the countries offering available data on this item, we find that young audiences in half the countries prefer programs of national origin,[3] as shown in Table 13.1.

---

[3]It should be noted that we only distinguished between "national" and "international" in asking informants about the origin of favorite programs. Thus, the term "international" encompasses programs from neighboring countries as well as transnational programs, and hence Table 13.1 cannot be taken as a simple indicator of national differences in terms of globalization of favorite television programs.

TABLE 13.1
Origin (National or International) of Favorite Program

		CH	DE	DK	ES	FI	GB	IL	SE
Aged 6-7									
	National	43	54	46	29	46	14	N/A	52
	International	N/A	58	54	46	71	54	86	48
Aged 9-10									
	National	10	55	42	66	29	57	59	63
	International	90	45	58	35	72	43	41	37
Aged 12-13									
	National	7	66	27	72	25	61	30	52
	International	94	34	73	28	75	39	70	48
Aged 15-16									
	National	7	69	30	75	22	59	19	46
	International	93	31	70	25	78	41	81	54
Average									
	National	8	60	36	68	26	57	29	53
	International	92	40	64	32	74	43	71	47

Spain tops the list when it comes to favoring domestically produced programs, followed by Germany, the United Kingdom, and Sweden. Spain has a long tradition of regional broadcasting, whereas the other three countries have strong national, public service traditions. So does Finland, however, where three quarters of young audiences prefer international television programs. It does not seem, then, that public service television in and of itself enhances national preferences of viewing. A more important factor seems to be the size of language communities. All four nationally oriented countries have a population size that allows for a varied domestic production including children's programs. Conversely, Denmark, Finland, Israel, and Switzerland are not only smaller countries but two of them (Israel and Switzerland) encompass quite separate language communities, each of which are too small to allow for, or prioritize, domestic programs that appeal to the young. In that type of checkered media landscape, inexpensive, transnational imports from the United States and elsewhere may operate as a common ground that appeals to the young irrespective of their ethnic and/or linguistic background. In the case of Switzerland, terrestrial channels from neighboring Germany, France, and Italy add to children's near-universal predilection for nondomestic television.

If this analysis is valid, then it follows that the division between young audiences' national and international television preferences hides a more profound issue concerning the possibilities and priorities of producers in the respective European countries to offer domestic television output that appeals to the young of both sexes and various ages. Only when audiences find few or no domestic programs or genres to their taste do they turn to imports whether of the transnational or neighboring country variety. This result may offer an important corrective to public discourses that, in general, blame the perceived threats to national identities on Americanization and, in particular, find fault with the imported television fiction and films that swamp large and small screens in Europe, without relating these media imports to the substance and variety of domestic output.

The clearest indication of this "international" pattern of choice is offered by 6- to 7-year-old boys. In all countries they prefer programs of international origin, not because they like what is foreign, but because they prefer cartoons above all other genres—and the majority of cartoons on offer are produced in the United States or Japan. As we saw in chapter 6, girls in general select a more varied media menu, hence the picture is less clear with 6- to 7-year-old girls. In Finland and Israel, for example, they follow the international pattern generally seen in these countries, whereas in the United Kingdom, the very young girls deviate from the general "national" pattern by preferring programs of international origin, possibly due to a heavier influence in the United Kingdom from cartoon channels such as Nickelodeon and the Disney Corporation. Furthermore, in most European countries, even national programs catering to the very young often contain some imported material (mostly cartoons). For example, the domestic Spanish programs *Con mucha marcha* (real fun) and *Club Megatrix* show cartoons produced in the United States or Japan.

As children grow older, their choice and use of media widen to include the use of music and electronic games (and, in many countries, books as well)—all markets that aspire to transnational production and marketing. With electronic games, the Anglo-American dominance is near universal and only multinational conglomerates such as Disney and Mattel bring out games for young children in a variety of national languages. As for music, again we see differences between big and small language communities. France is a prime example of a country in which music in the national language holds its ground even with many older children. In Denmark, on the other hand, perhaps as a result of parental emphasis on early acquisition of English skills, Anglo-American imports dominate the music tastes of middle-class children and of adolescents, and many domestic music bands, such as Aqua, sing in English to capture a larger market share. So, when studying young audiences' entire media landscape, the general conclusion to be drawn is that globalization—and that often means reception and use of prod-

ucts in English—increases with age and that even young children in countries with a large domestic share of television are more international in their
media fare than may immediately be assumed.

RECOGNITION OF OTHERNESS

If we wish to specify further the users' own evaluations of these general
trends, it is important to know whether or not children recognize differences
between domestic and foreign media output and, if they do, what they consider to be formal and substantive traits of "otherness." Naturally, one has to
take into consideration that such traits vary with different types of media.
Thus, translated books are not formally marked by their extraneous origins,
unlike media such as television and film where images and, in countries
using subtitles, language may be defined as formal traits of otherness. For
example, in Denmark, translated books make up more than 60% of all children's books, and translations from English make up nearly four out of every
six imports (*Dansk bogfortegnelse*, 1997, p. 19). However, all books look Danish at first sight.

In audiovisual media, subtitling is used in Israel and the smaller countries
of Northern Europe, except in television programs for very young children.
In Germany, France, Italy, and Spain, on the other hand, dubbing is the rule
(Luyken, 1991). Subtitles are an immediate marker of foreign products even
to young children, as they will often need adults or older siblings as inter-
preters. In countries using dubbing in film and television, what is spoken in
the national tongue tends to be regarded as a national product although differences in accents may be noted, especially by older children. In these
countries, visual signs of foreignness are noted more. For example, a middle-
class British girl, aged 13, noted about *Neighbours* and *Home and Away*:

> I mean you can tell it's Australian by the way the boxes and the chocolate bars
> are . . . you know in the coffee shop they've got like a fridge and then they've
> got like a row of chocolate bars, and you can tell because the boxes are made
> differently to ours and the wrappers are different.
>
> (Livingstone & Bovill, 1999)

So, when applying a child-centered, bottom-up view on media globalization,
we find little interest in origin of production, multinational economy, and
vertical integration of corporations. Children have other markers of otherness. Apart from language, they mostly note visual signs of differences in
media characters (e.g., physiognomy, hairdo, skin color), places (e.g., palm
trees, lots of traffic, wooden houses with thatched roofs) and objects (e.g.,
car brands, street signs, what people eat). Formal signs of signification—the

title of a film if it is not translated, the form of announcement and presentation—are remarked on, too. Thus, British children define the satellite channel Nickelodeon as being British because of its British editorial anchoring, whereas few doubt that MTV with its multinational hosts is no homegrown product.

Children's choice between domestic and international media output implies more or less explicit symbolic negotiations between known and unknown narrative repertoires and formal signs, social conventions, and world views. Obviously, children in these negotiations take their own everyday lives and media norms as points of reference and comparison. Still, it would be wrong to surmise a neat fit between production and reception in these negotiations: Domestic media products do not necessarily belong to the domain of the known, or foreign media products to domains of the unknown. For many youngsters, a soap opera such as *Beverly Hills 90210*, hugely popular in many European countries in the mid-1990s, may be readily incorporated into a known, everyday world because of its subject matter—recognizable conflicts concerning, for example, courting, parenting, and schooling (Povlsen, 1999). As a young Israeli woman, aged 17, professed, "[*Beverly Hills*] is fun. It's about youth, it's about what happens to you everyday, girlfriends, boyfriends, dating." What Ang termed the emotional realism of soaps (Ang, 1985) transcends formal exoticisms such as palm trees, fast cars, and artful demonstrations of beach volleyball. Conversely, domestically produced narratives about groups not normally depicted in the media may seem more outlandish and strange to young audiences than a soap opera produced in the United States or Australia.

The existence of many othernesses surfaces with particular poignancy for audience groups who have recently immigrated. Here, the increasing media globalization creates new possibilities and possible problems for children and young people situated as they are between the often contradictory (media) norms of parents and peers. For example, a French study on Maghreb immigrants carried out by Alkan (quoted in Jouët & Pasquier, 1999) demonstrated that the satellite channels Arab Sat and Turksat are preferred by many fathers, who as heads of families oversee and feel responsible for the general moral outlook of their wives and children, whereas mothers tend to stress the importance of French television channels as a means of integrating their children into French culture. Still, Alkan also described an example of adolescent children watching an intimate scene on French television with their mother and turning off the set so as to avoid confrontation—and turning it back on when she leaves the room (Jouët & Pasquier, 1999; Qureshi & Moores, 1999). As Chailley (1999) concluded in another French study, for immigrant children the otherness made visible on channels from their parental homelands is more readily accepted as part their own culture than is the otherness found in audiovisual products from other European countries and the United States (p. 377). Well-known genre conventions alone are no guarantee of securing cultural preference.

Results like these should caution against making simple analogies about domestic culture as a homogeneous and known domain of experience that may be neatly contrasted to foreign culture as an equally homogeneous unknown whose exoticism is defined and delimited through its complete difference from the domestic. According to Morley and Robins (1995), "Globalization, as it dissolves the barriers of distance, makes the encounter of colonial center and colonized pheriphery immediate and intense" (p. 108). Mediated globalization may be as much about exoticizing the seemingly well-known as about acculturation to the seemingly foreign.

ENTERTAINMENT IS GLOBAL, EDUCATION IS LOCAL?

The diverse use of different media and genres for different purposes has decisive implications for children's and young people's notions of media globalization. Music, fiction in film and books and on television, and electronic games are mostly associated with excitement, entertainment, and having fun (see chapter 4). Since much of this media fare is commercially produced and imported, young users tend to link these gratifications to consumerism and to products beyond the confines of their country. This is particularly true as children get older. Conversely, news and documentary genres are associated with information and more or less "useful knowledge," gratifications that are primarily sustained by national or local media institutions, most of which are furthermore linked to public service ideals and in a wider sense to the educative ideals promoted in school. As a 15-year-old Danish boy suggested:

> You have to keep up with things, don't you? I don't delve deeply into politics, but one has to know a little, or you would feel totally stupid coming to a job and they start talking about politics, and you just sit there in a corner in your own little, secluded world, like Rainman or something.

Seen within the perspective of globalization, these diverse associative frameworks imply that national culture and edification are closely linked, whereas entertainment is linked to global media products and their uses. A plausible conclusion to be drawn from these oppositions is that young users define national media output in general and information in particular as boring but necessary, whereas international media output in general and fiction in particular is fun. This, however, is not entirely the case: As mentioned earlier, children and young people do favor domestic output in countries where this output caters to the tastes of discrete ages and both sexes. In other countries (see following examples), domestic music, films, television series, and games are hugely popular, too, when they obey the genre conventions and thematic foci that appeal to the young. Thus, the domestic Israeli soap opera *Ramat Aviv Gimel* is highly popular with older children, as is the teen-soap *Hélène et les garçons* with French children (Pasquier, 1999). Young Danes stress their preference for the domestic pop group Aqua, not primarily because it is Danish, but because the group's music sounds "right," because their look singles them out as special on the international music scene, and because they offer a special mood of high energy (Lemish et al., 1998). These examples illustrate Robertson's (1992) argument that what is called local is in large degree constructed on a global or at least superlocal basis.

Robertson's argument may be carried even further. In the often complex negotiations between local, national, and global media and genres, negotiations that also involve maneuvering between public service and commercial output, it seems that many children's attitudes are pragmatically dependent on different moods, social uses, and needs. A striking example of this is seen in an interview with a group of strictly religious Israeli girls, aged 12, who professed the necessity for modest clothing and total obedience to God, only to express their admiration of Spice Girls and Jean-Claude van Damme's action movies a few minutes later. Similarly, a 15-year-old French girl stated her music preferences as follows:

[*Aqua*] is famous at the moment but I think it won't last. I only like their first song (it's funny). Hanson are very skilful brothers and they succeed quite well despite their youth. I like them but it's a pity they have stopped school. I like their songs. I like French music because you can memorize the lyrics quickly. I like Italian music because it's beautiful.

Such findings have several implications. First, genres and media types evolve in a dialogue between the local, the national, and the global, with Anglo-American norms gaining increasing importance as children grow older. Second, young media users do recognize traits of otherness and these are negotiated on a pragmatic basis. Third, recognition is deemed significant only insofar as it helps sustain the formation of their cultural identities within parameters that can be defined and accepted as "normal." Othernesses that are deemed too exotic tend to be written off as insignificant, unimportant, "weird." So even if young audiences develop an understanding and acceptance of cultural diversity through their pragmatic attitudes, it is still exercised within social boundaries that have to be constantly negotiated.

ENGLISH AS A LINGUA FRANCA

Particularly in a multilingual continent such as Europe, language and national identity are closely connected. For example, within one generation from the late nineteenth century onward, Sweden transformed its educational system from being based on classical languages to Swedish as the linguistic norm in an effort to strengthen national sentiments (Thavenius, 1995). The connection between language and national identity has operated discursively to sustain notions of homogeneity between geographically defined populations and official cultural norms; hence the symbolic importance for politicians to speak in their native tongue during negotiations. Naturally, such discourses are questioned by groups who for one reason or another do not fit the official discourses, but this does not in itself disprove a close connection between identity (if not national identity) and language. Therefore, the issue of globalization is fundamentally also an issue about linguistic norms, about differences in access and modes of expression.

English dominates most business transactions. It is the language of the international music and book industry as well as the production of electronic games. The majority of blockbuster films are from Hollywood, and the large home market for television production in the United States creates a critical export advantage, the effect of which on young viewers was demonstrated in prior several quotes. Last, but not least, English is the language of computer use, including use of the Internet.

The dominance of English is recognized in most European countries. In linguistic terms, for obvious reasons, the United Kingdom is a case apart in the present study. Of the other 11 countries, learning English as a first foreign language is statutory in Denmark, Israel, the Netherlands, Spain, and Sweden. In Finland, Flanders, and Switzerland, the other official languages of the respective countries are the first foreign languages learned at school, followed by English as a mandatory or optional second language. In France, children may choose English as their first foreign language and nearly everyone does so. The introduction to English varies from the age of 6 in Spain (with experiments beginning at the age of 3) to the age of 13 or 14 in Flanders.

Thus English serves as a common linguistic ground in a continent marked by a range of language communities. The widespread, official endorsement of English is used by older children to legitimate their own media use: For example, playing electronic games, it is claimed, helps train one's proficiency in English—a statement that many parents endorse and use as an argument for the family's digital acquisitions. Also, children make a point of using English in their everyday conversations even if few take it as far as this pair of middle-class Israeli girls, aged 12:

One day she and I went and decided that we are not too good in English. So we decided—from today on we speak English. So we spoke English all the time, and if one of us didn't understand we switched back to Hebrew and helped each other. That's what we do. Not only in English.

At the age of 10 or 11, when most children already have mastered reading and writing in their mother tongue, English assumes a symbolic position as a taste marker. Many children recognize differences between British, American, and Australian English (even if they pay little importance to origin of production): They find it "cool" to apply the correct English terms for genres (horror, action, science fiction) and formal properties (cut, fast forward, dubbing, delete) and to know the original titles of films and television series (electronic games are nearly always sold by their original titles). Many domestic products are measured against, and often found wanting when compared to, English media output, which is routinely associated with innovation, quality, and technical skills. For example, a 15-year-old Danish boy remarked, "I don't like Danish films so much, because the budgets are low, there are not so many good actors in Denmark." Similarly, a 15-year-old Israeli girl argued, "American series, that's quality. Let's say they will bring beautiful actors but they also have some class . . . they have to be more intellectual, more with acting talent."

In all 11 countries except Israel, British English is the more or less official standard taught at school. Conversely, American English dominates leisure-time media, and our qualitative data equally suggest that children and young people themselves adopt American English as their chosen dialect; it not only comes naturally to them through their media exposure, it also marks their own conversations as being different from official, educational dialogues. Many consider British English to be a snooty, "la-di-da" language, unlike the vernacular of American English. These qualitative findings are confirmed by other quantitative studies. For example, a national survey on Danes' attitudes to the English language ($N = 856$) carried out in 1995–1996 showed that the younger people are, the more they prefer American to British English (Preisler, 1999). Similarly, a pilot survey carried out in 1992 among 215 students in Hamburg, Germany demonstrated that four out of five hear British English from their teachers and a similar proportion associate American English with radio and television (Hasebrink, Berns, & Skinner, 1997). Still, this evaluation does not necessarily imply a preference for media products from the United States. Here, official cultural discourses seem to play a part, with Israeli children at one end of the spectrum ("British series—yuk," girl aged 16) and, at the other end, French children for whom English in general has less significance as a mark of distinction and who routinely denounce media output from the United States.

Interestingly, children's and young people's different evaluations of American and British English are in some countries mirrored in official, adult discourse. For example, in Switzerland the business community strongly supports the teaching of American English as a necessary stepping-stone for entering the international world of commerce, but the educational authorities favor British English. Here, young users' attempts to gain an oppositional cultural capital by using American English seem to make them best suited to enter the field in which economic capital holds sway.

Generally speaking, age differences surface clearly in the use of English. In Europe, two generations ago, a mark of a good education was the ability to speak Latin and Greek, and one generation later it was the mastery of at least two modern languages. Today, adults and children alike accept the predominance of English with more or less equanimity, and the question of dialects in English has now assumed a critical position in the cultural battle of distinction. Thus, American English may be assuming a position as a marker of age, a distinction formerly left to youthful media and modes of address. It seems a reasonable prophecy to gauge that in most European countries American English seems likely to win over British English, not least due to the increasing importance played by the Internet. So far, the Internet has been almost neutral in linguistic terms—an "emoticon," or "smiley," is not in Dutch, Finnish, or Italian—unlike an oral expression of disgust or joy. As the Internet is taken up by more and more Europeans and as streaming media become a technical possibility, oral modes of expression will increasingly substitute the written word in virtual communication, and hence linguistic differences will also come to play a part in this medium.

Already today, we see a close connection between young users' proficiency in English and their use of the Internet, even if no causal relationship has been found. For example, the Swiss survey found that the better children's self-professed abilities in English, the more they use the Internet: One out of every three children, who claims a good or very good written English proficiency, has used the Internet, whereas this is true for only one in six of children with little self-professed proficiency. The difference decreases with age, so that among 15- or 16-year-olds, one in five with little proficiency in English has used the Internet against one in four of pupils with a good or very good proficiency (Süss & Giordani, 2000). Undoubtedly, the symbolic importance paid to the Internet in public discourse gilds surfing, chatting, and playing games on the Internet with an aura of innovation that may spark young users' immediate interest. Whether this interest will persist naturally, however, depends on more than linguistic capabilities. Fundamentally, it depends on what may be found on the Net.

SAMENESS OR DIFFERENCE ON THE INTERNET?

Whether individual scholars anticipate a trajectory of media pessimism or optimism, few doubt that the Internet is the most decisive player in media globalization. Much speculation and somewhat less empirical investigation focuses on the ways in which the Internet may change not only the macroaspects of finance and power and mesoaspects of cultural production and social interaction, but also microaspects of perception and identity. In terms of research on children and young people, the microperspective has been the most prevalent: Do we face a global "digital generation" in Negroponte's (1995) words or, to speak with Tapscott (1998), a new Net generation, or *n-gen*? As is evident from the preceding chapters, the present study does not lend support to such grand claims: The advent of computer communication has meant a further and heterogeneous diversification of an already complex media landscape used by the young in Europe, not a replacement of old media by new.

Still, seen from young users' own perspective, the virtual forms of globalized communication that transcend geographical place and time do change the entire media landscape for the connected—and hence also for the unconnected, if only indirectly. Foremost among these is the possibility of interactive, mediated communication (chatting, sending e-mail, partaking in news groups) and the possibilities of media production, from the making of personal homepages to editing music taken from the Internet or grabbing Net pictures, morphing them, and possibly returning the results to the Net. These possibilities serve to blur existing boundaries between mass and personal forms of communication and between media reception and production.

So far, most youngsters using computer media and particularly the Internet have exercised the possibilities of virtual communication rather than production. Anders, aged 12, living in Denmark and by no means an intense computer user, has surfed the Internet at school when doing a project on snakes. Unlike books, homepages on the Net offered him "a normal person writing about what he experienced with snakes, that was pretty fun." Also, Anders likes the idea of contacting people in other countries via the Net "to see what somebody in the USA is doing in his everyday life." The furthest Anders's imagination takes him is to fantasize about playing chess with a person in China. This emphasis on similarity, on communicating with other children about mutual interests, is corroborated by two Swedish boys, aged 13:

Int: What do you talk about [on the Internet]?

A: Well, life in general, how old we are. If I speak with a boy, we speak about girls and the like. About hobbies and such. . . . . .

   If you meet on the Net, you may speak to somebody in China if that takes your fancy, it doesn't matter where they're from, just somebody to talk to. You can say what you like and stuff.

(Sjöberg, 1999, p. 29)

As is evident, Internet communication is, indeed, viewed as a global phenomenon, but it is the freedom to seek and find similarities across borders that is stressed more than the process of crossing boundaries in and of itself (see also Tobin, 1998). Experimentation with conceptions of the self does take place in chat groups, notably with older adolescents and in initial, short-term encounters where chatters may fake their names and ages, but the substance of chatting is often very close to home.

These findings concerning the impact on identity of virtual, globalized communication are rather different from those quoted, for example, by Turkle (1995). Turkle saw the computer as opening a vast number of windows to the world, thus facilitating experimentation with, and exploration of, identity positions that together advance a fragmented sense of the self: "The life practice of windows is that of a decentered self that exists in many worlds and plays many roles at the same time" (p. 14). Since Turkle made her empirical studies on young adult academics communicating via MUDs (multi-user-dungeons), the Internet has grown exponentially. That it is rapidly becoming an everyday option for sizable groups of ordinary youngsters in some cultures may induce us to modify or even revise such grand generalizations (see Drotner, 1999b).

Young users' vacillation between faking names and ages and yet focusing on IRL (in real life) interests may usefully be conceptualized as a form of role playing similar to that found with younger children who continuously alternate between dimensions of fantasy and reality when playing, for example, "house" or "robbers." Thus, Internet use in general, and chatting in particular, may be seen as a means to continue the joys of playing at an age when actual role playing is usually laid aside. Ultimately, for older children and adolescents, Internet use, like role playing in early childhood, rather than being a postmodern flight from or decentering of their everyday existence and the prospects of an adult identity, may operate as a way of coming to terms with them.

GLOBALIZATION OF PUBLIC SERVICE FOR THE YOUNG?

Young Europeans may be using the Internet to speak about themselves and their everyday experiences in emulation of IRL communication, but they mostly do so in English, which for most people outside the United Kingdom still means a linguistic limitation to their means and ranges of expression. Hence, the fundamental importance played by the Internet in processes of mediated globalization and the preponderance of English in virtual forms of communication takes us back to questions raised earlier in this chapter about the connection between the formation of cultural identities, language, and media. As mentioned at the beginning of this chapter, a complex constellation of media—public service and commercial, local, national and transnational—are today fundamental tools for the rising generations in their negotiations of who they are and what the world is like. This position, in turn, puts media culture at the center not only of cultural policies, but of wider questions of socialization, education, and cultural democracy.

How do European children and young people in future develop and sustain a full range of cultural expressions through the media? How do adults secure that the media not only address the rising generations as consumers but equally as citizens? How do we see to it that the young are able not only to understand and interpret media output made by others (i.e., adults), but are equally in a position to use the media themselves in accordance with basic traditions of informed citizenship? In answering questions such as these, one should seek to balance a respect for young media users' own preferences and adult responsibilities for creating a range of choice. We should not criticize children for choosing what they do from existing media menus, but we could optimize their possibilities of being able to select from a wide range of different media fare—and perhaps introduce them to tastes that they never knew existed.

A media-centered answer to those questions may start from an observation that the increasingly important transnational media are mostly commercial and, hence, the relations between commercial and public service media are central to our answers. Obviously, there is no neat divide between the two types. Most public service media nurture commercial interests in, for example, issues of export, merchandising, and sponsoring. Commercial producers may bring out quality programs that cater to a diversity of young audiences rather than to the lowest common denominator—a trend that globalization may actually encourage, as discrete target groups can now be reached transnationally, thus adding up to an economically viable audience. However, in one fundamental respect, public service and commercial media do differ, namely in their modes of addressing young audiences.

As mentioned earlier, commercial media hinge on notions of consumerism, public service media on notions of citizenship. To the extent that we wish to preserve and develop social and cultural democracy for all members of our societies, the notion of citizenship has to be sensitized to an age perspective. So far this has gone relatively unnoticed, but such a development would allow the young to become members of a constituency of citizens, despite their lack of legal rights. Fundamentally, this implies that the classic elements found in the definition of public service for adults in radio and on television must be extended to children and to all media: children and young people must be offered free and public access to a full range of media forms (from books and television to the Internet), to a diversity of genres, both fact and fiction, and to output of quality and relevance, and they must be offered these things in their own language.

Language does play a fundamental part in our development of identity. The virtual dominance of English in most commercial, computer-related media and its increasing presence in children's lives makes it particularly important that the young have access to other types of media products that address relevant parts of their culture—including the quirky, the unexpected, and the provocative. This is no mean feat in view of the decreasing number of underage citizens in most European countries and the concomitant rapid increase in transnational, commercial media production that caters to older, more affluent consumers. It is a particular challenge to extend public service to the Internet and other online services given the preponderance of commercial development in this diverse field.

Public service radio and television have traditionally been instrumental in developing and sustaining public fora of exchange and dialogue for adults where issues of difference and conflict may be discussed. Today, the public sphere is being transformed with the advance of the Internet and its possibilities of creating virtual—and often fairly young—transnational communities based on immediate interests and with differential access based on users' abilities or willingness to pay. Together, these developments strongly reinforce the necessity for free and universal access to public, cultural fora where virtual and IRL communities of all ages may interact. If public service media institutions are to have a platform and influence the virtual public sphere in future, they will have to include issues and modes of address that are relevant and appeal to the young, just as is already partly the case in radio and television. In smaller language communities this, for example, involves prioritizing national television fiction that caters to older children and adolescents, whereas in larger language communities it may involve output of greater cultural—including linguistic—diversity.

There are good reasons to surmise that public service institutions may benefit from strengthening their liaisons with other institutions traditionally catering to the public good such as libraries and museums. Also, public service corporations may learn from commercial online producers to think in terms of media integration and synergy. From a generational perspective, this means that catering to young tastes in television and radio may secure a viable online following by young audiences—and vice versa. Although these demands may seem excessive or daunting to public service producers, the alternative is equally overwhelming: National media in general and public service media in particular will be relegated by many young, European audiences to the safe but unimportant "useful" margins of their cultural landscapes.

BEYOND CULTURAL DIVERSITY

A child-centered answer to the question about developing and sustaining tools of interpretation and cultural interaction in an increasingly global media landscape involves a rethinking of media education, including what

UNESCO termed *the parallel school* of leisure-time media (Halloran & Jones, 1985). The print media—books, newspapers, journals, and maps—have been focal levers of cultural modernity. The Enlightenment ideals, which underpin most democratic societies to this day, view reading and writing as fundamental catalysts of citizenship and general character formation or, in German, *Bildung*. Access to the modes of communication across divisions of opinion is the precondition for any formation of consensus on which ideals of the public sphere are constructed (Habermas, 1989). Although the unified conceptions of these ideals have rightly been questioned (first and most thoroughly by Negt & Kluge, 1972), they have nevertheless become pillars on which educational systems have been founded since the 19th century. Their "reality effect" is with us even today.

In thoroughly mediated and increasingly globalized cultures, however, a proper understanding and use of print media seems insufficient as a means of democratic participation. If children and young people are to learn and participate in democratic action, they have to employ a much wider range of communication tools than reading and writing, even if these abilities are by no means rendered superfluous or obsolete. Viewed from an historical perspective, the entire range of media (print, audiovisual, digital) may be defined as late-modern catalysts of general character formation as well as concrete competences. Still, in public discourse this is a controversial issue because it serves to question established hierarchies of cultural capital. The rising generations are often the first to acquire new cultural abilities through their leisure use of media, whereas adults exercise a necessary role as gatekeeepers, controlling which of these cultural abilities are to be considered socially accepted competences and included for example within the educational systems (Drotner, 1999a).

As it is, children's and young people's media abilities are either marginalized as unimportant or demonized outright as dangerous aspects of individualized leisure-time consumption, or else they are objectified as communication tools in education. Examples of the marginalization approach are the debates on canonized literary works to be inculcated via national education (see Bloom, 1994). The best example of the "tools" approach is the way in which computer competences are defined: The computer is at best viewed as a piece of information technology for which children need to have a driver's license in order not to get lost on the information superhighway. Only rarely is the computer defined in educational terms as a fundamental medium of communication and part of an entire media landscape that pupils have to understand as part of their education. In both cases, changes would need a thorough revaluation of what general character formation and actual competences should be in a multicultural, global world. Meanwhile, the adults of tomorrow are busy building that world with radically different and highly divergent tools.

REFERENCES

Ang, I. (1985). *Watching Dallas*. London: Methuen.

Barker, M., & Petley, J. (Eds.). (1997). *Ill effects: The media/violence debate*. London: Routledge.

Bhabha, H. (1990). *Nation and narration*. London: Routledge.

Bloom, H. (1994). *The western canon: The books and school of the ages*. New York: Harcourt Brace.

Bolin, G. (1998). *Filmbytare: videovåld, kulturell produktion & unga män* [Film Swappers: Video Violence, Cultural Production and Young Men]. Umeå: Boréa. Dissertation.

Dansk bogfortegnelse: årskatalog 1996. (1997). [Danish National Bibliography 1996]. Ballerup: Danish Library Center/The Royal Library.

Chailley, M. (1999). Enfants aux ecrans [Children at the Screen]. *Reseaux, 17, 92–93*, 365–86. Special issue 'Les jeunes et l'ecran' ['The Young and the Screen'], eds. D. Pasquier & J. Jouët.

Demers, D. (1999). *Global Media: Menace or Messiah?* Cresskill, NJ: Hampton Press.

Drotner, K. (1992). Modernity and media panics. In M. Skovmand & K. C. Schroeder (Eds.), *Media cultures: Reappraising transnational media* (pp. 42–62). London: Routledge.

Drotner, K. (1999a). *Unge, medier og modernitet: pejlinger i et foranderligt landskab* [Youth, media and modernity: Tracing a changing trajectory]. Copenhagen: Borgen.

Drotner, K. (1999b). Internautes et joueurs: La nouvelle culture des loisirs chez les jeunes Danois. *Reseaux, 17, 92–93*, 133–72. Tr. (1999). Netsurfers and Game Navigators: New Media and Youthful Leisure Cultures in Denmark. *Reseaux: The French Journal of Communication, 7, 1*, 83–108.

Frèches, J. (1986). *La Guerre des Images* [Picture War]. Paris: Denoël.

Friedman, J. (1994). *Cultural identity and global process*. London: Sage.

Garnham, N. (1990). *Capitalism and communication: Global culture and the economics of information*. London: Sage.

Gershon, R. A. (1997). *The transnational media corporation*. Mahwah, NJ: Lawrence Erlbaum Associates.

Giddens, A. (1990). *The consequences of modernity*. Oxford: Polity Press.

Habermas, J. (1989). *The structural transformation of the public sphere*. Cambridge, MA: MIT Press. (Original work published 1962)

Hall, S. (1992). The question of cultural identity. In S. Hall, D. Held, & T. McGrew (Eds.), *Modernity and its futures*. Oxford: Polity Press.

Halloran, J. D., & Jones, M. (1985). *Learning about the media. Communication and society 16: Media education and communication research*. Paris: UNESCO.

Hannerz, U. (Ed.). (1990). *Medier och kulturer* [Media and cultures]. Stockholm: Carlssons.

Harvey, D. (1989). *The condition of postmodernity*. Oxford: Blackwell.

Hasebrink, U., Berns, M., & Skinner, E. (1997). The English language within the media worlds of European youth. In P. Winterhoff-Spurk & T. H. A. van der Voort (Eds.), *New horizons in media psychology: Research cooperation and projects in Europe* (pp. 156–174). Opladen: Westdeutscher Verlag.

Jensen, J. (1990). *Redeeming modernity: Contradictions in media criticism*. London: Sage.

Jensen, K. B. (Ed.). (1998). *News of the world*. London: Routledge.

Jouët, J., & Pasquier, D. (1999). Les jeunes et la culture de l'ecran [The young and the culture of the screen]. *Reseaux 17, 92–93*, 25–102. Special issue 'Les jeunes et l'ecran' ['The Young and the Screen'], eds. D. Pasquier & J. Jouët.

Kolar-Panov, D. (1997). *Video wars and the diasporic imagination*. London: Routledge.

Langer, J. (1998). *Tabloid television: Popular journalism and the 'other news'*. London: Routledge.

Lemish, D. et al. (1998). Global culture in practice: A look at children and adolescents in Denmark, France and Israel. *European Journal of Communication, 13*(4), 539–556.

Livingstone, S., & Bovill, M. (1999). *Young people and new media: Report of the research project 'Children, Young People and the Changing Media Environment'*. London: London School of Economics.

Livingstone, S., & Lunt, P. (1996). *Talk on television: Audience participation and public debate.* London: Routledge.

Luke, T. W. (1989). *Screens of power: Ideology, domination and resistance in international society.* Urbana: University of Illinois Press.

Lull, J. (Ed.). (1988). *World families watch television.* London: Sage.

Luyken, G.-M. (1991). *Overcoming language barriers in television: Dubbing and subtitling for the European audience.* Manchester, England: The European Institute for the Media.

McChesney, R. W. (1997). *Corporate media and the threat to democracy.* New York: Seven Stories Press.

Morley, D., & Robins, K. (1995). *Spaces of identity: Global media, electronic landscapes and cultural boundaries.* London: Routledge.

Negroponte, N. (1995). *Being digital.* New York: Knopf.

Negt, O., & Kluge, A. (1972). *Öffentlichkeit und Erfahrung: zur Organisationsanalyse von bürgerlicher und proletarischer Öffentlichkeit* [The Public Sphere and Experience: On Organizational Analysis of Bourgeois and Proletarian Public Spheres]. Frankfurt/M: Suhrkamp.

Pasquier, D. (1999). *La culture des sentiments: l'expérience télévisuelle des adolescents* [The Culture of Sentiment: Adolescents' Television Experience]. Paris: Éditions de la Maison des sciences de l'homme.

Povlsen, K. K. (1999). *Beverly Hills 90210: soaps, ironi og danske unge* [Beverly Hills 90210: Soaps, Irony and Young People]. Aarhus: Klim.

Preisler, B. (1999). *Danskerne og det engelske sprog* [Danes and the English Language]. Frederiksberg: Roskilde Universitetsforlag/Samfundslitteratur.

Qureshi, K., & Moores, S. (1999). Identity Remix: Tradition and translation in the lives of young Pakistani Scots. *European Journal of Cultural Studies, 2*(3), 311–330.

Robertson, R. (1992). *Globalization: Social theory and global culture.* London: Sage.

Schiller, H. (1969). *Mass communications and American empire.* New York: Beacon Press.

Schiller, H. (1989). *Culture, Inc.* New York: Oxford University Press.

Sjöberg, U. (1999). Att leva i cyberspace: en studie om hur yngre svenska tonåringer använder och upplever Internet [Living in Cyperspace: A Study of Swedish Teenagers' Use and Experiences of the Internet]. In C. Lykke Christensen (Ed.), *Børn, unge og medier: nordiske forskningsperspektiver* [Children, young people and media: Nordic research perspectives] (pp. 13–33). Gothenburg: Nordicom.

Süss, D., & Giordani, G. (2000). Sprachregionale und kulturelle Aspekte der Mediennutzung von Schweizer Kindern [Language and Culture Based Aspects of Media Use Among Swiss Children in Different Language Regions]. *Medienpädagogik. Zeitschrift für Theorie und Praxis der Medienbildung* [Media Education. Online Journal on Theory and Practice of Media Literacy] 1, www.medienpaed.com

Tapscott, D. (1998). *Growing up digital: The rise of the net generation.* New York: McGraw-Hill.

Thavenius, J. (1995). *Den motsägelsefulla bildningen* [Contradictory Education]. Stockholm, Stehag: Brutus Östlings Bokförlag Symposion.

Tobin, J. (1998). An American *Otabu* (or, a Boy's Virtual Life on the Net). In J. Sexton-Green (Ed.), *Digital diversions: Youth culture in the age of multimedia* (pp. 106–127). London: UCL Press.

Turkle, S. (1995). *Life on the screen: Identity in the age of the Internet.* New York: Simon & Schuster.

Wallerstein, I. (1991). The national and the universal: Can there be such a thing as world culture? In A. D. King (Ed.), *Culture, Globalization and the World System.* London: Macmillan.

CHAPTER

14

Children and Their Changing Media Environment

Sonia Livingstone

THE COMPARATIVE PROJECT

The present volume aimed to enhance understanding of the changing place of media in children and young people's lives, a subject of growing interest and concern to the public, policy makers, and the academic community alike. Since we began the empirical project reported here, new media have risen dramatically to the forefront of the public agenda. Regular headlines focus on the Internet, digital television, e-commerce, the virtual classroom, global consumer culture, and cyber-democracy. The result is a flurry of hype and anxiety, a pressure to be seen to be "doing something," a fear of not "keeping up." Although the potential benefits are much discussed, public concerns keep pace. Interactive media are seen to herald the rise of individualized and privatized lifestyles increasingly dependent on the economics of global consumerism, resulting in the demise of national culture and national media regulation. However, behind the speculation lies a dearth of knowledge about the diffusion and appropriation of new information and communication technologies (ICT). We know from studies of past "new" media that the outcomes of these processes are sometimes at odds with popular expectations, sometimes shaped by those expectations, and sometimes amenable to intervention if opportunities are recognized in time.

Why Children and Young People?

Children and young people merit attention for several reasons. Although too often left out of surveys of the population or the household, they represent a sizable segment of the population. In Europe, approximately half of all households contain parents and children, and some two thirds of the population live in these households (Kelly, 1998). Beyond considerations of population size, the discourse of rights has increasing purchase in relation to children and young people. In the media domain, this is exemplified by the internationally endorsed Children's Television Charter, which specifies that children should have high quality programs made specifically for them, to support the development of their potential and through which they can hear, see, and express their experiences and their culture so as to affirm their sense of community and place. Moreover, children and young people represent an increasingly influential segment of the population, whether viewed in terms of family dynamics, citizen rights, or as a consumer market. This influence can be conceptualized in two ways.

First, notwithstanding their heterogeneity, children and young people represent a distinctive and significant cultural grouping in their own right—a sizable market segment, a subculture even; thus it is too reductive to see them simply as passing through a developmental phase on the path toward adulthood. In key respects, children and young people lead the way in terms of new media: Households with children generally own more ICT, and many media goods, especially those that are relatively cheap and portable, are targeted at and adopted by the youth market. Indeed, children and young people are at the point in their lives where they are most motivated to construct identities, to forge new social groupings, and to negotiate alternatives to given cultural meanings; in all of these, the media play a central part.

Second, children and young people interact with adults within the household, with ICT situated in the midst of these cross-generation negotiations. Crucially, one cannot be certain of the conditions of access and use for individuals within a household given only household information; this is especially the case for children because traditionally, though perhaps decreasingly, they have lacked the power to determine activities in the home. Other than in single-person households, there are many intrahousehold issues of selection and negotiation regarding media acquisition and use, and given the multiplication of media goods, one must consider the diffusion of media not only across but also within households. In effect, in order to recognize the importance of both gender and generation as they subdivide the household, in addition to those factors that differentiate among households, one must encompass both individual and household levels of analysis.

Lastly, children and young people are the subject of specific policy intervention, premised on the assumption that they constitute a distinctive category of media audiences or users (Dorr, 1986). This is now being linked to the notion of children's rights, but essentially draws on a much longer tradition of policy designed to protect children from potential harm. Undoubtedly, our comparative project revealed a variety of issues that merit policy consideration, as discussed later. We find that children's and young people's access to outside leisure tends to be restricted, their use of media is frequently solitary and without parental mediation, their access to ICT is strongly but not always constructively mediated by the school while it is socially unequal at home, their confidence with computers may depend on the variable expertise of their parents, their content preferences are strongly gendered, their viewing is constrained by the availability of own-language programs, and in their construction of youth culture they draw increasingly on global media contents. However, each of these issues must be understood in its context, and each allows for qualification or alternative interpretation, so we caution against moral panics over any of these issues.

A Dual Focus on Media and on Childhood/Youth

Perhaps the main lesson learned from our wide-ranging study of young people in 12 nations is that media both shape and are shaped by the meanings and practices of young people's everyday lives. This presumably uncontroversial claim stands in contradiction to two widespread yet often implicit views of childhood and youth that we sought to contest in this volume. On one hand, we argued against a technologically determinist, mediacentric approach that attributes social change to technological innovation and underplays social and cultural contexts of use, thereby constructing such mythical objects of anxiety as the computer addict, square-eyed viewer, the Net-nerd, the Nintendo generation, the violent video fan, etc. (Buckingham, 1993). We met few of these during the course of our research. On the other hand, we argued against a cultural determinism (Neuman, 1991) that asserts a romantic view of childhood in which the media are so shaped by their contexts of use as to warrant no specific inquiry into their significance as either objects of consumption or purveyors of meanings. On this latter view, children are too sophisticated to be taken in by the messages of consumer culture, too interested in hanging out with friends in a nearby park to waste time watching television in their bedrooms; in short, they are too sensible to warrant public concern. Yet, whether or not "concern" is appropriate, certainly we met few children for whom the media are so unimportant or without influence.

In attempting a more even-handed approach, we learned from the culturalist and constructivist framework of the sociology of childhood (e.g., Corsaro, 1997; James, Jenks, & Prout, 1998; Qvortrup, 1995), with its stress on the child-as-agent, rather than child-as-object or child-as-adult-to-be. In defining itself against the rather sterile, reductionist conception of "the child" in mainstream media effects research, this framework has much in common with the sociological tradition of research on youth and youth culture (e.g., Förnas & Bolin, 1994; Osgerby, 1998), thus facilitating theoretical and empirical linkages between research on children and youth. In so doing, however, we rectified the curious neglect of the media in the sociology of childhood literature, following instead the tradition of research on youth culture in its recognition that the media contribute routinely to the culture of everyday life.

Thus, throughout this volume we adopted a dual focus, attempting to knit together the long-standing divisions in the academic literature between media-centered and child-centered approaches (see chapter 1). Our stress throughout has been on recognizing their interdependence in practice: The meanings of old and new media are grounded in the context of children's lives while, at the same time, children's lives today are thoroughly mediated (Livingstone, 1998). Most simply, we find over and again that, when we focus on the media, our story becomes one of "It depends on the context of use," whereas when we focus on family life or the home, our story instead becomes one of "Look how important the media are." This is no accident, for both are part of the same larger picture of modern, mediated childhood.

The child-centered approach leads us to recognize that the media represent just some of the consumer goods available in the home, some of the competing options for leisure activities, and some of the sources of social influence. Thus, it has the advantage of putting the media in their place, and so avoiding the hype, utopian or dystopian, surrounding new media. As this volume shows, children and young people are getting on with their lives on many fronts, chatting to their friends, arguing with their parents, worrying about school, and, yes, following their favorite television programs, just as they have for decades. The concerns and conditions of everyday life change more slowly than the timetable of technological developments, and the broad parameters of children's lives—growing up, becoming independent, shifting in focus from parents to peers—are more constant than suggested by popular speculation about how the media are changing childhood. Yet, the place of media in children's lives is far from negligible.

A media-centered analysis breaks down the generic concept of media, inquiring about media as both varieties of technology and as varieties (or genres) of content. As ICT enters everyday life, traditional conceptions of media as both objects of consumption and texts for interpretation are challenged (Silverstone, 1994). Indeed, rather than seeing these changes as the challenge of the new versus the old—the computer challenging the centrality of television, multiple channels challenging national, terrestrial ones, etc.—we might better see them in terms of a blurring of the boundaries in relation to which media have been traditionally conceptualized; for example, the blurring of leisure/work/learning spaces, of genres, and of print and audiovisual media.

This dual focus enriches both research perspectives, as discussed in this chapter. The study of information and communication technologies introduces new issues, too often overlooked in research on childhood, into the analysis of children's and young people's lifeworlds. These include the ICT-led reconceptualization of high and low socioeconomic status (SES) households into "information rich" and "information poor" homes, the equally problematic, though potentially constructive relation between home and school as conceptualized in ICT-based "informal" and "lifelong learning," and the refocusing of the distinctiveness of youth culture in terms of media-defined lifestyles and global consumer culture. Media research is similarly illuminated if we thoroughly contextualize media access and use within family life, peer relations, and the school environment. For example, children's access to new media at home or in school may or may not lead to more informed or creative uses; the acquisition of a PC may or may not affect time spent with books or television. We can only trace the links between access and use, as well as the consequences of new for older media, if we consider both the specific social contexts of use and the general cultural assumptions that shape the appropriation of new media into the home.

CROSS-NATIONAL COMMONALITIES IN YOUNG PEOPLE'S MEDIA ENVIRONMENTS

In chapter 1, as guidance for our 12-nation study, we classified approaches to cross-national research in terms of the search for commonalities and the search for differences. Our starting point was the identification of commonalities, recognizing how widely many findings apply across different national contexts. The foregoing chapters confirm that there are more similarities than differences in the significance of new media for young people across Europe; these are most apparent in the chapters dealing with young people's lifestyles and preferences (especially chapters 4, 5, 6, 12, and 13), suggesting that the centrality of media in peer culture in particular rests on widely shared symbolic uses of media (chapter 9).

Access and Use of Old and New Media

Historians of once-new media have traced the complex, and far from linear, process by which technologies are shaped socially and culturally before, during, and following their conception, design, packaging, marketing, purchase, and use (Flichy, 1995; Marvin, 1988). In this volume, we focused on two key phases of this cycle, diffusion and appropriation, both of which invite us to consider the contexts within which new media are acquired and used as much as the innovative features of these media themselves. *Diffusion* refers to the conditions according to which a new medium spreads through a society, typically following a common path from the innovators and early adopters through to the mass market (Rogers, 1995). *Appropriation* refers to the local practices of use that develop around a new medium once in the home, anchoring it within particular temporal, spatial, and social relations and thereby rendering it meaningful (Miller, 1987). Whereas questions of access are usually addressed in terms of diffusion, questions of use depend on the meanings-in-context that are mobilized by the appropriation of goods, though in practice these two processes are related.

As already noted, young people's media environments and usage are fairly consistent across the countries compared in our multinational project. The vast majority of European children have access to television, telephone, books, audio media, magazines, and video, these being primarily provided at home. Many have their own television set, though this varies from around a fifth in Switzerland to two thirds in the United Kingdom. At least half have access to a personal computer (PC), with the majority of children in some countries (BE, FI, IL, NL, SE), and around half in others (DE, ES, GB, IT) having a PC at home. Access to a multimedia PC is also growing, both at home and at school, and the diffusion of the Internet is accelerating. Compared with older media, however, access to newer, computer-based technologies is more variable in terms of both extent and location.

The continuing dominance of television over all other media in children's and young people's lives is indisputable. Notwithstanding the diversification of media in the home, television remains the medium most widely used, the one most often discussed with family and friends, and the one most often chosen for excitement and for relieving boredom. As watching television occupies, on average, more than 2 hours per day, it exceeds time spent with all other media combined (see chapter 4, Table 4.3). An average half an hour per day is spent playing computer games, whereas nongames use of the PC occupies around quarter of an hour of daily leisure time, and an average 5 minutes per day is spent on the Internet, though for those few who use it, the time spent in one session is considerably higher. Thus, across all countries, although nonscreen media remain important, it is screen-based media that are driving the changing media environment for children and young people, and interactive media such as computer/video games, PC use, and the Internet now occupy third place in terms of time expenditure, behind television and music (chapter 4).

"Average" figures for access and use mask underlying demographic variations, but these, too, are fairly consistent across countries. Generally, access to media somewhere in the home varies little by either age or gender of the child. Media provision in the home is, however, consistently dependent on SES: Homes higher in SES are considerably more likely to own most media, and this is particularly noticeable for computers (though not TV-linked games machines, more often found in low SES households). However, personal access to media in children's bedrooms is strongly affected by age and gender: Older children, and boys, own more media. Pasquier (chapter 7, this volume) notes two interesting exceptions, complicating a simple classification of "information rich" and "information poor": in lower SES families, children are more likely to have a computer in their bedroom, and a similar trend is evident for single-parent households. Whether this represents a privilege, in terms of private access, or a hindrance to its effective use, in terms of the absence of parental guidance, depends on the cultural capital of the family.

There are also clear differences between boys and girls in preferences for particular media and media contents. In terms of numbers of users, audio media, magazines, and books are more popular among girls and they spend more time with them. By contrast, screen media—computer/video games, PC (not for games), and the Internet—are all more used by boys, and even among users, boys use them for longer than girls. As for age, more teenagers make use of audio media, magazines, newspapers, PC (not for games), and the Internet, whereas younger children prefer books, comics, and computer/video games. Interestingly, although we find more users among the higher SES groups for books, comics, PC (not for games), and the Internet, children who use these media from lower SES homes spend just as long with them (see Appendix C).

Contextualizing Domestic Access and Use

It is a consistent story across the foregoing chapters that access to media underdetermines use. The observation that different factors affect access and use directs us toward relating the diffusion of new media to those contexts of childhood and youth within which they are appropriated. As we have seen, the impact of demographic variables works in opposite ways for access and use: For access, SES is the crucial variable; for use, age and gender matter greatly whereas, given equivalent access, SES makes little difference. Thus, the contextual factors underlying the diffusion process tend to reproduce familiar inequalities in access according to SES, whereas those that underlie the process of appropriation reproduce other, also familiar, differences that, for gender at least, also perpetuate inequalities.

Much of our effort was spent tracing the slippage between access in the home and use by children. Between the two lies the murky area of parental permission and values, physical and symbolic location of goods, lifestyle expectations, and personal preferences. Surveys may readily track diffusion of new media into the home, but the media actually used by children represent a subset of media at home. At the same time, children are adept at obtaining access to media not available to them at home—at friends' and relatives' houses, school, etc. By pinpointing those cases where children use a medium to which they do not have access at home and, conversely, those cases where they do not use a medium to which they do have domestic access, Johnsson-Smaragdi (chapter 5) shows how access is a neither a necessary nor a sufficient condition for use.

Consequently, one cannot presume use from a knowledge of access, nor that use will be guaranteed by a policy designed to ensure access. Rather, those social and cultural circumstances that determine the desirability of media, as opposed to their availability, must be considered. As shown in chapter 5, these vary by medium and, interestingly, it appears to be the PC and Internet that are most often not used by children even when available. On the other hand, those same new media are particularly sought out for use in other locations by children who lack home access. By contrast with new media, books tend to fall into the category of available but undesirable, being present in most homes but not always read; furthermore, cross-cultural variation is greatest for use and/or nonuse of print media. This suggests that whereas most young people are, to varying degrees, drawn into the new, globalized screen entertainment culture, the use of print media depends on longer-standing and more nationally specific cultural traditions, as discussed later.

These cultural perceptions and values underlying media choices have been traditionally addressed through the question of displacement. New media do not diffuse through a society without impacting on other, older media and, in chapter 4, Beentjes, Koolstra, Marseille, and van der Voort recall popular concerns over the arrival of television and its potential displacement of books (Himmelweit, Oppenheim, & Vince, 1958). Updating the story to the present day, they note that across all our countries, reading books declines steadily with age, that teenagers now read less than they did in earlier generations, and that there is some evidence of a displacement effect on reading for boys in particular. On the other hand, reading on a screen is becoming an increasing feature of teenage life, both at school and in leisure time, suggesting that the apparently adverse effect on books is not so much the triumph of the image over the word as of the screen over printed paper.

In treating all media as potentially in competition with each other, the displacement approach misses some crucial trends in young people's leisure lifestyles that a more contextual approach makes evident. In chapter 5, Johnsson-Smaragdi adopts a lifestyle analysis, grouping children and young people according to how they combine diverse media in their leisure time. She argues that "low" media users—the nearly half of the sample who spend an average 2$\frac{1}{2}$ hours daily with the media—are more likely to add new media to their previous media mix, showing an additive or accumulative pattern. On the other hand, heavier media users—who spend 5 to 7 hours per day with media—are more likely to specialize in one of a number of distinct ways, thereby concentrating much of their attention on selected media and so following a more exclusive pattern of use.

COMMON CULTURAL CONTEXTS
FOR THE APPROPRIATION OF NEW MEDIA

Because the contexts of everyday life are crucial to understanding the relation between access, meanings, and use, we explore the contexts of childhood and youth in several ways. As with the account of ICT diffusion in the previous section, these contexts can be examined initially through the lens of "the search for commonalities," although through our analysis of contexts of use, the markers of cross-national difference are also revealed, as discussed in the following section.

The primary context discussed in this volume is the one in which children initially come to be media users—the home. Pasquier (chapter 7), argues that, on one hand, the domestic context shapes the social meanings that attach to new media, while on the other hand, the introduction of new media transforms the meaning of the home, increasing its attractiveness as a site of leisure and reshaping family patterns of interaction so as to center on the media. However, the project has also explored the additional social contexts important in children's and young people's lives—peer culture and school. In tracing the intersections among these three contexts, we found many cross-national similarities.

First, as children grow older, their primary leisure context shifts from that of family to friends, with significant consequences for media use. Second, each of these contexts, separately and in combination, plays a part in the reproduction of long-standing sources of difference and inequality: Here we trace the implications of gender and SES inequalities as they impact on the use of ICT. Third, throughout Europe the home–school relation plays a key role in the appropriation of new ICT, with consequences for the extent to which the school may compensate for inequalities introduced by the home.

Growing Up: From Family to Friends

Notwithstanding the growth in bedroom culture (chapter 8) for both children and teenagers across in Europe, television remains at the center of family interaction, embedded in everyday domestic routines, including conversation, relaxation, meal times, and bedtime (see chapter 7). Television-oriented interaction tends to center on the mother and is greater in lower SES households. Similarly, we find that the new media are being assimilated into children's and young people's lives in comparable ways in different countries. Playing computer games, and using the computer more generally, tends to be more solitary than sociable; to the extent that it is sociable, it tends to be more peer-oriented than family-oriented, more male-oriented than female-oriented, and, for the PC particularly, more middle than lower class. Thus, children seek where possible to play computer games with friends, whereas television coviewing is more usually with family members.

This contrast points up how the leisure contexts of family and friends are significantly defined in relation to each other. This relationship is occasionally one of similarity: for example, television is young people's favorite topic of conversation with both friends and parents. It is more often one of complementarity, most clearly seen in the transition from the family-focused child who uses media to support play to the peer-focused teenager who uses media primarily to support talk. At other times, this relationship is one of competition or conflict, most clearly seen in parents' and children's negotiations over the when and where of leisure activities. Such conflicts between family and peer pressures over media use were common in our qualitative research. As Pasquier (chapter 7) notes, from a parental point of view, changes in both media provision and domestic culture are making the domestic regulation of media ever more difficult. Simultaneously, the very newness of these media makes the importance of such regulation apparent to parents.

Children's everyday tactics of resistance to parental control, easily underestimated from an adult viewpoint as just children being naughty, get to the heart of the domestic changes. For parents, the issue is one of responsibility for their children's moral education, whereas for children their growing autonomy is at stake; hence, this struggle is part of the growing democratization of the family (chapter 1). At present, we find that, for television, use in the bedroom is less mediated by parents than is living-room viewing, thus facilitating the process of "living together separately" (Flichy, 1995). Yet, because it raises new uncertainties for parents, use of the PC in the bedroom is subject to more, rather than less, parental mediation than is use of a PC located elsewhere, despite the practical difficulties of so doing (chapter 8). Whether such greater parental mediation can be sustained is uncertain, for not only are new media diverse and difficult to monitor, but also children are often more expert in ICT than their parents. Insofar as new media undermine parental regulation of children's media use, one can see these media playing a contributory role to the long-term cultural shift toward the democratization of the family.

If faced with a choice between friends and media, children choose friends, leaving media to fill the moments of boredom or loneliness (unless, as with the telephone and e-mail, the media can facilitate social interaction). However, if time with friends can include time with media, children often favor the combination, although the freedom children have to visit friends, the portability of media, and the peer-group valuation of media all make a difference. Thus, although many children and young people prefer to watch television or play computer games alone, they are nearly as likely to want to watch or play with a friend, suggesting a sociability that is not so much oriented toward isolation as oriented away from the family and toward friends In short, although the primacy of peer relations serves to put media "in their place," it is also obvious that one can no longer imagine youth culture without music, computer games, soap opera, or chat rooms, and that multiple-screen homes are becoming increasingly commonplace.

New Media, Old Inequalities

Discussion of "children and young people" readily permits the interpretation that all 6- to 16-year olds are affected equally by the opportunities and dangers that result from the arrival of new media in their homes. However, insofar as diffusion depends on a variety of political, economic, and cultural factors, it results in uneven or unequal access (Murdock, Hartmann, & Gray, 1995; Rogers, 1995; Schoenbach & Becker, 1989). In other words, our study suggests that, particularly in the home but also in the school, contexts of use tend to reproduce rather than undermine existing social inequalities.

We noted earlier that domestic access to media primarily varies by SES, although there are some gender differences in domestic access, whereas media use depends more on age and gender. Putting this the other way around, inequalities in gender arise predominantly, though not entirely, from differences in content preferences, and these are in turn dependent on leisure interests embedded in a similarly gendered peer culture (chapters 6, 9, and 12). By contrast, inequalities by SES arise predominantly from differences in domestic media access.

The SES differences in ICT access are consistent and substantial (chapter 3). However, the conditions of actual use of a medium within a household are far from transparent. Some children do not use a medium that is available in the household, for reasons that may concern parental permission or personal preference. Both these factors may in turn be shaped by cultural capital (Bourdieu, 1984) or expectations regarding appropriate interests and behavior. Other children may be regular users of media that the household does not in fact possess, drawing on networks of friends that both provide and are, in turn, constituted through such shared media use.

Interestingly, it appears that if lower SES children are provided with a computer, they make as much use of it as do higher SES children, with no differences in time spent on games or nongames uses. Furthermore, although access is strongly related to SES, choice of media for excitement or to relieve boredom is not. In other words, given access, it is media functions, not socioeconomic factors, that determine use. These functions, although independent of SES, are gendered, and so a parallel story emerges for gender. Specifically, although access to computers at home does not vary greatly for girls and boys, the choice of media for different purposes—with more boys than girls choosing computers for excitement and for relieving boredom—helps explain the differences in the time girls and boys spend with computer-based media.

Evidence of difference is not necessarily evidence for inequality, and in the case of gender, much of our qualitative research testifies to the positive, if very different, choices regarding media contents and preferences expressed by boys and girls. However, Lemish, Liebes, and Seidmann (chapter 12) do argue for evidence of inequality, because they uncover some of the struggles that these gender differences reveal, particularly on the part of girls. These include struggles to identify diverse role models in a consumer culture primarily addressed to boys, to find a voice in a culture that teaches them self-effacement, to define themselves through and against the images of femininity provided by the media, and to find confidence given that their preferred relationship-based narratives focus on uncertainty and self-doubt rather than the action-oriented leadership roles that dominate boys' preferred genres. Although this is countered somewhat by girls' attempts to find pleasure in boys' culture (because this dominates the media available to them), we see less evidence of a reverse trend, namely boys' interest in traditionally feminine media or media contents.

Nonetheless, Lemish et al. ask whether the focus should be on the overall consistency in gender differences or on the smaller areas where we find similarities between boys and girls. Although boys are more focused on technology, on action, and sport, and girls are more focused on communication, on chatting on the phone, and on soap opera, the cases of crossover may indicate a growing trend, facilitated by the common culture promoted by television, music, Internet, and e-mail, toward a lessening of gender differences, and this may be enhanced by the growing emphasis on communication and networking skills in ICT-mediated leisure and work.

As the conditions that reproduce them differ, these two types of inequality require different strategies to redress them. For gender inequalities, a two-pronged attack would seem appropriate: first, improving girls' access to computers, especially in their own rooms where they have control over the context of use; and second, improving the quality and variety of games that appeal to girls. For SES inequalities, the issue of access is primary. Noting that the PC is following a different path into the home from that of the rapidly universal television set some 40 years earlier, Pasquier (chapter 7) argues that social stratification is more persistent with the computer, requiring a concerted policy to redress it. At issue is partly the matter of cost, but Pasquier also stresses the importance of cultural capital in directing PC acquisition and use at home (Bourdieu, 1984). In Europe, most countries are dealing with SES inequalities in ICT through education policies, thus raising the tricky issue of the relation between provision at home and at school.

ICT at Home and School

The school has the potential to compensate for inequalities in domestic access to computers and in key respects, we find this potential is being realized. Although policy initiatives to provide resources and technical infrastructure vary across Europe, particularly in terms of whether ICT is introduced before or during secondary education, the scale of these initiatives has resulted in some 60% of European children using computers at school (chapter 10). However, the frequency of use remains relatively low at around once per week. As for the quality of computer use, chapter 10 details a series of difficulties facing schools in implementing the use of ICT in the classroom, while recognizing that this is still an early stage in ICT educational strategy.

The difficulties in introducing ICT into schools include the development of the curriculum, the training of teachers, and the acquisition and maintenance of up-to-date equipment. Also unresolved is whether computer literacy should be treated as a discrete set of skills taught in dedicated computer lessons, or as applicable across the curriculum and thus integrated into math, science, history, etc. Perhaps both strategies should be pursued simultaneously: Children cannot see the point of computers unless linked to interesting and significant contents, yet such linkages are hard to sustain when children lack basic skills to manipulate the computer interface.

Although it would have been beyond the scope of this project to evaluate the outcomes of different strategies for introducing ICT into children's lives, our findings suggest potential knowledge gaps arising from the relation between provision and support at school and at home (chapters 10 and 11). Particularly, Krotz and Hasebrink are pessimistic about whether schools can keep up with the pace of change within the home. In consequence, the inequalities introduced at home may outweigh the fact that access at school is more evenly distributed across the population. Similarly, the entertainment orientation of domestic ICT use may outweigh the educational uses at school. In this respect, use at home may provide an opportunity for the child to be the expert, compared to his or her parents, and to feel empowered by computers as entertaining tools, experiences that are rarer though not unheard of at school. However, the boundary between educational and entertainment uses of ICT remains problematic in the eyes of both parents and teachers, thus requiring further research to clarify their relationship.

CROSS-NATIONAL VARIATION IN YOUNG PEOPLE'S MEDIA ENVIRONMENTS

We advocated a dual focus on both media diffusion and use and contexts of childhood and youth, because, as seen earlier, an initial focus on the media takes us rapidly into an analysis of context, most obviously seen in the complex relation between access and use, whereas an initial focus on childhood quickly points up the centrality of the media in children and young people's lives. In this chapter thus far, the story has been one of cross-cultural commonalities, particularly as regards young people's lifestyles and usage preferences. However, both of these points of departure would lead us also to expect cross-national differences and, for this reason, chapter 1 outlined significant variation across the 12 nations being compared, in media and ICT environments, and in the contexts of childhood and family life. The remainder of this chapter discusses the cross-cultural differences observed within our study in relation to these two sources of variation, specifically national infrastructural provision of ICT (see especially chapters 3, 10, and 11) and social contexts of media use (see especially chapters 7, 8, and 9).

The Impact of National ICT Provision on Access at Home and School

There is no straightforward way of capturing the complexity of history, economics, and culture that accounts for the cross-national differences in ICT provision revealed by our study, although these may be encapsulated in the notion of readiness for an information society (see chapter 1). The notion of "the information society" (Webster & Robins, 1989) captures those social and political issues that arise from the diffusion and appropriation of new media including, most concretely, issues of technological innovation, investment, and infrastructure. More abstractly, the notion of the information society is often used more normatively, drawing on an assumption of societal progress, and more inclusively, encompassing issues of national development and globalization. Wary of such assumptions, other commentators rely on measures such as the index constructed by the World Economic Forum of "preparedness for the wired society" (chapter 1).

In the introductory chapter to this volume, we developed a similar measure, discriminating among countries in terms of the infrastructure and provision they make for children and young people in terms of access to and use of ICT. This pragmatic classification produced two main groups: "pioneers" of the new technologies (SE, FI DK, NL) and "laggards," relatively low on the new technologies (ES, FR, and IT). The United Kingdom was seen as a case apart, combining a heavy orientation toward television with rather high figures for new technologies. The remaining countries (BE-vlg, CH, DE, and IL) make up a less homogenous group, combining a multichannel environment with moderate use of new technologies.

However, relying on national statistics is problematic in relation to children. First, many national surveys only draw on the adult population, and second, some of the national statistics that have been combined to produce a single measure of, for example, "preparedness for the wired society," do not relate directly to children's lives. In our surveys, for example, we find that about half of all 6- to 16-year-olds in both Spain and the United Kingdom have access to a PC at home (chapters 3 and 4). Thus Spanish children are rather further "ahead" in domestic PC access, and British children rather "behind," compared with what one might have expected from national economic statistics. These findings suggest some limits to the simple image of a diffusion path from "backward" to "advanced," pointing up the multidimensional nature of readiness for an information society, and hence the importance of identifying those factors relevant to one's target group.

Nonetheless, as the foregoing chapters show, our findings do invite us on several counts to distinguish, in particular, the Nordic countries together with the Netherlands from other European countries, particularly France, Spain, and Italy. As predicted, the classification of "pioneers of new technologies" is borne out for children in the Nordic countries and the Netherlands, particularly in terms of domestic provision of computers but also in terms of time spent with interactive media, reflecting a more established culture of domestic and educational ICT. A similar picture emerges when we look at access to computers in school. This varies considerably, from only 1 in 3 pupils in Spain and Germany to more than three quarters in those countries identified as more advanced in ICT (chapter 1), namely the Nordic countries, the Netherlands, and the United Kingdom.

This apparent harmony between diffusion of ICT at home and at school, however, breaks down on closer examination, suggesting that national provision of ICT intersects with contexts of childhood and youth in complex ways. Certainly in some countries, the spread of ICT at home and school appears to go hand in hand. For example, it appears that the Nordic countries and the Netherlands lead in both, whereas Germany lags in both. In other countries, however, there is a discrepancy between provision at home and school. The United Kingdom, for example, is ahead in terms of PC use at school, but it lags behind for access to a PC at home, perhaps reflecting the screen-entertainment focus of families (centering on games machines, videos, and television) by contrast with the forward-thinking policies of business and education. By contrast, about half of all Spanish children have access to a computer at home but only one third have access at school, suggesting that here it may be parents who are the more forward-thinking.

Krotz and Hasebrink (chapter 11) characterize these differences in terms of public or institutional and private paths toward, or contexts for, new media use. For children, the former is primarily the school (though in some countries libraries also play an important role, as in Finland) whereas the latter is, of course, the home (though for adults such opportunities may also be provided elsewhere). Thus, our findings suggest that although in a few countries (e.g., UK), the institutional path has taken the lead, in most countries, the private path predominates, with schools struggling to provide access to computers equivalent to that available at home. This private path raises specific problems for the management of ICT use in educational contexts, as it means that many children come to school both better provided for at home than can be sustained at school and more experienced in ICT use than their classmates who lack a PC at home. Beyond issues of access, PC use at home and school complicates matters further, for the PC at school is used for a narrower range of applications, predictably more information-based, whereas the computer at home is used for a greater diversity of applications, including entertainment functions. As Krotz and Hasebrink point out, perhaps most significantly, it is children who have access to computers in both locations who feel most competent as computer users.

Those factors, according to which ICT is appropriated into particular social contexts, subject to specific national policies, and valued within certain cultural frameworks, are seen in chapter 11 as reason enough to challenge the general model of diffusion. Specifically, Krotz and Hasebrink critique the view of diffusion as a neutral or mechanistic and passive process, belying the complacent hope that all groups and societies will catch up eventually, as if there were a single endpoint to the process. Instead, they view diffusion as a constructive process within which the identification of a medium as *new* (i.e., new in social and cultural rather than purely technological terms; Livingstone, 1999) is crucial. Although in simple terms, most or all children and young people are now, in some way or another, new media users, they suggest that European countries are following diverse paths in the adoption of ICT. As a result, for a variety of social and cultural reasons, children and young people in different countries come to use ICT in somewhat different ways, as discussed next.

Cultures of Print and Screen

Part of what is at stake here are cultural conceptions of tradition, heritage, and value, all of which are intimately linked in the popular imagination with developments in media and communication technologies. As suggested before, this relationship between culture and ICT adoption is cross-nationally variable. In chapter 13, Drotner links this to national policies, suggesting that in the case of small language communities, these do not appear to have construed screen culture as inferior to that of print, having been more ready to invest in technologies that support transnational communication. Meanwhile, larger language communities, which in Europe tend also to be larger economic units, have devoted more attention—in terms of cultural policy and concern—to forms of communication represented by older, nationally based media (see also chapter 1). Certainly, in our project, there are indications that in the Nordic countries, cultural values and practices are establishing a positive connection between computers and books: Both are discussed among peers, and time spent with both is relatively high (see chapters 4 and 9). This contrasts with the situation particularly in the United Kingdom, where among children and young people, books are seen as boring and unrewarding, but computers provide interest and excitement. Indeed, insofar as we can discuss displacement in a cross-sectional study, Johnsson-Smaragdi suggests that it is in the United Kingdom that the evidence is strongest that children appear to adopt an exclusive pattern of use in which books tend to be displaced by screen media and television by the PC. In other countries, where access to new media is relatively high (e.g. FI, SE, NL, IL), these media appear to be more successfully combined with traditional print and screen media.

In a similar vein, when interpreting cross-national variation in the introduction of computers in schools, Süss suggests that the implicit values of traditional "print cultures" mitigate against recognizing and supporting children's positive uses of computers. This is evident in the cross-nationally variable quality of the informal opportunities for using computers in school, which tend to depend on teachers' assumptions regarding the relation between screen media, play, and learning. Again, we find the Nordic countries to be in the forefront in recognizing the educational potential of audiovisual media.

From these indications, we may draw the tentative conclusion that children in the Nordic countries and the Netherlands gain greater access to, and make more use of, ICT not only because ICT provision in their countries is comparatively high, but also because they live in a culture in which print and screen are not framed as in conflict. Enthusiastic adoption of both old and new media is, therefore, encouraged by the norms of the culture. By contrast, in France, Switzerland, and the United Kingdom, the culture tends to oppose the high value of print media, especially books, against the low value of screen media, especially television and computer games. This is certainly apparent in the value judgments of old and new media made by parents and teachers. The consequences of this may be seen in the ways in which children and young people from these latter countries combine media in their daily lives. When old and new media are framed as in competition with each other, we see a generation gap in which adults favor the old, both in terms of books and traditional children's broadcasting, and children opt for the new. The resulting trade-off undermines both children's pleasure in old media and adults' understanding of children's immersion in new media.

Diversity in Contexts of Childhood and Youth

Not only are cultural conceptions of tradition and value linked to popular views of ICT, but so, too, are cultural conceptions of home and family. How far do cross-national variations in domestic, peer, and educational practices frame young people's media use?

Beyond some intriguing interactions between SES and national habits of domestic media regulation, Pasquier identifies few cross-national differences in patterns of media *use* within the family home (chapter 7). Indeed, even where such differences were predicted, they were not to be found. For example, gender differences in computer use at home are no less evident in the Nordic countries, where gender relations in the society are more equal, than in the Mediterranean countries, where the social and employment status of women is very different (chapters 1 and 12). The apparent absence of differences may reflect the crudeness of a survey for exploring family practices, and the difficulties of conducting qualitative work in comparative perspective (see chapter 2); perhaps we should conclude more simply that family life is fairly constant across Europe.

However, it is noteworthy that some cross-cultural differences emerge when we explore the relationship between private and public leisure. Suoninen draws together a number of observations made throughout this project when she contrasts "traditional family-oriented cultures" (BE-vlg, ES, FR, and IT) and "peer-oriented cultures" (FI, SE, DK, and NL). The remaining countries (CH, DE, IL, and UK) are somewhat hybrid, being characterized as "moderate family-oriented cultures" (chapter 9). The primary importance of this distinction is the interaction with age. We saw how the transition from a family focus to a peer focus in the child's relationships with others is crucial to social development. However, those in peer-oriented cultures appear to make the transition during late childhood, whereas in family-oriented cultures, the shift comes only in the teenage years. Clearly, what is at issue here is differing conceptions of the meaning of "a child," parental perceptions of child development, and cultural judgments regarding the degree of autonomy to be accorded a young person. The key to understanding cross-national variation in such judgments, complicating our earlier conclusion in favor of pan-European consistencies, may lie in the observation that, of the three national groupings previously identified, the first group consists of predominantly Catholic countries, the second of Protestant countries, and the third brings together countries with strongly multicultural populations.

Similar cross-national differences emerge when we explore the extent to which a media-rich bedroom culture depends not just on domestic space and parents' working practices but also on the culture of childhood. In chapter 8, as in chapter 9, we seek to understand the meaning of media use within the home by framing it in the context of leisure opportunities outside the home. This analysis reveals Spain, for example, to be a strongly family-oriented culture where children spend comparatively little time watching favorite television programs alone in their bedroom. In the United Kingdom and in Germany, we see more evidence for privatized media use, partly because of cultural restrictions on children's freedom to meet friends in public locations.

To help us understand such variation, in our survey we asked children and young people which values they thought would be most important to them when they grew up. Although across all countries and ages, "having a happy family life" was preeminent, in several of the Northern European countries, there was relatively little consensus, and several values rivaled that of family life: in Germany, having "lots of money"; in France, having "an interesting job"; in the United Kingdom, having "lots of money" for the youngest group; "a good education" for 9- to 13-year-olds, and "an interesting job" for 15- to 16-year-olds; and in the Netherlands, "lots of money" matters most for the youngest group, to be replaced as they get older with "a good education" in addition to "a happy family life." By contrast, in both the Nordic (DK, FI, SE) and the Mediterranean countries (ES, IT, IL), "having a happy family life" was straightforwardly the dominant value. This is perhaps curious given that on the basis of both demographic and media use data, we have been led to contrast rather than align these two sets of countries. Although broad-brush characterizations of countries should be made with caution, a combination of all these various sources of data leads us to propose three national groupings, varying along the cultural trajectory towards individualization.

In the Mediterranean countries, where, as we saw in chapter 1, there is a high degree of family stability, albeit with relatively few children per family, and traditional gender relations as regards child-rearing, children are regarded as the rather precious center of a stable and traditional family structure that—as a unit rather than a collection of individuals—is taking advantage of the lifestyle choices offered by a consumerist and globalized culture. When children's media activities are examined in relation to the balance between family and peer culture, these are the countries with what Suoninen terms "traditional family-oriented cultures." By contrast, in the Nordic countries, distinctive for having relatively more working mothers, higher divorce rates, more wealth, and greater population homogeneity, the family—structured along democratic lines—represents a safe base within which children are regarded as valued citizens with the rights and the freedom to determine their chosen lifestyle. In terms of both media- and nonmedia-based leisure, this context frees young people to live within a more "peer-oriented culture" (chapter 9). However, it appears that rather less stable cultural contexts frame the lives of children in our third group (DE, UK, FR, NL). For a variety of reasons, different in each country, the cross-cutting demands of late modernity—in terms of gender relations, population diversity, wealth inequality, and so forth—offer a more heterogeneous or hybrid set of values for children and their families to live by. Although, as noted earlier, the links between contexts of childhood and media use are not straightforward, it is notable throughout this volume that the first two groups of countries are relatively consistent in both respects; it is the third group that is frequently most difficult to characterize and for which one must most often conclude regarding media access and use, "It depends."

YOUNG PEOPLE AND THE NEW MEDIA
IN LATE MODERNITY

Media environments and contexts of childhood are linked analytically insofar as both form part of the same larger picture of late modern, mediated
childhood, thus reinforcing the importance of a multidimensional, transnational approach to comparative analysis (Kohn, 1989). Notably, the cross-
national classifications that emerged from the media-centered and child-centered approaches to comparative analysis map onto each other. In some
respects, we found these links to be rather straightforward, pointing toward
the way in which such late modern developments as the democratization of
the family and national readiness for ICT go hand in hand. Specifically, it
appears that the countries that are most pioneering in ICT (FI, SE, DK, NL)
are also most democratic in their patterns of family life, endorsing a more
peer-oriented conception of childhood, whereas those that sustain a more
traditional conception of family life (e.g. ES, FR, and IT) are also more oriented toward the national television/low new technology position identified
in chapter 1. Although in other respects the mapping is not so neat, inviting
a more macrosociological account of European countries than can be
embarked on here, in what follows we develop the argument outlined in
chapter 1, that European countries are, to differing degrees, caught up in the
late modern processes of privatization, individualization, and globalization.

In theoretical terms, there is a clear distinction between *privatization*—the
shift from public or community spaces to privately owned (i.e., commercial
or domestic) spaces, and *individualization*—the loss of traditional sociostructural determinants of experience and action and the concomitant diversification of lifestyles freed from the factors that have hitherto defined identity
and taste (Giddens, 1993; Meyrowitz, 1985; Reimer, 1995; Ziehe, 1994). So, too,
is the notion of *globalization* conceptually distinct (Tomlinson, 1999). As
noted in chapter 1, these processes describe different ways of conceptualizing historical changes in social relations, the first focusing on the civic or citizenship roles versus that of the consumer, the second focusing on individual and diversified versus socially stratified culture, and the last focusing on
national versus global identities and community.

In practice, however, when we examine the domestic media uses by children and young people, we find these processes working together. The traditional conception of public life focuses on the community and on what is
communal, so that civic life reflects choices and habits shared with others.
In other words, there is a link between activities conducted in public, as part
of the public interest, and the social structures and traditions that we inher-
it and that bind us together. Meanwhile, the driving force of private interests
is toward the multiplication of markets and the diversification of taste categories, with the result that private life is increasingly centered on markers of

distinction and difference. Popular anxieties over the solitary nature of new media use draw on both these conceptions, linking anxieties about the loss of citizenship participation with those concerning the loss of community tradition and values. Thus, privatization supports individualization and vice versa. Similarly, models of public or civic media have traditionally been tied to national regulatory frameworks, although only a global media market, commercially funded, is proving able to support the diversity of individualized lifestyle preferences.

Living Together Separately

In the case of young people, the shift toward the private—particularly given their limited financial resources—means a shift toward home-based leisure. As suggested in chapter 8, this is driven both by the multiplication in media available at home and by growing restrictions placed on young people's access to public places. Media are, in consequence, a source of tension in the home, for although privatization makes the home increasingly important as a site of leisure, with the media clearly playing a key role, it also throws family members together at a time when individualization means that children's cultural preferences are increasingly unlikely to resemble those of their parents. The counterpressure, therefore, is for children and parents to spend their leisure time apart. As the multiplication of media goods in the home allows also for a diversification of tastes and habits at home that frees young people from following the lifestyle decisions of their parents, "bedroom culture" becomes an expression of individualized lifestyles on the part of young people.

Notwithstanding the cross-cultural differences discussed earlier regarding domestic contexts of media use, the commonalities remain strong, as all European countries are subject to the same late modern trends in the cultural conditions of everyday life. Most analyses of privatization and individualization center on the division marked by the front door, but for children and young people, the bedroom door is also key, marking a shift away from the public, communal space of the living room toward the solitary privacy of the bedroom. Thus, as households come to possess multiple televisions, telephones, video recorders, PCs, etc., we are moving rapidly away from the traditional image, with us since television's arrival in the 1950s, in which the family gathers in the main living room to coview the family television set, Dad monopolizes the remote control, sport wins out over soaps in the struggle to determine program choices, women's viewing is halted when the husband wants to see "his program," and children have to fit in. Under those conditions, concerns were raised regarding the operation of traditional generation and gender inequalities (Moores, 1988; Morley, 1986); now we see a new nostalgia for the lost days of togetherness in front of the set.

As argued in chapter 8, the so-called democratization of the family, in which young people increasingly have a say over how their lifestyle preferences are to be fairly accommodated along with those of parents, derives from the coincidence of a shift away from public forms of leisure, making domestic decision-making all the more important, and a shift toward diversification, multiplying the options available for which choices must be made. More generally, our findings suggest a shift over several decades from a domestic and leisure culture that for children and young people has been focused on the living room, on the family, and on a mixed diet of terrestrial television, music, and print media, toward one that encompasses a variety of leisure spaces within the home, diverse leisure companions, a greater degree of importance—in terms of time and attention—devoted to screen media, and an ever more mixed diet of television, video, computer, games, internet, music, and print.

In countries with a strong public service broadcasting tradition, none of this need give rise to concern, but at the same time as these domestic changes, we are witnessing a parallel shift in the media themselves. Traditionally part of the public and communal sphere, in Europe especially, the media are increasingly commercialized, specialized, and globalized. Where once the media were seen as the legitimate gateway through which public culture entered the privacy of the home, trends toward narrow-cast, globalized, and interactive media now potentially undermine public, communal culture by enhancing opportunities for individual lifestyle choices. From the viewpoint of media regulation, there is an unfortunate coincidence of two trends: for while bedroom culture makes domestic regulation of children's media use increasingly difficult for parents, the diversification and convergence of media makes regulation at the national or international level also increasingly difficult. The former trend leads parents to wish more than ever to rely on national regulators, whereas the latter trend is resulting in a growing pressure in policy circles to leave regulation to parents, albeit with support from various governmental and other agencies.

The Globalization of Youth Culture

Within Europe, there is a strong advocacy for facilitating free market competition among media conceived as commodities, this position being in tension with the view that media, now conceived as cultural products that convey value and identity, require protection. This latter view is itself complex: Given the European tradition of nationally produced public service media, the question of whether regulatory intervention is merited in order to protect public service broadcasting has become entangled with the question of how national regulation can or should support national against transnational media products. While these debates continue, we found that global media impact on children and young people in several ways.

Children's programs, traditionally a priority for public service broadcasting, are increasingly squeezed out in the new broadcasting climate (chapter 6). Consequently, we find that children turn to either imported cartoons or generic prime time programming not targeted at their age group. On the other hand, although national broadcasters have neglected youth programming, global channels are successfully targeting this audience, addressing them simultaneously as individuals with the latest lifestyle interests and as global citizens. Although academic comment on these shifts tends to deplore the former and celebrate the latter, one might instead suggest that the spread of global channels for children could generate a shared subculture equivalent to that of youth culture, whereas conversely, perhaps there should be as rigorous a defense of national, public service broadcasting for teenagers as for children. Although the vacuum left by national channels is more recent for children's than for youth programs, for both children and teenagers, global channels are stepping in to fill the gaps.

It is central to the processes of both globalization and individualization that youth culture is increasingly dissociated from national or class-based structures. Tastes and preferences thus become both heterogeneous within a culture and, simultaneously, shared across cultures. That it is appropriate to talk here of youth culture rather than, more simply, television preferences, is justified when we consider how such preferences are embedded in the leisure lifestyles of young people more generally. Most notably, we find that young people commonly use these global media contents in ways that transcend the medium that transmits them, pursuing intertextual themes (e.g., sports, stars, romance, cartoons) across such diverse media as television, computer games, comics, and the Internet.

Sports and music, which lead as topics of interest and whose popularity is evident also in television and game preferences (chapter 6), facilitate the process of individualization, as both allow for the expression of many fine distinctions according to different lifestyles, fan subcultures, and personal preferences. However, we also find evidence for a countertrend, in which the equally strong preference for drama and adventure revealed in young people's choices of favorite programs and games seems to suggest a common culture driven by underlying primordial themes (such as conflict, goal-seeking, competition, crisis, etc; Liebes & Katz, 1990). Both trends support, and depend on, the globalization of youth culture, the first through the diversification of transnational fan subcultures, the second through the homogenization of interests across nations, by centering on primordial themes.

The response of young people themselves to the increasingly globalized culture available to them—in terms of their perceptions, concerns, pleasures, and identities—is complex. Drotner (chapter 13) argues that language is a crucial variable. Those countries where children's favorite programs are domestic ones are not necessarily those with a strong public service tradition, but rather they are large countries in which it is economical to produce children's programs in their own language. Those countries in which children favor imported programs contain small language communities. Even then, the imported programs favored are not necessarily global/American productions. For example, Switzerland imports children's programs from Germany, a large, neighboring country that shares the same language. As Drotner notes (see also Silj, 1988), where there is a real choice between national and imported programs, children favor the national product. However, most children in most countries also find imported programs very attractive. This is often held to be because imported programs are seen as exotic, but Drotner suggests instead that children often find the underlying narratives of imported programs familiar, even if the settings are different, whereas on occasion they may find their domestic programs problematically unfamiliar.

Something more than language is at issue here. When several national teams used the survey to ask children, "If you had to live in another country, which would you choose?," the preference for "America" over Western European countries increased steadily as children grew older. Furthermore, we find that preferences for imported—particularly Anglo-American—programs increase with age. This apparent preference for Anglo-American norms, combined with the increasing priority given to teaching English in schools across Europe, is particularly important for new computer-based media and, especially, the Internet. Participation in global communication using the Internet, like the skills required to use the software, demands a good knowledge of English, and this currently limits the self-expression of many young people in Europe. Echoing Süss's comments regarding ICT in education (chapter 10), Drotner concludes that, in devoting efforts to teach children skills valuable in traditional contexts, insufficient attention is given to providing support in those domains where children are actively developing their skills, namely in the domain of new media technologies.

In short, the globalization of media culture has consequences for the kinds of children's programs available in a country, and here we argued that from the viewpoint of young people themselves, issues of language and cultural familiarity appear to matter more than traditional public service values. It also has consequences for youth culture insofar as this is increasingly constructed through the intertextual use of global themes, icons, fan objects, etc. Last, we suggested that the issues of language and of Anglo-American norms in media content are becoming increasingly important in relation to computer-based media. Debates over provision and regulation of national and global media will continue; in our project we witnessed some early consequences of the potent combination of a transformation in the economy, formats, and distribution of media resulting from globalization (Kinder, 1991; Kline, 1993) with what Drotner calls the "thorough mediation of contemporary juvenile culture" (chapter 13).

CONCLUSION

Both media environments and contexts of childhood vary cross-culturally, and so it has taken an enormously demanding, and often unwieldy, cross-national comparison to provide the empirical observations necessary to analyze their effects and their interdependence. Any attempt at an overview, therefore, threatens a serious injustice to the complexity and contingency of the observations and arguments offered throughout this volume. However, the overall balance of similarities and differences that emerges from the comparative project seems to invite the following general conclusion. On one hand, cross-national differences in both media environments and cultural traditions of leisure and family life frame children's media use, resulting in systematic variation in access and use. Yet, to a significant extent, use is underdetermined by access and, again to a significant extent, lifestyle choices are underdetermined by traditional conceptions of leisure and family life. Thus, within the freedom allowed by nationally specific constraints, we find that children and young people from different countries structure their media use in common ways and according to common meanings, reflecting a culture of childhood and youth that applies across the advanced industrialized countries of Western Europe. The late modern processes of privatization, individualization, and globalization helped us understand this transnational culture as it contextualizes the everyday lives of children and young people.

If we shift the focus from the spatial to the temporal dimension of this transnational culture, it should be evident that, because of continued, and linked, changes in both the media environment and contexts of childhood, we have largely eschewed the temptation to make simple historical comparisons, as invited, for example, in the now-and-then comparison implicit in the task of updating Himmelweit, Oppenheim, and Vince's *Television and the Child* (1958). Rather, by regarding the time scale of new media diffusion and appropriation as superimposed onto the time scale of late modernity, we were able to trace the emergence of a transnational media culture that reflects a variety of factors—the strengthening of the youth market, the diversification of leisure opportunities, the growing importance of the home as a privatized leisure space, and the spread of the English language, among others. Crucially, these factors are themselves far from independent of the media whose meanings and use they frame, for they are themselves fundamentally mediated by an increasingly globalized mass culture (Förnas & Bolin, 1994; Thompson, 1995).

Although, as noted at the outset of this chapter, many of the issues raised here merit consideration in terms of policy intervention as well as academic debate, we advocated caution in making value judgments regarding our findings. Many of the differences or changes on which we commented are a matter of degree, and although from relatively small quantitative differences significant consequences may follow, these often require the benefit of hindsight to identify with confidence. Perhaps the implications of our findings are best seen in terms of a balance of opportunities and dangers. For example, parents may know about and share less of their children's media culture than they once did, but children have more freedom to make their own choices; parents may find it harder to regulate their children's media use, but children gain more privacy; children may be reading fewer books, certainly in some countries, but gaining skills in information technology; children's national media culture may be being undermined, but they enjoy becoming global citizens; and so forth. Having made our findings available through the production of this volume, we hope to inform judgments about the balance of opportunities and dangers facing children and young people and, perhaps, to inform the formulation of policy that might tip the balance in favor of the opportunities.

REFERENCES

Bourdieu, P. (1984). *Distinction: A social critique of the judgement of tastes*. Cambridge, MA: Harvard University Press.

Buckingham, D. (1993). *Reading audiences: Young people and the media*. Manchester, England: Manchester University Press.

Corsaro, W. A. (1997). *The sociology of childhood*. Thousand Oaks, CA: Pine Forge Press.

Dorr, A. (1986). *Television and children: A special medium for a special audience*. Beverly Hills, CA: Sage.

Flichy, P. (1995). *Dynamics of modern communication: the shaping and impact of new communication technologies*. London: Sage.

Förnas, J., & Bolin, G. (Eds.). (1994). *Youth culture in late modernity*. Beverly Hills, CA: Sage.

Giddens, A. (1993). *The transformation of intimacy: Sexuality, love and eroticism in modern societies*. Cambridge: Polity Press.

Himmelweit, H. T., Oppenheim, A. N., & Vince, P. (1958). *Television and the child: An empirical study of the effect of television on the young*. London and New York: Oxford University Press.

James, A., Jenks, C., & Prout, A. (1988). *Theorizing childhood*. Cambridge: Cambridge University Press.

Kelly, M. J. (1998). Media use in the European household. In D. McQuail & K. Siune (Eds.), *Media policy: Convergence, concentration and commerce* (pp. 144–164). London: Sage.

Kinder, M. (1991). *Playing with power in movies, television and video games: From muppet babies to teenage mutant ninja turtles*. Berkeley, CA: University of California Press.

Kline, S. (1993). *Out of the garden: Toys, TV, and children's culture in the age of marketing*. London and New York: Verso.

Kohn, M. L. (1989). Introduction. In M. L. Kohn (Ed.), *Cross-national research in sociology* (pp. 17–31). Newbury Park: Sage.

Liebes, T., & Katz, E. (1990). *The export of meaning: Cross-cultural readings of DALLAS*. New York: Oxford University Press.

Livingstone, S. (1998). Mediated childhoods: A comparative approach to the lifeworld of young people in a changing media environment. *European Journal of Communication, 13*(4), 435–456.

Livingstone, S. (1999). New media, new audiences. *New Media and Society, 1*(1), 59–66.

Marvin, C. (1988). *When old technologies were new: Thinking about electric communication in the late nineteenth century.* Oxford: Oxford University Press.

Meyrowitz, J. (1985). *No sense of place: The impact of electronic media on social behavior.* New York: Oxford University Press.

Miller, D. (1987). *Material culture and mass consumption.* Oxford: Blackwell.

Moores, S. (1988). The box on the dresser: Memories of early radio and everyday life. *Media, Culture and Society, 10,* 23–40.

Morley, D. (1986). *Family television: Cultural power and domestic leisure.* London: Comedia.

Murdock, G., Hartmann, P., & Gray, P. (1995). Contextualizing home computers: Resources and practices. In N. Heap, R. Thomas, G. Einon, R. Mason, & H. Mackay (Eds.), *Information technology and society: A reader* (pp. 269–283). London: Sage.

Neuman, W. R. (1991). *The future of the mass audience.* Cambridge: Cambridge University Press.

Osgerby, B. (1998). *Youth in Britain since 1945.* Oxford: Blackwell.

Qvortrup, J. (1995). Childhood in Europe: A new field of social research. In L. Chisholm (Ed.), *Growing up in Europe: Contemporary horizons in childhood and youth studies.* Berlin and New York: de Gruyter.

Reimer, B. (1995). Youth and modern lifestyles. In J. Förnas & G. Bolin (Eds.), *Youth culture in late modernity* (pp. 120–144). London: Sage.

Rogers, E. M. (1995). *Diffusion of innovations* (Vol. 4). New York: Free Press.

Schoenbach, K., & Becker, L. B. (1989). The audience copes with plenty: Patterns of reactions to media changes. In L. B. Becker & K. Schoenbach (Eds.), *Audience responses to media diversification: Coping with plenty* (pp. 353–366). Hillsdale, NJ: Lawrence Erlbaum Associates.

Silj, A. (1988). *East of Dallas: The European challenge to American television.* London: British Film Institute.

Silverstone, R. (1994). *Television and everyday life.* London: Routledge.

Thompson, J. B. (1995). *The media and modernity: A social theory of the media.* Cambridge: Polity.

Tomlinson, J. (1999). *Globalisation and culture.* Chicago: University of Chicago Press.

Webster, F., & Robins, K. (1989). Plan and control: Towards a cultural history of the information society. *Theory and Society, 18*(3), 323–351.

Ziehe, T. (1994). From living standard to life style. *Young: Nordic Journal of Youth Research, 2*(2), 2–16.

APPENDIX A:
Country Abbreviations

Throughout the book the following abbreviations will be used for the 12 countries taking part:

BE-vlg	Flanders
CH	Switzerland
DE	Germany
DK	Denmark
ES	Spain
FI	Finland
FR	France
GB	The United Kingdom
NL	The Netherlands
IL	Israel
IT	Italy
SE	Sweden

The United Kingdom is used throughout the text, to indicate that the national survey included Northern Ireland. (Great Britain, although more consonant with the abbreviation GB, includes only England, Wales, and Scotland). It should also be remembered throughout that the Israeli sample included only the Jewish, and not the Arab, population.

APPENDIX B:
Participating Institutions and Research Teams

DENMARK

Institution
　　Centre for Child and Youth Media Services, University of Copenhagen.

Research team
　　Professor Kirsten Drotner and Dr. Gitte Stald

Funders
　　Danish Telecom (Tele Danmark), The Danish Ministry of Culture and the Danish Research Council for the Humanities

Contact
　　Professor Kirsten Drotner
　　Department of Literature, Culture & Media
　　University of Southern Denmark
　　55 Campusvej
　　DK 5230 Odense M.
　　Denmark
　　Tel: +45 6550 3642 (dir.)
　　　　 +45 6550 3430 (secr.)
　　Fax: +45 6593 5348
　　Email: drotner@litcul.sdu.dk

National report
Drotner, K. (2000). *Medier for fremtiden: børn og unge i det ændrede medielandskab* [Media for the future: Children and young people in the changing media landscape].

Publications
Drotner, K. (1999). Internautes et joueurs: La nouvelle culture des loisirs chez les jeunes danois, *Reseaux, 17*, 92–93, 133–72. Translated (1999) as Netsurfers and game navigators: New media and youthful leisure cultures in Denmark. *Reseaux, The French Journal of Communication, 7-1*, 83–108.

Drotner, K. (2000). Difference and diversity: Trends in young Danes' media cultures. *Media, Culture and Society, 22-2*.

FINLAND

Institutions
Department of Communication, University of Tampere
Research Unit for Contemporary Culture, University of Jyväskylä

Research team
Dr. Annikka Suoninen, Dr. Marja Saanilahti, and Professor Taisto Hujanen

Funders
The Academy of Finland, The National Children's Fund for Research and Development (ITLA) and the Finnish Public Broadcasting Company (YLE).

Contact
Dr. Annikka Suoninen,
Research Unit for Contemporary Culture
P.O. Box 35
University of Jyväskylä
FIN-40351 Jyväskylä
Finland
Tel: +358-14-260 1313
Fax: +358-14-260 1311
Email: suoninen@cc.jyu.fi

National report
Saanilahti, M. (1999). *Lasten ja nuorten muuttuva mediakulttuuri. Tutkimusraportti 1* [Changing media culture of children and youth. Research Report 1]. Publications of the Department of Communication Studies B 42/1999. Tampere, Finland: University of Tampere.

Publications
Suoninen, A. (2000). Norsun muisti. Lasten ja nuorten lukeminen ennen ja nyt [Lasting memories. Reading among children and youth now and then]. In M. Linko, T. Saresma, & E. Vainikkala (Eds.), *Otteita kulttuurista. Kirjoituksia nykyajasta, tutkimuksesta ja elämäkerrallisuudesta* [Grasping culture. Essays on contemporary culture, research and autobiography] (pp. 212–229). Publications of the Research Unit for Contemporary Culture no. 41. Jyväskylä, Finland: University of Jyväskylä.

Suoninen, A. (2001). Se pieni ero pelikellojen helinässä. Katsovatko pojat Quake-Quake-Maahan? [Boys, girls and computer games. Lost boys and the new Never-Never land?]. In E. Huhtamo & S. Kangas (Eds.), *Mariosofia - elektronisten pelien kulttuuri* (Mariosophy - the culture of electronic games). Helsinki, Finland: BTJ Kirjastopalvelu.

FLANDERS

Institution
University of Nijmegen.

Research team
Dr. Leen d'Haenens

Funders
The Department of Communication Studies, University of Ghent (Belgium) and The Department of Communication, University of Nijmegen (The Netherlands)

Contact
Dr. Leen d'Haenens
University of Nijmegen
Department of Communication
P.O. box 9104
6500 HE Nijmegen
The Netherlands
Tel: 00 31 24 36 12322 or 12372
Fax: 00 31 24 36 13073
Email: l.dhaenens@maw.kun.nl

National report
d'Haenens, L., Kokhuis, M., & van Summeren, C. (2000). *Vlaamse kinderen en jongeren in een veranderende mediacontext* [Flemish Children and Teenagers in a changing Media Context]. Nijmegen: Katholieke Universiteit Nijmegen (Sectie Communicatiewetenschap).

Publications
  Beentjes, J., d'Haenens, L., van der Voort, T., & Koolstra, C. (1999). Neder-
landse en Vlaamse kinderen en jongeren als gebruikers van interactieve
media [Dutch and Flemish children and adolescents as users of interactive
media]. *Tijdschrift voor Communicatiewetenschap, 27-2*, 105–24.
  d'Haenens, L. (2000). Flemish children and young people's media use patterns in their domestic family contexts. In H.-B. Brosius (Ed.), *Kommunikation
über Grenzen und Kulturen* [Communication crossing borders and cultures]
(pp. 293–308). Konstanz: UVK Medien.

FRANCE

Institution
  Centre National de la Recherche Scientifique (National Center for Scien-
tific Research), Ecole des Hautes Etudes en Sciences Sociales (School for
High Studies in Social Sciences) Paris

Research team
  Professor Dominique Pasquier, Professor Josiane Jouët, & Dr. Eric Maigret and others

Funders
  France Television, Canal Plus, CNET, Telerama

Contact
  Professor Dominique Pasquier
  CEMS
  54 boulevard Raspail
  Paris 75006
  Tel: 33 1 64905917
  Fax: 33 1 49 54 26 70
  Email: pasquier@ehess.fr

National report
  Pasquier, D., & Jouët, J. (Eds.). (1999). Les jeunes et l'Ecran [Young people
and the screen]. *Reseaux, 92/93, 24–102*.

Publications
  Pasquier, D., Buzzi, C., d'Haenens, L., & Sjöberg, U. (1998). Family lifestyles
and media use patterns. An analysis of domestic media among Flemish,
French, Italian and Swedish children and teenagers. *European Journal of
Communication, 13*(4), 503–519.

Jouët, J., & Pasquier, D. (1999). Youth and screen culture. *The French Journal of Communication, 7*(1), 31–58.

GERMANY

Institution
    Hans-Bredow Institut für Medienforschung, University of Hamburg

Research team
    Dr. Friedrich Krotz & Dr. Uwe Hasebrink

Funders
    Hamburgische Anstalt für neue Medien (HAM), Ministerium für Arbeit, Gesundheit and Soziales in Nordrhein-Westfalen and Freiwillige Selbstkontrolle Fernsehen (FSF)

Contact
    Dr. Friedrich Krotz,
    Hans-Bredow-Institut
    Heimhuder Str 21
    D - 20148 HAMBURG
    Tel: 00 49 40 450 217-0
    Fax: 00 49 40 450 217-77
    Email: F.Krotz@Hans-Bredow-Institut.de

National report
    Krotz, F., Hasebrink, U., Lindemann, T., Reimann, F., & Rischkau, E. (1999). *Neue und alte Medien im Alltag von Kindern und Jugendlichen. Deutsche Teilergebnisse einer europäischen Studie* [New and old media in the everyday of children and young people. German Results of a European study]. Hamburg: Hans-Bredow-Institut.

Publications
    Johnsson-Smaragdi, U., d'Haenens, L., Krotz, F., & Hasebrink, U. (1998). Patterns of old and new media use among young people in Flanders, Germany and Sweden. *European Journal of Communication, 13*(4), 479–501.
    Krotz, F. (1998). Computervermittelte Kommunikation im Medienalltag von Kindern und Jugendlichen in Europa [Computer mediated communication in the everyday of children and young people in Europe]. In P. Rössler (Ed.), *Online Kommunikation* [Online communication] (pp. 85–102). Opladen: Westdeutscher Verlag.

ISRAEL

Institutions
Tel Aviv University and The Hebrew University of Jerusalem

Research team
Dr. Dafna Lemish & Professor Tamar Liebes

Funders
Yad Hanadiv Foundation, The Israeli Council for Cable Broadcasts and The NCJW Research Institute for Innovation in Education, School of Education at the Hebrew University of Jerusalem

Contact
Dr. Dafna Lemish
Department of Communication
Tel Aviv University
PO Box 39040
Israel 69978
Tel: 00 972 3 6406407
Email: Lemish@post.tau.ac.il

National report
Lemish, D., & Liebes, T. (1999). *Children and youth in the changing media environment in Israel.* Jerusalem: The NCJW Research Institute for Innovation in Education, School of Education, The Hebrew University of Jerusalem.

Publications
Lemish, D., Drotner, K., Liebes, T., Maigret, E., & Stald, G. (1998). Global culture in practice: A look at children and adolescents in Denmark, France and Israel. *European Journal of Communication, 13*(4), 539–556.
Liebes, T. (1999). "Will I be pretty, will I be rich"—Teenage girls' cultural images of future success. *Reseaux, 17*, 189–216 (in French).

ITALY

Institution
Department of Sociology and Social Research, University of Trento

Research team
Professor Renato Porro, Dr. Barbara Ongari, Dr. Pierangelo Peri, Dr. Carlo Buzzi, & Dr. Francesca Sartori

Funders
University of Trento, Department of Sociology and Social Research
Radiotelevisione Italiana (RAI)

Contact
Dr. Pierangelo Peri
University of Trento
Department of Sociology and Social Research
Via Verdi, 26
38100 Trento
Italy
Tel: 00 39 0461 881470
Fax: 00 39 0461 881348
Email: pierangelo.peri@soc.unitn.it

Publications
Pasquier, D., Buzzi, C., d'Haenens, L., & Sjöberg, U. (1998). Family lifestyles and media use patterns. An analysis of domestic media among Flemish, French, Italian and Swedish children and teenagers. *European Journal of Communication, 13*(4), 503–519.

Buzzi, C. (Ed.). (2001). *Bambini e nuovi media* [Young people and new media]. Roma: Eri.

THE NETHERLANDS

Institution
Center for Child and Media Studies, Leiden University

Research team
Professor Tom van der Voort, Dr. J. W. J. Beentjes, Dr. Cees Koolstra, & Dr. Nies Marseille

Funders
The Dutch Ministry of Education, Culture and the Sciences, and The Dutch Broadcasting Organisation (NOS)

Contact
Professor Tom H. A. van der Voort
Center for Child and Media Studies
Leiden University
Wassenaarseweg 52
2333 AK Leiden

The Netherlands
Tel: +31 71 5274078
Fax: +31 71 5273945
Email: vdvoort@fsw.leidenuniv.nl

National reports
  Beentjes, J. W. J., Koolstra, C. M., Marseille, N., & van der Voort, T. H. A. (1997). *Waar blijft de tijd? De tijdsbesteding van kinderen en jongeren van 3 tot 17 jaar* [Where's the time gone? Time expenditure of children and young people aged 3–17]. Leiden, The Netherlands: Leiden University, Center for Child and Media Studies.
  Beentjes, J. W. J., Koolstra, C. M., Marseille, N., & van der Voort, T. H. A. (1998). *Media en vrije tijd: Het mediagebruik van kinderen en jongeren in de leeftijd van 3 tot en met 17 jaar* [Media and lesiure time: Media use of children and young people aged 3–17]. Hilversum, The Netherlands: The Dutch Broadcasting Organisation (NOS).

Publications
  Beentjes, J. W. J., d'Haenens, L., van der Voort, T. H. A., & Koolstra, C. M. (1999). Dutch and Flemish children and adolescents as users of interactive media. *Communications: The European Journal of Communication Research, 24*, 145–166.
  Van der Voort, T. H. A., Beentjes, J. W. J., Bovill, M., Gaskell, G., Koolstra, C. M., Livingstone, S., & Marseille, N. (1998). Young people's ownership and uses of new and old forms of media in Britain and the Netherlands. *European Journal of Communication, 13*(4), 457–477.

SPAIN

Institution
  Department of Journalism and Department of Sociology of the Faculty of Social Sciences and Communication, University of the Basque Country

Research team
  Professor Carmelo Garitaonandia, Dr. Patxi Juaristi, & Jose A. Oleaga

Funders
  The University of the Basque Country and Euskal Irrati Telebista [The Basque Radio and Television Public Corporation]

Contact
  Professor Carmelo Garitaonandia
  Department of Journalism

University of the Basque Country
P.O. Box 644
48080 Bilbao
Spain
Email: pupgagac@lg.ehu.es

National report
In preparation

Publications
Garitaonandia, C., Juaristi, P., Oleaga, J. A., & Pastor, F. (1998). Las relaciones de los niños y de los jóvenes con las viejas y nuevas tecnologías de la informacion [Children and teenagers' relationship with old and new communication technologies]. *Spanish Journal of Communication Studies, ZER, 4,* 131–161.

Garitaonandia, C., Juaristi, P., & Oleaga, J. A. (1999). Qué ven y cómo juegan los niños y los jóvenes españoles [What Spanish children and young people watch and how they play]. *Spanish Journal of Communication Studies, ZER, 6,* 67–97.

SWEDEN

Institution
Media and Communication Studies, University of Lund

Researchers
Professor Ulla Johnsson-Smaragdi and M.Sc., PhD student Ulrika Sjöberg

Funders
The Swedish Council for Research in the Humanities and Social Sciences (HSFR)

Contact
Professor Ulla Johnsson-Smaragdi
Media and Communication Studies
Department of Sociology
University of Lund
PO Box 114
221 00 Lund
Email: Ulla.Johnsson-Smaragdi@soc.lu.se or Ulla.Johnsson-Smaragdi@svi.vxu.se

National report
Johnsson-Smaragdi, U., & Sjöberg, U. *Young Swedes in a new media environment. Statistics and comments* (Preliminary title. Forthcoming)

Publications
    Johnsson-Smaragdi, U., d'Haenens, L., Krotz, F., & Hasebrink, U. (1998). Patterns of old and new media use among young people in Flanders, Germany and Sweden. *European Journal of Communication, 13*(4), 479–501.
    Johnsson-Smaragdi, U. (1999). Young people & new media in Sweden (in Italian). In C. Buzzi (Ed.), *Gli adolescenti e i new media* [Adolescents and the new media]. ERI/RAI. (Also available in English through the author).

SWITZERLAND

Institutions
    IPMZ-Institute of Communication, University of Zurich.
    SLA-Secondary Teacher Training Department at the University of Berne.
    ISSCom-Institute of Communication at the University of Lugano

Research team
    Dr. Daniel Süss (Project Director), Giordano Giordani and Professor Heinz Bonfadelli

Funders
    IPMZ-Institute of Communication at the University of Zurich, Secondary Teacher Training Department at the University of Berne, TA-Media AG Zurich, Euro-Beratung Zurich and Intermundo Berne (Swiss Coordination Office for "Youth for Europe")

Contact
    Dr. Daniel Süss
    IPMZ-Institute of Communication
    University of Zurich
    P.O. Box 507
    CH-8035 Zurich
    Switzerland
    Email: suess@ipmz.unizh.ch

National report
    Süss, D. (2000). *Kinder und Jugendliche im sich wandelnden Medienumfeld. Eine repräsentative Befragung von 6–16 jährigen und ihren Eltern in der Schweiz* [Children and young people in a changing media environment. A representative survey on 6- to 16-year-olds and their parents in Switzerland]. Zürich: Institut für Publizistikwissenschaft und Medienforschung. (Institute of Communication)

Publications
Süss, D., Suoninen, A., Garitaonandia, C., Juaristi, P., Koikkalainen, R., & Olcaga, J. A. (1998). Media use and the relationships of children and teenagers with their peer groups. A study of Finnish, Spanish and Swiss cases. *European Journal of Communication, 13*(4), 521–538.

Süss, D. (2000). Kindlicher Medienumgang und elterliche Kontrolle in der Schweiz [Children's media use and control from parents in Switzerland]. In H.-B. Brosius (Ed.), *Kommunikation über Grenzen und Kulturen* [Communication crossing borders and cultures] (pp. 309–323). Konstanz: UVK Medien.

UNITED KINGDOM (CO-ORDINATORS OF THE EUROPEAN STUDY)

Institution
Media@lse, The London School of Economics and Political Science

Research team
Professor Sonia Livingstone and Dr. Moira Bovill, together with colleagues from the Department of Social Psychology, London School of Economics and Political Science

Funders of the national research
Conducted in association with the Broadcasting Standards Commission, the project was assisted financially by The Advertising Association, The British Broadcasting Corporation (BBC), The Broadcasting Standards Commission, British Telecommunications plc, ITVA, ITV Network Limited, Independent Television Commission, Yorkshire/Tyne-Tees Television, The Leverhulme Trust and The London School of Economics and Political Science (STICERD)

Funders of the international workshops
The European Commission (DGX and Youth for Europe Programme, DGXXII), The European Parliament and The European Science Foundation.

Contact
Professor Sonia Livingstone
Media@lse
Department of Social Psychology
The London School of Economics and Political Science,
Houghton Street
London WC2A 2AE
Tel: 0207 955 7710
Fax: 0207 995 7565
Email: s.livingstone@lse.ac.uk

National report
Livingstone, S., & Bovill, M. (1999). *Young people new media*. Full report (circa 400 pp) and summary report (56 pp) published by LSE. Contact Ms Carol Whitwill, S465, LSE, Houghton Street, London WC2A 2AE.

Publications
Livingstone, S., & Gaskell, G. (1997). Children and the television screen: Modes of participation in the media environment. In S. Ralph, J. L. Brown, & T. Lees (Eds.), *Tune in or Buy in?* (pp. 7–24). Luton: University of Luton Press.

Livingstone, S. (1999). Les jeunes et les nouveaux medias: Sur le leçons à tirer de la télévision pour le PC [Young people and new media: Do lessons drawn from television apply to computers?]. *Reseaux, 92/93*, 101–132.

APPENDIX C:
Measurement of Time Use

MEASURING EXPOSURE TO MEDIA

There is no standard method for measuring media exposure, and there is considerable controversy within the media literature and industry. Any exercise in measuring time spent with media involves a series of judgments concerning appropriate measurement tools and the degree and types of error associated with each.[1] The particular tools we developed for this project were based on consideration of the variety of measurement instruments used by the broadcasting industry, by market researchers, and by academic researchers in our 12 countries, as well as practical considerations to do with the age of the children in the survey sample. Following qualitative work with focus groups and in parent interviews, asking about time use in different ways, the British team then tested several ways of measuring time use in a pilot survey using the BBC's Television Opinion Panel.

In practice there were two significant constraints on the kinds of measures we could use. First, what questions readily make sense to children and therefore are easily and validly answered? Second, what questions could be answered in a relatively short period of time, considering the overall length of the survey and the number of different media involved. For example, the

---

[1] See for example, Kubey and Cziksentmihalyi (1990) and Barwise and Ehrenberg (1988) for discussion of the measurement of media use, and Ang (1991) for a highly critical account of both academic and industry attempts to measure time spent with television.

British survey took about 45 minutes on average, and contained some 200 questions in total, of which nearly 70 measured media exposure. It was therefore necessary to use a relatively small set of precoded response options to keep questions both comprehensible and quick to deliver.

The number of days in the week spent with a medium was ascertained by asking, *"We are interested in all the things you do when you're not at school/in your leisure time. How often do you do [activities] in your free time?"* Respondents were given seven options, which were assigned the following values:

	Code
6 or 7 days a week	6.5
4 or 5 days a week	4.5
2 or 3 days a week	2.5
About once a week	1.0
About once a month	0.1
Less than once a month	0.25
Never do this	0

Those over the age of 8 were asked, *"And on a day when you [do activity], about how long altogether do you usually spend?"* In this case 9 options were provided, which were coded as follows:

	Code
Never do this	0
A few minutes	0.1
Around half an hour	0.5
Around 1 hour	1
Around 2 hours	2
Around 3 hours	3
Around 4 hours	4
Around 5 hours	5
More than 6 hours	6

We are confident that these measures allowed us to construct a fairly reliable measure of time use, although any measuring tool contains biases and limitations. In the British survey, parents were asked a parallel set of questions, and in the United Kingdom and the Netherlands, children kept a time use diary; comparisons across measures revealed a substantial agreement across time measures (Livingstone & Bovill, 1999; Van der Voort et al., 1998).

"Average minutes per day" variables were computed by multiplying the hours and days variables, dividing the product by 7, and multiplying the result by 60—(Days × hours)/7 × 60. For time spent with television, hours/

minutes were asked separately for a weekday (Monday to Friday) and for the weekend. In this case the computation was as follows:

$$((\text{Days} \times \text{weekday hours} \times 5) + (\text{Days} \times \text{weekend hours} \times 2))/49 \times 60.$$

The measure thus created (average minutes per day spent) allows us to compare the relative amounts of time spent with different media. It should, however, be remembered that very different use patterns may result in similar figures. For example, if on average one medium is used on 1 day a week for around 42 minutes and another for only 7 minutes on 6 days a week, the average number of minutes per day spent on both media will be 6 minutes.

In Appendix C, figures are given first for users only, and secondly for the whole population (i.e., including nonusers, who are given a score of 0).

Figures are included for the following media: television, video, music (on radio, tapes, CDs, or records), PC (not for games), Internet, video and computer games, and books (not for school).

Where differences are statistically significant, this is reported, except in the case of Denmark and France. The data for these countries were not available for inclusion in the comparative database, precluding the creation of new composite variables and tests of significance.

REFERENCES

Ang, I. (1991). *Desperately Seeking the Audience*. London: Routledge.

Barwise, T., & Ehrenberg, A. (1988). *Television and its Audience*. London: Sage.

Kubey, R., & Cziksentmihalyi, M. (1990). *Television and the quality of life: How viewing shapes everyday experience*. London: Lawrence Erlbaum Associates.

Livingstone, S., & Bovill, M. (1999). *Young people, new media*. An LSE Report, available from http://psych.lse.ac.uk/young_people.

Van der Voort, T., Beentjes, J., Bovill, M., Gaskell, G., Koolstra, C. M., Livingstone, S., & Marseille, N. (1998). Young people's ownership and uses of new and old forms of media in Britain and the Netherlands. *European Journal of Communication, 13*(4), 457–477.

TABLE C.1

Average Number of Minutes per Day Spent With Television for Users Only and All, by Gender, Age, and SES

	Gender		*Age*			*SES*		
	M	F	9-10	12-13	15-16	H	M	L
BE(vlg)								
Users only	146	133	*127*	*134*	*152*	138	141	141
All	146	133	*127*	*134*	*152*	138	141	141
CH								
Users only	<u>122</u>	<u>105</u>	**90**	**121**	**125**	<u>100</u>	<u>111</u>	<u>133</u>
All	<u>121</u>	<u>104</u>	**89**	**121**	**124**	<u>100</u>	<u>110</u>	<u>131</u>
DE								
Users only	138	127	**118**	**133**	**147**	<u>120</u>	<u>137</u>	<u>160</u>
All	138	127	**118**	**133**	**147**	<u>120</u>	<u>137</u>	<u>160</u>
DK								
Users only	163	150	143	158	168	152	159	161
All	160	147	139	156	166	149	156	156
ES								
Users only	141	136	132	137	146	-	-	-
All	140	136	131	137	146	-	-	-
FI								
Users only	143	148	**120**	**159**	**156**	<u>138</u>	<u>160</u>	<u>140</u>
All	141	148	**118**	**159**	**155**	<u>136</u>	<u>159</u>	<u>140</u>
FR								
Users only	97	86	74	91	103	72	93	102
All	97	86	74	91	103	72	93	102
GB								
Users only	164	156	<u>143</u>	<u>165</u>	<u>170</u>	**137**	**155**	**171**
All	164	156	<u>143</u>	<u>165</u>	<u>170</u>	**137**	**155**	**171**
IL								
Users only	153	167	<u>162</u>	<u>176</u>	<u>142</u>	<u>138</u>	<u>162</u>	<u>176</u>
All	153	167	<u>162</u>	<u>176</u>	<u>142</u>	<u>138</u>	<u>162</u>	<u>176</u>
IT								
Users only	105	112	-	*116*	*103*	102	107	118
All	104	112	-	*114*	*103*	101	106	116
NL								
Users only	113	114	<u>102</u>	<u>123</u>	<u>116</u>	**93**	**111**	**126**
All	112	113	<u>101</u>	<u>122</u>	<u>114</u>	**92**	**109**	**125**
SE								
Users only	139	133	**110**	**137**	**142**	<u>122</u>	<u>138</u>	<u>164</u>
All	138	133	**109**	137	**141**	<u>122</u>	<u>136</u>	<u>164</u>

Note. Bold $p < 0.001$, underlined $p < 0.01$, italics $p < 0.05$.

TABLE C.2
Average Number of Minutes per Day Spent With Video for Users Only and All, by Gender, Age,
and SES

	Gender			Age			SES		
	M	F	9-10	12-13	15-16	H	M	L
BE(vlg)								
Users only	33	27	24	33	31	27	34	29
All	30	25	23	30	29	25	32	26
CH								
Users only	**37**	**24**	34	30	26	27	28	38
All	**32**	**20**	29	26	22	23	24	31
DE								
Users only	<u>22</u>	<u>15</u>	18	18	20	18	18	22
All	<u>20</u>	<u>13</u>	15	17	19	17	16	19
DK								
Users only	53	46	51	48	49	44	50	66
All	49	40	45	43	45	40	46	55
ES								
Users only	34	30	37	32	27	-	-	-
All	30	27	34	29	24	-	-	-
FI								
Users only	<u>45</u>	<u>31</u>	**47**	**40**	**27**	40	36	38
All	<u>42</u>	<u>30</u>	<u>43</u>	<u>38</u>	<u>26</u>	36	35	36
FR								
Users only	-	-	-	-	-	-	-	-
All	-	-	-	-	-	-	-	-
GB								
Users only	40	38	43	39	36	<u>27</u>	<u>39</u>	<u>44</u>
All	32	29	34	31	28	<u>24</u>	<u>31</u>	<u>33</u>
IL								
Users only	*61*	*47*	62	54	44	46	52	61
All	44	36	45	44	32	33	40	47
IT								
Users only	26	27	-	28	26	<u>24</u>	<u>24</u>	<u>36</u>
All	23	25	-	25	23	<u>22</u>	<u>22</u>	<u>32</u>
NL								
Users only	19	15	16	18	16	15	17	18
All	18	15	15	18	16	15	16	17
SE								
Users only	**55**	**34**	41	45	46	*32*	*43*	*55*
All	**52**	**32**	34	43	45	*31*	*41*	*52*

Note. Bold $p < 0.001$, underlined $p < 0.01$, italics $p < 0.05$.

TABLE C.3
Average Number of Minutes per Day Spent With Music (on radio, tapes, CDs, or records) for
Users Only and All, by Gender, Age, and SES

	Gender		Age			SES		
	M	F	9-10	12-13	15-16	H	M	L
BE(vlg)								
Users only	68	72	**40**	**60**	**97**	*70*	*60*	*88*
All	67	71	**39**	**59**	**96**	*69*	*58*	*86*
CH								
Users only	<u>86</u>	<u>105</u>	**68**	**81**	**135**	106	94	99
All	<u>82</u>	<u>102</u>	**63**	**79**	**132**	103	90	93
DE								
Users only	<u>52</u>	<u>59</u>	**38**	**52**	**73**	59	45	66
All	<u>50</u>	<u>55</u>	**35**	**49**	**70**	56	44	60
DK								
Users only	73	99	57	88	116	87	92	75
All	69	97	53	85	114	84	89	69
ES								
Users only	-	-	-	-	-	-	-	-
All	-	-	-	-	-	-	-	-
FI								
Users only	**87**	**148**	**74**	**121**	**159**	<u>103</u>	<u>113</u>	<u>146</u>
All	**82**	**145**	**69**	**116**	**156**	<u>97</u>	<u>110</u>	<u>143</u>
FR								
Users only	-	-	-	-	-	-	-	-
All	-	-	-	-	-	-	-	-
GB								
Users only	<u>71</u>	<u>89</u>	**42**	**70**	**121**	77	77	83
All	**61**	**84**	**34**	**63**	**116**	68	70	74
IL								
Users only	*95*	*119*	**52**	**103**	**149**	<u>120</u>	<u>94</u>	<u>130</u>
All	**73**	**106**	**36**	**91**	**135**	<u>97</u>	<u>79</u>	<u>112</u>
IT								
Users only	**92**	**117**	-	**92**	**119**	102	103	112
All	**85**	**114**	-	**86**	**115**	98	100	106
NL								
Users only	<u>83</u>	<u>101</u>	**49**	**83**	**142**	87	90	96
All	<u>83</u>	<u>100</u>	**49**	**83**	**142**	87	90	96
SE								
Users only	-	-	-	-	-	-	-	-
All	-	-	-	-	-	-	-	-

Note. Bold $p < 0.001$, underlined $p < 0.01$, italics $p < 0.05$.

TABLE C.4
Average Number of Minutes per Day Spent With PC (not for games) for Users Only and All, by Gender, Age, and SES

	Gender		Age			SES		
	M	*F*	*9-10*	*12-13*	*15-16*	*H*	*M*	*L*
BE(vlg)								
Users only	**45**	**21**	*19*	*33*	*42*	37	28	33
All	**29**	**12**	*11*	20	26	23	17	18
CH								
Users only	**28**	**13**	17	19	23	21	22	12
All	**18**	7	**6**	**12**	**17**	<u>18</u>	<u>14</u>	<u>5</u>
DE								
Users only	21	18	11	20	22	18	14	16
All	11	8	**3**	**10**	**15**	10	6	7
DK								
Users only	34	17	18	24	32	26	27	21
All	25	11	9	18	25	19	17	12
ES								
Users only	<u>46</u>	<u>27</u>	33	31	43	-	-	-
All	<u>26</u>	<u>15</u>	<u>14</u>	<u>17</u>	<u>29</u>	-	-	-
FI								
Users only	**37**	**16**	29	25	26	**36**	**22**	**17**
All	**34**	**14**	25	23	22	**33**	**20**	**15**
FR								
Users only	-	-	-	-	-	-	-	-
All	-	-	-	-	-	-	-	-
GB								
Users only	*36*	*24*	<u>21</u>	<u>26</u>	<u>43</u>	26	36	30
All	<u>15</u>	<u>8</u>	<u>7</u>	<u>10</u>	<u>18</u>	<u>15</u>	<u>16</u>	<u>8</u>
IL								
Users only	*47*	*32*	32	42	42	33	43	37
All	<u>25</u>	<u>13</u>	15	21	18	15	21	15
IT								
Users only	**47**	**20**	-	39	29	38	34	25
All	**24**	**8**	-	<u>19</u>	<u>12</u>	*21*	*15*	9
NL								
Users only	<u>21</u>	<u>14</u>	<u>12</u>	<u>18</u>	<u>21</u>	16	16	20
All	<u>16</u>	<u>11</u>	**8**	**14**	**18**	14	13	14
SE								
Users only	**48**	**22**	<u>23</u>	<u>31</u>	<u>41</u>	33	31	50
All	**36**	**17**	**11**	**25**	**35**	30	22	36

Note. Bold $p < 0.001$, underlined $p < 0.01$, italics $p < 0.05$.

TABLE C.5
Average Number of Minutes per Day Spent With Internet for Users Only and All, by Gender, Age, and SES

	Gender		Age			SES		
	M	*F*	*9-10*	*12-13*	*15-16*	*H*	*M*	*L*
BE(vlg)								
Users only	17	4	9	8	19	15	14	6
All	3	*	1	1	3	2	2	1
CH								
Users only	16	8	0	13	12	17	12	4
All	4	1	**0**	3	**5**	7	**2**	**1**
DE								
Users only	9	6	7	6	10	6	16	6
All	2	*	*	**1**	**3**	1	1	1
DK								
Users only	21	10	18	15	16	15	15	17
All	15	5	6	10	13	9	9	10
ES								
Users only	17	16	*32*	*10*	*15*	-	-	-
All	5	3	6	3	5	-	-	-
FI								
Users only	13	10	13	9	14	16	10	8
All	*10*	6	6	*7*	*12*	*11*	6	*5*
FR								
Users only	-	-	-	-	-	-	-	-
All	17	15	20	18	14	19	18	12
GB								
Users only	12	12	25	13	7	12	19	7
All	3	1	2	2	2	3	3	1
IL								
Users only	*35*	*17*	38	23	28	28	31	20
All	**14**	**4**	7	7	12	12	9	5
IT								
Users only	17	21	-	23	15	11	21	6
All	4	3	-	4	3	3	4	1
NL								
Users only	4	3	4	4	3	*6*	*2*	*4*
All	1	*	*	1	1	2	*	1
SE								
Users only	**24**	**14**	11	19	22	15	17	19
All	**17**	**9**	**3**	**14**	**18**	11	11	11

Note. Bold $p < 0.001$, underlined $p < 0.01$, italics $p < 0.05$.

TABLE C.6
Average Number of Minutes per Day Spent With Computer of Video Games for Users Only and
All, by Gender, Age, and SES

	Gender			Age			SES		
	M	F	9-10	12-13	15-16	H	M	L
BE(vlg)								
Users only	**38**	**17**	*16*	*31*	*33*	30	24	31
All	**26**	**10**	10	20	20	18	16	17
CH								
Users only	**48**	**18**	37	30	34	36	33	30
All	**39**	**12**	24	25	24	29	25	19
DE								
Users only	**50**	**18**	*31*	*36*	*46*	42	36	41
All	**40**	**21**	<u>20</u>	<u>27</u>	<u>34</u>	32	24	29
DK								
Users only	87	27	65	65	47	57	58	62
All	78	18	50	52	34	45	43	47
ES								
Users only	**51**	**24**	45	37	37	-	-	-
All	**41**	**13**	32	27	23	-	-	-
FI								
Users only	**74**	**17**	48	51	41	53	47	37
All	**68**	**15**	44	46	35	46	43	34
FR								
Users only	-	-	-	-	-	-	-	-
All	-	-	-	-	-	-	-	-
GB								
Users only	**58**	**29**	43	43	56	33	55	48
All	**46**	**15**	29	33	29	22	34	32
IL								
Users only	**89**	**39**	<u>65</u>	<u>79</u>	<u>47</u>	48	*74*	*57*
All	**67**	**21**	**46**	**57**	**24**	<u>28</u>	<u>52</u>	<u>33</u>
IT								
Users only	**59**	**24**	-	*48*	*36*	44	43	37
All	**49**	**14**	-	**37**	**23**	32	29	26
Users only	**38**	**17**	23	30	30	28	27	*27*
All	<u>36</u>	<u>14</u>	22	28	24	24	25	*25*
SE								
Users only	**66**	**19**	45	48	43	49	36	59
All	**60**	**14**	32	40	35	43	30	50

Note. Bold $p < 0.001$, underlined $p < 0.01$, italics $p < 0.05$.

TABLE C.7
Average Number of Minutes per Day Spent With Books (not for school) for Users Only and All,
by Gender, Age, and SES

	Gender		Age			SES		
	M	F	9-10	12-13	15-16	H	M	L
BE(vlg)								
Users only	21	29	*21*	*33*	*22*	<u>18</u>	<u>35</u>	<u>27</u>
All	<u>15</u>	<u>25</u>	<u>20</u>	<u>30</u>	<u>14</u>	**14**	**30**	**22**
CH								
Users only	**21**	**34**	<u>31</u>	<u>33</u>	<u>21</u>	35	28	26
All	**18**	**32**	**28**	**31**	**19**	32	25	23
DE								
Users only	**15**	**24**	17	23	17	21	14	13
All	**12**	**22**	15	20	14	19	12	11
DK								
Users only	19	23	25	21	18	20	21	23
All	13	20	20	17	14	17	16	18
ES								
Users only	-	-	-	-	-	-	-	-
All	-	-	-	-	-	-	-	-
FI								
Users only	**29**	**49**	*50*	*41*	*30*	47	35	37
All	**22**	**47**	<u>46</u>	<u>36</u>	<u>24</u>	42	29	32
FR								
Users only	-	-	-	-	-	-	-	-
All	-	-	-	-	-	-	-	-
GB								
Users only	29	28	29	31	25	30	32	26
All	13	18	18	17	12	*21*	*18*	*12*
IL								
Users only	*28*	*41*	35	42	30	33	35	41
All	**15**	**29**	25	26	17	21	22	23
IT								
Users only	-	-	-	-	-	-	-	-
All	-	-	-	-	-	-	-	-
NL								
Users only	**20**	**29**	27	2	23	27	26	23
All	**18**	**28**	26	23	20	26	24	20
SE								
Users only	**13**	**28**	<u>31</u>	<u>21</u>	<u>18</u>	19	19	19
All	**9**	**26**	<u>24</u>	<u>19</u>	<u>13</u>	17	14	15

Note. Bold $p < 0.001$, underlined $p < 0.01$, italics $p < 0.05$.

Author Index

Subject Index

Page numbers in [   ] indicate tables

A

Action programmes, 174, 269, 276
Age
  access/ownership, 56-66 *passim,*
    72-76, 82-83, 312, 313
  attitudes toward school, 233, 234
  bedroom culture and privatiza-
    tion of media use, 179, 182-199,
    [183]
  and content preferences, 144-145,
    [144], 146, 149-156 *passim,*
    [151], [154]
  gender and media use, 264, 269,
    279
  and global media, 287-292
    passim, 298
  and media use styles, 122, 135, 134
  and new media in school, 223-227
  new media users, 248-249, 253,
    254, 256, 257, 261
  nonuse of media, 137
  and peer group relations, 202,
    204, 204n, 205, 207-218 *passim,*
    324
  percentage of users per medium,
    93-95
  and relative value of media to
    children, 67-71, 77, 79, 82, 93
  research project, 33-34, 49
  comparative perspective, 11
  quantitative methodology, 45
  television/computers and
    family life, 162, 167, 168, 170,
    176

and time expenditure, 86, 87, 90,
  91, 97, 98, 106, 108, 352-358
  passim
uses and gratifications of media,
  86, 89-90, 99, 101, 102, 104, 106,
  107, 312-313
Appropriation, 312
  common cultural contexts, 315-319
Aqua, 291, 295
Audio media, 82, 86-108 *passim,*
  115, 312, 313; *see also* Radio;
  Music
Audiovisual media
  in school, 221, 235
Australian programmes, 292, 293

B

BBC, Television Opinion Panel, 349
Bedroom culture, 57, 179-182, 324,
  327; *see also* Personal ownership
  of media
  definition of bedroom culture,
    179-182
  experience and significance of
    media use in bedroom, 195-199,
    [197]
  and parental media regulation,
    191-195, [194], 328
  relationship between number of
    media in bedroom and time
    spent there, 37, 185-188, [187]
  and serious computer use, 188
  and social isolation of children,
    189-191, [190]